Microsoft SQL Server 2000
Database Design

Rozanne M. Whalen

Rozanne Whalen is the President of Software Solutions, Inc., in New Orleans, Louisiana. She is a Microsoft Certified Systems Engineer (MCSE), Microsoft Certified Database Administrator (MCDBA), Microsoft Certified Trainer (MCT), Novell Certified NetWare Instructor (CNI), and Novell Certified NetWare Engineer (CNE). She has written instructor-led courseware for the Computer Professional department of Element K for the past four years. She is also the editor (and a contributor) of Element K's *Inside Microsoft Windows 2000* journal, and the author of *MCSE SQL Server 2000 Administration for Dummies*, published by Hungry Minds. Rozanne actively teaches instructor-led training to prepare students for the MCSE and MCDBA exams. She has a Bachelor of Science degree in Chemistry from Loyola University, and a Master of Business Administration with a concentration in Information Systems from the University of New Orleans.

MICROSOFT SQL SERVER 2000: DATABASE DESIGN

Course Number: 077462
Course Edition: 1
For software version: 2000

ACKNOWLEDGEMENTS

Project Team

Curriculum Developer and Technical Writer: Rozanne M. Whalen • **Copy Editor:** Christy D. Flanders • **Reviewing Editors:** Elizabeth M. Swank, Taryn Chase and Angie J. French • **Quality Assurance Analyst:** Frank Wosnick • **Print Designer:** Daniel P. Smith

Project Support

Managing Editor: Clare S. Dygert • **Acquisitions Editor:** Tina Maria Nelson

Administration

Senior Director of Content and Content Development: William O. Ingle • **Director of Certification:** Mike Grakowsky • **Director of Design and Web Development:** Joy Insinna • **Manager of Office Productivity and Applied Learning:** Cheryl Russo • **Manager of Databases, ERP, and Business Skills:** Mark Onisk • **Director of Business Development:** Kent Michels • **Instructional Design Manager:** Susan L. Reber • **Manager of Publishing Services:** Michael Hoyt

NOTICES

Your comments are important to us. Please contact us at Element K Press LLC, 1-800-478-7788, 500 Canal View Boulevard, Rochester, NY 14623, Attention: Product Planning, or through our Web site at **http://support.elementkpress.com**.

MICROSOFT SQL SERVER 2000: DATABASE DESIGN

CONTENT OVERVIEW

Microsoft SQL Server 2000: Database Design

CONTENTS

CONTENTS

CONTENTS

CONTENTS

INTRODUCTION

Welcome to the Element K Content training team.

Our goal is to provide you with the best computer training available—and we know exactly what that takes. Our corporate heritage is based in training. In fact, we use our Student Manuals every day, in classes just like yours, so you can be confident that the material has been tested and proven to be effective.

If you have any suggestions on how we can improve our products or services, please contact us.

ABOUT THIS COURSE

This course teaches you how to use the Transact-SQL language to query and program Microsoft SQL Server 2000 in a Windows 2000 Server environment. This course also assists you in preparing for the Microsoft Certified Systems Engineer and Microsoft Certified Database Administrator Exam #70-229, Designing and Implementing Databases with Microsoft SQL Server 2000 Enterprise Edition.

Course Prerequisites

To ensure your success, we recommend you first take the following Element K courses or have equivalent knowledge: *Windows 2000: Installation and Administration*, or the *Windows 2000 for Windows NT Administrators* Element K course, or have equivalent knowledge. You should also know the basics of querying a SQL server by using the SELECT, INSERT, and UPDATE SQL statements. If you aren't familiar with using these commands, you should first take the *Microsoft SQL Server 2000: Querying with Transact-SQL* Element K course.

Course Objectives

When you're done working your way through this book, you'll be able to:

*   Identify the features of Microsoft SQL Server 2000.
*   Use Transact-SQL to query a SQL server.
*   Design, create, and manage databases.
*   Create and manage tables.
*   Implement data integrity techniques.
*   Design and implement indexes.
*   Query multiple tables through the use of joins.
*   Design subqueries.
*   Use aggregate functions in queries and create user-defined functions.
*   Create and manage views.
*   Design and implement stored procedures.
*   Create triggers.

ABOUT THIS COURSE

- Manage transactions and locks.
- Implement queries across multiple servers.
- Optimize queries.
- Analyze query performance.

COURSE SETUP INFORMATION

Hardware and Software Requirements

To run this course, you will need:

- At least 128 MB of RAM for each student computer (256 MB strongly recommended). At least 256 MB for the instructor's computer.
- A 2 GB or larger hard drive for each of the student computers, and a 4 GB or larger hard drive for the instructor's computer.
- A Pentium 300 MHz processor or faster.
- A VGA or higher resolution video card and monitor.
- A mouse or compatible tracking device.
- A 12 X (or faster) CD-ROM drive.
- A network adapter and network cabling.
- A licensed copy of Windows 2000 Server or Advanced Server for each student and the instructor.
- Windows 2000 Service Pack 1 or later.
- A licensed copy of Microsoft SQL Server 2000 Enterprise Edition for each student and the instructor.
- For the instructor's computer only, a display system to project the instructor's computer screen and PowerPoint slides.

Class Requirements

In order for the class to run properly, perform the procedures described below.

For the instructor's computer:

1. Install Windows 2000 Server on the C drive using the following parameters:
   - Install a new copy of Windows 2000 Server (clean install).
   - Accept the license agreement.
   - Enter the product key, if necessary.
   - Convert or format the C drive to NTFS. (Your C drive should be at least 4 GB in size.)
   - Select the regional settings appropriate for your location.
   - Use a name and organization appropriate for your setup.
   - Select Per-Server licensing, and add enough licenses to cover all the computers in the classroom.

- Use INSTRUCTOR as the computer name. Use password as the Administrator's password.

- On the Windows 2000 Components page, select (don't check) Networking Services and click Details. Check Domain Name System and click OK. Select Internet Information Services (IIS), and then click Details. Check NNTP Service, and then click OK. Click Next to install the Windows 2000 components.

- Set the appropriate date, time, and time zone for your location.

- On the Networking Settings page, select Custom Settings. Assign a static IP address that is unique on your network and an appropriate subnet mask. (We strongly recommend using a dummy IP addressing scheme such as 200.200.200.#, and using 200.200.200.100 for the instructor's computer.) Use this same IP address (200.200.200.100) for the Preferred DNS Server address.

- Install the computer into the default workgroup of WORKGROUP.

- Complete the installation and log on as Administrator. Select I Will Configure This Server Later, and click Next. Uncheck Show This Screen At Startup and close the Windows 2000 Configure Your Server window.

2. Configure a root DNS zone and a forward lookup zone:

   - From the Administrative Tools menu, choose DNS.

   - Right-click on your server and choose Configure The Server.

   - Click Next to start the Configure DNS Server Wizard.

   - On the Root Server page, verify that This Is The First DNS Server On This Network is selected. Click Next.

   - On the Forward Lookup Zone page, verify that Yes, Create A Forward Lookup Zone is selected and click Next.

   - Select Standard Primary and click Next.

   - On the Zone Name page, in the Name text box, type classroom.com. (This will create a zone for the classroom.) Click Next.

   - Click Next to accept the default zone filename.

   - On the Reverse Lookup Zone page, select Yes, Create A Reverse Lookup Zone and click Next.

   - Select Standard Primary and click Next.

   - In the Network ID text box, type 200.200.200. Click Next.

   - Click Next to accept the default zone filename.

   - Click Finish.

3. Configure the root zone, classroom.com, and 200.200.200.x Subnet zones to accept dynamic updates:

   - In DNS, expand your server, and expand Forward Lookup Zones.

   - Verify that the root and classroom.com zones are there.

   - Right-click on the root zone and choose Properties. In the Allow Dynamic Updates drop-down list, select Yes. Click OK to close the Properties dialog box.

   - Configure the classroom.com zone to accept dynamic updates.

- Below Reverse Lookup Zones, verify that you see the 200.200.200.x Subnet zone.
- Configure this zone to accept dynamic updates.
- Close DNS.

4. Install the instructor's computer as a domain controller for the classroom. com domain.

   - From the Start menu, choose Run.
   - In the Open text box, type *dcpromo* to start the Active Directory Installation Wizard.
   - Create a new domain, a new domain tree, and a new forest.
   - Use classroom.com for the DNS name of the domain.
   - Accept the default domain NetBIOS name of CLASSROOM.
   - Accept the default locations for the Active Directory database, its log, and the SYSVOL folder.
   - Set permissions to be compatible with only Windows 2000 servers.
   - Set the Administrator password for the Directory Services Restore Mode to *password*.
   - Restart the computer when prompted. Log back on as Administrator.

5. Change your root, classroom.com, and 200.200.200.x Subnet zones to Active Directory-integrated:

   - In DNS, right-click on a zone and choose Properties.
   - Click Change. Select Active Directory-integrated and click OK.
   - Click OK to confirm that you want to change the zone type.
   - Click OK to close the Properties dialog box.
   - Repeat these steps for all zones.

6. Install Service Pack 1 for Windows 2000.

7. Create a Group Policy to enable all users to log on locally at the domain controllers:

   - From the Administrative Tools menu, choose Active Directory Users And Computers.
   - Expand your domain and right-click on the Domain Controllers Organizational Unit (OU). Choose Properties to open the Domain Controllers Properties dialog box.
   - Select the Group Policy tab.
   - Verify that the Default Domain Controllers Policy object is selected and click Edit.
   - Below the Computer Configuration node, expand Windows Settings→ Security Settings→Local Policies. Select User Rights Assignment.
   - In the details pane, double-click on Log On Locally. If necessary, check Define These Policy Settings. Click Add to open the Select Users Or Groups dialog box.

- Click Browse. In the list of names, double-click on the Domain Users group. Click OK to close the Select Users Or Groups dialog box. Click OK again.
- Click OK to close the Security Policy Setting dialog box.
- Close the Group Policy window.
- Click OK to close the Domain Controllers Properties dialog box.
- Leave Active Directory Users And Computers open.

8. In Active Directory Users And Computers, create a user account for each student in the class, the instructor, and for the SQL Server services.

- Name the student accounts Student# (where # is each student's assigned number) and the instructor's account Instructor. Name the SQL Server service account SQLService. Assign a password of password to each account.
- Add these accounts to the Domain Admins group.
- Close Active Directory Users And Computers.

9. Create a folder named C:\Setup. Copy the \English\Ent folder (including all files and subfolders) from the SQL Server 2000 Enterprise Edition CD-ROM to C:\Setup. Share the C:\Setup\Ent folder as SQL2000.

10. Install SQL Server 2000 Enterprise Edition on the computer.

- Click SQL Server 2000 Components, and then click Install Database Server.
- Install SQL Server to your local computer.
- Create a new instance of SQL Server.
- If necessary, enter your name and company name on the User Information page.
- Agree to the Software License Agreement.
- Install the Server and Client Tools.
- Create a default instance of SQL Server 2000.
- Choose the Typical Installation Type.
- Configure the SQL Server services to use the domain user account named SQLService with a password of password.
- Choose Windows Authentication Mode.
- Configure the server to use a Processor with one processor.
- When the installation is complete, start the SQL Server services.
  - From the Microsoft SQL Server program group, choose Service Manager.
  - Verify that the SQL Server service is selected, and then click Start/Continue.

11. Copy the student data files from the course CD-ROM to C:\Data.

For each student's computer:

1. Install Windows 2000 Server on the C drive using the following parameters:
- Install a new copy of Windows 2000 Server (clean install).

ABOUT THIS COURSE

- Accept the license agreement.
- Enter the product key, if necessary.
- Convert or format the C drive to NTFS. (Your C drive should be at least 2 GB in size.)
- Select the regional settings appropriate for your location.
- Use a name and organization appropriate for your setup.
- Select Per-Server licensing, and add enough licenses to cover all the computers in the classroom.
- Use a computer name of SQLSERVER#, where # is a number from 1 up to the total number of students in the classroom. Use password as the Administrator's password.
- On the Windows 2000 Components page, click Next. (Accept all of the default Windows 2000 components including Internet Information Server.)
- Set the appropriate date, time, and time zone for your location.
- On the Networking Settings page, select Custom Settings. Assign an IP address of 200.200.200.# to each student, where # is each computer's assigned number.
- Use 255.255.255.0 as the subnet mask and 200.200.200.100 for the Preferred DNS Server address.
- Install the computer into the CLASSROOM domain. Enter Administrator for the domain user name, and password for the password.
- Complete the installation and log on as Administrator. Select I Will Configure This Server Later, and click Next. Uncheck Show This Screen At Startup and close the Windows 2000 Configure Your Server window.

2. Install Service Pack 1 for Windows 2000.

3. Install the Windows 2000 Administrative Tools.
   - From the Start menu, choose Run.
   - In the Open text box, type \\instructor\c$ to connect to the administrative share for the root of the instructor's hard disk.
   - Access the \winnt\system32 folder on the instructor's computer. Double-click on the Adminpak file to install the Administrative Tools.

4. Install SQL Server 2000 Enterprise Edition on each student computer.
   - Connect to the SQL2000 share on the instructor's computer.
   - Double-click on Autorun.
   - Click SQL Server 2000 Components, and then click Install Database Server.
   - Install SQL Server to your local computer.
   - Create a new instance of SQL Server.
   - If necessary, enter your name and company name on the User Information page.
   - Agree to the Software License Agreement.
   - Install the Server and Client Tools.

- Create a default instance of SQL Server 2000.
- Choose the Typical Installation Type.
- Configure the SQL Server services to use the domain user account named SQLService with a password of password.
- Choose Windows Authentication Mode.
- Configure the server to use with one processor.
- When the installation is complete, start the SQL Server services.
  - From the Microsoft SQL Server program group, choose Service Manager.
  - Verify that the SQL Server service is selected, and then click Start→Continue.

5. Copy the student data files from the course CD-ROM to C:\Data.

HOW TO USE THIS BOOK

You can use this book as a learning guide, a review tool, and a reference.

As a Learning Guide

Each lesson covers one broad topic or set of related topics. Lessons are arranged in order of increasing proficiency with *Microsoft SQL Server 2000*; skills you acquire in one lesson are used and developed in subsequent lessons. For this reason, you should work through the lessons in sequence.

We organized each lesson into explanatory topics and step-by-step activities. Topics provide the theory you need to master *Microsoft SQL Server 2000*, and activities allow you to apply this theory to practical hands-on examples.

You get to try out each new skill on a specially prepared sample file. This saves you typing time and allows you to concentrate on the technique at hand. Through the use of sample files, hands-on activities, illustrations that give you feedback at crucial steps, and supporting background information, this book provides you with the foundation and structure to learn *Microsoft SQL Server 2000* quickly and easily.

As a Review Tool

Any method of instruction is only as effective as the time and effort you are willing to invest in it. For this reason, we encourage you to spend some time reviewing the book's more challenging topics and activities.

As a Reference

You can use the Concepts sections in this book as a first source for definitions of terms, background information on given topics, and summaries of procedures.

ICONS SERVE AS CUES:

Throughout the book, you will find icons in the margin representing various kinds of information. These icons serve as at-a-glance reminders of their associated text.

Topic:
Represents the beginning of a topic

Check Your Skills:
Represents a Check Your Skills practice

Task:
Represents the beginning of a task

Apply Your Knowledge:
Represents an Apply Your Knowledge activity

Student Note:
Highlights information for students

Glossary Term:
Represents a definition; this definition also appears in the glossary

Quick Tip:
Represents a tip, shortcut, or additional way to do something

Warning:
Represents a caution; this note typically provides a solution to a potential problem

Web Tip:
Refers you to a Web site where you might find additional information

Instructor Note:
In the Instructor's Edition, gives tips for teaching the class

Overhead:
In the Instructor's Edition, refers to a PPT slide that the instructor can use in the lesson

Additional Instructor Note:
In the Instructor's Edition, refers the instructor to more information in the back of the book

An Overview of SQL Server

Data Files:
none

Lesson Time:
2 hours

Overview

In this lesson, we will take a look at the who, what, and where of SQL Server. We're going to start by examining exactly what SQL Server is, and then move on to looking at each of its components (such as databases, database objects, and services). We'll also show you how SQL Server works by describing its architecture. Finally, we'll look at the tasks you'll be expected to perform as a database developer.

Objectives

To understand the capabilities of Microsoft SQL Server, you will:

1A   Define the components of SQL Server.

In this topic, we will begin by examining what exactly SQL Server is and the features it offers you. We will also explore how you can integrate SQL Server not only with Windows 2000, but also with the other Microsoft Server applications such as Microsoft Exchange Server. In addition, we will explore the core services used by SQL Server. Finally, we will provide you with an overview of the utilities that you can use to administer SQL Server 2000.

1B   Define the types of objects you can implement within a database.

In this topic, we will examine the different types of objects you can implement within a database (such as tables, indexes, and views). We will also explore the system databases and their contents. Finally, we will show you how to work with a database by creating a database diagram within SQL Server Enterprise Manager.

1C   Define the components that make up SQL Server's architecture.

As a developer, it's important that you understand SQL Server's architecture in order to develop sound applications. In this topic, we will define each of the SQL Server architecture components. We will also show you how each of these components works together to enable a client and server to communicate.

1D   Identify the administrative tasks for managing SQL Server, and to examine the procedures you use to implement security.

In the database environment, you'll find that there are two distinct roles: the database administrator and the database designer. In this topic, we will look at the responsibilities of each role. We will also provide you with a review of how you implement security in SQL Server 2000.

TOPIC 1A

Exploring the Components of SQL Server

If you're thinking about implementing a database on your network, you should understand the role that a database server such as Microsoft SQL Server plays. Microsoft SQL Server is a client/server database management system. A client/server database management system consists of two components: a front-end component (the client), which is used to present and manipulate data; and a back-end component (the database server), which is used to store, retrieve, and protect the databases. For example, you can use Microsoft Access or a custom application written in Visual Basic on a client workstation to access databases on a Microsoft SQL server. In a client/server system, the majority of the data processing is done on the server instead of the clients. This means that a client/server system can reduce your network traffic (because only the results of queries must be sent to the clients). In addition, client/server systems are easier to scale because you can upgrade their performance simply by upgrading the server's hardware.

You can use SQL Server 2000 to support databases of almost any size. In fact, SQL Server easily supports terabyte-size databases. (Of course, for such large databases, you'll want to configure SQL Server on clustered servers.) You'll find that your SQL Server database (and the applications you use with that database) typically takes one of two forms:

We focus on all of the techniques for designing and using an OLTP database in this course.

- An Online Transaction Processing (OLTP) system, in which users continually make changes to the data in the database. For example, the database system for recording customers' orders at Amazon.com is an OLTP system.

- An Online Analytical Processing (OLAP) system, in which you primarily focus on analyzing the data in the database. You typically don't make many changes to such databases. For example, let's say that you have four different retail stores, each with its own inventory and order database. In this environment, you would use an OLAP system to combine the data from each of the four databases for performing analysis such as sales trends, customer demographics, and so on.

You'll frequently hear Microsoft SQL Server 2000 referred to as a relational database management system (RDBMS). An RDBMS uses established relationships between the data in a database to ensure the integrity of the data. For example, if you're setting up an order-entry database system, you'll probably define a relationship between the customer and invoice tables so that a sales clerk can't enter a customer account number in the invoice table if that customer doesn't exist in the customer table. These relationships enable you to prevent users from entering incorrect data.

The commands you primarily use to query a database on a database server are part of the *Structured Query Language (SQL)*. The Structured Query Language is a standardized set of commands used to work with databases. Microsoft SQL Server 2000 supports an enhanced version of SQL referred to as *Transact-SQL.* You use Transact-SQL commands to create, maintain, and query databases. You can use these commands either directly by manually entering commands in tools such as SQL Query Analyzer, or indirectly by using a client application such as Microsoft Access that is written to issue the necessary SQL commands. The American National Standards Institute (ANSI) and the International Standards Organization (ISO) are responsible for defining the standards for SQL. Microsoft SQL Server supports the most recently published standards for ANSI SQL. Because this standard was published in 1992, you'll sometimes hear the version of SQL implemented in SQL Server referred to as SQL-92.

In addition to Transact-SQL, you can also use the following languages to query SQL Server:

- Extensible Markup Language (XML)—Developed by the World Wide Web Consortium (W3C) to standardize the language used to develop Web documents.

- Multidimensional Expressions (MDX)—A language that enables you to define objects for analyzing data.

- SQL Distributed Management Objects (SQL-DMO)—A collection of objects that perform management and replication tasks. When you're developing a custom application, you can call these objects to perform a management task (such as creating a login account) instead of having to write a program from scratch to perform the same task.

SQL:
Structured Query Language is a language you use to add, modify, retrieve, and delete data from a relational database management system.

Transact-SQL:
Microsoft's enhanced version of ANSI SQL-92.

Features of Microsoft SQL Server

SQL Server includes many features that make it a powerful database management system for enterprise networks and smaller networks. These features include everything from supporting a wide variety of operating systems to integration with Windows 2000 and the Microsoft Server applications.

Support for Multiple Platforms

You can install the server component of Microsoft SQL Server 2000 on a variety of operating systems, including:

- Windows 98 and Windows Me.

- Windows NT 4.0, including the Workstation, Server, and Enterprise Edition versions.

- Windows 2000 Professional and the Windows 2000 Server family.

You can also install the client utilities of SQL Server 2000 on a wide variety of operating systems. The client utilities enable you to query and manage SQL servers. You can install the client utilities on computers running Windows 3.x, Windows 9x, Windows Me, Windows NT versions 3.x or later, Windows 2000, and DOS. You can even connect to SQL Server via Web browsers. SQL Server also supports third-party clients such as those running UNIX or Apple Macintosh.

Integration with Windows 2000

Microsoft designed SQL Server to integrate with both Windows 2000's security and the Active Directory itself. This integration with Windows 2000's security makes it possible for you to create your user accounts only in Windows 2000 and use them for granting access to SQL Server. In addition, you can rely on Windows 2000 to authenticate your users instead of SQL Server 2000. By using Windows 2000 to authenticate your users, you can take advantage of its enhanced security features such as encryption. SQL Server's integration with the Active Directory enables your users to search the Active Directory for SQL servers.

SQL Server also integrates with Windows 2000 utilities and services. For example, you can use the SQL Server counters within System Monitor to evaluate the performance of your server. Use the Application log in the Event Viewer to troubleshoot SQL Server errors. You can also integrate SQL Server 2000 with Windows 2000 services. For example, by integrating SQL Server with Internet Information Services, you make it possible for your users to query databases from a Web browser.

SQL Server consists of several services in Windows 2000. You can manage these services by using Windows 2000 utilities such as the Computer Management MMC. You can also manage these services using SQL Server's utilities.

Integration with Microsoft .NET Enterprise Servers

Microsoft designed SQL Server 2000 to integrate with its .NET Enterprise Server applications. We describe how you can take advantage of this integration in the following table.

Server Application	Enables SQL Server to
Microsoft Exchange Server	Send email messages to notify you when problems occur or when a scheduled job is completed.
Microsoft Host Integration Server 2000	Integrate with IBM mainframes or AS/400 applications and data using the Systems Network Architecture (SNA) protocol.
Microsoft Systems Management Server (SMS)	Store software and hardware inventory collected by SMS.
Microsoft Windows 2000 with Internet Security and Acceleration (ISA) Server	Provide secure access to SQL Server data. You use ISA Server as both a firewall to protect your internal network, and a Web cache to provide Internet access to your users.

Scalability

The maximum amount of RAM and disk space supported by SQL Server 2000 varies depending on the edition you're installing.

Microsoft SQL Server is scalable, which means your database management system can grow with your company. SQL Server is multi-threaded and can take advantage of Windows 2000's threading and scheduling services. Microsoft SQL Server also supports a parallel database architecture. If your server has multiple processors, SQL Server will issue database commands to all processors simultaneously. Finally, the Standard edition of SQL Server 2000 can address up to 2 gigabytes (2 GB) of RAM and 32 terabytes (32 TB) of hard-disk space.

Replication

Depending on your network, you might find that you need more than one SQL server. For example, you'll typically need multiple SQL servers if your network consists of two or more sites connected by WAN links. You might also choose to configure more than one server for fault tolerance. If you find that you need more than one SQL server for your network, you can configure SQL Server to auto-matically copy information from one SQL server to another. The process of copying data from one SQL server to another is called replication. Replication automates the process of copying data from one SQL server to another so that you don't have to manually copy data to your SQL servers.

Centralized Management

You can manage all of your SQL servers by using the Microsoft SQL Server Enterprise Manager utility. This utility provides you with a graphical interface for performing such management tasks as creating and maintaining databases and their objects, optimizing the server, and configuring replication.

Reliability

SQL Server includes reliability features such as transaction processing, online backups, and log shipping. Transaction processing enables SQL Server to detect and roll forward or back any incomplete transactions in a database. An incom-plete transaction can occur if your server shuts down improperly (like when the power fails). SQL Server uses transaction processing to prevent databases from becoming corrupt. Online backups enable you to back up your server's databases without shutting down the server or disconnecting users. The log shipping feature makes it easy for you to set up mirrored SQL servers. Your primary server is called the production server, and the backup server is called the standby server. With log shipping, SQL Server automatically copies all changes to a database on the production server to your standby server.

SQL Server 2000 supports Windows Clustering (a feature of Windows 2000 Advanced Server and Datacenter Server). This feature enables you to configure two servers (called nodes) into a cluster. This capability is referred to as failover clustering, because it enables SQL Server to continue running in the event of a failure.

Automating Tasks

One of the wonderful features of SQL Server is its ability to schedule jobs. You can use this feature to schedule jobs to run at a specific time or on a regular basis. For example, you can schedule jobs to import or export data, back up a database, or replicate information between servers. You can also configure SQL Server to notify you when a scheduled task is completed; SQL Server can send this notice via email, pager, or the net send command. SQL Server includes a sophisticated alerts management system that enables you to configure your server to automatically monitor for problems on the server, and even run jobs in the event a problem occurs.

TASK 1A-1:

Exploring the Features of Microsoft SQL Server

1. You're planning to install Microsoft Access on your client workstations; your clients will use Microsoft Access to work with a database that's currently stored on your Windows 2000 server. Why should you consider implementing Microsoft SQL Server in this environment?

2. You have a client that is considering downsizing a corporate database from a minicomputer to a Microsoft SQL Server on a microcomputer. Your client is concerned about performance. What features of SQL Server should you describe to your client?

Components of SQL Server

Microsoft SQL Server's environment consists of both services and administrative tools. Let's start exploring SQL Server by identifying its services.

The SQL Server Services

SQL Server consists of four core components. In the Windows 2000 environment, these components are services. If you install SQL Server on Windows 98 or Me, Setup installs these components as applications. The following table describes the four core components.

Service	Responsible for
MSSQLServer	Processing all Transact-SQL statements, managing database files, allocating the server's resources to clients, and ensuring data integrity. The MSSQLServer service is the database engine.
SQL Server Agent	Managing all scheduled jobs, monitoring for alerts, and notifying operators.
Microsoft Search	Providing support for full-text queries through creating and maintaining the necessary indexes.
Microsoft Distributed Transaction Coordinator	Enabling clients to include several types of data in a single transaction.

TASK 1A-2:

Exploring the SQL Server Services

Setup: SQL Server was installed on your computers during classroom setup.

1. **Log on to Windows 2000 as student# with a password of password.** (Replace # with your assigned student number.) Make sure that you log on to the Classroom.com domain. If you see the Configure Your Server dialog box, uncheck Show This Screen At Startup and then close the dialog box.

2. From the Microsoft SQL Server program group, **choose Service Manager** to start the SQL Server Service Manager utility. You can use this utility to view the status of your server's services, and to start, pause, or stop any of the services.

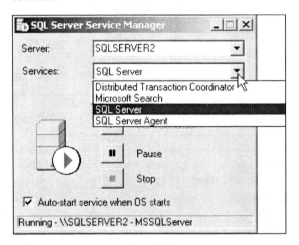

3. **Look at the status of the Distributed Transaction Coordinator, Microsoft Search, SQL Server, and SQL Server Agent services.** (Use the Services drop-down list to select each service.) You should see that the Microsoft Search and SQL Server services are currently running on your server.

4. **Close SQL Server Service Manager.**

Administrative Tools

SQL Server also includes many utilities for administering your server. The utilities consist of graphical tools, wizards, and command-line utilities. These utilities use a special object interface called SQL Distributed Management Objects (SQL-DMO); this interface is implemented as a dynamic link library (DLL) which uses objects and methods for performing such administrative tasks as creating databases, configuring replication, scheduling jobs, and defining alerts. All of the SQL Server utilities use SQL-DMO to perform such tasks on your server. In addition, you can develop applications to call SQL-DMO to perform administrative tasks.

Graphical Tools

SQL Server 2000 includes several powerful utilities you can use to administer almost every component of your server. The following table describes the graphical utilities included with SQL Server 2000.

Utility	Enables You to
Client Network Utility	Manage the configuration of each client's Network Library.
SQL Server Enterprise Manager	Perform management tasks on all SQL servers on your network. For example, you can create and manage your server's databases, monitor the space used within devices, configure your server, and manage replication. SQL Server Enterprise Manager is a Microsoft Management Console (MMC) snap-in.
SQL Server Network Utility	Manage the configuration of the server's Network Libraries.
SQL Query Analyzer	Analyze the plan of a query, view statistics about a query's performance, and execute/manage queries.
SQL Server Service Manager	Start, stop, and pause the SQL Server services.
SQL Server Profiler	Monitor and analyze the server's performance.
SQL Server Setup	Install and configure SQL Server.

SQL Server Wizards

In addition to the above graphical utilities, SQL Server also includes several wizards and assistants for performing administrative tasks. These wizards make it easy for you to perform many administrative tasks by walking you through them step-by-step.

Wizard	Enables You to
Configure Publishing and Distribution Wizard	Configure a server to publish its data. (Published data is called a publication.) After you've configured a server as a publisher, other SQL servers can subscribe to its publications.
Create Database Wizard	Create a database and its transaction log.
Create Job Wizard	Create and schedule administrative jobs for performing such tasks as backing up a database and truncating the transaction log.
Database Maintenance Plan Wizard	Configure and schedule maintenance tasks such as backups, consistency checking, and log shipping for a database.
Index Tuning Wizard	Obtain SQL Server's recommendations for indexing a database. You can even use this wizard to create the indexes it recommends.

Command-line Utilities

In addition to the graphical utilities included with SQL Server, you can enter commands in a Command Prompt window. The following table describes some of the command-line utilities you can use to administer your SQL Server.

Command	Enables You to
bcp	Copy data between database management systems or applications by using text files.
osql	Use ODBC to connect to your server to run SQL statements.

Other Utilities

The following table describes other utilities you can use to help you administer your SQL server.

Utility	Enables You to
SQL Server Books Online	View and query SQL Server's documentation online.
Transact-SQL Help	View context-sensitive help in SQL Query Analyzer. You access this help by pressing [Shift][F1] in SQL Query Analyzer.

TASK 1A-3:

Identifying Administrative Utilities

1. **Match each SQL Server utility with the types of tasks you can use it to perform.**

____	SQL Server Enterprise Manager	a.	Enables you to configure the server's Network-Library.
____	Client Network Utility	b.	Use to track activity on your SQL server.
____	bcp	c.	Enables you to configure and manage all SQL servers on your network.
____	SQL Server Profiler	d.	Use to query SQL Server at the command line.
____	osql	e.	Enables you to automate administrative tasks such as backups.
____	Index Tuning Wizard	f.	Import text files into a SQL database.
____	Database Maintenance Plan Wizard	g.	Use to automate the creation of indexes for a database.
____	SQL Server Network Utility	h.	Use to configure the client's Network Library.

Registering Servers

When you run SQL Server Enterprise Manager on a SQL server, it will automatically register and display that server in the console tree. You must register any other servers you want to manage from within SQL Server Enterprise Manager. You'll also have to register your SQL server if you install the SQL Server administrative tools on a client workstation.

To register a server in SQL Server Enterprise Manager, right-click on the SQL Server Group container in the console tree. From the shortcut menu, choose New SQL Server Registration to start the Register SQL Server Wizard. You use this wizard to specify the server you want to connect to as well as how you want to be authenticated on that server. After you've registered a server, SQL Server Enterprise Manager saves the registration information so that you can see that server the next time you open SQL Server Enterprise Manager.

TASK 1A-4:

Using SQL Server Enterprise Manager

1. From the Microsoft SQL Server program group, **choose Enterprise Manager** to open SQL Server Enterprise Manager.

2. **Look at the SQL Server Enterprise Manager interface.** SQL Server Enterprise Manager uses the Microsoft Management Console (MMC) interface. MMC enables you to "snap in" administrative tools so that you can perform a variety of administrative tasks from within a single utility. When you first open SQL Server Enterprise Manager, you see the MMC displayed with the Microsoft SQL Server's snap-in loaded. The left pane in SQL Server Enterprise Manager is called the console tree, and the right pane is called the details pane.

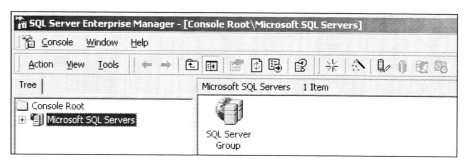

3. In the console tree, **expand Microsoft SQL Servers** to display a list of the server groups in SQL Server Enterprise Manager. By default, SQL Server Setup creates only the SQL Server Group. You can also create your own server groups to organize your SQL servers.

4. **Right-click on the SQL Server Group and look at the shortcut menu.** You can choose New SQL Server Registration to start the Register SQL Server Wizard. Use this option to register other SQL servers within SQL Server Enterprise Manager.

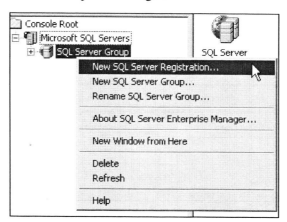

5. **Close the shortcut menu.**

6. **Expand the SQL Server Group** to display a list of servers registered in the group. By default, SQL Server Enterprise Manager automatically registers your local server in this group; SQL Server Enterprise Manager logs you in to your server by using your Windows 2000 account.

7. **Look at the green arrow on your server's icon.** The green arrow indicates that your server is currently running.

8. In the console tree, **right-click on your server.** From the shortcut menu, **choose Edit→SQL Server Registration Properties.**

9. **Look at the Registered SQL Server Properties dialog box.** You can use this dialog box to register your server with a different login account and password, switch between Windows Authentication and SQL Server Authentication security, move your server to a different server group, and set server configuration options.

You can specify a different login account and password only with SQL Server Authentication. If you're using Windows Authentication, you can log in to your SQL server only with your current Windows 2000 user account. You can't specify a different Windows user account.

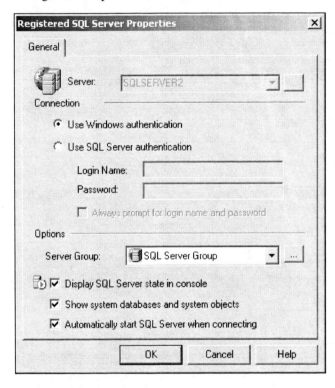

10. **Click Cancel** to close the Registered SQL Server Properties dialog box.

11. **Expand your server** to display the folders for configuring your server. For example, you use the Security folder to configure your server's login accounts.

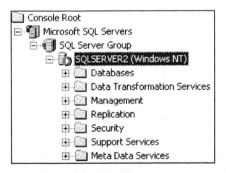

12. **Minimize SQL Server Enterprise Manager.**

SQL Query Analyzer

You use SQL Query Analyzer to run SQL queries as well as to optimize the performance of the queries. A query is simply a command you send to your server. This query can request data from the server, change data, or delete information. Queries consist of one or more SQL statements. The query window in SQL Query Analyzer consists of one or more panes. The pane in which you type your query is called the Editor pane, and SQL Query Analyzer displays the results of your query in the Results pane, as shown in Figure 1-1. Other panes you can configure SQL Query Analyzer to display include:

- Messages pane, for displaying any error messages.

- Execution Plan pane, for displaying SQL Server's plan for executing a query in a graphical format.

- Trace pane, for tracking server trace information.

- Statistics pane, for displaying statistics about the tasks performed by the server to process a query.

Figure 1-1: *The Query window consists of at least two panes: the Editor pane and the Results pane.*

One of the new features in SQL Server 2000 is that you can display an Object Browser window within SQL Query Analyzer. This is a wonderful enhancement to SQL Query Analyzer because it enables you to browse for the names of the objects you want to query.

Default Databases

When you install SQL Server, the Setup utility automatically creates several system and sample user databases. System databases contain information used by SQL Server to operate. You create user databases and they can contain any information you need to collect. You can use SQL Query Analyzer to query any of your SQL databases, including the system and sample databases. The following table describes the type of information stored in each of the default databases.

Database	Contains
distribution	History information about replication. SQL Server creates this database on your server only if you configure replication.
master	Information about the operation of SQL Server, including user accounts, other SQL servers, environment variables, error messages, databases, storage space allocated to databases, and the tapes and disk drives on the SQL server.
model	A template for creating new databases. SQL Server automatically copies the objects in this database to each new database you create.
msdb	Information about all scheduled jobs, defined alerts, and operators on your server. This information is used by the SQL Server Agent service.
Northwind	A sample database for learning SQL Server.
pubs	A sample database for learning SQL Server.
tempdb	Temporary information. This database is used as a scratchpad by SQL Server.

TASK 1A-5:

Using SQL Query Analyzer

1. From the Microsoft SQL Server program group, **choose Query Analyzer** to run SQL Query Analyzer.

2. **Look at the Connect To SQL Server dialog box.** You use this dialog box to specify which SQL server you want to connect to as well as how you want to log in to the server. In the SQL Server text box, **type .** to specify your local server. Below Connect Using, **select Windows Authentication.**

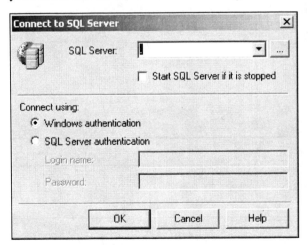

3. **Click OK** to log in to your server with Windows Authentication.

4. **Look at the SQL Query Analyzer interface.** By default, SQL Query Analyzer displays the Editor pane in the Query window and the Object Browser window. (You don't see the Results pane because you haven't yet executed a query.) SQL Query Analyzer also connects you to your login account's default database. Your login account was assigned the master database as its default database during classroom setup.

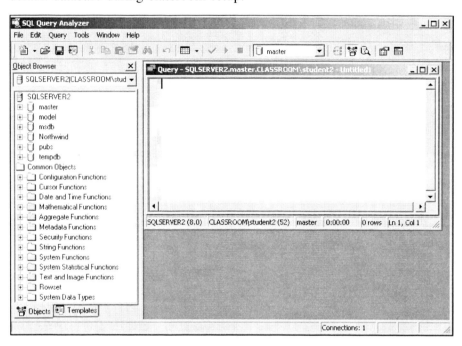

5. In the Object Browser window, **expand the pubs database.** You now see a list of folders containing the different types of objects within the pubs database.

6. Expand the User Tables folder and the dbo.authors table within it. You can use the Object Browser window to display a list of the columns, indexes, constraints, and triggers for this table. You can also use the Object Browser window to identify other objects that are based on this table (such as views, stored procedures, and indexes). We're going to talk more about the types of objects you can create within a database in the next topic.

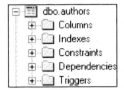

The Object Browser window displays both the owner's name (the user who created the object) and the object's name itself for each object. For example, the notation "dbo.authors" means that the table is owned by the user named dbo, and the table name is authors.

7. Expand the Columns folder to display a list of the columns that make up the authors table. You can use this information to help you write a query to query the authors table.

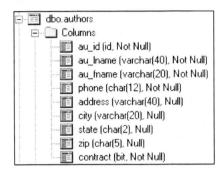

8. From the Database drop-down list, **select pubs.** You're going to query the pubs database.

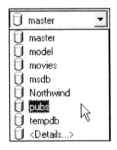

9. In the Editor pane, **type the following query:**

```
SELECT au_id, au_lname, au_fname
FROM authors
```

You use the SELECT SQL statement to display rows in a table. By using SELECT au_id, au_lname, au_fname, you specify that you want the results set to contain only those columns.

10. Choose Query→Execute to have SQL Server process your query. (You can also execute queries by pressing [Ctrl]E, [F5], or by clicking the Execute Query button on the toolbar.)

11. **Look at the Results pane.** SQL Query Analyzer displays the results of your query in a separate pane in the window.

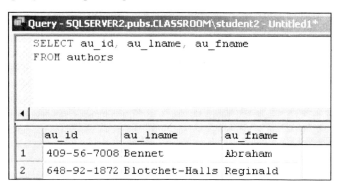

12. **Choose Edit→Clear Window** (or press [Ctrl][Shift][Delete]) to clear your previous query from the Editor pane. Notice that clearing the Editor pane doesn't clear the Results pane.

13. **Minimize SQL Query Analyzer.**

TOPIC 1B

SQL Server Database Structure

database:
A collection of related database objects such as tables, views, and indexes. Each database in SQL Server consists of at least one data file and a transaction log file.

table:
An object within a database that contains rows and columns of information.

Now that we've looked at what SQL Server does for you as a database server, let's take a look at the components of a database in more detail. Most importantly, you use SQL Server to store one or more databases. In the Microsoft SQL Server environment, the term *database* refers to a collection of tables and other database objects such as indexes. A *table* consists of rows and columns; these rows and columns contain the data for the table. A database can contain a virtually unlimited number of tables; each table can contain a maximum of 1,024 columns (fields). You can also define up to 250 indexes per table. You create an index by specifying the columns with which you want to sort the data within a table.

You will typically create a database to contain all of the associated tables, indexes, and other database objects for a particular application. For example, let's say that you're planning to create a system for managing customer orders. In this scenario, your database might consist of tables for storing customer information, inventory, tax schedules, and invoices. You might also create indexes based on customer numbers, part numbers, and invoice numbers. As you can see, a single database can contain multiple tables and indexes. We talk about creating many of the different database objects in detail later on in the course.

Tables

One of the most critical components of a database is its tables. That's because SQL Server uses tables to store data. You create a table to contain a set of related information. When you create a table, you define its columns. Columns refer to the individual pieces of information (fields) you want to track for a specific table. For example, if you want to create a table to store customer information, you should define columns to store such information as an account number, name, address, city, state, zip code, and telephone number for each customer.

You can control how information is stored in a particular column by configuring the following properties in the following table.

Property	Enables You to Specify
Data type	The type of data that can be entered into the column. For example, if you configure a column's data type as decimal, users can enter only numeric information into the column. You must also specify a data type when you define variables.
Constraint	Rules for validating data entry. You use constraints to enforce data integrity between tables. For example, if you have a customer table and an invoice table, you can create a constraint on the invoice table such that users can enter a customer ID number in the invoice table only if that ID number exists in the customer table.
Default	A default value for a column. For example, if you are creating a table to store customer information, you might want to set default values for the city and state columns.
Rule	Valid values for data entry. You can use rules to make sure that your users enter specific values into a column. For example, if you want to restrict users to entering either 1, 2, or 3 in a column, you could create a rule stating that only those numbers are valid for the column.

Indexes

Because each table can contain anywhere from a few hundred rows up to millions of rows, you use indexes to speed up table searches. You can define indexes for your tables so that you can search faster for information within the tables. For example, if you have a customer information table, you can create an index on the customer's account number. When you create an index, you specify a key. You use this key to identify the column or columns in the table on which you want to base your index.

nonclustered index:
A separate database object that contains the key columns on which you want to index a table, along with a value to identify each row in the table. A nonclustered index doesn't change the order of the actual rows in the table.

clustered index:
An index that changes the way SQL Server stores the rows in a table. This index isn't a separate database object. Instead, SQL Server uses this index to determine the order in which it stores the rows that make up a table. You can define only one clustered index per table.

You can create indexed views only in the SQL Server 2000 Enterprise and Developer editions.

materializing:
The process of retrieving the rows and columns from one or more tables to display the results set for a view.

You can create two types of indexes within SQL Server: *nonclustered* and *clustered.* When you create a nonclustered index, you specify a key for sorting the data. SQL Server creates the index as a separate object within the database; this index contains the sorted key information for each row in the table, and a pointer that identifies the row within the table. When you query a table for a specific row, SQL Server can search the index to find the row rather than searching the table itself—much like you use the index in the back of a book to find a specific page. When you create a nonclustered index, you don't change the order of the data within the table.

If you create a clustered index, in contrast, you force SQL Server to store the data within the table in the order specified by the index. For example, you could create a clustered index for a customer information table by using the customer account number as the key. When you add data to the table, SQL Server automatically places the new rows in order by account number. A clustered index controls the order in which data is stored within a table. You can create only one clustered index per table. You should always create a clustered index for a table. By creating a clustered index, you configure SQL Server to automatically store the data in a table in a specific order. Although both clustered and nonclustered indexes enable you to search tables faster, the clustered index provides better performance because it is part of the table itself and not a separate database object.

Because SQL Server stores the rows in a table in order by its clustered index, you'll find that a clustered index improves the performance of queries that typically return a group of rows instead of a single row. For example, you might define a clustered index on a customer table based on the ZIP code column if you frequently retrieve customers' information by ZIP code.

Views

You can define views within a SQL Server database. A view enables you to specify how you want to see the data within one or more tables. You define a view by choosing the tables within the database you want to view and then the columns within those tables. For example, if you create a customer order database that contains customer, inventory, and invoice tables, you might want to create a view that contains the customer account number and name from the customer table and the orders placed by that customer from the invoice table. Views help you secure your server by enabling you to grant users permissions to a view without having to grant them permissions to the tables on which a view is based.

In a sense, you can think of a view as a "virtual" table, because each view uses the same format as a table (meaning it consists of columns and rows). In addition, you query a view just as you would a table. For example, you can use the statement SELECT * FROM object_name, where object_name is either a table or a view name. SQL Server retrieves the columns and rows that make up a view each time you query the view. This process is called *materializing* the view; and depending on the view and the tables on which it's based, the process can place quite a heavy load on your server. For this reason, one of the enhancements Microsoft added to SQL Server 2000 is support for creating indexes on a view. A clustered index on a view forces SQL Server to store the view's results set in a database just like it stores tables. We're going to talk more about how you create indexed views later on in the course.

Stored Procedures

Another type of database object you can create within a SQL Server database is a stored procedure. You can create a stored procedure to perform a series of Transact-SQL commands on your server. You can execute a stored procedure within SQL Server tools such as SQL Query Analyzer, or call a stored procedure from a custom program such as one written in Visual Basic. SQL Server compiles and caches a stored procedure the first time you run it to improve its performance.

Triggers

You can configure SQL Server to perform specific Transact-SQL statements when a user adds, deletes, or changes the contents of a table. Because these Transact-SQL statements are run only when an action is performed against a table, Microsoft refers to these statements as triggers. You use a trigger to perform such tasks as verifying the accuracy of the data in your table or keeping records of changes.

User-defined Functions

One of the enhancements in SQL Server 2000 is support for user-defined functions. You can create your own functions to perform complex calculations—and then save them as one of a database's objects. The advantage to defining your own functions is that you can then re-use a function within a custom application instead of having to write the calculations performed by the function.

Identifying SQL Server Objects

Now that we've explored the different types of objects you can create, let's take a moment to explain the different types of names you can use to refer to objects. You use objects' names in stored procedures, programs, and queries. SQL Server enables you to identify objects by using either their fully qualified names or their partial name. A *fully qualified name* for an object consists of four components: the SQL server name, the database name, the owner name, and the object name. Each component in the fully qualified name for an object must be separated by a period (in other words, server.database.owner.object). For example, if you have a table named "customer" that is stored in a database named "receipts" on a server named "sales," then the fully qualified name for the table is:

```
sales.receipts.owner_name.customer.
```

The owner of an object is typically the same as the owner of the database. By default, the owner of a database is usually the database user account named dbo (which is short for database owner).

You don't always have to use an object's fully qualified name. Instead, you can use a partial name to identify an object. When you use a partial name, you can omit some of the components of an object's fully qualified name. For example, if you're currently working on the sales server, if your current database is the receipts database, and if you're the owner of the customer table, then you could identify the customer table simply by its partial name—customer. A partial object name can be any of the following:

fully qualified name:
An object name that contains the server, database, owner, and object names. Because this name consists of four components, you'll sometimes hear the fully qualified name for an object referred to as the four-part object name.

If you omit any of the "in-between" names in a partial name, you must still indicate it by putting a period in the name.

- server.database..object
- server..owner.object
- server...object
- database.owner.object
- database..object
- owner.object
- object

When you use a partial name, SQL Server assumes the following:

- If you don't specify a server name, SQL Server assumes the object is on your local server (the server to which you're connected).
- If you don't specify a database name, SQL Server assumes your current database.
- If you don't specify an owner name, SQL Server assumes the owner is the SQL user associated with your login account.

Most of the time you'll find that you identify objects by using a partial name, such as database.owner.object or just the object name itself. You typically use a fully qualified name only when you're creating distributed queries (queries that query data distributed across multiple servers).

TASK 1B-1:

Discussing the Components of SQL Server

1. **What is a database? What types of objects can a database contain?**

2. **Compare and contrast clustered and nonclustered indexes.**

3. **You would like to create a table named bookstores in the pubs database. Assuming that dbo is the owner of the database and that the database is on your current server, what name should you use to identify this table?**

4. **Why might you create a clustered index on a view?**

5. In SQL Server Enterprise Manager, **expand your server's Databases folder** to display a list of the databases on your server.

6. **Look at your server's databases.** You should see four system databases (master, model, msdb, and tempdb) as well as two user databases (Northwind and pubs). These databases were automatically created on your server when SQL Server was installed during classroom setup.

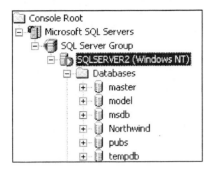

7. **Expand the Northwind database** to display a list of the types of objects you can define within the Northwind database.

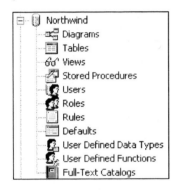

8. **Select the Tables object and take a look at the details pane.** You should see a list of both system tables within the Northwind database (such as those that begin with *sys*) as well as data tables (such as Customers). These tables are created automatically when you install SQL Server.

9. **Assuming that you want to access the Customers table in your server's Northwind database, what is the table's fully qualified name?**

10. **If you're currently working on your server and you're the owner of the Customers table, what partial names could you use to refer to this table?**

11. **Switch to SQL Query Analyzer.**

12. **What is your current database?**

13. **In the following space, write a query to view all rows in the Customers table in the Northwind database (given that your current database is pubs).**

14. In SQL Query Analyzer, **execute the query you wrote in step 13.**

15. **Clear the Query window.**

16. **Minimize SQL Query Analyzer.**

System Tables

Within each database, SQL Server maintains information about that database in system tables. (These tables are copied to new databases from the model database.) These system tables make up the database catalog. Another term you'll hear for the database catalog is metadata, which means information about information. In other words, a database's metadata describes the database's structure, components, users, security, and so on. The following table describes some of the system tables in each database catalog.

System Table	Contains a Row for Each
sysusers	Windows 2000 user, SQL Server user, Windows 2000 group, or role that you've defined as users of the database.
sysobjects	Object in the database.
syspermissions	Permission you grant or deny to any database user.

In addition to the database catalog, SQL Server also maintains a system catalog in the master database. SQL Server uses the system catalog to keep track of everything to do with the configuration of your server. Most importantly, the system catalog contains metadata for tracking all other databases on your server. For this reason, the master database is critical to the operation of SQL Server. The following table describes some of the system tables stored in the system catalog.

System Table	Contains a Row for Each
sysdatabases	Database on the SQL server.
sysxlogins	Login account that can log in to the SQL server.
sysmessages	Error or warning message. You can also create your own error messages. (You might do so if you're developing a custom application.) If you do, SQL Server adds your error messages to the sysmessages table in the master database.

We're going to show you how to create your own error messages in the "Stored Procedures" lesson.

Retrieving Metadata

You can view the metadata stored in system tables by querying them just like any other database table. One word of caution, though. Microsoft strongly recommends that you don't write scripts that query the system tables directly in order to avoid potential problems with querying the same tables in future versions of SQL Server, because Microsoft has stated that the structure of system tables can change with new versions of SQL Server. For this reason, Microsoft recommends that you use the *system stored procedures*, system functions, and system information schema views included with SQL Server 2000 to query the system tables instead of writing your own scripts. The following table describes some of the system stored procedures that you can use to query system tables. If you're like most people, you'll find that you frequently need to use these stored procedures, so you should memorize the stored procedures in this table.

system stored procedures: *Stored procedures written by Microsoft that are installed when you install SQL Server 2000. You can use these stored procedures to perform most of the administrative tasks on your server.*

You'll find that the majority of Microsoft's system stored procedures have names that begin with "sp_." For example, sp_help is a system stored procedure.

System Stored Procedure	Enables You to View Information About
sp_help	A database's objects. This stored procedure returns a list of all objects in the database, along with each object's owner and type.
sp_help *object*	A database object. Use this stored procedure to view not only the owner, type, and creation date of the object, but also its structure. For example, if you use sp_help with a table name, SQL Server displays a list of the columns that make up the table.
sp_helpdb *database*	The files and size of a database. Use sp_helpdb to view a list of the database's files, their location, and size information.
sp_helpindex *table*	The indexes defined for the specified table. Use the results to determine index type, along with the columns on which each index is based.

Let's take a look at an example where you view information about the authors table in the pubs database. You can see this table's structure by running the following query:

```
sp_help authors
```

You can also view metadata by using system functions. You query a system function by using the SELECT Transact-SQL statement. For example, to view the length of a column named 'au_lname' in the authors table within the pubs database, you can execute this query by using the following syntax:

```
SELECT COL_LENGTH('authors','au_lname')
```

The following table describes some of the functions you can use to query a database's metadata.

System Function	Enables You to Obtain
COL_LENGTH(*'table'*, *'column'*)	The width of a column.
DATALENGTH(*data_type*)	The length of an expression of any data type.
DB_ID(*'database_name'*)	The unique ID number assigned to a database.
STATS_DATE(*'table_id'*, *'index_id'*)	The date when the statistics for an index were last updated.
USER_NAME(*user_id*)	The user name for a given user ID.

A third technique you can use to view metadata is to use the information schema views that are included with SQL Server. These views enable you to examine metadata for all objects in a database. Like system functions, you use these views with the SELECT statement, as follows:

```
SELECT *
FROM information_schema.columns
```

We describe some of the views you can use to query metadata in the following table.

System Information Schema View	Enables You to View
information_schema.columns	Information about the columns defined in a database.
information_schema.tables	A list of the tables in a database.
information_schema.tables_privileges	Security information for the tables in a database.

TASK 1B-2:

Identifying the Default Databases and System Tables

1.   **In your own words, define the term metadata.**

2.   **What is the difference between the system catalog and a database catalog?**

3.   In SQL Server Enterprise Manager, **expand the master database and select the Tables object.** You should see a list of the tables within the master database. By default, SQL Server 2000 displays the system databases and tables in SQL Server Enterprise Manager (instead of hiding them).

4.   **What is the role of the sysdatabases table in the master database?**

5. In the details pane, **right-click on the sysdatabases table and choose Open Table→Return All Rows** to display all of the rows in the sysdatabases table. You should see a row for each of the databases on your server. In addition, you see the unique ID number SQL Server assigns to each database (in the dbid column) as well as when the database was created (in the crdate column).

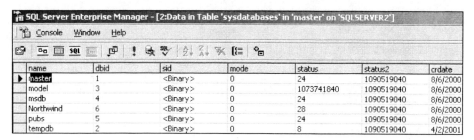

name	dbid	sid	mode	status	status2	crdate
master	1	<Binary>	0	24	1090519040	8/6/2000
model	3	<Binary>	0	1073741840	1090519040	8/6/2000
msdb	4	<Binary>	0	24	1090519040	8/6/2000
Northwind	6	<Binary>	0	28	1090519040	8/6/2000
pubs	5	<Binary>	0	24	1090519040	8/6/2000
tempdb	2	<Binary>	0	8	1090519040	4/2/2001

6. **Close the sysdatabases table.** Make sure you close the window with the title Data in Table 'sysdatabases', not SQL Server Enterprise Manager.

7. In the console tree, **right-click on your server and choose Edit SQL Server Registration Properties.**

8. **Look at the available options for your server's registration.** You can use the Show System Databases And System Objects option to control whether or not SQL Server Enterprise Manager displays the system databases and tables.

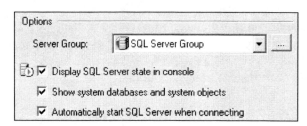

9. **Uncheck Show System Databases And System Objects, and then click OK.**

10. **Look at your server's Databases folder.** You no longer see the master, msdb, model, and tempdb system databases.

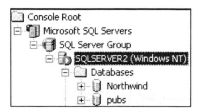

11. **Expand the Northwind database and select the Tables object.** You see only the user data tables in the Northwind database (the system tables are now hidden).

12. **Reconfigure SQL Server Enterprise Manager to display the system databases and objects.**

13. **Switch to SQL Query Analyzer.**

14. From the Database drop-down list, **select Northwind.**

15. Execute the following query:

```
SELECT table_name, table_type
FROM information_schema.tables
```

This query enables you to view a list of the tables and views defined in the Northwind database.

	table_name	table_type
1	Alphabetical list of products	VIEW
2	Categories	BASE TABLE
3	Category Sales for 1997	VIEW
4	Current Product List	VIEW
5	Customer and Suppliers by City	VIEW
6	CustomerCustomerDemo	BASE TABLE
7	CustomerDemographics	BASE TABLE
8	Customers	BASE TABLE

16. Minimize SQL Query Analyzer.

Creating Database Diagrams

One of the wonderful tools included in SQL Server Enterprise Manager is its Create Database Diagram Wizard. You use this wizard to create a diagram containing some or all of the tables in a database, the structure of those tables, and their relationships with other tables. For example, in the pubs database, the authors table has a relationship with the titleauthor table that's based on the author ID column.

You create a database diagram by expanding the database in SQL Server Enterprise Manager. Next, right-click on the Diagrams icon below the database, and choose New Database Diagram. Use the Create Database Diagram Wizard to select the tables you want to view in your diagram. After you create your database diagram, you can use the Query Designer to build queries based on the tables in your database. You can also use the Query Designer to join tables in the query based on the relationships between the tables.

TASK 1B-3:

Creating and Working with a Database Diagram

Objective: To create a database diagram based on the Northwind sample database.

1. In SQL Server Enterprise Manager, in the console tree, **expand the Northwind database.**

2. Right-click on the Diagrams object and choose New Database Diagram to start the Create Database Diagram Wizard.

3. On the Welcome page, **click Next.**

4. On the Select Tables To Be Added page, below Available Tables, **select the Categories table.**

5. Below Available Tables, **press [Shift] and select the Suppliers table** to select all of the user tables in the Northwind database—but not the system tables. (The system tables all have names that begin with "sys.")

6. **Click Add** to add the tables to your diagram.

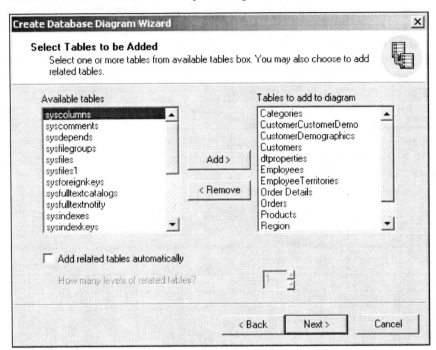

7. Below Available Tables, **select the Territories table and click Add** to add this table to your diagram.

8. **Click Next, and then click Finish.**

9. **Take a look at your database diagram.** You should see all of the tables in the Northwind database, their structures, and how each table links to other tables in the database. (Because there are so many tables, your diagram might be too small to read.)

10. On the toolbar, **click the Zoom button.**

11. From the drop-down list, **choose 75%** to enlarge your database diagram.

12. **Based on the relationships between the tables you see in the diagram, which tables will you need to query if you want to see a list of orders, the dates the orders were placed with the Northwind company, and the names of the customers?**

13. In the database diagram, **select the Orders table.** If you select a table by clicking on its title bar, you should see that the first column in the table is selected and that you have a blinking cursor in that column. You should see that only the Orders table is highlighted in your diagram.

14. **Right-click on the Orders table and choose Task→Open Table** to display the rows in the Orders table.

15. On the toolbar, **click the Show/Hide Diagram pane button** to display the Diagram pane. (The Show/Hide Diagram pane button is the second button from the left on the toolbar.) The Diagram pane enables you to view the structure of the table you are querying and to add tables to the query. You can also use the Diagram pane to specify which columns from each of the tables you want to view in the query.

16. **Look at the Diagram pane.** You now see a split screen consisting of the Diagram pane in the top half and the rows in the Orders table in the bottom half. The Diagram pane shows the structure of the Orders table. You can use the check boxes to the left of each column to specify which columns you want to see in your query results.

As you work through this Task, you might see a message asking if you want to continue working with this results set. This message appears if there's a time delay between your first query to see all columns and rows in the Orders table and your next query. Because you no longer need to see all rows in the Orders table, you can click No when you get this message.

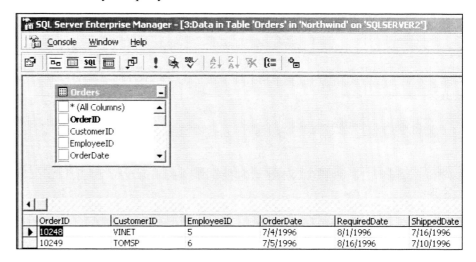

17. In the Diagram pane, **right-click anywhere in the empty space and choose Add Table** to display a list of tables in the Northwind database.

18. From the list of tables, **select Customers and then click Add** to add the Customers table to the query.

19. **Click Close** to close the Add Table dialog box.

20. **Look at the Diagram pane.** You now see the Orders and Customers tables in the Diagram pane—and that the Orders table is linked to the Customers table by the column Customer ID.

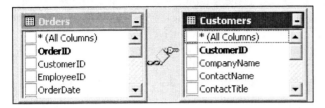

21. In the Orders table in the Diagram pane, **check the OrderID and OrderDate columns.** In the Customers table, **check the CompanyName and ContactName columns** to add the Order ID, Order Date, Company Name, and Contact Name columns to your query.

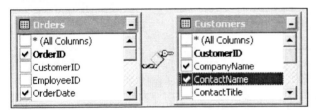

22. On the toolbar, **click the Show/Hide SQL pane button.** (This is the fourth button from the left on the toolbar.)

23. **Look at the SQL pane.** The SQL pane enables you to view the Transact-SQL statement you've built in the Diagram pane. You use the SELECT Transact-SQL statement to query the table to display specific rows. Because you initially viewed all columns in the Orders table, the SELECT statement contains the command to show all columns (SELECT *,).

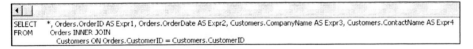

24. **Right-click the SQL pane and choose Properties.** In the Properties dialog box, **uncheck Output All Columns** to modify the SELECT statement so that it no longer displays all columns.

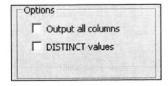

25. **Click Close** to close the Properties dialog box.

26. On the toolbar, **click the Show/Hide SQL pane button** again to close the SQL pane.

27. **You want to display the results of your query in alphabetical order by company name. Within each company's orders, you would like to see the orders sorted by order date. Of the columns in both tables, which columns should you use to perform this sort?**

28. In the Diagram pane, in the Customers table, **select (don't uncheck) the Company Name column.** On the toolbar, **click the Sort Ascending button** to configure SQL Server to sort the results set by the Company Name column. (The Sort Ascending button has A-Z on it.)

29. **Look at the Company Name column.** SQL Server displays "A - Z" next to the Company Name column to indicate that it's going to sort your query by this column.

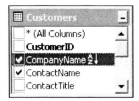

30. In the Orders table, **configure SQL Server to sort by order date in ascending order.**

31. On the toolbar, **click the Run button** to execute the query. (The Run button is the one with the exclamation point.)

32. **Take a look at the results of your query.** You should see a list of orders sorted first by company name and then by order date.

33. **Close the Query window (don't close SQL Server Enterprise Manager).**

34. In the Database Diagram window, on the toolbar, **click the Save button** to save your diagram. **Enter** *Northwind* for the name of your database diagram, **and then click OK.**

35. **Close the Database Diagram window.**

APPLY YOUR KNOWLEDGE 1-1

Suggested time:
20 minutes

Querying a Database Diagram

Objective: To create a database diagram based on the pubs database. You're also going to use this diagram to build a query to display each author's last name, first name, and the title of their books.

1. In SQL Server Enterprise Manager, build a database diagram of the pubs database. Add all tables except for those that begin with "sys" to the database diagram.

2. Based on this diagram, which should you use in a query if you want to see a list of the authors' names and the titles of their books?

3. How are these tables linked together?

4. Build a query that shows each author's last name, first name, and the title of his/her books. Sort the results set by the author's last name and the title.

5. Save the database diagram as pubs.

6. Close the Database Diagram window.

TOPIC 1C

SQL Server Architecture

Because SQL Server is a client/server database management system, components of its architecture reside on both the client and the server itself, as shown in Figure 1-2. We're going to start exploring the architecture by examining the client components, and then move on to the server's architecture.

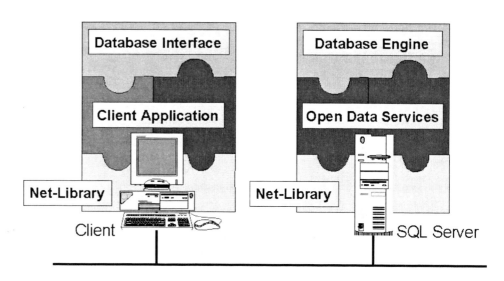

Figure 1-2: *SQL Server architecture.*

Client Architecture

Internet applications might use the Hypertext Transport Protocol (HTTP) to access SQL Server data instead of a database API.

On the client, the SQL Server architecture consists of three layers: the client application, a database interface, and a Net-Library. At the client application layer, your clients use an application such as the SQL Server utilities, Microsoft Access, or a custom application (developed in programs such as Visual Basic) to access the SQL server. At its most basic, the client application enables your users to send SQL queries to the server and displays those queries' results sets. Your client application can send these SQL statements to a SQL server by using a variety of methods and languages, including Transact-SQL, Extensible Markup Language (XML), and English Query. XML enables you to send queries as part of a URL or template over the Hypertext Transport Protocol (HTTP). In other words, XML enables you to query a SQL server from a Web browser. English Query enables you to query SQL Server by using a question such as "How many customers live in Utah?" instead of its equivalent Transact-SQL query:

```
SELECT *
FROM customers
WHERE state = "UT"
```

The client application works in conjunction with a database Application Programming Interface (API) to access the data on the server. If you're developing an application from scratch, you can choose your application's API. If you're using applications such as Microsoft Access or the SQL Server utilities, you use whatever database API the programmer chose for those applications. So what is a database API? An API defines the language and functions the client application can use to access the resources on the SQL server. SQL Server 2000 supports a variety of database APIs, including OLE DB, ODBC, and DB-Library. ODBC is an industry-standard, non-proprietary interface for accessing a variety of data sources, including SQL Server. Developed by Microsoft, the OLE DB interface also enables you to access a variety of data sources, and has the advantage of being object-oriented. In fact, you might think of OLE DB as an object-oriented version of ODBC. Because OLE DB is accessible only from C and C++, you must use Microsoft's ActiveX Data Objects to encapsulate OLE DB for use in languages such as Visual Basic, Active Server Pages, and Visual Basic Scripting. The DB-Library API was also developed by Microsoft, but is specifically designed to work only with SQL Server. For this reason, many programmers choose to invest their time in learning OLE DB and ODBC, because they can use these APIs to communicate with a much wider variety of data sources. You'll find that very few new applications have been written to use the DB-Library API.

As a client, you communicate with a SQL server by using a *Net-Library* (also called a Net-Lib or a Network Library). SQL Server uses Net-Libraries to prepare client requests for sending by the appropriate network protocol, and to receive responses from the server. You can configure both the client and the SQL server to use more than one Net-Library, but both the client and the server must have a Net-Library in common. SQL Server supports TCP/IP, Named Pipes, IPX/SPX (NWLink), Banyan Vines, and AppleTalk ADSP. We're going to talk more about Net-Libraries in the next lesson.

Net-Library:
A Dynamic Link Library (DLL) that enables a client and a SQL server to communicate over a specific network protocol.

Tabular Data Stream Protocol

SQL Server uses the Tabular Data Stream (TDS) protocol to send data between the client and the server. TDS packets, in turn, are then encapsulated in the protocol stack used by the Net-Library. For example, if you're using SQL Server on a TCP/IP-based network, TDS packets are encapsulated in TCP/IP packets.

Server Architecture

On the server, the SQL Server architecture consists of the Database Engine (which is made up of two components: the Relational Engine and the Storage Engine), Open Data Services (ODS), and the server's Net-Library. The Relational Engine is responsible for checking the syntax of Transact-SQL queries, designing an optimized execution plan for each query, executing queries, and enforcing security. The Storage Engine handles everything to do with the server's files, including allocating space, reading and writing data, logging and recovery, and backup and restore operations. ODS acts as an interface between the server's Net-Library and its applications. Its job is to manage communications on the network between the server and its clients. Specifically, the server receives client requests and responds through Open Data Services. The server's Net-Library accepts connection requests from a client's Net-Library.

Client/Server Communications

Let's take a few minutes to look at how all of these components that make up SQL Server's architecture work together. For example, let's say that you're working on a client computer and you use SQL Query Analyzer to send a query to a SQL server. Here's how the communications between your client computer and the server take place:

1. When you execute the query within SQL Query Analyzer, it sends your query to the appropriate database API on your computer. (The database API your client computer chooses depends on the application you're using.) The database API is responsible for using the appropriate provider, driver, or DLL to encapsulate your query into one or more Tabular Data Stream (TDS) packets. Your computer then forwards these TDS packets to the client computer's Net-Library.

2. The client computer's Net-Library is responsible for encapsulating the TDS packets using the appropriate network protocol. For example, if you're using the TCP/IP Sockets Net-Library, your computer encapsulates the TDS packets using the TCP/IP protocol. Your client computer then sends these packets to the server's Net-Library; the server's Net-Library strips out the network protocol portion of the packets so that only the TDS packets remain.

3. Your server's Open Data Services strips out the TDS packet information so that it can retrieve your query from the packets. After Open Data Services extracts your query, it sends it to the Relational Engine, which has the job of determining the best execution plan for processing your query and then compiling it. Next, the Relational Engine executes the query based on this optimized execution plan. At this point, the Relational Engine talks to the Storage Engine to retrieve the data.

4. The Storage Engine retrieves the data that satisfies your query and stores it in data buffers. It then passes this data along to the Relational Engine. The Relational Engine combines the data it receives from the Storage Engine into a single results set, and sends this results set on to Open Data Services.

5. Open Data Services takes the data it receives from the Relational Engine and sends it to the server's Net-Library, which is responsible for encapsulating the data with the appropriate network protocol. The server then sends the resulting packets to the client.

TASK 1C-1:

Understanding the SQL Server Architecture

1. **What is the role of the Net-Library?**

2. **What database APIs does SQL Server support?**

Designing a Database Application

You'll find that there are several factors you should consider when designing a database application. These factors include:

• Selecting an application architecture. This architecture determines how much of your application resides on the server, and how much on the client. We're going to look at your choices for application architecture in more detail in just a moment.

• Designing the database for optimum performance. You should consider how you can best take advantage of your server's hardware at this point. For example, does your server have a drive array? If so, you should plan to spread your database across the array.

• Determining the types of objects you should create within the database, and their relationships to each other. As part of your planning, make sure you consider any constraints you might want to define to enforce data integrity. You should also consider how you want to secure the database.

• Creating the database and its objects.

• Optimizing the application and the database. At this stage, you should make sure that you test the critical steps performed by your application and database to verify that they can keep up with the workload. Make sure that you've created the necessary indexes to enhance performance—and that you've designed your database to take advantage of your server's hardware.

- Designing a strategy for deploying the application.

Choosing an Application Architecture

When you design an application, there are several different client/server architectures you can choose from. These architectures vary as to how much of the data processing is done by the SQL server as compared to the client. Before you look at the architectures, it is important that you understand that all client/server applications consist of three logical layers:

- Presentation—the user interface (this layer usually resides on the client);
- Business—the application's logic and rules for working with the data (this layer can be on the server, client, or both); and
- Data—the actual database itself, its rules for database integrity, and stored procedures (this layer is typically only on the server).

Application architectures are usually categorized based on the number of computers that are involved in the application. For example, an application that consists of a portion running on the server and on the client is usually referred to as 2-Tier. The following table describes the different application architectures.

Application Architecture	Description
Intelligent Server (2-Tier)	An application that resides on both the server and the client, but the majority of the processing (the Business and Data layers) is performed by the server. Only the Presentation layer resides on the client.
Intelligent Client (2-Tier)	An application that resides on both the server and the client, but the majority of the processing (the Presentation and Business layers) is performed by the client. Only the Data layer resides on the server. Example: Microsoft Access.
N-Tier	An application that resides on a database server (the Data layer), an application server (the Business layer), and the client (the Presentation layer).
Internet	An application where the Business and Presentation layers reside on a Web server, the Data layer on a database server, and the client uses a Web browser to access the information. Example: Web sites that use SQL databases.

End-users don't typically access SQL Server directly. Instead, they access SQL Server by using an application that you've designed to meet their specific requirements. You can design your application to access SQL Server by using any of the following:

- Transact-SQL, Microsoft's enhanced version of the SQL language. Keep in mind that you can develop stored procedures consisting of Transact-SQL statements, and then call these stored procedures from other programs (such as those written in Visual Basic).

- XML. This language enables users to query your server to insert, update, delete, or simply view SQL Server data by executing URL queries or template files within a Web browser. The Web browser then uses the Hypertext Transfer Protocol (HTTP) to communicate with your server.

- MDX. You use this language to define multidimensional objects (called cubes) for analyzing data in an OLAP environment.
- OLE DB and ODBC APIs.
- ActiveX Data Objects (ADO) and ActiveX Data Objects Multidimensional (ADO MD).
- English Query.

TASK 1C-2:

Exploring the Application Architecture

1. **Why are applications sometimes referred to as 2-tier?**

2. **Where do the three layers of an application reside in an Intelligent Server (2-Tier) application?**

TOPIC 1D

Identifying SQL Server Management Tasks

In most database management systems, you'll find that there are two distinct management roles: the database developer and the database administrator. Depending on the size of your network and your database management system, you might find that one person can perform the roles of both the database developer and administrator. In order to clear up any confusion you might have, and also to explain why we cover the specific topics in this course, we want to take a moment to define the responsibilities of both the database developer and the database administrator. The database developer is responsible for the following tasks:

- Designing databases—including the types of objects the application needs, and the design of those objects.
- Creating and managing database objects (such as tables and indexes).
- Working with the data in the databases.
- Testing and optimizing the application that accesses the database.
- Optimizing database performance.

In contrast to the database developer, the database administrator manages the overall functioning of the database server. Some of the tasks the database administrator is responsible for include:

- Installing, configuring, and optimizing SQL Server.
- Creating and managing databases and their files.
- Transferring data from other database management systems into SQL Server.
- Replicating data.

- Managing security.
- Maintaining backups.
- Automating management tasks.
- Optimizing the performance of the SQL server.

This course focuses on the tasks you perform as a database developer. As a result, we're going to spend most of our time looking at how you create and manage databases and their objects, implement data integrity, design, create, and manage indexes, and so on. Although we touch on some of the steps you must perform to administer SQL Server 2000, this type of information isn't the focus of the course. For more information on installing and configuring SQL Server, see the Element K course *Microsoft SQL Server 2000: System Administration.*

TASK 1D-1:

Determining SQL Server Management Tasks

1. **You're planning to implement SQL Server on your network. As the database developer, what are some of the tasks you will be responsible for?**

2. **If you're the database developer and not the administrator, what are some of the tasks you aren't responsible for?**

An Overview of SQL Server Security

Although managing security is primarily a database administrator's task, as a database developer, it's important that you understand how SQL Server's security works. SQL Server's security consists of three layers:

- Login security, which enables you to control who can log in to the SQL server.
- Database access security, which enables you to control who can access each database on your server.
- Permissions security, which enables you to control what a user or group of users can do to a database and the Transact-SQL commands the user or group can use.

You implement login security by configuring your server's authentication mode, and by defining login accounts for your users. Let's start by taking a look at the authentication mode. Microsoft SQL Server 2000 supports two login authentication modes, as described in the following table.

Authentication Mode	Enables Users to Log In to the SQL Server Using
SQL Server and Windows	Either a SQL or Windows login account.
Windows Only	A Windows login account.

If you configure your server to use SQL Server and Windows Authentication (also known as mixed-mode authentication), your server will accept both SQL Server and Windows login accounts. With Windows Only Authentication, your server will accept only Windows login accounts. This means that your users must have user accounts within the Windows 2000 domain so that Windows 2000 can authenticate them. You configure your server's authentication mode during installation, but you can always change it later by modifying your server's properties within SQL Server Enterprise Manager.

One of the biggest advantages of Windows Authentication is that SQL Server relies on Windows 2000 to authenticate your users, which means that you can take advantage of all of the Windows 2000 security features—such as password encryption, password expiration dates, minimum password length, and account lockout. In addition, Windows Authentication enables your users to access the SQL server without having to remember a separate login account and password. In contrast, SQL Server Authentication enables clients who can't log on to a Windows 2000 domain (such as those running UNIX or connecting over the Internet) to connect to your SQL server. Finally, with Windows Authentication, you can map Windows 2000 groups to login accounts, which means that you can enable a whole group of users to log in to SQL Server by defining only one login account.

When a user logs in to SQL Server by using her Windows account, the client uses a trusted connection. This is a trusted connection because Windows 2000 performs the user authentication, not SQL Server. In other words, SQL Server is trusting Windows 2000 to validate the user's account. Windows 2000 uses the trusted connection to forward the user's account and group membership information to SQL Server. When the user's account information is forwarded to SQL Server, SQL Server checks its sysxlogins table in the master database to verify that the user's Windows 2000 account (or a group of which the user is a member) has a valid login account.

When a user logs in to a SQL server by using SQL Server Authentication, the user establishes a non-trusted connection. This type of connection is referred to as non-trusted because SQL Server performs the user authentication. Similar to Windows Authentication, SQL Server verifies that the user's SQL login account is defined in the sysxlogins table. If the user doesn't have a login account in the sysxlogins table, SQL Server doesn't permit the user to log in.

You specify the login authentication mode when you install SQL Server. You can change your server's login authentication mode by modifying its properties within SQL Server Enterprise Manager. Keep in mind that if you change your server's authentication mode, you must stop and restart the server. Let's take a look at how you go about modifying your server's authentication mode.

TASK 1D-2:

Configuring Your Server's Authentication Mode

1. If necessary, **switch to SQL Server Enterprise Manager.**

2. In the console tree, **right-click on your server and choose Properties** to display the SQL Server Properties dialog box.

3. **Select the Security tab and take a look at your options.** You can config-ure your server to use both SQL Server and Windows Authentication (mixed) or Windows Only Authentication. You can use the audit settings to configure SQL Server to record successful login attempts, failed login attempts, or all login attempts.

Remember, if you change your server's authentication mode, you must stop and restart the SQL Server service before it will reflect your change.

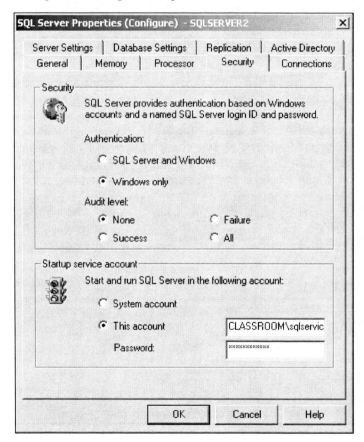

4. **Choose SQL Server And Windows** to configure your server to support both SQL and Windows login accounts.

5. **Click OK** to save your changes.

6. **Click Yes** when prompted to confirm that you want to stop and restart the SQL Server service.

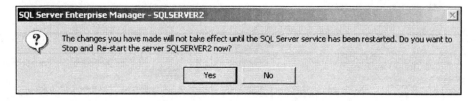

Creating Login Accounts

The second component of login security is login accounts. SQL Server supports two types of login accounts: SQL Server and Windows. You create a Windows login account by adding a user or group's Windows 2000 account as a login on your server. (If you want to add several Windows 2000 users as login accounts on your SQL server, you'll find it's much faster if you make them a member of a group and then add that group as a login account.) You create a SQL Server login account by defining the account name and password. You can create login accounts by using SQL Server Enterprise Manager, the `sp_grantlogin` stored procedure to add a Windows user or group account, or the `sp_addlogin` stored procedure to create a SQL login account.

TASK 1D-3:

Creating a SQL Login Account

1. In SQL Server Enterprise Manager, in the console tree, **expand your server's Security folder.**

2. **Select the Logins object** to view a list of the login accounts on your SQL server in the details pane. By default, SQL Setup creates a SQL login account named sa (system administrator) with full permissions to manage the server. In addition, Setup creates a login account for the Windows user account for the service account (this is the account the SQL Server services use to log in to your server). Finally, Setup creates a Windows login account for the Windows 2000 Administrators group. As a result, all members of the local Administrators group on your SQL server can log in to your SQL server.

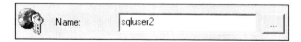

Logins	3 Items				
Name	Type	Server Access	Default Database	Default Language
BUILTIN\Administrators	Windows Group	Permit	master	English
CLASSROOM\sqlservice	Windows User	Permit	master	English
sa	Standard	Permit	master	English

3. **Right-click on the Logins object and choose New Login.**

4. In the Name text box, **type** *sqluser#*. (Replace # with your assigned number.)

5. Below Authentication, **select SQL Server Authentication** to configure your new login account to use SQL Server authentication.

6. In the Password text box, **type** *password* to assign a password to the SQL Server login account.

SQL Server Authentication	
Password:	xxxxxxxx

7. **Click OK** to create your new login account.

8. In the Confirm New Password text box, **type *password*, and then click OK.** You must retype the password so that you can make sure that you typed the password correctly.

9. **Switch to SQL Query Analyzer.**

10. **Choose File→Disconnect** to disconnect your current login session within SQL Query Analyzer.

11. In the message box, **click No.** You don't need to save your previous queries. By default, SQL Query Analyzer always prompts you to save your queries to a script file whenever you exit the program.

12. **Choose File→Connect** to open the Connect To SQL Server dialog box. You can use this dialog box to log in with your Windows account, or to log in with a SQL login account.

13. In the Connect To SQL Server dialog box, **choose SQL Server Authentication.** In the Login Name text box, **type *sqluser#*.** In the Password text box, **type *password.***

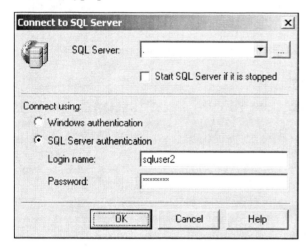

14. **Click OK** to log on to SQL Server using a SQL login account. (At this point, your sqluser# user can't do much on your server because you haven't given this account any permissions to your server's databases.)

15. **Close SQL Query Analyzer.**

APPLY YOUR KNOWLEDGE 1-2

Suggested time:
10 minutes

Creating a Login Account for a Windows 2000 Account

Objective: To create a Windows 2000 user account. You will then create a login account for this user in SQL Server Enterprise Manager. Finally, you will test the new login account by logging on to Windows 2000 and running SQL Query Analyzer.

For this Lab, You Will Need the Following Information	Use this Value or Another Value Provided by Your Instructor
A Windows 2000 account name	Your first name
A password	password

1. In Active Directory Users And Computers, create a user with your name. Use your first name as your logon name. Set your password to password. Add this user as a member of Domain Admins. Close Active Directory Users And Computers.

2. In SQL Server Enterprise Manager, add a login account for the new user's Windows 2000 account by right-clicking on the Logins folder below your server and choosing New Login. In the Name text box, type your first name. From the Domain drop-down list, choose Classroom. Click OK to save your new login account.

3. Close SQL Server Enterprise Manager.

4. Log off, and then log back on to Windows 2000 as the user with your first name and a password of password.

5. Verify that you can log in to your SQL server by running SQL Query Analyzer. (Make sure you choose Use Windows Authentication in the Connect To SQL Server dialog box.)

6. Close SQL Server Query Analyzer.

7. Log off from Windows 2000 and log back on as student#.

Configuring Database Users and Permissions

Now that you've seen how to create both Windows and SQL Server login accounts, your next task is to learn how to make these login accounts database users. One of the easiest ways you can add a login account as a database user is to make them a member of a database role (which makes the login account a user of the database). You add a login account as a database user by using either SQL Server Enterprise Manager or the sp_grantdbaccess stored procedure. You must be a database owner or a member of the db_accessadmin database role to add a login account as a database user.

Each database contains a special database user called the dbo. This user has all permissions for working with the database. The sa SQL Server login account and all members of the sysadmin server role use the dbo user account for all databases on your server. Another special database user you can create is the guest user. You can use the guest database user to grant guest access to a database. You'll typically use the guest database user account when you want to grant temporary access to a database. Creating a guest account enables all users with logins who aren't users of the database to access that database. For this reason, you should create a guest account only after you've carefully considered the security of your server.

You can't add a guest database user to the master and tempdb databases.

You can implement permissions by assigning individual statement and object permissions to users, or by adding database users as members of a role. Statement permissions enable you to control whether users can execute statements for creating objects. For example, you can grant users the CREATE DATABASE and

CREATE TABLE statement permissions. Object permissions enable you to control what users can do with existing objects. For example, you can grant users the SELECT and INSERT permissions so that they can view the contents of a table and insert rows into it. For more information on statement and object permissions, see the Element K *Microsoft SQL Server 2000: System Administration* course.

SQL Server 2000 includes both server roles (for administering the server itself) and database roles (for working with and administering individual databases). You can also create your own user-defined database roles. The following table describes the server roles to which you can assign users.

Server Role	Nickname	Enables the Login Account to
Bulk Insert Administrators	bulkadmin	Perform bulk insert operations.
Database Creators	dbcreator	Create and alter databases.
Disk Administrators	diskadmin	Manage database files.
Process Administrators	processadmin	Manage SQL Server processes.
Security Administrators	securityadmin	Manage and audit server logins.
Server Administrators	serveradmin	Configure server-wide settings.
Setup Administrators	setupadmin	Install SQL Server replication.
System Administrators	sysadmin	Perform any action on your server.

In the following table, we describe the database roles to which you can assign users. Keep in mind that other than the public role, you can't modify the permissions associated with each role. If you find that you need roles with specific permissions, you can create your own user-defined roles.

Database Role	Enables the Database User to
public	Use the default permissions assigned to the role.
db_accessadmin	Add or remove database users, groups, and roles.
db_backupoperator	Back up and restore the database.
db_datareader	Read data from any table in the database.
db_datawriter	Add, change, or delete data from any table in the database.
db_ddladmin	Add, change, or drop database objects.
db_dbowner	Perform any database role activity.
db_securityadmin	Assign statement and object permissions to users.

In addition to the database roles that give users permissions, two database roles deny privileges. We describe these roles in the following table.

Database Role	Prevents the Database User from
db_denydatareader	Reading data from any table in the database.
db_denydatawriter	Adding, changing, or deleting data from any table in the database.

How SQL Server Validates Permissions

Each time a user attempts an action that issues a SQL statement (whether the action is issuing a statement directly, such as in a query, or by using a utility such as SQL Server Enterprise Manager), SQL Server first verifies that the user has the necessary permissions to execute the statement. If the user has the necessary permissions, SQL Server processes the user's request. If the user doesn't have the necessary permissions, SQL Server sends an error message to the user.

TASK 1D-4:

Working With Server and Database Roles

1. **Start SQL Server Enterprise Manager.**

2. In the console tree, **expand your server's Security folder** to display a list of the objects related to security.

3. **Select the Server Roles object and take a look at the details pane.** You should see a list of the server roles to which you can add users.

Server Roles	8 Items	
Full Name /	Name	Description
Bulk Insert Administrators	bulkadmin	Can perform bulk insert operation.
Database Creators	dbcreator	Can create and alter databases.
Disk Administrators	diskadmin	Can manage the disk files.
Process Administrators	processadmin	Can manage the processes running in SQL Server.
Security Administrators	securityadmin	Can manage the logins for the server.
Server Administrators	serveradmin	Can configure the server-wide settings.
Setup Administrators	setupadmin	Can manage extended stored procedures.
System Administrators	sysadmin	Can perform any activity in the SQL Server installation.

4. In the details pane, **double-click on System Administrators** to display the Server Role Properties dialog box. You can add or remove login accounts from this role. By default, SQL Setup adds the built-in Administrators Windows 2000 group, service account, and the sa SQL login account as members of the System Administrators role.

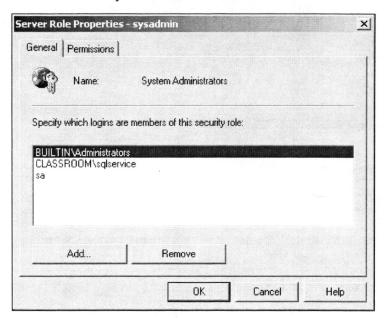

5. **Click Cancel** to close the Server Role Properties dialog box.

6. In the console tree, **select the Logins object** to display a list of your server's login accounts in the details pane.

7. **Double-click on sqluser#. Look at the tabs in the SQL Server Login Properties dialog box.** You can use this dialog box to add the login account to both server roles and database roles (by using the Database Access tab).

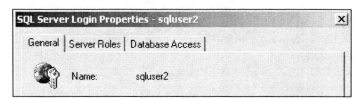

8. **Select the Database Access tab.** You use this page to configure the login account as a database user and add them to a database role.

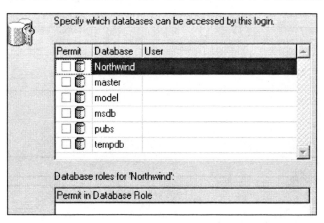

9. In the list of databases, **check pubs** to add sqluser# as a user of the pubs database.

10. **Look at the changes in the dialog box.** You should see that SQL Server Enterprise Manager automatically made sqluser# a member of the public database role for the pubs database.

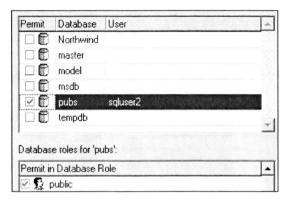

11. In the Permit In Database Role list, **check db_owner** to add sqluser# as a member of the db_owner role.

12. **Click OK** to close the SQL Server Login Properties dialog box.

13. **Close all open windows.**

Summary

In this lesson, we examined the components and services that make up SQL Server, and the default databases and tables. We also explored the types of tasks you're responsible for as a database developer and examined the utilities you can use to accomplish those tasks. Finally, we provided you with an overview of the security features you can implement within SQL Server 2000.

LESSON 1 REVIEW

1A **List two features that make SQL Server a powerful database management system.**

1B In the SQL Server environment, what do the terms database and table mean?

1C What three layers make up the client/server application architecture?

1D List and explain the two login security modes you can implement in SQL Server.

YOUR NOTES:

Exploring Transact-SQL

Data Files:
create_table.sql
select_lab.sql
update_delete_lab
insert.sql
select.sql
permissions.sql
deny_revoke_lab.sql
variables.sql
execute_lab.sql
statement.sql

Lesson Time:
3 hours

Overview

As a database developer, it's critical that you understand how to use the Transact-SQL language to work with SQL Server and its databases. In this lesson, we will explore how you use Transact-SQL to query your server. We'll also introduce you to the types of SQL commands you can use, along with the basics for executing those statements.

Objectives

To learn the Transact-SQL language, you will:

2A   **Use the tools included with SQL Server 2000 for executing SQL statements.**

SQL Server 2000 includes two primary tools for executing SQL queries: SQL Query Analyzer, a graphical utility, and osql, a command-line utility. In this topic, we will show you how to work with both tools.

2B   **Execute Transact-SQL statements.**

In this topic, we will show you how to use the three types of SQL statements (Data Definition Language, Data Manipulation Language, and Data Control Language) to work with SQL Server 2000.

2C   **Use Transact-SQL to develop programs.**

The Transact-SQL language includes elements that enable you to design flexible programs. For example, you can use a variable to store a value based on user-entered information—and then use that variable within a program. In this topic, you will learn how to declare and use variables. In addition, you will implement control-of-flow statements such as IF...ELSE to control the steps performed by a program.

TOPIC 2A

Working with Transact-SQL

Now that we've explored what SQL Server is and why you would use it, let's move on to looking at how you access the data on a SQL server. You access data by using Microsoft's enhanced version of the Structured Query Language, Transact-SQL. Transact-SQL is SQL Server's implementation of the ANSI SQL-92 standard. You can use the SQL language in a variety of relational database management systems, including Microsoft SQL Server, Oracle, and Sybase. You use the SQL language to work with the data on your server. For example, you can use the SELECT SQL statement to retrieve data from your server.

When you send a statement to your server for processing, the statement is called a query. Actually, a query can consist of one or more SQL statements. SQL Server includes two utilities you can use to query your server: SQL Query Analyzer and the osql command-line utility. In addition, you can use SQL queries in a wide variety of application development environments such as Visual Basic.

SQL Query Analyzer

SQL Query Analyzer enables you to work with queries in a graphical environment. You can select text to copy and paste just as you would within a word processing application. In addition, SQL Query Analyzer offers you the following advantages:

- SQL Query Analyzer automatically assigns different colors to query components. In addition, you can customize these colors to suit your own taste.

- You can open multiple query windows, each with a separate connection to your server; you can even establish each connection with different user credentials.

- You can parse (test) queries for accuracy before executing them.

- You can display the results of a query in grid or text format.

- SQL Query Analyzer can execute all or only parts of a script based on the components you select.

- You can generate a graphical execution plan to see how SQL Server will process your query. You can use this information to optimize your queries.

- SQL Query Analyzer includes an Object Browser window that you can use to view the names of databases and objects. In addition, you can view the structure of objects such as tables.

You can purchase the ANSI SQL-92 standard document from ANSI by going to **http://webstore.ansi.org/ ansidocstore/find.asp** *and searching for the document name. Search for "ANSI X3. 135-1992 (R1998)."*

TASK 2A-1:

Using SQL Query Analyzer

Setup: You are logged on to Windows 2000 as student#.

1. **Start SQL Query Analyzer and log in by using Windows Authentication.**

2. In the Editor pane, **type the following query:**

```
USE pubs
SELECT *
FROM authors
```

3. **Choose Query→Parse** to test the syntax of your query. If you've entered the query correctly, you see a message stating that the command completed successfully. If you have a syntax error, SQL Query Analyzer displays the line number and the nature of the error. You can then correct the error before attempting to execute your query. **Correct any syntax errors.**

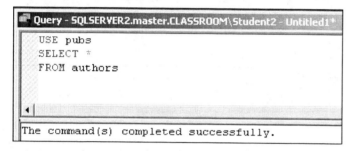

4. **Choose Query→Execute** to execute your query. SQL Server processes your query and returns the results in the Results pane. Notice that you now see the pubs database displayed in the Database drop-down list.

5. **Look at the colors SQL Query Analyzer assigns to your SQL keywords. For example, look at the `USE` and `SELECT` keywords as compared to objects (such as pubs and authors).** By default, SQL Query Analyzer displays SQL keywords in blue and text in black.

6. Choose **Tools→Options** to display the Options dialog box for configuring SQL Query Analyzer. **Select the Fonts tab.** You can use the Fonts page to customize the colors SQL Query Analyzer assigns to components of queries.

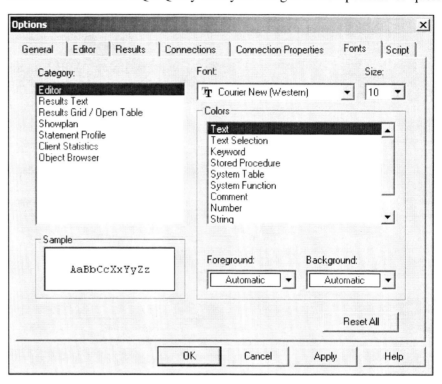

7. Below Colors, **choose Keyword and look at your choices.** The default foreground color (the letters of the keyword) is blue and the font is Courier New (Western).

8. **Click Cancel** to close the Options dialog box.

9. In the Editor pane, **add the following lines to your previous query:**

```
SELECT *
FROM titles
```

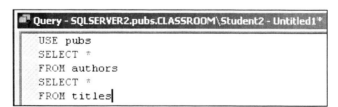

10. **Execute the query.**

11. **Look at the Results pane.** You see all rows in both the authors and the titles tables listed. (Use the vertical scroll bar in the Results pane to display all of the results from both queries.)

12. In the Editor pane, **use your mouse to highlight only the following lines (as shown in the graphic):**

```
SELECT *
FROM titles
```

13. Execute the query. You should see that SQL Query Analyzer returns only the rows in the authors table. You can selectively execute query statements in the Editor pane by highlighting their lines.

14. On the toolbar, **click the Clear Window button** to clear your previous query from the Editor pane.

15. Minimize SQL Query Analyzer.

Osql

In addition to SQL Query Analyzer, you can use the osql utility to execute SQL statements, stored procedures, and script files. In contrast to SQL Query Analyzer, osql is a command-line utility. You use osql either by logging in to your server and then executing commands in interactive mode, or by logging in and executing commands as part of the osql syntax. The basic syntax for osql is as follows:

```
osql -S server_name -U login_id -P password
```

You should use this syntax if you want to log in to your server by specifying a SQL login account. In contrast, if you want to log in to your server by using Windows Authentication, use this syntax instead:

```
osql -S server_name  -E
```

All of the parameters you use with the osql command are case-sensitive. These parameters can be preceded by either a hyphen (-) or a slash (/). The following table defines the optional parameters you can use with osql.

Parameter	Enables You To
-U login_id	Specify the SQL login account you want to use to log in to the SQL server. If you don't specify both the -U and -P parameters, you must use the -E parameter. SQL Server will then use your current Windows account to log you in to the SQL server (and won't prompt you for a password).
-P password	Provide the password for the SQL login account you specified with the -U parameter.
-E	Log in by using your current Windows account (rather than specifying a SQL login account). Because SQL Server uses Windows 2000 to authenticate your user account, Microsoft refers to this type of connection as trusted.

Parameter	Enables You To
-S server_name	Specify the name of the SQL server to which you want to connect. You must use the -S parameter when you run the osql command on a computer other than the SQL server.
-?	Display a help screen containing all of the osql parameters.
-i input_file	Specify the name of a file that contains Transact-SQL statements or stored procedures. For example, you use -i when you want osql to run a SQL script file.
-o output_file	Identify the name of a file for receiving output from osql.
-b	Configure osql to automatically exit and return a DOS ERRORLEVEL value if an error occurs when osql processes SQL statements. Osql sets the DOS ERRORLEVEL value to 1 if it encounters an error with a severity of 10 or greater; in contrast, osql sets DOS ERRORLEVEL to 0 if the error's severity is less than 10.
-Q "query"	Run the specified query. Use this option when you want to connect to a SQL server and run a query by using a single command. For example, you can use the command osql -S server_name -E -Q "SELECT * FROM pubs.dbo.authors" to connect to your server and display a list of all of the authors in the pubs database.

When you use osql in interactive mode, it displays line numbers as shown in Figure 2-1. You type your SQL statements, one to each line. Osql does not execute your query until you type the SQL keyword GO on a separate line. After you're done querying your server in osql, type EXIT to disconnect and close the osql utility.

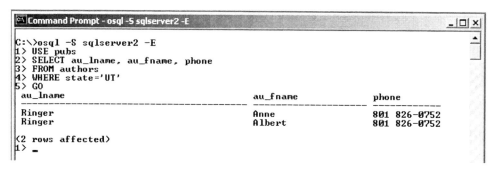

Figure 2-1: *Type your SQL statements on separate lines in osql.*

TASK 2A-2:

Using Osql

1. **Write an osql statement for logging in to your partner's SQL server by using a trusted connection.**

2. **Open a Command Prompt window.**

3. **Connect to your partner's server by using the osql statement you recorded in step 1.** You should see a 1> prompt when you're successfully connected to your partner's server.

4. At the 1> prompt, **enter USE pubs** to specify that you want to use your partner's pubs database and to advance to the second line in osql.

5. At the 2> prompt, **enter SELECT au_lname, au_fname, phone.**

6. At the 3> prompt, **enter FROM authors** to specify that you're querying the authors table.

7. At the 4> prompt, **enter GO.** Osql now processes all lines of your query. When it's done displaying all rows of the authors table, you should see a 1> prompt. This means that you can now enter a new query.

8. At the 1> prompt, **enter EXIT** to disconnect from your partner's server and close osql.

9. **Close the Command Prompt window.**

TOPIC 2B

Transact-SQL Statements

You can group SQL statements into three categories:

- Data Definition Language (DDL) statements, which enable you to create database objects.
- Data Manipulation Language (DML) statements, which enable you to query or modify data.
- Data Control Language (DCL) statements, which enable you to determine, set, or revoke users' permissions to SQL databases and their objects.

We're going to start our tour of the SQL language by exploring the statements you can use to create database objects. After you've created objects, we'll move on to showing you how to work with those objects by using DML statements. We'll then examine how you can protect objects by using security and the DCL statements.

Throughout this course, we're going to provide you with the ANSI SQL syntax for Transact-SQL statements. Microsoft strongly recommends that you use the ANSI-compliant syntax whenever you're developing programs or scripts in order to make them as compatible as possible with other SQL-based systems.

Data Definition Language Statements

The primary DDL statements are CREATE, ALTER, and DROP. You'll always use these statements in conjunction with an object type and an object name. The general syntax for these statements is:

```
CREATE object_type object_name
```

You replace object_type with the type of object you're creating. For example, you create a table by using the statement CREATE TABLE table_name. You might need to specify other parameters as part of the CREATE statement, depending on the object type. For example, when you create a table, you'll need to not only specify the new table's name, but also the columns you want to define in that table. So, to create a new table named *customers* in the pubs sample database, you might use the following syntax:

```
USE pubs
CREATE TABLE customers
(
lname varchar(20), fname varchar(20), address varchar(20),
city varchar(15), state char(2),
zip char(9), phone char(10)
)
```

Be aware that you must be a member of either the sysadmin server role or the dbcreator, db_owner, or db_ddladmin database roles to use any of the DDL Transact-SQL statements. Although we talk about this in more detail later in the course, we want to point out that you'll see better performance with SQL Server if all of your objects have the same owner. When objects that depend on each other (such as a view based on a table) have different owners, SQL Server must evaluate a user's permissions for both objects before the user can access the view. For this reason, if you have more than one user creating objects, you should make sure that the object owner is the same for both objects. If necessary, you can change an object's owner by using the sp_changeobjectowner stored procedure.

Naming Objects

Microsoft recommends that you use its standard naming rules when you name objects. Object names that conform to these rules are referred to as standard identifiers. A standard identifier must meet the following requirements:

- Names must be between one and 128 characters in length (including letters, numbers, and symbols). You can't include spaces in a standard identifier.

- The first character of the object's name must begin with a letter (a-z or A-Z).

- Any subsequent characters you use in the name can be any character including letters, numbers, or the @, $, #, or _ symbols.

SQL Server requires that you begin the names for variables, temporary tables and procedures, and global temporary objects with specific symbols, as follows:

- Variables must begin with @.

- Temporary objects must begin with #.

- Global temporary objects must begin with ##.

In addition to these requirements, the names you assign to temporary objects can't be more than 116 characters (including the # or ## symbols).

If you use a name that doesn't conform to the rules for standard identifiers, you must delimit the name by using either square brackets ([ ]) or double quotes (" "). Names that contain spaces or use reserved words must also be delimited. As such, Microsoft refers to them as delimited identifiers. For example, if you name a table customer addresses, you'll have to delimit the table's name whenever you refer to it (because the name contains a space):

```
SELECT *
FROM [customer addresses]
```

You can always use the square brackets as delimiters; however, SQL Server doesn't permit you to use double quotes as delimiters unless you've turned on support for them. You can turn on support for double quotes by executing the following query: SET QUOTED_IDENTIFIER ON. By default, SET QUOTED_IDENTIFIER is off. You must turn it on for each user.

Designing Naming Conventions

While you'll find that everyone has their own opinion as to how you should name objects, we've found that there are a few guidelines that come in handy. Keep the following suggestions in mind when you name objects:

- Keep names short but meaningful.

- Try to develop a standard, so that it's easy for you and your users to identify object types.

- Include something in the object name that indicates its object type. For example, you might want to include "view" or "vw" in the names of views because they're often mistaken for tables.

- Make your object names (and even user names) unique.

- Use singular names for objects and their properties. If you name some objects in a database with plural names and others with singular names, it will be difficult for you to remember the object names. For example, in the pubs sample database, several of the tables have plural names (authors, discounts, publishers, and so on) and others have singular names (employee, titleauthor, roysched, and so on). Because these names aren't consistent, you might have difficulty remembering which names have an "s" on the end and which don't.

- Avoid using spaces in object names. As we've said, if you use spaces, you must delimit those names with square brackets or double quotes whenever you use them in a query.

TASK 2B-1:

Creating a Simple Table

Setup: The student data files were copied to your computer during classroom setup.

1. In SQL Query Analyzer, **choose File→Open.** When you're prompted to save your query, **click No.**

2. **Access the Student Data folder (C:\Data)** or as specified by your instructor.

3. In the list of files, **double-click on create_table** to open the script file. This file contains the SQL statement for creating a table named practice within the pubs database.

4. **Look at the script file as your instructor reviews each of the statements.** The USE pubs line of the script switches your current database to the pubs database. Next, because SQL Server requires that you execute the CREATE TABLE statement as its own batch separate from all other SQL statements, we separate the USE pubs and the CREATE TABLE statements by using the GO statement. Finally, the CREATE TABLE statement creates a table named practice that consists of two columns: lname and fname.

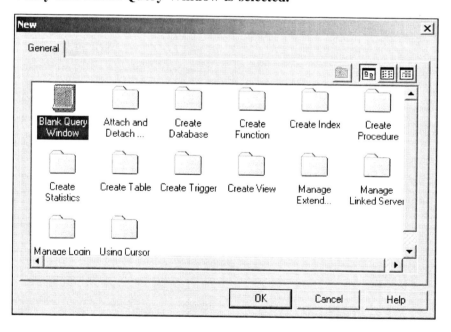

5. **Execute the script file.** You can execute the script by choosing Query→ Execute, clicking the Play button on the toolbar, or by pressing [Ctrl]E.

6. **Look at the Results pane.** You should see that your commands completed successfully.

7. **Choose File→New.** You're going to open a new Query window.

8. **Verify that Blank Query Window is selected.**

9. **Click OK** to open a second Query window.

10. **Close the Query window containing the create_table script file.**

11. In the new Query window, **to display the structure of the practice table, execute the following query:**

```
sp_help practice
```

12. **Look at the Results pane.** SQL Query Analyzer displays five grids. The first grid enables you to view the name of the table, its owner, the table type, and the date and time you created the table. The second grid enables you to view a list of the table's columns and their data types.

Next, the third grid enables you to determine if you've defined any identity columns on the table. An identity column enables SQL Server to automatically increment a value that you specify for each new row you add to the table. You can use the fourth grid to determine if you've configured any of the table's columns as each row's "globally unique identifier" (RowGuidCol). This designation indicates that the values within this column aren't only unique within the table, but also across the entire database.

Finally, you use the fifth grid to determine in which filegroup the table resides. You can distribute a database across multiple files, each in separate filegroups, in order to optimize its performance. Unless you specify otherwise, SQL Server creates new objects in the primary filegroup.

	Name	Owner	Type	Created_datetime
1	practice	dbo	user table	2001-04-09 20:13:15.593

	Column_name	Type	Computed	Length	Prec	Scale	Nullable
1	lname	varchar	no	20			yes
2	fname	varchar	no	20			yes

	Identity	Seed	Increment	Not For Repli
1	No identity column defined.	NULL NULL		NULL

	RowGuidCol
1	No rowguidcol column defined.

	Data_located_on_filegroup
1	PRIMARY

13. **Clear the Query window.**

Data Manipulation Language Statements

Now that you've seen how to use DDL to create objects, let's move on to how you go about working with those objects. You manipulate objects by using the DML statements: INSERT, SELECT, UPDATE, and DELETE. By default, only the members of the sysadmin server role or dbcreator, db_owner, db_datawriter, or db_datareader roles can execute DML statements. Let's take a look at each of these statements in more detail.

Using INSERT

You use the INSERT statement to add rows to a table. Here's the syntax:

```
INSERT INTO table_name
(column_list)
VALUES (values_list)
```

In this syntax, you replace `table_name` with the name of the table to which you want to add rows. If you aren't inserting information into all columns in the table, replace `column_list` with a list of columns to which you're inserting information for the new rows. If you're inserting information into all columns in the table, you don't have to specify the column names. Finally, replace `values_list` with a list of values for the columns. You must enclose the values for all columns with non-numeric data types in quotes.

TASK 2B-2:

Inserting Data

1. **Write an `INSERT` statement for inserting your name into the practice table.**

2. In SQL Query Analyzer, **use the `INSERT` statement you recorded in step 1 to add a row to your table.** Remember, you can choose Query→Parse to check your syntax.

3. **Use the `INSERT` command to add another name to your table.** You should have a total of two rows in your practice table. We're going to look at how you view these rows next.

4. **Clear the Query window.**

Using SELECT

You can use the `SELECT` Transact-SQL statement to display the contents of a table. At its most basic, you use `SELECT` to display all columns and all rows in the table by executing the following query:

```
SELECT *
FROM table_name
```

In contrast, if you want to display only selected columns for a table, execute this query instead:

```
SELECT column_list
FROM table_name
```

In this query, you replace `column_list` with a list of column names separated by commas. For example, to list each author's last name and first name from the authors table in the pubs database, you could execute this query:

```
SELECT au_lname, au_fname
FROM pubs.dbo.authors
```

You can use the string concatenation operator (+) to group two character-based columns into a single column. (The character-based data types include varchar, char, nvarchar, nchar, text, and ntext.) You can also add constants to the combined columns. For example, to combine the au_fname and au_lname columns from the authors table to display a single column with the first and last names separated by a space, use this query:

```
SELECT au_fname + ' ' + au_lname
FROM pubs.dbo.authors
```

If you concatenate two columns together, SQL Query Analyzer no longer displays the column names in the Results pane. You can specify a column heading for the combined columns by using an AS clause. To use a two (or more) word column heading, you must enclose the name in quotes. For example, if you want to use the column heading Names of Authors, you should use this syntax:

```
SELECT au_fname + ' ' + au_lname AS 'Names of Authors'
FROM pubs.dbo.authors
```

Sorting the Results

You can use the clause ORDER BY followed by one or more column names to change the order of the results set. For example, to list the authors in alphabetical order, use this syntax:

```
SELECT *
FROM authors
ORDER BY au_lname
```

By default, SQL Server sorts in ascending order. You can specify descending order by adding the DESC keyword to the end of your ORDER BY clause. You can also sort by multiple columns by separating them with commas. For example, to list all authors in alphabetical order by last name and then first name, use the following syntax:

```
SELECT *
FROM authors
ORDER BY au_lname, au_fname
```

TASK 2B-3:

Selecting Data

1. **Write a query for viewing all rows in the practice table.**

2. In SQL Query Analyzer, **execute the query you recorded in step 1.**

3. **Write a query for listing all rows in the practice table with the first and last names concatenated together. Use Name as the column heading in the results set.**

4. **Execute the new query you recorded in step 3.**

5. **Write a query for sorting all rows in the practice table in descending order by last name.**

6. **Execute the new query you recorded in step 5.**

7. **Clear the Query window.**

Using a WHERE Clause With the SELECT Statement

You can create more powerful `SELECT` queries by using a `WHERE` clause to choose specific rows in a table. When you use a `WHERE` clause, you can specify a value to identify one or more rows in the table. Use the following syntax to execute a `SELECT` query with a `WHERE` clause:

```
SELECT column_list
FROM table_name
WHERE column_name conditional_operator value
```

If the column you use in the `WHERE` clause is one of the character data types, you must enclose the value in quotes. In contrast, if the column you use is one of the numeric data types, you can't enclose the value in quotes. For example, if you wanted to view all customers in the customers table who live in California, you should type:

```
SELECT *
FROM authors
WHERE state = 'CA'
```

In this query, you must enclose the value 'CA' in quotes because the state column uses the character data type.

Conditional Operators

The following table describes the conditional operators you can use in SQL Server in a `WHERE` clause.

Symbol	Description
=	Equal to
!=	Not equal to
<>	Not equal to
<	Less than
>	Greater than
<=	Less than or equal to
>=	Greater than or equal to

You can use multiple conditions in your `WHERE` clause by using the operators `AND`, `OR`, and `AND NOT`. For example, you might use the following query to select all rows from the authors table where the authors live in Oakland, CA:

```
SELECT *
FROM authors
WHERE state = 'CA' AND city = 'Oakland'
```

Operator Precedence

If you use multiple operators in a query, SQL Server evaluates them in order as follows:

1. Parentheses—if you've grouped conditional statements together by parentheses, SQL Server evaluates the contents of the parentheses first.

2. Arithmetic—multiplication (uses the operators *, /, or %).

3. Arithmetic—addition (uses the operators + or -).

4. Other—string concatenator (+).

5. Logical—NOT.

6. Logical—AND.

7. Logical—OR.

For example, if you want to find the names of all authors in the pubs database who live in the states of California or Utah, and who have contracts on file, use the following syntax:

```
SELECT au_lname, au_fname
FROM authors
WHERE (state = 'CA' OR state = 'UT') AND contract = 1
```

In contrast, consider this query:

```
SELECT au_lname, au_fname
FROM authors
WHERE state = 'CA' OR state = 'UT' AND contract = 1
```

In this example, SQL Server would find all authors who either live in California (regardless of whether they have a contract on file), or live in Utah and have a contract on file. This is because SQL Server evaluates conditions that use the logical AND before it evaluates those that use the logical OR. If you want to be sure of how SQL Server will process your queries containing multiple operators, you should use parentheses.

SQL Server and Case-sensitivity

When you install SQL Server, you can configure it to use a collation that is either case-sensitive or case-insensitive. If you install SQL Server as case-insensitive (the default setting), it will preserve the case you use when you add or change the data in columns; however, when you search for rows by using a WHERE clause, you can use either uppercase or lowercase values in your WHERE clause. For example, using WHERE city = 'Oakland' or WHERE city = 'oakland' will return the same rows in your SELECT statement.

Functions

Transact-SQL includes many functions that enable you to manipulate or perform calculations. You use functions as part of a SELECT statement. SQL Server supports the following three types of functions: rowset, aggregate, and scalar.

Aggregate Functions

Aggregate functions enable you to perform calculations on multiple rows but return only a single value in response. Some of the aggregate functions include: AVG ( ), COUNT ( ), MIN ( ), MAX ( ) and SUM ( ). For example, if you want to calculate the average price of a book in the titles table of the pubs database, you can use the following query:

```
SELECT AVG(price)
FROM titles
```

You should be aware that if a table's columns permit null values (where no data is entered into the column), the results of your aggregate function's calculations might be inaccurate. SQL Server doesn't include any columns with null values in its calculations. For example, you might think that using the MIN ( ) function to find the lowest-priced book in the titles table would return a book with a price of null. (Your query would be SELECT MIN(price) FROM titles.) However, SQL Server ignores null values, so you get the lowest-priced book with an actual value in the price column instead.

Rowset Functions

You use rowset functions just as you would a table in a SQL statement. Use rowset functions to perform distributed queries where you're retrieving data from a remote server. Before you can use a rowset function to perform a distributed query, you must first link the remote server to your server by using the sp_addlinkedserver stored procedure. After you've linked the remote server, you can use the OPENQUERY ( ) function to retrieve data from the server. Use the following syntax:

```
SELECT *
FROM OPENQUERY(linked_server_name, 'query')
```

Scalar Functions

Scalar functions perform calculations on only one value and return only one value. You typically use scalar functions to return system information or to determine the status of components such as cursors. For example, you can use the DB_NAME ( ) function to identify the name of the current database. In the following table, we describe the types of scalar functions you can use in SQL Server.

For detailed information on each of these types of functions along with their syntax, please see the "Functions" topic within Books Online. We're going to look at how you use Books Online later on in this lesson.

Type of Scalar Function	Enables You to	Examples
Configuration	View information about your connection and the server's configuration.	`@@SERVERNAME`
Cursor	View information about cursors.	`CURSOR_STATUS('local' | 'global', 'cursor_name')`
Date and Time	Perform calculations or extract portions of a date or time. You can use these functions to perform date math functions (such as determining the difference between two dates), or to extract a portion of a date (such as to identify only the month within a date value).	`YEAR(date)`
Mathematical	Perform calculations based on the parameters you specify within the function.	`ROUND(numeric_expression, length)`
Metadata	View information about databases and their objects.	`COL_LENGTH('table, column)`
Security	Identify information about users and role memberships.	`IS_MEMBER('group' | 'role')`
String	Perform operations on character data.	`UPPER(column | variable | expression)`
System	Determine information about objects and system settings.	`CONVERT(data_type, expression [,style])`
System Statistical	Retrieve statistics for your server.	`@@CONNECTIONS`
Text and Image	Work with text and image data.	`TEXTPTR(column)`

Let's take a look at some examples of these functions. One use for the CONVERT( ) function is to format dates. As part of this function, you must specify the style of date you want. For example, style 107 uses the format *Mon DD, YY*, where "Mon" is the abbreviation for the name of the month. In contrast, style 101 uses the format *MM/DD/YY*. In the following syntax, we use the CONVERT( ) function to display the order date in the Northwind..orders table in style 107. We show you the results of this statement in Figure 2-2.

```
SELECT orderID, CONVERT(varchar(30), orderdate, 107)
      AS 'Order Date'
FROM Northwind..orders
```

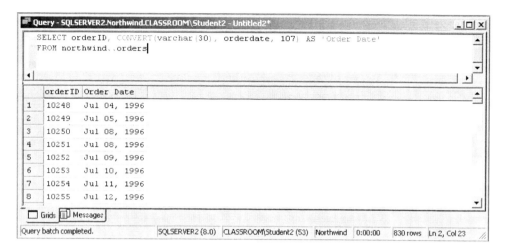

Figure 2-2: *You can use the* CONVERT( ) *function to display a date in a variety of formats.*

Here's another example. The following statement shows you how to use the USER_NAME( ) and APP_NAME( ) functions to view the name of the user you're currently logged on as and the application you're using.

```
SELECT USER_NAME( ), APP_NAME( )
```

We show you the results of this statement in Figure 2-3. In this example, SQL Server displays the user name as dbo because we're logged on as a member of the sysadmin server role.

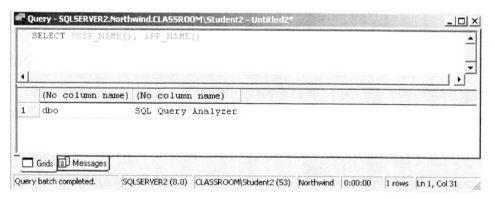

Figure 2-3: *You can use system functions to view your current user name and application.*

APPLY YOUR KNOWLEDGE 2-1

Suggested time:
30 minutes

Using the SELECT Statement

> **Objective:** To use the SELECT statement to work with the data in the authors and titles tables from the pubs database.

1. In SQL Query Analyzer, verify that you have the pubs database selected. Use a stored procedure to view the structure of the authors table in the pubs database. What stored procedure did you use?

2. In the space below, write a SELECT statement that will enable you to view a list of all authors' first names, last names, and telephone numbers. Concatenate the authors' first and last names and use the column heading Name. Execute this query in SQL Query Analyzer.

3. In the space below, write a SELECT statement for viewing all authors who live in California but not in Oakland. Include the authors' first names, last names, city, and state in your results. Concatenate the authors' first and last names, and use Name for the column heading. Concatenate the city and state columns and use City and State for the column heading. Separate the city and state with a comma.

   Execute this query in SQL Query Analyzer. How many rows are in your results?

4. View the structure of the titles table. (You can use the Object Browser window or sp_help titles.)

5. In the space below, write a query to select all books with a price greater than 20 dollars. Include the title of the book and its price in your results.

   Execute the query in SQL Query Analyzer. How many rows are in your results?

6. In the space below, write a query to select all books with a price of at least 15 and no more than 20 dollars, and year-to-date sales greater than 2000 dollars. Include the title of the book, its price, and year-to-date sales in your results.

   Execute the query in SQL Query Analyzer. How many rows are in your results?

7. In the space below, write a query to determine the average price of all of the books in the titles table.

Execute this query in SQL Query Analyzer. What is the average price?

8. Clear the Query window.

Using UPDATE

You can use the UPDATE Transact-SQL statement to modify the contents of a row. Use the following syntax:

```
UPDATE table_name
SET column_name= value, ...column_name  = value
WHERE column_name conditional_operator value
```

In this example, you replace *table_name* with the name of the table you want to update. Replace *column_name* with the name of the column you want to update, followed by the new value for the column. Finally, you must identify which row in the table you want to update by using the WHERE clause. In the WHERE clause, you must specify a column name, a conditional operator (such as =), and a value for that column. For example, if you want to change the zip code for an author in the authors table whose ID number is 172-32-1176, type:

```
UPDATE authors
SET zip = '78912'
WHERE au_id = '172-32-1176'
```

Using DELETE

You can use the DELETE Transact-SQL statement to delete a row from the table. Here's the syntax:

```
DELETE FROM table_name
WHERE column_name = 'value'
```

You replace *table_name* with the name of the table. Identify the row you want to delete by replacing *column_name* with the name of a column and *value* with a value that identifies one or more rows in the table. For example, to delete an author with the ID number of 172-32-1176, type:

```
DELETE FROM authors
WHERE au_id = '172-32-1176'
```

APPLY YOUR KNOWLEDGE 2-2

Updating and Deleting Rows

Objective: To add a new row to the practice table, change its values, and then delete it.

1. In SQL Query Analyzer, use INSERT to add a new row to the practice table. Use Practice for the first name and User for the last name. What query did you use?

If you don't specify a WHERE *clause with the* UPDATE *statement, SQL Server changes all rows in the table with the value you specify.*

When you use a WHERE *clause, you can specify values by using any case (including uppercase, lowercase, or mixed-case), as long as you selected a case-insensitive sort order when you installed Microsoft SQL Server.*

If you don't specify a WHERE *clause with the* DELETE *statement, SQL Server deletes all rows in the table.*

Suggested time:
15 minutes

2. Verify that you inserted the row correctly by using the SELECT statement. Write the query you used in the space below.

3. In the space below, write a query to change the Practice User's first name to Joe. Execute this query in SQL Query Analyzer, and then verify your change with the SELECT statement.

4. In the space below, write a query to delete the new row. Execute this query in SQL Query Analyzer.

5. Verify that you deleted the row by using the SELECT statement.

6. Clear the Query window.

Data Control Language Statements

You use DCL statements to set users' permissions. You can assign permissions to a specific user or database role. Keep in mind that you must be a member of the sysadmin server role or dbcreator, db_owner, or db_securityadmin database roles to use the DCL statements. These statements consist of GRANT, DENY, and REVOKE. You view the assigned permissions for an object by using the sp_helprotect stored procedure. Here's the following syntax for viewing users' permissions: sp_helprotect 'object'

Replace *object* with the name of the object for which you want to view the permissions assignments. For example, the following statement enables you to view the permissions assigned to the authors table in the pubs database: sp_helprotect authors

Statement Permissions

The permissions you can assign to users consist of both statement and object permissions. Statement permissions enable you to control whether users can use the following Transact-SQL statements:

- CREATE DATABASE
- CREATE DEFAULT
- CREATE PROCEDURE
- CREATE RULE
- CREATE TABLE
- CREATE VIEW
- BACKUP DATABASE
- BACKUP LOG

The object you specify when you use the sp_helprotect *stored procedure must be in your current database. You can't use an object's fully qualified name (database.owner. object) to view the permissions assigned to objects that aren't in your current database.*

In addition to controlling whether users can use these statements, statement permissions also control whether users can perform the equivalent tasks in SQL Server utilities. For example, if you give a user the CREATE DATABASE statement permission, the user can use the command in SQL Query Analyzer, and the user can also create a database within SQL Server Enterprise Manager.

Because creating a database updates system tables in the master database, you can assign the CREATE DATABASE statement permission only in the master database. In addition, you must make the user to whom you want to assign the permission a user of the master database.

Object Permissions

Now that we've looked at statement permissions, let's move on to object permissions. You use object permissions to control the tasks users can perform on objects within a database. For example, you might grant object permissions to permit some users to insert, delete, or update the information in a table, while restricting other users from performing those tasks. Object permissions enable you to control whether users can use the Transact-SQL statements that apply to database objects. The following table describes these statements and the objects on which you use them.

Transact-SQL Statement	Database Objects
DELETE	Tables and views
DUMP TABLE	Tables
EXECUTE	Stored procedures
INSERT	Tables and views
SELECT	Tables, views, and columns
UPDATE	Tables, views, and columns

Object permissions apply to any Transact-SQL statement, stored procedure, or utility that uses those statements. So, if you have the permission to delete a table, you can delete the table by using either the DROP TABLE statement in a query, the Delete option in SQL Server Enterprise Manager, or a stored procedure that issues the DROP TABLE statement.

Using GRANT

So how do you go about assigning permissions? You do so by using the GRANT SQL statement. Here's the syntax you use to grant statement permissions:

```
GRANT {ALL|statement[, ...n]}
TO user_name[, ...n]}
```

You can use the GRANT Transact-SQL statement to grant all statement permissions or only selected statement permissions. If you want to grant a user more than one statement permission, list the permissions separated by commas. In this syntax, you replace *user_name* with the name of one or more users (or a database role) to whom you want to grant the permissions. For example, to grant the CREATE DATABASE and CREATE TABLE permissions to the user named Sally, use the following syntax:

```
GRANT CREATE DATABASE, CREATE TABLE
TO Sally
```

To grant object permissions to a user or database role, use this syntax instead:

```
GRANT
{
{ALL|permission[, ...n]} [(column_name[, ...n])]
ON {table_name|view|stored_procedure|extended_procedure}
}
TO user_name[, ...n]
```

Replace *permission* with one or more object permissions. You can optionally assign permissions for specific columns in a table or view rather than all columns. If you want to assign permissions for specific columns, list their names and separate them by commas. Replace *table_name*, *view*, *stored_procedure*, or *extended_procedure* with the name of the object to which you want to grant the user permissions. Replace *user_name* with the name of the user or database role. For example, to grant the INSERT, UPDATE, and DELETE object permissions to David for the authors table, use the following syntax:

```
GRANT INSERT, UPDATE, DELETE
ON authors
TO David
```

You must first use the database in which the object exists or use the object's fully qualified name to identify it when using the GRANT statement. You don't have to assign the SELECT permission because SQL Server automatically grants it to the public database role for each object in the database.

TASK 2B-4:

Assigning Permissions to the Public Database Role

1. In SQL Query Analyzer, **execute the following SQL statement:**

    ```
    sp_helprotect 'practice'
    ```

    This query enables you to view the current permissions assignments for the practice table. Because you haven't assigned any permissions to users or roles for this table, you see a message stating that there are no matching rows to report. (SQL displays this message because it stores permissions in rows in the table named syspermissions in each database.)

    ```
    Server: Msg 15330, Level 11, State 1, Procedure sp_helprotect, Line 346
    There are no matching rows on which to report.
    ```

2. **In the space below, write the SQL statement for giving the public database role the SELECT, INSERT, UPDATE, and DELETE permissions to the practice table in the pubs database.**

3. **Execute the query you recorded in step 2** to assign permissions to the public database role.

4. **Execute the query:**

    ```
    sp_helprotect 'practice'
    ```

    You should see that the public role now has the DELETE, INSERT, SELECT, and UPDATE object permissions.

5. **Clear the Query window.**

Using DENY

If you want to prevent a user or role from accessing an object or from using a statement permission, you can deny the user's permissions. Denying permissions removes all permissions granted to the user or role and prevents the user from inheriting any permissions.

To deny permissions, begin by selecting a database. You can deny permissions only in your current database. Then, use the following syntax to deny permissions:

```
DENY {ALL|statement[, ...n]}
TO user_name[, ...n]
```

You can assign the CREATE DATABASE *permission only in the master database.*

For example, to deny the CREATE DATABASE permission for the user Andy, you should use the following syntax:

```
DENY CREATE DATABASE
TO Andy
```

You can deny object permissions by using this syntax:

```
DENY { {ALL|permission[, ...n]} [(column_name[, ...n])]
ON {table_name|view|stored_procedure|extended_procedure} }
TO user_name[, ...n]
```

For example, to deny the UPDATE and DELETE object permissions to David for the authors table, use the following syntax:

```
DENY UPDATE, DELETE
ON authors
TO David
```

Using REVOKE

You can revoke granted or denied permissions from a user or role. While revoking a granted permission is similar to denying the user permission, the end result is different. If you deny a user's permission, the user can't inherit permissions for an object. In contrast, if you revoke a user's permission, the user can inherit permissions for that object.

To revoke permissions, begin by selecting a database. Next, use the REVOKE Transact-SQL statement to deny permissions. Here's the syntax:

```
REVOKE {ALL|statement[, ...n]}
FROM user_name[, ...n]
```

For example, to revoke the CREATE DATABASE statement permission from Sally, use the following syntax:

```
REVOKE CREATE DATABASE
FROM Sally
```

Here's the syntax for revoking object permissions:

```
REVOKE { {ALL|permission[, ...n]} [(column_name[, ...n])]
ON {table_name|view|stored_procedure|extended_procedure} }
FROM user_name[, ...n]
```

APPLY YOUR KNOWLEDGE 2-3

Suggested time:
15 minutes

Denying and Revoking Permissions

Objective: To deny permissions to the public database role for the practice table. You will then revoke all permissions from the public role.

1. In the space below, write the SQL statement for denying the DELETE permission from the public database role for the practice table. Execute this query in SQL Query Analyzer.

2. Verify the change to the public database role's permissions by executing the sp_helprotect stored procedure.

3. Write the SQL statement for revoking the UPDATE and INSERT permissions from the public database role for the practice table. Execute the query in SQL Query Analyzer.

4. Verify that you've changed permissions by using the sp_helprotect stored procedure.

5. What's the difference between denying and revoking permissions?

6. Clear the Query window.

7. Minimize SQL Query Analyzer.

Working with Books Online

One of the utilities included with SQL Server 2000 is Books Online. You can use Books Online to read about techniques for installing, managing, and optimizing SQL Server, as well as how to design, create, manage, and optimize databases. Books Online consists of four navigation trees: Contents, Index, Search, and Favorites. The navigation trees are displayed in the left pane of the interface. You can use the Contents tree to browse the topics covered in Books Online. When you select a topic, Books Online displays its contents in the right pane of the interface. Use the Index tree to search for specific terms; in contrast, you can use the Search tree to search for *any* word in Books Online. Finally, you can add specific topics as Favorites; Books Online displays those topics in the Favorites navigation tree.

When you use Books Online to find the syntax of SQL statements, you will find that Microsoft uses various formats to identify the components of each statement. The following table describes some of the formats used to represent the components of a SQL statement.

Component	Format	Example
SQL keywords	All uppercase letters	`SELECT`
User-supplied parameters of SQL statements (such as database, table, and column names)	All lowercase letters	`SELECT *` `FROM authors`

Optional syntax	Enclosed in square brackets [ ]	`CREATE TABLE`
		`[server.database.owner.]`
		`table_ name...`

Options that are alternatives to each other	Separated by the vertical bar character (|)	`WITH [NO_LOG |` `TRUNCATE_ONLY`

APPLY YOUR KNOWLEDGE 2-4

Suggested time:

30 minutes

Using SQL Server Books Online

Objective: To use Books Online to read and research the Transact-SQL language.

1. From the Microsoft SQL Server program group, start Books Online.

2. In the left pane, select the Contents tab if necessary. Expand Transact-SQL Reference. Within the Transact-SQL Reference, select the Functions topic and read about the various functions included in SQL Server 2000.

   Which function can you use to find the highest price of a book in the titles table in the pubs database?

3. How can you use this function to find the highest price of a book in the titles table of the pubs database?

4. In SQL Query Analyzer, use this function to find the highest price of a book. How much is the book?

5. In Books Online, by using the Index tab, find the syntax for the osql utility. What command should you use to run osql, find the highest price of a book in the titles table, and close osql?

Execute this command from a Command Prompt window. (You should get the same price for the book as you had gotten for your answer in step 4.)

6. Close the Command Prompt window.

7. Use the Search tab to search for Transact-SQL tips. What are some of the techniques Microsoft recommends you use to improve the performance of queries?

8. Close Books Online.

9. In SQL Query Analyzer, clear the Query window.

TOPIC 2C

Programming in Transact-SQL

You can use Transact-SQL to program scripts and stored procedures for performing specific tasks on your server. Components of SQL programs include the SQL statements themselves, along with variables, control-of-flow statements, and comments. We're going to start exploring how you program in SQL by looking at variables and how you might use them.

Variables

You use *variables* for assigning values. Because you can assign different values to variables, using them in your programs makes those programs more flexible; you can write your programs such that users input the values for variables. Microsoft refers to variables as "local" because they're available to you only in your current batch of SQL statements or stored procedure. Variables are not only local to your batch of statements or stored procedure, but also to your connection. This means that a variable you declare can't be accessed by another user's connection. Uses for local variables include acting as a counter for a loop to count (or control) how many times the loop is performed, holding a value for testing control-of-flow statements, and saving a data value to be returned by a stored procedure.

variable:
A programming entity to which you assign a value.

Before we go into how you define and work with variables, we want to take a moment to talk about the term global variable. Prior to SQL Server 2000, Microsoft's documentation referred to entities with names that began with two @ signs as global variables. For example, Microsoft originally called the entity @@SERVERNAME a global variable. This term isn't technically accurate because, by definition, a variable is something to which you can assign a value. In SQL Server 2000, Microsoft corrected this error, and you'll now find that they call these entities functions instead of global variables. Keep in mind that these functions (the ones that begin with @@) are parameterless, which means that you can view their contents by executing a statement such as SELECT @@SERVERNAME. We describe some of the available functions in the following table.

Function	Contains
@@CONNECTIONS	The number of logins to your server since its last startup.
@@ERROR	The error number of the last executed Transact-SQL statement.
@@ROWCOUNT	The number of rows affected by your last SQL statement.
@@SERVERNAME	The name of your SQL server.
@@VERSION	The type of CPU installed in your server, and the date, time, and version of the SQL Server software.

Working with Local Variables

Now that we've looked at what variables are and why you use them, let's move on to how you implement them. Before you can use a variable in SQL, you must first define it. You define a local variable by assigning it a name and a data type. Begin the name of a local variable with a single at (@) sign. You use the DECLARE Transact-SQL statement to define a local variable. Here's the syntax:

```
DECLARE @variable_name data_type
```

In this syntax, you replace *variable_name* with the name you want to assign to the variable and *data_type* with the variable's data type. For example, to define a variable in which you plan to store a last name, you might use the following syntax: DECLARE @temp_name varchar(20).

This statement assigns the name @*temp_name* to the variable and defines its data type as varchar (variable character) with a maximum width of 20 characters.

After you've declared a variable, you can assign a value to it by using several techniques. For example, you can assign a constant value to a variable by using the syntax: SELECT @temp_name = 'Whalen'.

Alternatively, you can use this syntax:

```
SELECT @temp_name = au_lname
FROM authors
WHERE au_id = '172-32-1176'
```

This syntax enables you to store the contents of a column into a variable based on a condition in your WHERE clause. In this example, you'll end up storing the last name, White, into the variable @temp_name. (Remember that you must declare the variable before you can assign a value to it.)

You can also use the SET statement to assign a value to a local variable. For example, you might use the following syntax to list all authors who live in a particular state:

```
DECLARE @temp_state char(2)
SET @temp_state = 'ca'
SELECT au_lname, au_fname, state
FROM pubs.dbo.authors
WHERE state = @temp_state
```

These statements enable you to define a local variable named @temp_state, set its value, and then query the authors sample table for a list of authors who live in the state defined in the variable.

You can use the DECLARE *statement to declare multiple variables by separating them with commas. For example, this statement declares two variables:* DECLARE @fname varchar(20), @lname varchar(20).

TASK 2C-1:

Using Variables

1. **What query should you use to define a variable named @vlname for storing an author's last name and setting its initial value to Hunter?**

2. **How can you use this variable to find an author with this last name in the authors table? (Hint: the name of the last name column in the authors table is au_lname.)**

3. **In SQL Query Analyzer, execute together the queries you recorded in steps 1 and 2.**

4. **What query could you use to determine how many logins have occurred on your server since its last startup?**

5. **Execute the new query you recorded in step 4.** You might find the number of connections higher than you expected. This is because the value of this variable is increased each time you log in to your server. So, if you've opened and closed SQL Query Analyzer several times, you increase the number of logins on your server.

6. **Clear the Query window.**

Executing SQL Statements

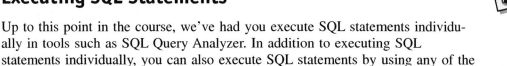

Up to this point in the course, we've had you execute SQL statements individually in tools such as SQL Query Analyzer. In addition to executing SQL statements individually, you can also execute SQL statements by using any of the following techniques: dynamically, through batches, transactions, and scripts.

Dynamic SQL Statements

Microsoft refers to a dynamic SQL statement as one that's constructed during the execution of a script. For example, you might design a stored procedure with variables so that you can construct a SELECT statement that incorporates those variables. Using dynamic statements increases the flexibility of SQL because it enables you to construct a statement when a SQL script or stored procedure is run.

You build a dynamic statement by combining the EXECUTE Transact-SQL keyword with strings and variables. SQL Server determines the values of the variables whenever it processes the statement. Here's the syntax:

```
EXECUTE ({@variable | 'Transact-SQL string'}
      + {@variable | 'Transact-SQL string'}...)
```

In this syntax, you should replace *@variable* with the name of a local variable (remember, you must have declared a value for the variable first). Replace '*Transact-SQL string*' with the static components of a SQL statement. For example:

```
DECLARE @vname varchar(20), @vtable varchar(20), @vdbase
varchar(20)
SET @vname = "'White'"
SET @vtable = 'authors'
SET @vdbase = 'pubs'
EXECUTE ('USE '+ @vdbase + 'SELECT * FROM ' + @vtable + '
WHERE au_lname = '  + @vname)
```

In this example, you must enclose the value for the @vname variable in both double and single quotes because you need the value of the variable to include the single quotes. In other words, you want the value of @vname to be 'White' not White (without any quotes). You need the single quotes around White so that the WHERE clause will be WHERE au_lname = 'White' when SQL Server dynamically constructs the statement.

You should consider the following when constructing dynamic SQL statements:

- The SQL statement along with all variables must consist of character data. If you want to use numeric data in the dynamic statement, you must convert it to character data first.

- You can nest multiple dynamic statements.

- You can't use functions in a dynamic statement.

Batches

batch:
A series of SQL statements you send to the server so that the server can process them together.

A SQL *batch* is simply a set of SQL statements executed together. You can run a batch interactively or as part of a script. When you send SQL statements individually to the server for processing, your server incurs a certain amount of overhead to process those statements. In contrast, if you combine several SQL statements into a batch, your server incurs this overhead only once for the entire batch—instead of for each individual statement that makes up the batch. Batches enhance the performance of your server because SQL Server can parse, optimize, compile, and execute the statements together rather than individually. If you have a syntax error within a batch, SQL Server won't process any of the statements in the batch.

The techniques you use to identify a batch within programs vary. For example, you use the SQL EXECUTE command within an ODBC application to identify a batch.

You define a batch in tools such as SQL Query Analyzer by using the GO command. This command isn't a SQL statement. Instead, it's simply a signal that identifies the end of a batch within the Microsoft SQL Server client utilities (such as SQL Query Analyzer and osql). SQL Server treats all statements from a previous GO statement as a single batch—or all statements since the start of your query session or script until the first GO as a batch.

For example, you can use the following syntax to cause SQL Server to execute the statements as a batch:

```
USE pubs
SELECT MAX(price) AS 'Highest Book Price'
FROM titles
PRINT ' '
SELECT MIN(price)AS 'Lowest Book Price'
FROM titles
PRINT ' '
 SELECT AVG(price)AS 'Average Book Price'
FROM titles
GO
```

You should be aware of the following considerations when defining batches:

- You can't combine the following SQL statements into a single batch: CREATE PROCEDURE, CREATE VIEW, CREATE TRIGGER, CREATE RULE, and CREATE DEFAULT. Each statement requires that you follow it by the GO command. For example, if you want to create a database, table, and a trigger, you must use the following syntax:

```
CREATE DATABASE database_name
CREATE TABLE table_name (column list)
GO
CREATE TRIGGER trigger_name
GO
```

- If you declare and use local variables within a batch, those variables are available only to you as part of the batch. If you reference a local variable after a GO command, you'll get an error message.

- You must precede stored procedures with the EXECUTE (or EXEC) keyword if you run them within a batch unless the stored procedure is used in the first line of the batch. For example, consider the following query:

```
SELECT *
FROM pubs..practice
EXECUTE sp_help 'practice'
GO
```

Because you're using the sp_help stored procedure within a batch, you must precede it with the EXECUTE keyword, as follows:

```
SELECT *
FROM pubs..practice
EXECUTE sp_help 'practice'
GO
```

Transactions

SQL Server processes transactions like a batch; in other words, SQL Server treats the statements within a transaction as a single unit. But here's the key difference between a transaction and a batch: you can undo the changes made by all of the statements within a transaction, but you can't undo the actions of the statements within a batch. The entire transaction must succeed or fail as a whole in order to maintain data integrity. You can define multiple batches within a single transaction.

You mark the beginning of a transaction by preceding the SQL statements with the BEGIN TRANSACTION statement. You end a transaction by using either the COMMIT TRANSACTION or ROLLBACK TRANSACTION statement. If you use ROLLBACK TRANSACTION, SQL Server undoes any of the changes or rows affected by the transaction. Use the following syntax to define a transaction:

```
BEGIN TRANSACTION
        SQL statement #1
        SQL statement #2
        ...
COMMIT TRANSACTION
```

You use transactions when you must make sure that all of the statements complete successfully. If any one of the statements fail, you don't want any of the statements to execute. You typically see transactions used in applications that involve money. For example, in an application for handling checking and savings bank accounts, you would use a transaction to write the SQL statements for transferring money from one account to the other.

Scripts

A SQL script is simply a text file containing a series of SQL statements. You can open the file within SQL Query Analyzer and then re-execute its statements. You can also use osql to run script files.

APPLY YOUR KNOWLEDGE 2-5

Suggested time:
20 minutes

Running SQL Statements

Objective: To design and execute a dynamic SQL statement. You will also execute a batch of statements.

1. Write a query to execute a dynamic SQL statement for querying the titles table in the pubs database for all books. Have SQL Server display only the title and price columns, and sort the results in descending order by price. Declare variables for storing the database, table, and columns you want to include in the SELECT statement. Verify that your query works by executing it in SQL Query Analyzer.

2. Write a query to insert two new rows into the practice table in the pubs database. Add the necessary commands to have SQL Server treat the query as a batch. Execute the query in SQL Query Analyzer.

3. In SQL Query Analyzer, verify that the new rows were inserted into the practice table. Write the query you used in the space below.

4. Clear the Query window.

Control-of-Flow Statements

You use control-of-flow statements to control how SQL Server executes the statements in a stored procedure. Control-of-flow statements include:

- IF...ELSE
- BEGIN...END
- WHILE
- CASE

Let's take a look at each of these statements in more detail.

IF...ELSE

Use the IF...ELSE statement to have SQL Server first determine if a condition is true or false, and then perform an action for each value. For example, you could use the following IF...ELSE statement to display one message if an author lives in California and a different message if the author doesn't:

```
DECLARE @temp_state char(2)
SELECT @temp_state = state
FROM authors
WHERE au_lname='White'
IF @temp_state='ca'
        PRINT 'This author lives in California.'
ELSE
        PRINT 'This author does not live in California.'
```

SQL Server displays the statement between the IF and ELSE statement if the condition @temp_state='ca' is true, and the statement after the ELSE if the condition is false. SQL Server treats only the first statement after the ELSE keyword as what it should do if the condition is false. (In this example, the PRINT keyword simply displays a message on the screen. You can use the PRINT keyword to display either a message contained within quotes or the value of a variable.)

BEGIN...END

If you want SQL Server to process more than one statement if a condition is true or false, define a block of statements by using the BEGIN...END keywords. These keywords enable you to group SQL statements together within an IF...ELSE statement. For example:

```
IF (SELECT COUNT(*) FROM authors WHERE contract = 0) > 0
        BEGIN
        PRINT 'These authors do not have contracts
          on file:'
        PRINT ' '
        SELECT au_lname, au_fname, au_id
        FROM authors
        WHERE contract = 0
        END
ELSE
        PRINT 'All authors have contracts on file.'
```

This block of code enables you to run multiple SQL statements based on whether the condition is true or false by using the BEGIN...END keywords. In this example, the IF condition counts the number of rows in the authors table where the contract column has a value of zero (0). If the count is greater than zero, you will see a message stating that there are authors who don't have contracts on file, followed by a list of those authors.

WHILE

You can use a WHILE statement to repeatedly perform a task until a specific condition is met. For example, you might use a WHILE statement to add rows to a table. Here's the syntax:

```
SET NOCOUNT ON
GO
DECLARE @counter INT
SET @counter=0
WHILE (@counter<20)
BEGIN
        INSERT INTO pubs..practice
        VALUES('Last'+CAST(@counter as char(2)), 'First')
        SET @counter = @counter+1
END
SET NOCOUNT OFF
```

Using the statement SET NOCOUNT ON prevents SQL Server from displaying the message stating the number of rows affected by the INSERT statement. Use the CAST(*variable*) AS *data_type*) clause to convert the integer variable @counter to character format.

CASE

The CASE statement evaluates an expression to see if it is true or false. Based on the result, it uses a specific value for true or false. For example, the following query returns the full name of the state an author in the pubs database lives in, rather than the state abbreviation:

```
SELECT au_fname + ' ' + au_lname AS Name, 'State of Residence' =
        CASE
                WHEN 'CA' THEN 'California'
                WHEN 'IN' THEN 'Indiana'
                WHEN 'KS' THEN 'Kansas'
                WHEN 'MD' THEN 'Maryland'
                WHEN 'MI' THEN 'Michigan'
                WHEN 'OR' THEN 'Oregon'
                WHEN 'TN' THEN 'Tennessee'
                WHEN 'UT' THEN 'Utah'
        END
FROM pubs..authors
ORDER BY state, au_lname
```

If you want to use a numeric value to determine which case is used, but have SQL Server display a character-based message, you must use the following syntax:

```
SELECT au_fname+' '+au_lname AS Name, 'Contract Status' =
        CASE
        WHEN (contract=1) THEN 'Contract on file.'
        WHEN (contract=0)
          THEN 'We do not have a contract with this author.'
        END
FROM pubs..authors
```

Notice that you must use the syntax 'Contract Status' = in the SELECT statement. This is because the CASE statement returns character data even though the conditional statement evaluates a numeric column.

APPLY YOUR KNOWLEDGE 2-6

Suggested time:
20 minutes

Using Control-of-Flow Statements

Objective: To create a query to display different messages based on a book's year-to-date sales.

1. Write a query to list the books in the titles table. Include the title and year-to-date sales columns in the results set; sort the results set in descending order by the year-to-date sales column. Make sure you include a line to use the pubs database. Use the CASE control-of-flow statement to display messages of your choice based on each book's year-to-date sales. Sort the rows in descending order by year-to-date sales. Record your messages in the following table.

Condition	Message
year-to-date sales <= 200	
year-to-date sales > 200 and <= 1000	
year-to-date sales > 1000 and <= 5000	
year-to-date sales > 5000	

2. Execute your query in SQL Query Analyzer.

3. Use SQL Server Books Online to determine how you can add a case for handling null values in the ytd_sales column for the titles table.

4. Edit your query to include the syntax for handling null values. Execute the query again to verify that your change works.

5. Don't clear the Query window.

Creating SQL Scripts

You can create a SQL script by using any text editor such as Notepad or SQL Query Analyzer. If you create your script within Notepad, make sure you save it with the extension .sql. By default, SQL Query Analyzer automatically appends the .sql extension to scripts when you save them. You can load and execute a script from within SQL Query Analyzer or by using the osql command-line utility.

Comments

You should always document your work by including comments in scripts. SQL Server supports two types of comments: inline and block. An inline comment is one that you place on the same line as a SQL statement. You must precede it with two hyphens. For example, use the following syntax for inline comments:

```
SELECT *
FROM authors
WHERE contract = 0 -- Find authors without contracts.
```

You can use a block of comments when you want to isolate several comments from your SQL statements. Identify a block of comments by preceding them with /* and ending them with */. By convention, you'll typically see lines within the block of comments preceded by **. For example:

```
/*
** This syntax typically indicates a block of comments
** in a script.Use the /* to indicate the start of the
** block, and a */ to indicate the end of the block.
*/
```

When you're debugging a script, you might find it helpful to prevent SQL Server from executing some of the lines of your script. Use the block comment indicators to comment out those lines. For example:

```
/*
USE pubs
SELECT AVG(price)
FROM titles
*/
```

Remember, SQL Server won't execute the statements between the block comment indicators.

TASK 2C-2:

Saving a Script File

1. In SQL Query Analyzer, **verify that you still see your query from Lab 6.**

2. Above the query, **insert the following block of comments:**

    ```
    /* Query to display a message based on each book's
    year-to-date sales.
    ** Designed by your_name on date.
    */
    ```

    Replace *your_name* with your name, and *date* with today's date. (Notice that SQL Query Analyzer automatically displays your comments in light green.)

```
/* Query to display a message based on each book's year-to-date sales.
** Designed by Rozanne Whalen on 4/16/01.
*/
USE pubs
SELECT title, 'Year-to-date sales' =
        CASE
                WHEN (ytd_sales<=200) THEN 'message'
                WHEN (ytd_sales>200 and ytd_sales<=1000) THEN 'message'
                WHEN (ytd_sales>1000 and ytd_sales<=5000) THEN 'message'
                WHEN (ytd_sales>5000) THEN 'message'
                WHEN (ytd_sales IS NULL) THEN 'message'
        END
FROM titles
ORDER BY ytd_sales DESC
```

3. **Choose File→Save As** to display the Save Query dialog box. **Look at the Save In drop-down list. Verify that your current folder is C:\Data.**

4. Look at the Save In drop-down list to verify that your current folder is C:\Data. In the File Name text box, **type *sales* and then click Save.** SQL Query Analyzer automatically appends the .sql extension to your script file. By default, SQL Query Analyzer saves the file in the ANSI file format.

5. On the toolbar, **click the New Query button** to open a new, blank Query window.

6. **Close the Query window containing the SQL statements for your script.**

7. **Choose File→Open** to display the Open Query File dialog box.

8. From the list of query files, **select the sales script and click Open** to load your script into SQL Query Analyzer.

9. **Execute the script** to re-run your query. You should see that SQL Query Analyzer switches to the pubs database and then runs your query.

10. **Close SQL Query Analyzer.**

APPLY YOUR KNOWLEDGE 2-7

Using Osql to Execute a Script

Objective: To use osql to execute the sales SQL script.

Suggested time:
10 minutes

1. In the space below, write the command you should use to execute the sales SQL script. As part of the command, log on to your server using Windows Authentication.

If you need help with this command, refer to the osql topic in Books Online.

2. Open a Command Prompt window and execute the command you wrote in step 1.

3. Close all open windows.

Working with XML

SQL Server 2000 enables you to configure Microsoft Internet Information Services (IIS) to access data on your SQL server. After you configure this support, users can query your server over the Hypertext Transfer Protocol (HTTP). This means that users can enter queries as a URL in the Address text box of their Web browser. You can also develop Web pages that display SQL Server data. Whether you use a query within a Web browser or you develop Web pages to display SQL Server data, the language you must use is called the Extensible Markup Language (XML).

virtual directory:
A virtual directory is an alias to a folder that can be accessed through your IIS server.

For more information on configuring a virtual directory for SQL Server, please see the Element K "SQL Server 2000: System Administration" course.

Before users can access your server through HTTP using XML, you must first configure a *virtual directory* for SQL Server. Let's explore what a virtual directory is first. A virtual directory is nothing more than an alias that points to a folder somewhere on your network. (This folder can be on your IIS server, SQL server, or any other server.) We call a virtual directory an alias because the name your users use to access this directory doesn't indicate where that folder is stored—or the actual path to that folder. For example, you access a virtual directory when you enter a URL such as **www.microsoft.com/sql**. In this example, "sql" represents the name of the virtual directory, yet that reference could point to any server (or multiple servers) on Microsoft's network. You configure a virtual directory by using the IIS Virtual Directory Management for SQL Server utility.

So, in order to set up an IIS server to access a SQL server, you must first configure a virtual directory. Your first step is to create a folder to store the files you want to make accessible through the virtual directory. Next, you use the IIS Virtual Directory Management for SQL Server utility to define the virtual directory and point it to this folder. As part of the virtual directory's configuration, you specify the types of access you want to permit when users query your server with a URL. SQL Server supports three types of access:

- *Directly accessing objects in databases (such as tables and views).* You typically won't enable support for direct database access in order to make your server as secure as possible.

- *Executing XML Path (XPath) Language queries.* With these types of queries, users access schema files in the URL instead of accessing a database directly. You can think of schema files as essentially a view that's based on one or more tables within a database.

- *Executing template files.* To support these queries, you create a document that contains the SQL statements you want users to be able to execute along with XML formatting. When users call this template in a URL, the SQL statements you've included in the template file are executed.

Designing an XML Query

While this course isn't meant to teach you XML programming, we want to provide you with an overview of using the SELECT statement in an XML query. You use a SELECT statement to display SQL data on a Web page. As part of your query, you must specify the format in which you want to display the data, as follows:

```
SELECT columns
FROM table
FOR AUTO | EXPLICIT | RAW
```

In the following table, we describe the differences between the AUTO, EXPLICIT, or RAW XML formats.

Format	Description
AUTO	Displays each of the rows in the query's result set as nested XML elements, and uses each column's name to identify the attributes in the result set. (In comparison, the RAW format simply identifies each row in the result set as "row.")
EXPLICIT	Displays each of the rows in the query's result set based on the explicit formatting you specify.
RAW	Displays each of the rows in the query's results set as an XML element with the generic identifier of "row."

You can optionally add the keyword XMLDATA to any of these formats to enable SQL Server to include not only the data, but also information about the structure of the table(s) behind the data. SQL Server returns this schema information before it displays the results set. Here's the syntax:

```
SELECT columns
FROM table
FOR AUTO | EXPLICIT | RAW [, XMLDATA]
```

Let's say that you want to use the following query to retrieve data in the XML format. This query retrieves a list of stores' ID numbers, their names, and all orders on file from the pubs database:

```
SELECT store.stor_id AS StoreID, stor_name AS Name,
order.ord_num AS OrderNum,
        order.qty AS Quantity
FROM stores AS store JOIN sales AS orders
ON store.stor_id = orders.stor_id
ORDER BY stor_name
FOR XML format
```

Let's take a look at using the RAW and AUTO formats in more detail. In Figure 2-4, you can see what the results set for this query looks like when we use the clause FOR XML RAW. Notice that each row in the results set is contained in its own tag named "row." In addition, SQL Server repeats the ID number and name of each store for each order they have on file. Now, take a look at the results set you see in Figure 2-5. We used the clause FOR XML AUTO in this example. When you use the AUTO format, SQL Server displays the results set in a hierarchy: You should see that each store has its own tag containing the StoreID and Name information (the store tag is called the parent tag), and then indented below each store tag is a tag for each order on file (each order represents a child tag). Using the AUTO format also provides you with greater flexibility because you have control over the labels assigned to each of the tags.

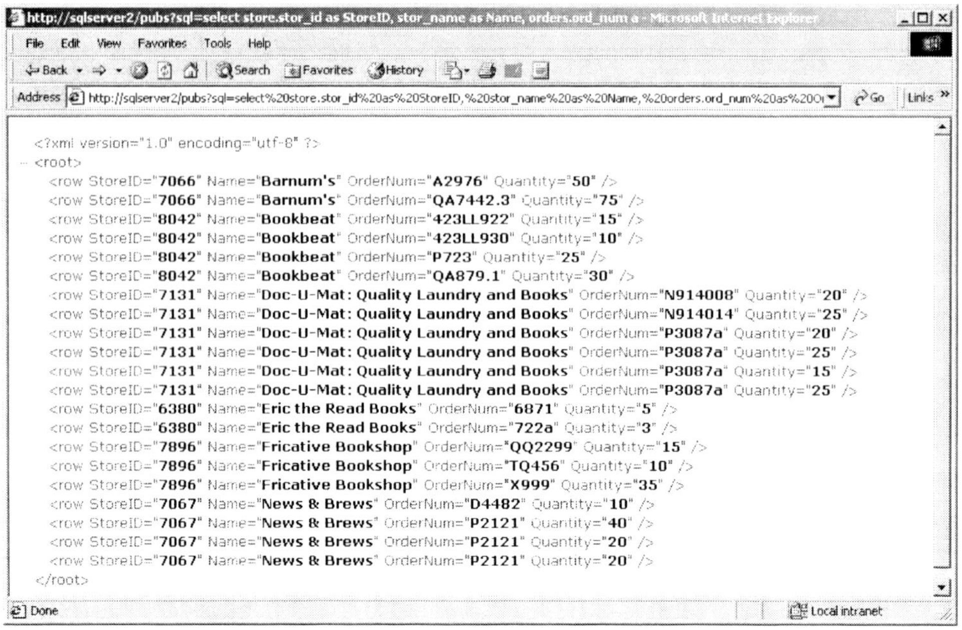

Figure 2-4: *Displaying data with the* RAW XML *format.*

Figure 2-5: *Displaying data with the* AUTO XML *format.*

There are a few restrictions you can run into when using the FOR XML clause as part of a URL query. You can't use the FOR XML clause within:

- A subquery for an INSERT, UPDATE, DELETE, SELECT, or SELECT...INTO statement. For example, you can't execute the following query:

```
SELECT *
FROM table_name1
WHERE ... (SELECT * FROM table_name2 FOR XML RAW)
```

- A COMPUTE BY or FOR BROWSE clause.

- A stored procedure that you call by an INSERT statement.

- As part of the SELECT statement you use to define a view.
- A cursor.

TASK 2C-3:

Choosing an XML Format

1. **Which XML format do you think was used in the query to generate the results set you see in the graphic below? How can you tell?**

```
<row CustomerID="ALFKI" ContactName="Maria Anders" />
<row CustomerID="ANATR" ContactName="Ana Trujillo" />
<row CustomerID="ANTON" ContactName="Antonio Moreno" />
<row CustomerID="AROUT" ContactName="Thomas Hardy" />
<row CustomerID="BERGS" ContactName="Christina Berglund" />
<row CustomerID="BLAUS" ContactName="Hanna Moos" />
```

2. **You've been asked by the Web development team for your company to provide them with data from your company's customers table in XML format. They don't want the data in hierarchical order, but they would like you to include information about the customers table's schema. What FOR XML clause should you use?**

Summary

In this lesson, we provided you with an overview of using the Transact-SQL language to work with both SQL Server and its data. You learned how to use the two primary tools for executing queries: SQL Query Analyzer and osql. You also explored the various types of SQL statements you can use, including Data Definition Language, Data Control Language, and Data Manipulation Language statements. Finally, we explored the types of programming commands you can use to program in Transact-SQL.

LESSON 2 REVIEW

2A In what scenario would you use osql instead of SQL Query Analyzer?

2B What are the three categories of SQL statements? Give an example of each.

2C How can you document SQL scripts?

Designing and Implementing Databases

Data Files:
create_database.sql
filegroup.sql
set_options.sql
increase_size.sql

Lesson Time:
2 hours

Overview

One of your first tasks as a database developer is to create the databases you need. In this lesson, we will show you how to go about designing your databases and optimizing their design for performance. Next, we'll discuss how to create databases and their filegroups using Transact-SQL. Finally, we will explore how you manage databases by expanding, shrinking, and dropping them.

Objectives

To design, create, and manage databases, you will:

3A Identify the issues for designing databases.

One of the first factors you should consider when designing your databases is their size. In this topic, we will discuss how to estimate the size of your databases so that you can configure the size of its files. We will also examine how you can design your database so as to optimize its performance.

3B Create and configure databases.

After you've designed your strategy for implementing a database, your next task is to create the database. In this topic, we will create a database by using Transact-SQL. We will also show you the techniques you can use to configure database options.

3C Manage databases.

Because databases change over time, it's important that you know how to either increase or decrease the size of a database. In this topic, we will show you how to automatically or manually change the size of a database. You'll also learn how to increase the size of a database's transaction log. Finally, you'll learn how to delete a database if you no longer need it.

 TOPIC 3A

Identifying Database Design Issues

Before you can create databases, you should understand SQL Server's terminology for databases and their components. We're going to start by looking at this terminology, and then move on to how you go about creating databases on your server.

Databases and Files

A database is a collection of database objects; these objects include tables, indexes, views, and stored procedures. At a minimum, each database consists of a primary data file with an extension of .mdf. In addition to its primary data file, you can optionally configure SQL Server to store a database in a secondary data file. These files use the extension of .ndf. You might choose to use a secondary data file if you want to distribute a database across multiple physical drives. Placing the data files on separate hard drives can help improve the performance of a database because SQL Server can perform file I/O operations on both drives simultaneously.

Transaction Logs

In addition to a database's primary data file, you must also create a transaction log for each database. The transaction log consists of at least one file. SQL Server automatically assigns the extension of .ldf to each transaction log file. Let's take a moment to explore the role of the transaction log. SQL Server uses the transaction log to make it possible to either recover (roll forward) or undo (roll back) a transaction. This capability of rolling back or rolling forward transactions enables SQL Server to protect your database from corruption in the event of a server crash.

Here's how transaction logging works: When you change a database, the first thing SQL Server does is to copy the pages of the database that you're changing into a portion of RAM called the buffer cache. (Depending on what's happening on your server, these pages might already be cached in RAM.) Next, SQL Server records your change to both the data pages and the transaction log in RAM. It then writes the change to the database's transaction log on your server's hard disk. At this point, SQL Server considers your change committed. Only after writing the change to the transaction log can SQL Server then write the changed data pages in RAM out to the database on your server's hard disk. What's most important for you to understand is that SQL Server *always* writes the change to the transaction log on the hard disk before it writes that same change to the database. It's this strategy of writing to the transaction log before writing to the database that makes it possible for you to recover a failed transaction (or to undo a transaction, for that matter). Because SQL Server writes to the transaction log before it writes to your database, you'll sometimes hear a database's transaction log referred to as a write-ahead log.

SQL Server identifies two types of transactions: explicit and implicit. An explicit transaction is a group of one or more Transact-SQL statements that begin with the `BEGIN TRANSACTION` statement and end with the `COMMIT TRANSACTION` statement. SQL Server doesn't commit the changes you make in an explicit transaction's SQL statements until it processes the `COMMIT TRANSACTION` statement. As a result, you can roll back the transaction at any time prior to the `COMMIT TRANSACTION` statement. Remember, though, you must always use `COMMIT TRANSACTION` after you use `BEGIN TRANSACTION`. For example, if you precede an `INSERT` statement with the `BEGIN TRANSACTION` statement, SQL Server won't add the new row to your table until you execute the `COMMIT TRANSACTION` statement.

You use an implicit transaction when you use SQL statements by themselves without the `BEGIN TRANSACTION` statement. SQL Server considers all statements you execute part of a transaction until you issue either a `COMMIT TRANSACTION`, `COMMIT WORK`, or `ROLLBACK TRANSACTION` statement. The good news is that SQL Server doesn't enable implicit transactions by default. Instead, SQL Server turns on what's called the autocommit transaction mode. In this mode, SQL Server treats each individual SQL statement (along with its parameters) as a separate transaction. For example, if you execute a query and don't use the `BEGIN TRANSACTION` and `COMMIT TRANSACTION` statements, nor do you turn on implicit transactions, SQL Server autocommits the transaction. Why is this better? It's better because it means you don't have to worry about executing a `COMMIT TRANSACTION` statement for SQL Server to commit your changes.

TASK 3A-1:

Designing Databases

1. **You're planning to implement a customer service application within SQL Server. What components do you need to create to support this application? What file extensions will SQL Server use?**

2. **Explain the function of a transaction log.**

Estimating the Space Requirements for Databases

One of your tasks when you create a database is to specify its initial size. SQL Server creates your database's data file based on this initial size. For example, if you create a database named sqldata with a size of 50 MB, SQL Server creates a 50 MB data file to store the database. You should estimate your space requirements prior to creating your databases to avoid over-allocating disk space. If you find that your space requirements change, however, you can either shrink or grow your databases. You can also configure SQL Server 2000 to automatically grow or shrink your databases, and we'll talk more about that later on in this lesson.

Microsoft recommends that you configure the size of a database's transaction log as 10 to 25 percent of the size of the database. For example, if you estimate that your database will use 150 MB of disk space, you should configure the transaction log's size to be between 15 and 37.5 MB. If you frequently update the database, you'll find that you should use a transaction log size that's close to 25 percent of the database's size.

How SQL Server Measures Disk Space

SQL Server uses disk space in 8 KB *pages*. SQL Server uses some pages to keep track of the space allocated within a database, and other pages to store user and index data. Within a database, SQL Server allocates space for database objects such as tables and indexes in extents. An *extent* is a contiguous block of eight pages for a total of 64 KB of disk space, as shown in Figure 3-1. A database consists of 16 extents per megabyte. SQL Server uses both uniform and mixed extents. With a uniform extent, SQL Server dedicates the entire extent to an object. SQL Server uses a mixed extent to store up to eight objects. By default, SQL Server stores any new objects you create in a mixed extent. If that object grows to where it needs more than eight pages (64 KB), SQL Server stores the object's additional pages in a uniform extent.

page:
The minimum block of disk space that SQL Server copies from your server's hard disk to RAM, and vice versa. In SQL Server 2000, SQL Server uses 8 KB pages.

extent:
An allocation of disk space made up of eight contiguous 8 KB pages for a total of 64 KB.

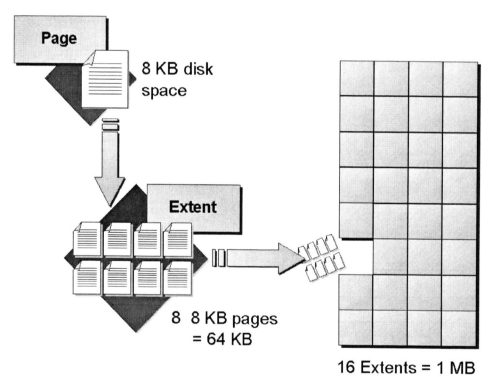

Figure 3-1: *Measurements of disk space.*

How SQL Server Manages Disk Space

Let's take a look at how SQL Server uses the pages within a database in more detail. When you create a database file, SQL Server automatically creates the first extent as a mixed extent. Within this file, SQL Server reserves the first page for storing file information such as any file attributes you configure, the name of the database to which the file belongs, the file's filegroup, minimum size, and file growth increment. This page is called the *File Header page*. In addition to the File Header page, SQL Server also uses a second page called the *Page Free Space (PFS) page* to keep track of the amount of free space available in the pages that make up the file. SQL Server can manage up to 8,000 contiguous pages per PFS page (approximately 64 MB of data). If your database exceeds this size, SQL Server adds PFS pages as necessary.

SQL Server also uses two other types of pages to identify free extents and mixed extents with available pages: *Global Allocation Map (GAM) page* and *Secondary Global Allocation Map (SGAM) page*. SQL Server uses a GAM page to keep track of all extents within a file. For each extent, SQL Server uses a bit to indicate whether the extent is allocated or not. If an extent is allocated, SQL Server marks the bit as 0; in contrast, if the extent is free, SQL Server marks this bit as 1. A single GAM page can manage up to 63,904 extents (roughly 4 GB of data). SQL Server can allocate additional GAM pages as needed. SQL Server uses the SGAM page to keep track of up to 63,904 mixed extents that have at least one page free. (If a mixed extent has a free page, SQL Server can store data on that page.) Like GAM pages, SQL Server uses a bit with a value of 1 to indicate that a mixed extent has one or more free pages. If an extent is a uniform extent or has no free pages, SQL Server marks this bit with a value of 0.

Keep in mind that the GAM and SGAM pages work together to help SQL Server identify available extents. For example, if an extent's bit has a value of 1 on the GAM page, this means that the extent is available for storing data—even if the SGAM page has a value of 0 for the same extent. This is because SQL Server doesn't update the information on the SGAM page until it actually begins to store data in the extent. In the following table, we describe the possible combinations of an extent's bits on both the GAM and SGAM pages, and what each combination means.

GAM Bit	SGAM Bit	Result
1	0	This extent is available for storing data.
0	1	This extent is a mixed extent with at least one free page available for storing data.
0	0	This extent is not available for storing data. The extent could be either a full mixed extent or a uniform extent.

In summary, when you create a database file, SQL Server uses at least the first four pages of that file to keep track of information about the file along with its space usage. These pages are numbered sequentially beginning with 0, as follows:

- Page 0: File Header page
- Page 1: Page Free Space page
- Page 2: Global Allocation Map page
- Page 3: Secondary Global Allocation Map page

We show you what these pages look like within the file's extent in Figure 3-2.

File Header page:
The first page in the first extent of a file. SQL Server uses this page to store information about the file, including the name of the database to which it belongs, the filegroup, and sizing information.

Page Free Space (PFS) page:
SQL Server keeps track of the available space in the file's pages within the PFS page. Each PFS page can keep track of a maximum of 8,000 contiguous pages in the file. If necessary, SQL Server adds multiple PFS pages to keep track of free space.

Global Allocation Map (GAM) page:
SQL Server uses this page to keep track of all extents within a file and identifies whether or not each extent is allocated.

Secondary Global Allocation Map (SGAM) page:
SQL Server uses the SGAM page to keep track of all mixed extents, along with whether or not each mixed extent has at least one free page.

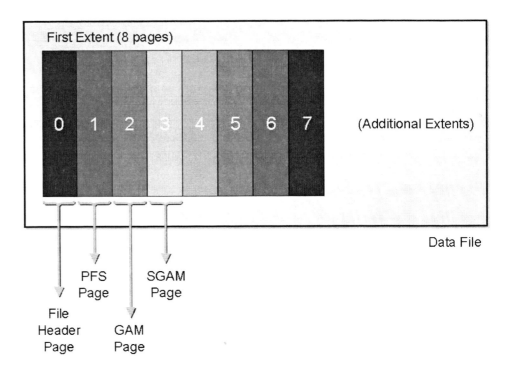

Figure 3-2: *File space pages.*

TASK 3A-2:

Identifying the Space Requirements for Databases

1. How does SQL Server address the storage space on your hard drive?

2. What factors should you consider when estimating the size of a database?

3. At what point does SQL Server use a uniform extent to store a table's data?

Optimizing Databases

SQL Server 2000 includes features that enable you to optimize the performance of its databases. These features include such techniques as: ·

*   Creating multiple data files.
*   Creating filegroups.

- Installing a drive array in your server.

- Using separate hard disks for transaction logs and the tempdb database.

One factor to bear in mind with a database system is that your server must perform frequent file Input and Output (I/O) operations. Any technique you implement that improves the speed of file I/O will improve the speed of the database system itself. So the one thing all of these different techniques have in common is that they enable you to improve the speed of file I/O in SQL Server. Let's examine each of these techniques in detail.

Creating Multiple Data Files and Filegroups

In general, you should spread as much of your database across as many hard disks as you can. You can do so by creating multiple files for your database, and placing each file on a separate hard disk. For example, if your server has four hard disks, you'll see better performance if you create four data files for the database, and place each data file on each of the four hard disks. You can further enhance performance by placing tables and their associated nonclustered indexes in separate data files on separate hard disks. This strategy enhances performance because SQL Server can access a table's nonclustered index on a separate hard disk from that of the table itself.

When you create a database, SQL Server automatically creates a default *filegroup* that contains your database's primary data file. You can add secondary data files to this default filegroup, or you can create secondary files within a new user-defined filegroup. You use filegroups to administer groups of secondary data files as a unit. For example, if you have a very large database, instead of backing up the entire database, you can back up by filegroups. Although filegroups don't inherently improve the performance of your database, keep in mind that creating a user-defined filegroup requires that you create at least one secondary data file. Creating this secondary data file on a separate hard disk does improve the performance of a database.

You can use filegroups only for storing data files. SQL Server doesn't permit you to store a database's transaction log file within a filegroup. You can, however, create multiple transaction log files for a database, and then place these files on separate hard disks.

filegroup:
A collection of one or more database data files. You use filegroups to group data files together so that you can administer them as a single unit.

Implementing Drive Arrays

If you don't want the administrative workload for creating multiple files and filegroups, a different strategy for improving file I/O performance is to implement a hardware drive array in your server. A drive array, also known as a Redundant Array of Independent Disks (RAID), enables your server to write data across multiple hard disks simultaneously. While both Windows 2000 and Windows NT enable you to implement a software RAID (disk striping with parity), this strategy increases the workload on your server, which can degrade your server's overall performance. Microsoft recommends that you implement a hardware RAID instead of a software RAID on your SQL server.

SQL Server 2000 supports RAID levels 0, 1, 5, and 10. Each of these RAID levels varies as to performance enhancements and fault tolerance. With RAID level 0, disk striping, your server writes (stripes) data across multiple hard disks. This strategy greatly improves the performance of both reading and writing to the hard disks, but doesn't offer you any fault tolerance. If any one of the hard disks in the drive array fails, your server won't be able to access any of the data on any of the hard disks in the drive array. RAID level 1, disk mirroring or disk duplexing, enables your server to mirror the data on one hard disk onto a second hard disk. RAID level 1 doesn't improve file I/O performance, but it does offer excellent fault tolerance. In this strategy, if one disk fails, your server can still access the data on the other hard disk.

RAID level 5, disk striping with parity, enables your server to stripe data along with parity information across multiple hard disks. If one of the hard disks in the array fails, your server can reconstruct its information by using the parity information on the other disks in the array. RAID level 5 enhances your server's fault tolerance. It also increases your server's performance when reading data, but not when writing data. Your server will be slower when writing data because it must write the parity information across the hard disks.

With RAID 10, you configure your server to mirror two drive arrays. In other words, RAID 10 is a combination of both RAID 1 (disk mirroring) and RAID 0 (disk striping). RAID 10 enables you to increase the fault tolerance of disk striping by mirroring the drive array. In addition, RAID 10 offers you the fastest disk I/O because your server doesn't have to write parity information to the hard disks. The only drawback to RAID 10 is its cost. For example, if you want to implement RAID 10, you'll need to mirror a four-disk array with a second four-disk array—for a total of eight hard disks.

Using Separate Hard Disks for the Transaction Log and Tempdb

Another strategy you can use to enhance file I/O performance is to place your database's transaction log on its own hard disk separate from that of the database. SQL Server writes to a database's transaction log sequentially. For this reason, your server will perform better if the transaction log is on its own dedicated hard disk. This strategy enables the hard disk's read-write heads to stay in place for writing to the transaction log. Keep in mind that most production database servers typically have only one user database, so this means that you'll need to store only one database's transaction log on a separate hard disk.

Microsoft also recommends that you isolate your server's tempdb database from your user databases to improve performance. Remember, SQL Server uses the tempdb database as its scratchpad for performing tasks such as sorting a table, rebuilding indexes, and so on. You'll improve the overall performance of SQL Server if you can isolate this database on its own hard disk or disk array. Don't worry about fault tolerance with the tempdb database; SQL Server empties it out each time you restart your server.

If you have the luxury of designing your "ideal" SQL server, here's what we recommend: a RAID 10 disk array for storing your server's operating system, SQL Server software, and user database; a mirrored pair of hard disks for the database's transaction log; and a separate hard disk or disk array for the tempdb database.

TASK 3A-3:

Optimizing Database Performance

1. You're responsible for designing the server on which your company will use SQL Server and a customer service database. You want to minimize your administrative workload while still providing the best possible performance for your server. What should you do?

TOPIC 3B

Creating Databases

Now that we've looked at the factors you should consider before creating a database (such as capacity and file placement), let's move on to the nuts and bolts of creating a database. You can create a database by using the CREATE DATABASE Transact-SQL statement, the Create Database Wizard, or SQL Server Enterprise Manager. You can use SQL Server Enterprise Manager to both access the Create Database Wizard and to create a database by using dialog boxes. You start the Create Database Wizard in SQL Server Enterprise Manager by first selecting your server in the console tree, and then choosing Tools→Wizards. From the list of wizards, expand the Database category, select the Create Database Wizard, as shown in Figure 3-3, and then click OK. To use the dialog boxes in SQL Server Enterprise Manager to create a database, right-click on the Databases folder below your server. From the shortcut menu, choose New Database. For more information on creating databases by using SQL Server Enterprise Manager, please see the Element K course *Microsoft SQL Server 2000: System Administration*.

You must be logged on as a member of either the sysadmin or dbcreator server roles in order to create a database.

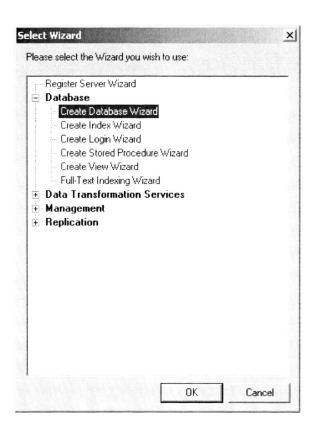

Figure 3-3: *Starting the Create Database Wizard.*

Creating a Database Using Transact-SQL

You can create a database and its transaction log by using the CREATE DATABASE Transact-SQL statement. You use this statement in either SQL Query Analyzer or the osql command-line utility. SQL Server keeps tracks of any new databases you create in the sysdatabases table and the space allocated to each database in the sysusages table. These tables are both stored in the master database; for this reason, you should always back up the master database after creating a new database.

When you create a database, you must specify information about the database such as its logical name, filegroup, primary data file name, size, maximum size, and the increments with which you want it to grow. Use the following syntax with the CREATE DATABASE statement:

The CREATE DATABASE command isn't case-sensitive; however, most documentation of SQL displays commands and parameters in uppercase letters and values in lower-case letters.

For readability, we've added spaces around the equal signs (=) in all SQL statement examples. When you write your statements, these spaces aren't necessary.

```
CREATE DATABASE logical_database_name
ON
        PRIMARY (NAME = logical_file_name,
        FILENAME = 'path\file_name',
        SIZE = size,
        MAXSIZE = maxsize,
        FILEGROWTH = filegrowth_increment)
LOG ON
        (NAME = logical_file_name,
        FILENAME = 'path\file_name',
        SIZE = size,
        MAXSIZE = maxsize,
        FILEGROWTH = filegrowth_increment)
```

In this example, we're creating a single data file within the default filegroup. (SQL Server calls the default filegroup "primary.") We're going to show you how to create secondary data files and user-defined filegroups in just a moment. In the following table, we describe the parameters you use in this CREATE DATABASE statement.

Assign the extension .mdf to primary database files, .ndf to secondary database files, and .ldf to transaction log files.

Parameter	Use to Specify
Database Name	The logical name of the database. You use this name to access the data in the database. For example, you use this name to query the database in SQL Query Analyzer.
Logical File Name	The logical name of the primary data file.
File Name	The name and path assigned to the operating system file in which SQL Server will store your database. This file is part of the primary filegroup. You must also specify a file name for the transaction log; this file is not part of the database filegroup.
Size	The initial size of the database file. You can specify the size in KB or MB. This file must be at least as big as the model database. By default, SQL Server configures the model database as 1.5 MB in size. The model database's primary data file is .75 MB, and its transaction log file is also .75 MB.
Maxsize	The maximum size to which you want SQL Server to be able to grow the file. You can specify maxsize in KB or MB. If you don't specify a maxsize, SQL Server configures the database file for unrestricted file growth (which means it can grow until your server's hard disk is completely full).
File Growth Increment	The increment with which you want SQL Server to grow the file. You can specify the increment in either MB, KB, or as a percentage. You can't specify a file growth increment that exceeds the value you specify for the file's maximum size. If you set the file growth increment to zero, SQL Server can't increase the database file's size. If you don't specify a file growth increment, SQL Server sets it to a default value of 10 percent and a minimum value of one extent (64 KB).

For example, to create a database named movies with a 15 MB primary data file in the primary filegroup, and a 3 MB transaction log file, here's the syntax:

```
CREATE DATABASE movies
ON
 PRIMARY (NAME = movies_data,
 FILENAME =
  'c:\Program Files\Microsoft SQL Server\mssql\Data\movies.mdf',
 SIZE = 15MB,
 MAXSIZE = 20MB,
 FILEGROWTH = 20%)
LOG ON
 (NAME = movies_log,
 FILENAME =
  'c:\Program Files\Microsoft SQL Server\mssql\Data\movies.ldf',
 SIZE = 3MB,
 MAXSIZE = 5MB,
 FILEGROWTH = 20%)
```

This example creates a database with a logical name of movies. The logical name of the database's data file is movies_data, and the physical name of the data file is movies.mdf. The database is 15 MB in size, can grow to 20 MB, and must grow in increments of 20 percent of the database size. This example also creates a transaction log file with a logical name of movies_log, and a physical file name of movies_log.ldf. The transaction log is 3 MB in size, can grow to 5 MB, and must also grow in increments of 20 percent of the transaction log size.

APPLY YOUR KNOWLEDGE 3-1

Suggested time:
10 minutes

Creating a Database

Objective: To create a database for use throughout this course.

Setup: If necessary, log on to your computer as Student# with a password of password.

1. Given the information in the following table, write the syntax you should use to create this database by using Transact-SQL. Notice that this database contains only one data file and it's stored in the primary filegroup.

Parameter	Value
Database name	movies
Primary data file's logical name	movies_data
Primary data file's path and file name	C:Program Files\Microsoft SQL Server\mssql\Data\movies_data.mdf
Database initial size	25 MB
Database maximum size	40 MB
Database file growth increment	1 MB
Transaction log logical name	movies_log
Transaction log path and file name	C:Program Files\Microsoft SQL Server\mssql\Data\movies_log.ldf
Transaction log initial size	6 MB
Transaction log maximum size	8 MB
Transaction log file growth increment	1 MB

2. If necessary, open SQL Query Analyzer and log in to your server with Windows Authentication. Write and parse the query you wrote in step 1.

3. When your syntax is correct, execute your query.

4. In SQL Query Analyzer, choose File→Save As. From the Save In drop-down list, verify that you've selected the My Documents folder. In the File Name text box, type movies; and then click Save to save the commands for creating the movies database as a SQL script.

5. Close the Query window.

6. Reconnect to your SQL server. (Choose File→Connect, and log on to your server using Windows Authentication.)

Creating Multiple Data Files and Filegroups

If you decide to create multiple data files for a database, you can create them all within the primary filegroup, or you can create one or more user-defined filegroups to contain the data files. In the following example, we show you how to create a secondary data file within the primary filegroup:

```
CREATE DATABASE logical_database_name
ON
        PRIMARY (NAME = logical_file_name,
        FILENAME = 'path\file_name.mdf',
        SIZE = size,
        MAXSIZE = maxsize,
        FILEGROWTH = filegrowth_increment)
        (NAME = logical_file_name,
        FILENAME = 'path\file_name.ndf',
        SIZE = size,
        MAXSIZE = maxsize,
        FILEGROWTH = filegrowth_increment)
LOG ON
        (NAME = logical_file_name,
        FILENAME = 'path\file_name',
        SIZE = size,
        MAXSIZE = maxsize,
        FILEGROWTH = filegrowth_increment)
```

Notice that you add a secondary data file name simply by adding a second file specification (the information that's contained within the parentheses). Make sure you name the secondary data file with the extension .ndf.

In this next example, we show you how to create a secondary data file in a user-defined filegroup:

```
CREATE DATABASE logical_database_name
ON
        PRIMARY (NAME = logical_file_name,
        FILENAME = 'path\file_name.mdf',
        SIZE = size,
        MAXSIZE = maxsize,
        FILEGROWTH = filegrowth_increment)
FILEGROUP filegroup_name
        (NAME = logical_file_name,
        FILENAME = 'path\file_name.ndf',
        SIZE = size,
        MAXSIZE = maxsize,
        FILEGROWTH = filegrowth_increment)
LOG ON
        (NAME = logical_file_name,
        FILENAME = 'path\file_name',
        SIZE = size,
        MAXSIZE = maxsize,
        FILEGROWTH = filegrowth_increment)
```

As you can see, you create a user-defined filegroup simply by adding the clause FILEGROUP filegroup_name, and then following it with a file specification for creating a file within that filegroup.

Adding Files and Filegroups to an Existing Database

Now that you've seen how to create a database with multiple data files and filegroups, let's take a look at how you add a data file or filegroup to an existing database. You add either a file or a filegroup by using the ALTER DATABASE statement. If you want to add a new file and place it in a new filegroup, you must add the filegroup first—and then add the new file to that filegroup. Here's the syntax for adding a new filegroup:

```
ALTER DATABASE logical_database_name
ADD FILEGROUP new_filegroup_name
```

You add a new file to a database by using the ALTER DATABASE statement as well. If you don't specify a TO FILEGROUP clause as part of the statement, SQL Server automatically creates the new file within the database's default filegroup. Here's the syntax for adding a file to a database:

```
ALTER DATABASE logical_database_name
ADD FILE
        (NAME = logical_file_name,
        FILENAME = 'path\file_name.ndf',
        SIZE = size,
        MAXSIZE = maxsize,
        FILEGROWTH = filegrowth_increment)
TO FILEGROUP filegroup_name
```

Configuring the Default Filegroup

By default, SQL Server configures the primary filegroup as your database's default filegroup. Unless you specify otherwise, SQL Server stores any new database objects you create in the default filegroup. Because your database's system tables (such as those that keep track of the database's users and permissions) are stored in the primary filegroup, you want to make sure that this filegroup doesn't run out of space. For this reason, you might want to configure a user-defined filegroup as the default instead of the primary filegroup. You can do so by modifying the filegroup's properties using the ALTER DATABASE statement or SQL Server Enterprise Manager. Here's the syntax for using the ALTER DATABASE statement to change the default filegroup:

```
ALTER DATABASE database_name
MODIFY FILEGROUP filegroup_name DEFAULT
```

Viewing Information about Files and Filegroups

SQL Server includes two system stored procedures that you can use in SQL Query Analyzer to view information about files and filegroups. Use the following stored procedure to identify the physical names and attributes of the current database's data files: sp_helpfile. You can optionally specify a file name to view information about that specific file.

You can view information about the current database's filegroups by using the following stored procedure: sp_helpfilegroup. You can optionally specify a filegroup name so that you can view information about only that filegroup.

APPLY YOUR KNOWLEDGE 3-2

Suggested time:
15 minutes

Adding a Filegroup and Data File to a Database

Objective: To add a second filegroup and a data file within it to the movies database. You're also going to set this new filegroup as the default filegroup for the movies database.

1. In SQL Query Analyzer, design and execute a query to add a filegroup named Data to the movies database. Write the query you used in the following space.

2. Design and execute a query to add a data file with a logical name of movies_data2 and a physical file name of movies_data2.ndf. Create this file with an initial size of 10 MB, and don't specify a maximum size (so that the file growth is unlimited). Add this file to the Data filegroup. Write the query you used in the following space.

3. Use `sp_helpfile` and `sp_helpfilegroup` to view information about the files and filegroups for the movies database. (Hint: Make sure you use the movies database first.)

4. Clear the Query window.

Configuring Database Options

If you want to set certain options for all new databases you create, set them on the model database. SQL Server then sets these options for any new databases you create.

Now that you've created a database, you can configure its options. (Actually, you can also set these options when you use the CREATE DATABASE statement to create a database.) For example, you can configure a database as read-only if you don't want users to be able to make changes to its data. You can configure an existing database's options by using either SQL Server Enterprise Manager or the ALTER DATABASE statement. You can display and modify a database's options in SQL Server Enterprise Manager by right-clicking on the database and choosing Properties from the shortcut menu. Use the following syntax to configure database options by using Transact-SQL:

```
ALTER DATABASE database_name
SET option[, status]
```

You'll find that some of the database options can be enabled simply by specifying the keyword. Others require that you specify a status value (such as ON or OFF). For example, here's the syntax to configure the movies database as read-only:

```
ALTER DATABASE movies
SET READ_ONLY
```

Microsoft divides the database options you can configure into categories. Within each category, you'll find several different options you can set. The following table describes each of the option categories and some of the common options you might configure. (For each option, we provide you with the SQL keyword you should use in the SET clause when configuring the option.)

Category	Option	Enables You to Configure
Auto	AUTO_SHRINK	Whether SQL Server can automatically decrease the size of the database. This option is disabled by default. You must specify ON or OFF for this option.

Category	Option	Enables You to Configure
Cursor	CURSOR_CLOSE_ON_COMMIT	SQL Server to automatically close open cursors whenever it commits their transactions. This option is disabled by default. Specify either ON or OFF for this option.
Recovery	RECOVERY FULL | BULK_LOGGED | SIMPLE	How much data SQL Server keeps in the database's transaction log. The more information SQL Server maintains in the transaction log, the greater the recoverability of your data. If you use the Full Recovery Model, SQL Server logs all transactions in your database's transaction log. With the Bulk-Logged Recovery Model, SQL Server logs all transactions in the transaction log except for bulk operations. Finally, with the Simple Recovery Model, SQL Server clears all transactions from the log as soon as it commits them. By default, SQL Server configures all databases to use the Full Recovery Model.
SQL	ANSI_NULL_DEFAULT	Support for null columns in a database. Null means that no data has been stored in the column. By configuring a column to permit nulls, you permit users to not enter data in that column. By default, SQL Server disables this option, which means that all database columns are set to not permit nulls unless you specify otherwise.
State	SINGLE_USER | RESTRICTED_USER | MULTI_USER	The database so that it can be used by only a single user, or by only certain users (those users who are members of the db_owner, dbcreator, or sysadmin roles), or by all users. By default, SQL Server configures a database as multi-user.
	READ_ONLY | READ_WRITE	The database as read-only or read-write. Use the READ_ONLY option to enable users to view data but not make any changes to the data. By default, SQL Server configures new databases as READ_WRITE.

Viewing Database Option Settings

You can use the DATABASEPROPERTYEX ( ) function to determine the status of a database's options. Here's the syntax:

```
SELECT DATABASEPROPERTYEX('database_name', 'property')
```

Replace database_name with the database for which you want to view an option's status. Replace property with any of the following properties:

- IsAutoShrink
- IsCloseCursorsOnCommitEnabled
- Recovery

- IsAnsiNullDefault
- Updateability (to determine if a database is read-only or read-write)
- UserAccess

TASK 3B-1:

Setting Database Options

1. In SQL Query Analyzer, **verify that you're using the movies database.**

2. **Execute the following query:**

```
SELECT DATABASEPROPERTYEX('movies', 'UserAccess')
```

You can use this query to determine if the database is configured as single-user, restricted user, or multi-user.

3. **Look at the Results pane.** You should see that the movies database is configured for multi-user access (the default setting).

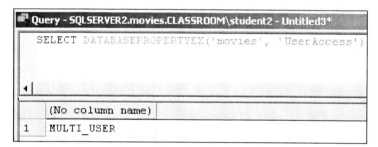

4. Let's set the movies database for single-user access. **Execute this new query:**

```
ALTER DATABASE movies
SET SINGLE_USER
```

You should see a message stating that the command completed successfully.

5. **Execute a new query to verify that the movies database is single-user:**

```
SELECT DATABASEPROPERTYEX('movies', 'UserAccess')
```

6. **Click the New Query button on the toolbar** to attempt to open a Query window with a second connection to the movies database.

7. **Look at the SQL Query Analyzer message box.** After a few moments, you should see a message stating that the movies database is open and configured to support only one user at a time. You can't connect to the movies database because you have an existing connection to the database and have configured it as single-user.

8. **Click OK** to close the message box.

9. **Close the new Query window.**

10. **Write and execute a new query to reconfigure the movies database for multi-user access. Record the query you used in the space below.**

11. **Write and execute a query to configure the movies database to use the Simple Recovery Model. Record the query you used in the space below.**

Displaying Information About Databases and Transaction Logs

SQL Server 2000 includes several stored procedures that you can use to view information about your databases. We describe these stored procedures in the following table.

Stored Procedure	Enables You to View
sp_helpdb	The name, size, owner, database ID, creation data, and database options. If you run the sp_helpdb stored procedure against the master database, you can view information about all databases on your server. If you want to view information about only one database, you can run the sp_helpdb procedure with a specific database's name by typing sp_helpdb *database_name*.
sp_spaceused	A summary of the storage space used by a database and its transaction log and objects. You can use sp_spaceused by itself or followed by the name of a database, transaction log, or object.

TASK 3B-2:

Using Stored Procedures to View Database Information

1. In SQL Query Analyzer, **verify that you're using the movies database.**

2. In the Query window, **execute the following query:**

   sp_helpdb

   This query enables you to view information about all databases on your server.

3. Look at the Results pane. You should see a list of your server's databases (in alphabetical order). Notice that the new database you created displays your Windows 2000 account information as the owner, whereas the databases created during the installation of SQL Server display the sa login ID as the owner. You can also see the options configured for each database by looking at the Status column.

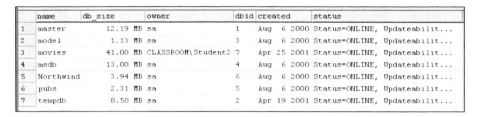

	name	db_size	owner	dbid	created	status
1	master	12.19 MB	sa	1	Aug 6 2000	Status=ONLINE, Updateabilit...
2	model	1.13 MB	sa	3	Aug 6 2000	Status=ONLINE, Updateabilit...
3	movies	41.00 MB	CLASSROOM\Student2	7	Apr 25 2001	Status=ONLINE, Updateabilit...
4	msdb	13.00 MB	sa	4	Aug 6 2000	Status=ONLINE, Updateabilit...
5	Northwind	3.94 MB	sa	6	Aug 6 2000	Status=ONLINE, Updateabilit...
6	pubs	2.31 MB	sa	5	Aug 6 2000	Status=ONLINE, Updateabilit...
7	tempdb	8.50 MB	sa	2	Apr 19 2001	Status=ONLINE, Updateabilit...

4. Clear the Query window.

5. In the following space, write a query for displaying information about only the movies database.

6. In SQL Query Analyzer, **execute the query you recorded in step 5.** This query enables you to view the name of the database and its size, along with the names and sizes of each of the files that make up the database.

7. In the Query pane, **execute a new query:**

```
sp_spaceused
```

The `sp_spaceused` procedure enables you to view the size of the movies database. You can also view the amount of space within the movies database that's reserved for data and indexes. Because you've just created the movies database, it contains only the system tables and indexes automatically copied by SQL Server into the movies database from the model database.

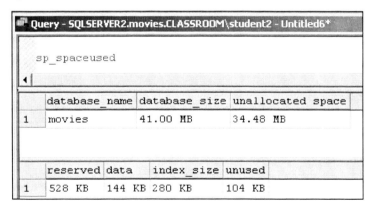

Query - SQLSERVER2.movies.CLASSROOM\student2 - Untitled6*

```
sp_spaceused
```

	database_name	database_size	unallocated space
1	movies	41.00 MB	34.48 MB

	reserved	data	index_size	unused
1	528 KB	144 KB	280 KB	104 KB

8. Clear the Query window.

TOPIC 3C

Managing Databases

As you implement databases on your SQL server, you might find that the size needs for those databases change. Management tasks include:

- Increasing (expanding) or decreasing (shrinking) the size of a database.
- Increasing the size of a transaction log.
- Dropping (deleting) a database.

Changing the Size of a Database

You can either increase (expand) or decrease (shrink) the size of a database. In order to do so, you must be the owner of the database or a member of the sysadmin server role to modify its size. In addition, you must be using the master database to change the size of any other database. When you change the size of a database or transaction log, you should always back up the master database both before and after the change. This way, if any problems occur due to the change in size, you can restore the master database to recover from the failure.

You can increase the size of a database by using any of the following techniques:

- Automatically, by setting the automatic growth option on the database, its transaction log, or both.
- Manually, by increasing the size of the database, its transaction log, or both.
- Manually, by configuring secondary database files, log files, or both.

Automatically Expanding a Database and its Transaction Log

You can configure SQL Server to automatically expand your database and transaction log files as needed by using either the ALTER DATABASE statement or SQL Server Enterprise Manager. As you know, you can configure the database and its transaction log with an initial size, a maximum size, and a growth increment.

Use the following syntax to expand your files by using the ALTER DATABASE statement:

```
ALTER DATABASE database_name
     MODIFY FILE
     (NAME = 'logical_name',
     SIZE = size,
     MAXSIZE = maxsize,
     FILEGROWTH = filegrowth_increment)
```

You can configure a database file to support unrestricted file growth by using the clause MAXSIZE = UNLIMITED, or by not specifying a maximum size. (If you don't specify a maximum size, SQL Server automatically configures the database file for unrestricted file growth.) Be aware that if you configure a file to support unrestricted file growth, it can continue to grow until your server runs out of disk space. As an alternative, you might want to set a maximum size that's less than your server's available disk space and configure a file growth increment; that way, SQL Server can expand the database without the risk of your server running out of disk space.

If you want to configure SQL Server to automatically expand a transaction log by using the ALTER DATABASE statement, replace *logical_name* in the above syntax with the name of the database's transaction log.

Manually Expanding a Database and its Transaction Log

If you configure SQL Server not to automatically grow a database or its transaction log, you can manually expand them by using either SQL Server Enterprise Manager or the ALTER DATABASE statement. To manually expand a database or its transaction log in SQL Server Enterprise Manager, perform the following steps:

1. In SQL Server Enterprise Manager, below your server's Databases folder, right-click on the database you want to expand. From the shortcut menu, choose Properties.

2. Use the Data Files page to expand the database by increasing each data file's size in the Space Allocated (MB) text box. Use the Transaction Log page to expand the transaction log. Expand the transaction log by increasing its size in the Space Allocated (MB) text box.

You can manually increase the size of the database or its transaction log by using the following ALTER DATABASE statement:

```
ALTER DATABASE database_name
MODIFY FILE
      (NAME = 'logical_name',
      SIZE = size )
```

If you think about it, another technique you can use to expand a database is to add secondary data files. Remember, you can create these database files in the primary filegroup or in a user-defined filegroup. As we've said, you use secondary database files as a strategy to distribute a database across multiple hard drives to enhance performance. Create secondary database files by using either SQL Server Enterprise Manager or the ALTER DATABASE statement. To create secondary database files by using the ALTER DATABASE statement, use the following syntax:

```
ALTER DATABASE database_name
ADD FILE
      (NAME = 'logical_name',
      FILE NAME = 'path\filename',
      SIZE = size,
      MAXSIZE = maxsize,
      FILEGROWTH = filegrowth_increment)
```

Because we covered creating secondary data files and filegroups in the previous topic, we aren't going to cover them here. But keep in mind that you use secondary data files and filegroups as a technique for manually expanding a database.

Suggested time:
10 minutes

APPLY YOUR KNOWLEDGE 3-3

Maintaining the Size of Databases and Transaction Logs

Objective: To use the ALTER DATABASE statement to change the size of the movies database and its transaction log.

1. In SQL Query Analyzer, execute the query sp_helpdb movies to view the total size of the movies database, along with the size of each of its files.

2. You want to increase the size of the movies database by increasing the size of the movies_data2 secondary data file from 10 MB to 15 MB. What SQL statement should you use?

3. Execute this query in SQL Query Analyzer.

4. Verify that you've increased the size of the movies_data2 file by executing the query `sp_helpdb movies`.

5. You want to increase the maximum size of the movies database's transaction log from 8 MB to 10 MB. What SQL statement should you use?

6. Execute this query in SQL Query Analyzer.

7. Verify your changes by using `sp_helpdb`.

8. Clear the Query window.

Monitoring the Size of a Transaction Log

You should keep a close eye on the amount of space used in your database's transaction logs in order to make sure they don't run out of space. (Of course, this is only an issue if you haven't configured the transaction log to support unrestricted file growth.) If a transaction log runs out of space, your users won't be able to make any changes to the associated database. If you need to increase the size of a transaction log, use SQL Server Enterprise Manager or the ALTER DATABASE Transact-SQL statement.

You can monitor the amount of space used in a transaction log by using SQL Server Enterprise Manager, Windows 2000 System Monitor, or the DBCC SQLPERF(LOGSPACE) statement. This statement enables you to view a list of databases, the total log size in MB, and the percent of space used within each log file. In System Monitor, you can monitor each database's transaction log by using the SQL Server: Databases object and then choosing the appropriate database instance. The following table describes some of the counters associated with the SQL Server: Databases object and how you can use them to monitor transaction logs.

Counter	Enables You to Monitor
Log File(s) Size (KB)	The size of the transaction log. You might want to monitor this counter if you've configured SQL Server to automatically increase the size of your transaction log.
Percent Log Used	The percentage of the transaction log space that's currently in use.

You can monitor these counters in System Monitor's Chart view, or you can create an alert in the Alert view. For example, you can configure System Monitor to generate an alert if the Percent Log Used counter exceeds 75 percent.

Certain situations can generate extra transactions that can cause your transaction logs to fill up sooner than normal. For example, if you're importing data into a table with indexes, SQL Server logs all inserts and index changes in the transaction log. If you're going to import a large amount of data, you might consider deleting the table's indexes, importing the table, and then rebuilding the indexes in order to avoid filling up the transaction log. Another situation that can cause your transaction logs to fill up is adding or modifying text or image data by using the WRITETEXT or UPDATETEXT statement with the WITH LOG option. SQL Server doesn't typically log images in order to reduce the amount of space used in the transaction log.

APPLY YOUR KNOWLEDGE 3-4

Using System Monitor to Monitor Transaction Logs

Suggested time:
15 minutes

Objective: To use System Monitor to monitor the movies database's transaction log.

You access System Monitor by choosing Performance from the Administrative Tools program group.

1. In System Monitor, create a chart to monitor the transaction log for the movies database. Monitor both the size of the transaction log (by using the Log File Size counter) and the percentage of the log file in use (by using the Percent Log Used counter). You can select multiple counters by holding down the [Ctrl] key.

2. What percentage of the movies database's log file is currently in use?

3. In System Monitor, create an alert to notify you when the transaction log for the movies database is more than 75 percent full.

4. Close System Monitor.

Shrinking Databases or Files

Remember, you configure a database's options by displaying its properties within SQL Server Enterprise Manager or by using the ALTER DATABASE statement.

If you find that you've allocated too much space to a database, you can shrink the entire database or one of its files. Shrinking a database updates its information in the master database. For this reason, make sure that you back up the master database before and after you shrink a database. You can configure SQL Server to automatically shrink a database, or you can manually shrink the database by using the DBCC SHRINKDATABASE statement. You configure SQL Server to automatically shrink a database by checking the Auto-shrink database option. You can shrink an individual database file by using the DBCC SHRINKFILE statement.

If you manually shrink a database or one of its files, make sure that you don't attempt to make it smaller than the size of the model database or the amount of data currently stored in the database or file. When you use the DBCC SHRINKDATABASE statement, SQL Server shrinks the database as a deferred job that runs in the background on your server. Because shrinking the database runs as a deferred job, you might not see changes to your database immediately. Use the following syntax to shrink an entire database:

```
DBCC SHRINKDATABASE (database_name, target_percent
[, NOTRUNCATE|TRUNCATEONLY])
```

Replace *database_name* with the logical name you assigned to the database. Replace *target_percent* with the amount of free space you would like to have in the database after SQL Server shrinks it. You can optionally add the parameters NOTRUNCATE or TRUNCATEONLY. Using the NOTRUNCATE option configures SQL Server to keep the freed file space in the database rather than returning the space to the operating system. Using TRUNCATEONLY configures SQL Server to return any freed space to the operating system, shrinks the database file to the last allocated extent, and reduces the file size without moving any data. SQL Server doesn't attempt to move data to any unallocated pages. DBCC SHRINKDATABASE ignores the *target_percent* parameter when you use the TRUNCATEONLY option.

You can shrink one of the database's files by using the DBCC SHRINKFILE statement. Use the following syntax to shrink a database file:

```
DBCC SHRINKFILE (file_name, target_size
[,EMPTYFILE|NOTRUNCATE|TRUNCATEONLY])
```

Replace *file_name* with the name of the database or transaction log file you want to shrink. You can use the EMPTYFILE option to configure SQL Server to move all data from the file to other files within its filegroup so that you can then delete the file altogether. You then delete the file by using the ALTER DATABASE statement. The NOTRUNCATE and TRUNCATEONLY options work the same in DBCC SHRINKFILE as they do with DBCC SHRINKDATABASE.

TASK 3C-1:

Configuring SQL Server to Automatically Shrink a Database File

1. In SQL Query Analyzer, **execute the following query:**

    ```
    ALTER DATABASE movies
    SET AUTO_SHRINK ON
    ```

    Enabling this option makes it possible for SQL Server to automatically shrink the database as needed.

2. **Clear the Query window.**

Deleting a Database

If you find that you no longer need a database, you can delete it to reclaim disk space on your server. SQL Server also refers to deleting a database as dropping the database. When you delete a database, SQL Server removes its information from the sysdatabases table in the master database. Because of this change, make sure you back up the master database both before and after you delete a database. SQL Server automatically deletes all of the database's files when you delete the database. You can optionally delete the backup and restore history for the database as well. You must be logged in to the SQL server as the sa user or a member of the sysadmin or db_owner roles to delete a database.

You can't delete a database if it is in the process of being restored, is open by any user, or is publishing any of its tables in replication. You also shouldn't delete any of the system databases (although you can delete the msdb database).

You delete a database by using either SQL Server Enterprise Manager or the DROP DATABASE command. To use the DROP DATABASE command to delete a database, execute the following statement: DROP DATABASE database_name.

Replace *database_name* with the name of the database you want to delete. You can delete multiple databases by listing the name of each database, separating the name of each database with a comma.

TASK 3C-2:

Deleting a Database

1. In SQL Query Analyzer, **verify that the master database is your current database.**

2. **Execute the following query:**

    ```
    DROP DATABASE movies
    ```

3. **Execute a new query:**

    ```
    sp_helpdb
    ```

    This stored procedure enables you to view a list of the databases defined on your server. You should see that you no longer have a movies database.

4. **Clear the Query window.**

APPLY YOUR KNOWLEDGE 3-5

Suggested time:
15 minutes

Using a Script File to Create a Database

Objective: To use the movies.sql script file you created earlier in the lesson to re-create the movies database on your server.

1. In SQL Query Analyzer, open the movies.sql script file.

2. Modify the script file to include the following changes:
   - Increase the maximum file size to the transaction log to 10 MB.
   - Add the commands to create the movies_data2 secondary data file. Configure this file with an initial size of 15 MB and support for unrestricted file growth. Create this file within a filegroup named Data.

   Record the changes you made to the script in the following space.

3. Save your changes to the movies.sql script file.

4. Execute the script.

5. Use `sp_helpdb` to verify that you see the movies database again.

6. Close all open windows.

Summary

In this lesson, you learned just about everything you need to know about creating databases. We began by defining the planning you should do when designing a database. We also talked about how you can optimize a database's design by using multiple files or filegroups, or by implementing RAID. Next, you learned how to create a database by using the CREATE DATABASE Transact-SQL statement. Finally, you learned how to manage databases by setting options with the ALTER DATABASE statement, and how to expand, shrink, and delete a database.

LESSON 3 REVIEW

3A What formula can you use to estimate how big you should make a database's transaction log?

3B You would like to make sure that your database's transaction log doesn't use all of the available disk space on your server. How can you prevent this from happening?

3C What are some of the management tasks you might perform on databases?

Creating and Managing Tables

Overview

As database systems go, tables are pretty much the heart and soul of the database. In this lesson, we will examine the system data types you can use to define the columns in a table. We'll show you how to create and use user-defined data types to standardize the structure of tables within a database. We'll also discuss how to create and maintain a table by using Transact-SQL.

Data Files:

data_types.sql
movie_tables.sql
modify_table.sql

Lesson Time:
3 hours

Objectives

To create and manage tables, you will:

4A   **Identify the data types you can use to define the columns in a table.**

In this topic, you will learn how you go about designing tables by reviewing the principles of data modeling. Next, you'll learn the different data types you can use when defining a table's columns. Finally, you'll learn how to create both user-defined data types and tables themselves by using Transact-SQL.

4B   **Maintain tables.**

After you've created your tables, odds are that you'll need to make changes to their structure. In this topic, we will show you how to add, modify, and drop columns from a table. We will also walk you through creating a script file that you can use to re-create a database's tables and objects.

TOPIC 4A

Design and Create Tables

Because your primary goal when you implement a database management system is to give users access to information, the tables and the data within them are the heart of SQL Server. When you create a table, you must define the types of information (columns) you want to store in each row in the table. For example, if you are creating a table to store customer information, you might create columns to store the customer's first name, last name, phone number, and address information.

Designing a Table

normalization:
The process of organizing the information in tables within a relational database in order to minimize the duplication of data across those tables.

You should always plan the design of tables for a database before you actually create them. You can begin the design by examining the data you want to store in each table. Because SQL Server is a relational database, meaning you can link tables together, you should try to *normalize* your tables. When you normalize tables, you prevent duplications of data both within each table and across multiple tables. For example, assume that you are responsible for designing the tables for a point-of-sale system for a movie rental store, and you would like to have tables that contain the following information:

- Customer names and addresses

- Videotape inventory

- Invoices for each customer's movie rentals

You would like the customer table to contain the customer's name, telephone number, and address. For the movie table, you would like to track each tape's unique ID number and title. You would like the invoice table to identify the customer and the movies rented. When you design the invoice table, you should try to minimize the duplication of information contained in other tables. So, you might design the invoice table to contain only the customer's phone number and the tape numbers of the movies rented. By using the customer's telephone number, you can link the invoice table to the customer table, and then query the customer table for the customer's name and address. Likewise, by using the tape numbers for the movies rented, you can query the movie table for the titles.

When you design normalized tables, you prevent the duplication of data across multiple tables. But, if you want to be able to link multiple tables together, as in the movie rental store example, the tables must have at least one column in common. For example, by creating a phone number column in both the customer and invoice tables, you link the information in both tables together by that column.

There are three normal forms, each one having a greater degree of normalization. In First Normal Form (1NF), you must configure the columns in a table so that each contains different information. For example, if you want to store each customer's birthdate in the customer table, you must design the table so that only one column contains the customer's birthdate in order for the table to conform to 1NF. In Second Normal Form (2NF), you can't configure a table where one of its columns is derived from another column. Continuing with our example, if you configure the customer table with a birthdate column, you can't configure a second column to contain the customer's birth year in order to conform to 2NF. Finally, in Third Normal Form (3NF), you can't configure tables with any duplicate information. For example, let's say that your database contains the customer and employees tables. If you want to store birthdate information for both tables, in 3NF, you must put the birthdate information in its own separate table—and then link the customer and employee tables to this table. While we could go on in much greater detail about normalizing tables, here's the most important thing you should understand: When you normalize tables, you prevent the duplication of data across those tables. Preventing duplication reduces the disk space requirements for your data and helps to eliminate data entry errors.

Consider the Output

Another factor you should consider when designing a table is how you might want the data from a table to be displayed. For example, if you create a customer table that contains a single column for storing the customer's name, you might not be able to display a list of customers in alphabetical order by their last names. If users enter the customers' names as *first_name last_name*, you will be able to display the customers only in alphabetical order by their first names. You could also have problems with inconsistent data entry—some users might enter customers' names as *last_name, first_name*, while other users might enter the names as *last_name first_name* (with no comma). In this scenario, you should create separate columns for each portion of the customer's name, including first name, middle name or initial, last name, and possibly a suffix (for storing "Jr." or "III").

TASK 4A-1:

Normalizing Table Designs

1. Given the structure of the following tables, what changes should you make to normalize their design?

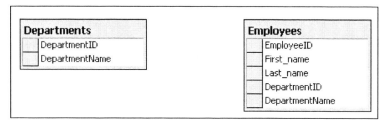

2. As a consultant, you've been asked to analyze the design of a database for a local junior college. One of the complaints the college administration has is that they have students that take more than five classes, but the design of the Students table enables them to enroll students in only five classes. You can see the structure of two of the database's tables in the following graphic. How should you normalize the design of these two tables? Do you need any additional tables to improve the design of this database?

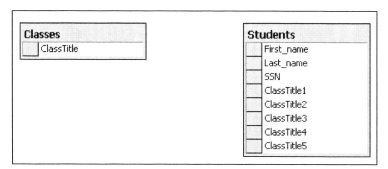

Defining Columns for a Table

Now that we've looked at what you should consider when designing a table, let's move on to the nuts and bolts of defining a table's columns. When you create the columns for a table, you must give each column a name and identify the type and length of data you want to store. You can create a maximum of 1,024 columns within a table; the maximum size of each row can't exceed 8,060 bytes.

The names you assign to columns can be up to 31 characters long. You should try to keep your column names as short as possible while still making the names meaningful. For example, if you're creating a column to store each customer's last name in the customer table, you might want to name the column last_name or lname. Because you can build views with columns from different tables, you might also want to put a portion of the table name in the column name. For example, you might want to name the last name column for the customer table cust_lname so that you can easily identify that the column is from the customer table and contains last name information.

You use data types to identify what type of data (values) users can enter into the column. For example, you can use the integer data type to specify that users can enter only numbers into a column. In contrast, if you use the character data type, users can enter both numbers and letters, along with other characters, into the column. So, if you want users to enter only numbers into a column, you should use the integer (or one of the other numeric) data types.

SQL Server supports two categories of data types: system and user-defined. The system data types are included with SQL Server. You create user-defined data types based on the system data types. You use user-defined data types to make it easier for you to standardize column definitions across multiple tables. For example, if you plan to create a column to store telephone numbers in multiple tables, you might create a user-defined data type and then use this data type within your column definitions for the tables. SQL Server separates the system data types into the following categories: binary, character, date and time, numeric, integer, monetary, and special.

When you define a column, you can specify whether the column will accept null values or not. If you configure a column to accept null values, SQL Server permits users to leave that column blank during data entry. If you configure the column to not accept null values, SQL Server requires users to enter information into the column during data entry. When you create a table by using the CREATE TABLE Transact-SQL statement, SQL Server configures the columns to not permit nulls by default unless you specify otherwise. In contrast, when you create a table in SQL Server Enterprise Manager, SQL Server configures columns to accept null entries by default.

Each of the data types has a keyword associated with it that you use as part of the CREATE TABLE statement. As you learn about each of the data types, you'll see that you can use either a SQL Server keyword or an ANSI keyword to configure a column to use a data type. The ANSI keyword conforms to the SQL-92 standard for defining a column's data type.

You can exceed the maximum row size of 8,060 bytes if you specify a column's data type as text or image. You can configure text or image columns with a maximum size of 2 GB.

Binary Data Types

SQL Server supports binary and varbinary data types. Use the binary data types if you plan to store hexadecimal information in a column. Choose binary if the data you plan to store is a fixed length; use varbinary for variable length binary data. You can configure binary and varbinary columns with a width of up to 8,000 bytes. Use the following syntax to specify the binary data types as part of the CREATE TABLE statement (where *n* represents the width of the column).

Data Type	SQL Keyword	ANSI SQL-92 Keyword
Binary	binary (n)	binary (n)
Varbinary	varbinary (n)	binary varying (n)

Character Data Types

The actual amount of space SQL Server uses to store a binary or varbinary column is the width you specify plus four bytes. For example, if you configure a column as binary (5), the total space used to store this column is nine bytes.

The character data types enable you to configure columns to support letters, numbers, and special characters such as the question mark (?). You can define two types of character data types in SQL Server: character (char) and variable length character (varchar). You can configure the two data types with a maximum width of 8,000 characters. When you use the character data type for a column, each character or space in that column uses one byte of storage space. For example, if you configure a column to use the character data type with a width of 10 characters, regardless of whether you enter data into that column or not, SQL Server uses 10 bytes per row to store that column. For this reason, you should use the character data type when you expect the data entered into a column for each row to be consistent, so that the server doesn't have to constantly recalculate the width of the column.

In contrast to the character data type, a column that uses the variable length character data type uses disk space based on the data in the column. For example, if you don't enter data into a column that's configured to use the varchar data type with a size of 10 characters, SQL Server doesn't use any disk space to store that column. When you configure a column to use the varchar data type with a size of 10 characters, SQL Server can't store more than 10 characters in that column. So, if you enter more than 10 characters into the column, SQL Server automatically truncates the data after the 10th character.

Use the following syntax to specify the character data types as part of the CREATE TABLE statement (where *n* represents the width of the column).

Data Type	SQL Keyword	ANSI SQL-92 Keyword
Character	char (n)	character (n)
Varchar	varchar (n)	character varying (n), char varying (n)

Unicode Character Data Types

SQL Server 2000 also enables you to define a column's data type as Unicode. You should use the Unicode character data types if you plan to store characters in a column that are from multiple character sets. The Unicode character data types include nchar (fixed length) and nvarchar (variable length). You can configure each data type to store up to 4,000 characters (4,000 characters is 8,000 bytes in length).

Use the following syntax to specify the Unicode character data types as part of the CREATE TABLE statement (where *n* represents the width of the column).

Data Type	SQL Keyword	ANSI SQL-92 Keyword
Unicode character	nchar (n)	national char (n), national character (n)
Unicode varchar	nvarchar (n)	national character varying (n), national char varying (n)

Date and Time Data Types

SQL Server enables you to configure columns to support date information. You should always use the date data types for columns if you want the ability to perform date calculations. For example, if you're creating a table to store employee information and you would like to be able to calculate how long an employee has worked for your company, you must create a column with a date data type to store the employee's hire date.

SQL Server supports two date data types: datetime and smalldatetime. The following table describes the differences between these data types.

Data Type	Size (in bytes)	Supported Values
datetime	8 (4 bytes each for date and time)	Date: 1/1/1753 AD to 12/31/9999 AD; Time: in milliseconds past midnight
smalldatetime	4 (2 bytes each for date and time)	Date: 1/1/1900 AD to 6/6/2079; AD Time: number of minutes past midnight

You can enter the date for datetime or smalldatetime columns by using either words (such as January 1, 2002) or numbers (such as 1/1/2002 or 1-1-2002). If you don't specify the first two digits of the year, SQL Server automatically assumes the first two digits are 20 if the last two digits are 49 or less and 19 if the last two digits are 50 or greater. For example, if you enter a date as 1/1/02, SQL Server automatically converts the date to 1/1/2002.

If you enter a date but not a time, in datetime or smalldatetime columns, SQL Server uses the default time of 12:00 A.M. If you enter a time but not a date, SQL Server uses the default date of January 1, 1900. If you don't enter either a date or a time, SQL Server uses the default value of January 1, 1900 12:00 A.M.

You can configure SQL Server to display the values in the datetime or smalldatetime columns in several different formats. For example, you can display dates in both alphabetic and numeric formats. You can display times in several different formats, including hours:minutes and hours:minutes:seconds:thousandths of seconds.

Use the following syntax to specify the date and time data types as part of the CREATE TABLE statement.

Data Type	SQL Keyword
Datetime	datetime
Smalldatetime	smalldatetime

There are no ANSI keywords equivalent to the datetime and smalldatetime data types. You don't have to specify a width for the column as both datetime and smalldatetime have pre-defined widths of 8 bytes and 4 bytes respectively.

Exact Numeric Data Types

Numeric data types enable you to store numbers with decimal places in columns. SQL Server supports two types of numeric data types: exact and approximate. The exact numeric data types enable you to store fixed-point numbers in a column. A fixed-point number is one in which you define the number of digits both before and after the decimal point. In contrast, the approximate numeric data types enable you to store floating-point numbers in a column. A floating-point number is one in which you don't define the number of digits before and after the decimal point; instead, you specify the number of digits of precision for the column. If you attempt to store a number that exceeds the number of digits of precision, SQL Server automatically rounds the number up. While you will find that floating-point numbers aren't as accurate as fixed-point numbers, columns that use floating-point data types can support a larger range of numbers than columns using fixed-point data types.

SQL Server includes two exact (fixed-point) numeric data types: decimal and numeric. Although the data types have different names, decimal and numeric are functionally equivalent and you can use them interchangeably. When you choose the decimal (or numeric) data type, you must specify the precision and scale for the column. The value you enter for precision identifies the maximum number of digits, including the digits both before and after the decimal place, you can enter into the column. The value you enter for the scale identifies the maximum number of digits you can enter into the column after the decimal place. For example, if you choose the numeric data type with a precision of 8 and a scale of 2 for a column, the largest number you can enter into the column is 999,999.99. If you don't enter values for the precision and scale when you choose the numeric data type for a column, SQL Server automatically configures the column with a precision of 18 and a scale of 0.

The number of bytes required to store a column that's using the numeric (or decimal) data type varies depending on the number of digits of precision you specify. The following table describes the space used by the numeric data type for varying digits of precision.

Digits of Precision	Size (in Bytes)
1 - 9	5
10 - 19	9
20 - 28	13
29 - 38	17

Use the following syntax to specify the exact numeric data types as part of the CREATE TABLE statement (where *p* represents the digits of precision and *s* represents the scale).

Data Type	SQL Keyword	ANSI SQL-92 Keyword
Exact numeric	decimal (p, s)	dec; dec (p, s)
	numeric (p, s)	none

Approximate Numeric Data Types

SQL Server includes two approximate (floating-point) data types: real and float. The real data type enables you to store numbers in a column with up to 24 digits of precision. The float data type enables you to store numbers in a column with a maximum of 53 digits of precision. The following table describes the two approximate data types.

Because the approximate data types aren't precise, you shouldn't use a column with the approximate data type as a table's primary key.

Data Type	Digits of Precision	Size (in Bytes)	Supported Values
real	1 to 24	4	-3.40E+38 to 3.40E+38
float	25 to 53	8	-1.79E+308 to 1.79E+308

Use the following syntax to specify the approximate numeric data types as part of the CREATE TABLE statement (where *n* represents the digits of precision).

Data Type	SQL Keyword	ANSI SQL-92 Keyword
Approximate numeric	real (n)	float (24)
	float (n)	float (n)
	float (53)	double precision

Integer Data Types

In contrast to the numeric data types, SQL Server uses the integer data types to store whole numbers. Because columns with these data types can contain only numbers, you can perform arithmetic operations on the values in the columns. SQL Server includes four integer data types that differ in the size of the numbers they can store and the amount of disk space they require to store those numbers. The following table explains the four supported integer data types.

Data Type	Size (in Bytes)	Supported Values
bigint or big integer	8	-2^{63} to 2^{63}-1 or -9,223,372,036,854,775,808 to 9,223,372,036,854,775,807
int or integer	4	-2^{31} to 2^{31}-1 or -2,147,483,648 to 2,147,483,647
smallint	2	-2^{15} to 2^{15}-1 or -32,768 to 32,767
tinyint	1	0 to 255

To minimize the amount of space used by a column, you should choose the smallest data type that fits your needs. If you need to store whole numbers in a column, you can choose between these four data types based on the possible range of values for that column. For example, if the largest number you'll store in the column is 22,000, you should use the smallint data type.

Use the following syntax to specify the integer data type as part of the CREATE TABLE statement (where *n* represents the digits of precision).

Data Type	SQL Keyword	ANSI SQL-92 Keyword
Big Integer	bigint	none
Integer	int	integer
Smallint	smallint	none
Tinyint	tinyint	none

Monetary Data Types

You use the monetary data types, money and smallmoney, to store money information rounded to the thousandth decimal place. Actually, most client applications display money values rounded to the nearest cent. The following table describes the money data types.

Data Type	Size (in Bytes)	Supported Values
money	8	-922,337,203,685,477.5808 to 922,337,203,685,477.5807
smallmoney	4	-214,748.3648 to 214,748.3647

To specify either the money or smallmoney data types as part of the CREATE TABLE statement, use either money or smallmoney as the keywords. ANSI SQL-92 doesn't have an equivalent keyword for the monetary data types.

Text and Image Data Types

If you need to store large amounts of information or graphics for each row in a table, you can use the text or image data types for the columns. The text data type enables you to store up to 2 GB of data in a column. By default, SQL Server allocates an 8 KB page to store text data from a column. As you need more space, SQL Server dynamically links additional 8 KB pages to the table. If you plan to store Unicode characters in a text column, use the ntext data type. This data type enables you to store up to 1 GB of Unicode data in a column.

You use the image data type to enable you to store graphics with tables. Similar to the text data type, you can store up to a 2 GB graphic in a column. SQL Server allocates an 8 KB page to store the image and dynamically allocates additional pages as needed.

Use the following syntax to specify the text and image data types as part of the CREATE TABLE statement.

Data Type	SQL Keyword	ANSI SQL-92 Keyword
Text	text	none
Unicode text	ntext	national text
Image	image	none

Special Data Types

SQL Server includes several special data types that enable you to store different types of data within a column. We define these data types in the following table.

Data Type	Size (in Bytes)	Enables You to Store
bit	1	1 or 0 values (use when a column will contain only these two values). For example, the contract column in the authors table uses the bit data type.
cursor	Up to 8	Output parameters that reference a cursor.

The ANSI SQL-92 keyword for timestamp is rowversion.

Data Type	Size (in Bytes)	Enables You to Store
sysname	256	Database object names. SQL Server automatically creates this data type based on the variable-length Unicode data type.
timestamp	8	A unique counter value that SQL Server updates each time you modify a row. (No relation to time data types.)
uniqueidentifier	16	A Globally Unique IDentification number (GUID) for the entire database. We're going to talk more about generating values for columns later on in this lesson.

Collation Settings

One of the new changes in SQL Server 2000 is that you can specify a collation setting for a column that's distinct from that of the server—and even the database itself. You might do so if you want to be able to store data that uses a different character set from that of the database or server. If you don't specify a collation for a column, SQL Server uses the database's collation for the column.

User-defined Data Types

You can create your own data types based on the system data types. Use your own data types to make sure that columns are consistent across a database. You can optionally create user-defined data types in the model database; SQL Server will then automatically copy those data types to all new databases. SQL Server stores user-defined data types in the systypes table in each database. We're going to look at user-defined data types in more detail next.

Designing Efficient Tables

You should keep in mind that SQL Server stores tables in 8 KB pages. The smaller your row size (the sum of the widths of all columns), the greater the number of rows SQL Server can store on a page. A greater row density per page enables SQL Server to retrieve more rows with a single I/O operation, and it also increases the number of rows SQL Server can cache in RAM for a given amount of memory. As you can see, you should try to keep your row size as small as possible based on the data you want to store in your table. Don't arbitrarily increase the size of your columns without considering the impact on performance. Also keep in mind that if the data you'll be storing in a column varies in length, you should use one of the variable length data types.

Another factor you should consider when designing your tables is planning for growth. For example, if you choose a data type such as smallint for the customer account number, the maximum number of customers you can have on file is 32,767. In this scenario, it would be better for you to use the integer data type—or better yet, use the character data type so that you can use not only numbers, but also letters and other characters as part of a customer's account number.

APPLY YOUR KNOWLEDGE 4-1

Designing Tables

Setup: In this activity, you're going to design the tables you will need in the movies database.

You're responsible for designing the necessary tables for the movies database. Your company, a video rental store, would like to be able to automate the process of renting movies. You would like to be able to maintain the movie inventory, customers, and rental invoices. In addition to standard reports such as customer mailing labels and movie inventory, your boss would like to be able to print reports such as rentals per day, rentals by hour of day, rentals by movie type (such as comedy or drama), and customers by ZIP code. You have decided that your database will consist of the following five tables.

We split the customer rentals into two tables so that you can normalize the data. You will use the rental table to store information such as the date of the rental and the customer information. Use the rental_detail table to store information about the invoice number and the movie rented. You'll need to link the rental and rental_ detail tables together.

Table Name	Contains
Movie	A list of the movie inventory at the rental store.
Customer	Customer information.
Category	A list of movie categories (such as comedy, horror, etc.). You're going to link this table to the movie table so that you can identify the type of movie as part of the inventory information.
Rental	Invoice information.
Rental_detail	A list of the movies rented per rental invoice. This table will be linked to the rental table.

1. What columns and data types will you use in the movie table?

Column Name	Data Type

2. What columns and data types will you use in the customer table?

Column Name	Data Type

3. What columns and data types will you use in the category table?

Column Name	Data Type

4. What columns and data types will you use in the rental table?

Column Name	Data Type

5. What columns and data types will you use in the rental_detail table?

Column Name	Data Type

6. What, if any, user-defined data types do you think you should create? Why?

Implementing User-defined Data Types

If you plan to use user-defined data types in your tables, you should create them before you create your tables themselves. You use the sp_addtype stored procedure to create user-defined data types. Use the following syntax:

```
sp_addtype name, 'data type', 'NULL' | ' NOT NULL'
```

Replace *name* with the name you want to assign to your user-defined data type; replace *data type* with one of the system data types. Use either NULL or NOT NULL to control whether or not users can leave the column blank during data entry. You should always explicitly state whether you want a column to be null or not null. In general, you shouldn't permit null values in your columns, and you should always explicitly specify whether you want a column to permit nulls or not.

Remember, if you use the sp_addtype *stored procedure as part of a batch, you must precede it with the* EXEC *keyword.*

SQL Server stores user-defined data types for each database in the systypes table. You can view information about the data types by using the following query:

```
SELECT *
FROM systypes
```

You can also use the `sp_help` stored procedure to view a database's user-defined data types. This stored procedure lists the user-defined data types at the end of the results set, as shown in Figure 4-1.

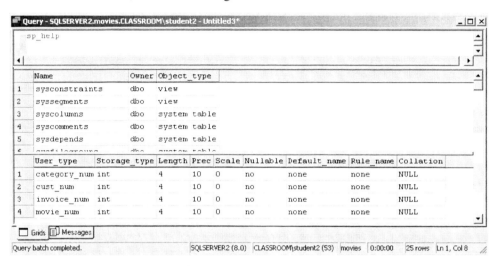

Figure 4-1: *Viewing user-defined data types.*

Deleting a User-defined Data Type

If you find that you no longer need it, you can use the `sp_droptype` stored procedure to delete a user-defined data type. Use the following syntax:
`sp_droptype name`.

APPLY YOUR KNOWLEDGE 4-2

Suggested time:
15 minutes

Creating User-defined Data Types

Objective: To create the necessary user-defined data types for the movies database.

Setup: You're logged on to Windows 2000 as student#. You've created a database named movies.

1. Start SQL Query Analyzer and connect to your server by using Windows Authentication. From the Database drop-down list, select the movies database.

2. Write a query for creating a user-defined data type named movie_num based on the integer data type; don't permit nulls in this data type.

3. In SQL Query Analyzer, execute this query against the movies database.

4. In SQL Query Analyzer, create user-defined data types named category_num, cust_num, and invoice_num based on the integer data type; configure these data types to not permit nulls.

5. What query can you use to view a list of the user-defined data types in the movies database?

6. Execute the query you recorded in step 5.

7. Clear the Query window.

Creating a Table

You can create a table by using either SQL Server Enterprise Manager or the CREATE TABLE Transact-SQL statement. Each database can have up to two billion tables; each table can contain 1,024 columns. For each table, you can configure its columns up to 8,060 bytes per row.

To create a table with SQL Server Enterprise Manager, begin by expanding the database in which you want to create the table. In the console tree, right-click on the Tables object; from the shortcut menu, choose New Table. You can then define the table's properties by using the New Table dialog box.

Use the following syntax to create a table by using the Transact-SQL commands in a Query window:

```
CREATE TABLE table_name
(column_name (column_properties),
next_column_name (column_properties))
```

When you define the name of the table, you can optionally specify the name of the database in which you want to create the table; to do so, use the format *database_name..table_name*. For example, to create a table named customer within the movies database, you would type CREATE TABLE movies..customer. For each column, replace *column_properties* with the data type of the column and, optionally, the size of the column. Depending on the data types of the columns you're creating, you might not need to specify a size. For example, if you're creating a column with the integer data type, you don't need to specify a size. In contrast, if you're creating a column with the character data type, you must specify the size (number of characters) you want to be able to store in the column. You can add either NULL or NOT NULL after a column's properties to specify whether or not you want the column to support null values. You should always explicitly specify whether you want a column to permit null values when you use the CREATE TABLE statement. If you want to configure a column to use a user-defined data type, simply specify the name of the data type for the column properties.

You can view a table's properties by using the sp_help stored procedure. Here's the syntax: sp_help 'table_name'

Automatically Generating Column Values

You can configure a column to start with an initial value and have SQL Server automatically increment that value by using the IDENTITY property. You typically use the IDENTITY property for a column you want to use as a table's primary key. Use this syntax to configure the IDENTITY property:

```
CREATE TABLE table_name
(column_name data_type
IDENTITY (seed [, increment]) NOT NULL
...)
```

You must use either the integer (bigint, int, smallint, or tinyint), numeric, or decimal data types for a column on which you configure the IDENTITY property. If you use the numeric or decimal data types, you must set the scale to zero. Replace *seed* with the initial value you would like SQL Server to use for the column; replace *increment* with the value by which you want SQL Server to increment the column for each new row. You must specify both the seed and the increment, or neither. If you don't specify the seed and increment, SQL Server uses a seed value of 1, and an increment of 1.

For example, in the following syntax, we're creating a table that contains a CustomerID column as an IDENTITY column, plus a column for storing the customer name. Notice that the IDENTITY column's seed value is 1000, and the increment is 1:

```
CREATE TABLE customer
(CustomerID int IDENTITY(1000, 1) NOT NULL,
CustomerName varchar(40))
```

You should consider the following when you use the IDENTITY property:

- You can configure only one column per table with the IDENTITY property. You can't update this column, nor can you configure it to permit null values.

- Using the IDENTITY property by itself doesn't guarantee that a column will be unique. If you want to guarantee uniqueness, create a unique index.

- You can use either the IDENTITY column's name or the IDENTITYCOL keyword to query this column. Using the IDENTITYCOL keyword enables you to query the IDENTITY column without having to know its name.

After you've defined an IDENTITY column, you can use several techniques to find out information about it:

- You can use the IDENT_SEED( ) and IDENT_INCR( ) functions to view the seed and increment properties respectively for an IDENTITY column.

- Use the @@identity system function to determine the value of the last row added to a table.

- The SCOPE_IDENTITY( ) function enables you to identify the last identity value inserted into a column within your current scope. Likewise, you can use the IDENT_CURRENT( ) function to determine the last IDENTITY value generated within the scope. (Your current scope is the stored procedure, batch, trigger, or function you're currently executing.)

You can use the UNIQUEIDENTIFIER data type as an alternative to the IDENTITY property. This data type enables you to store a 16-byte hexadecimal value in the column. The UNIQUEIDENTIFIER data type doesn't automatically generate an initial value. Instead, you populate it by using the NEWID( ) function. The best way to use the NEWID( ) function is to set it as the default value for the column by defining a default constraint.

APPLY YOUR KNOWLEDGE 4-3

Suggested time:
30 minutes

Creating the Tables for the Movies Database

Objective: To use the CREATE TABLE statement to create the necessary tables in the movies database.

1. In the following space, write the CREATE TABLE statement for creating the movie table. Don't permit null values in any columns. Use the following table to define the columns and their data types.

Column Name	Data Type
movie_num	movie_num IDENTITY(100,1)
title	varchar(40)
category_num	category_num
rating	varchar(5)
date_purch	smalldatetime
rental_price	smallmoney

2. Execute your query in SQL Query Analyzer. Make sure that you create the table in the movies database. (You might want to parse your query before you run it to double-check your syntax.) Use sp_help 'movie' to verify the new table's structure.

3. Use the CREATE TABLE statement to create the following tables: customer, category, rental, and rental_detail. Use the following tables to define the columns and data types. Write the queries you use to create each table.

Customer:

Column Name	Data Type	Permit Nulls?
cust_num	cust_num IDENTITY(300,1)	No
lname	varchar(20)	No
fname	varchar(20)	No
address1	varchar(30)	Yes
address2	varchar(20)	Yes
city	varchar(20)	Yes
state	char(2)	Yes
zip	char(10)	Yes
phone	varchar(10)	No
join_date	smalldatetime	No

Category:

Column Name	Data Type	Permit Nulls?
category_num	category_num IDENTITY(1,1)	No
description	varchar(20)	No

Rental:

Column Name	Data Type	Permit Nulls?
Invoice_num	invoice_num IDENTITY(1,1)	No
cust_num	cust_num	No
rental_date	smalldatetime	No
due_date	smalldatetime	No

Rental_detail:

Column Name	Data Type	Permit Nulls?
invoice_num	invoice_num	No
line_num	int	No
movie_num	movie_num	No
rental_price	smallmoney	No

4. Verify the structure of all tables by using the `sp_help` stored procedure.

5. Clear the Query window.

TOPIC 4B

Maintaining Tables

After you've created a table, you can change its structure by using either SQL Server Enterprise Manager or the `ALTER TABLE` Transact-SQL statement. You can change any of the column properties within SQL Server 2000; however, you should be aware that actions such as changing column data types can cause you to lose the data in that column.

Adding a Column

You can add a column to a table by using SQL Server Enterprise Manager or the `ALTER TABLE` statement. Use the following syntax to add a new column to a table with the `ALTER TABLE` statement:

```
ALTER TABLE table_name
ADD column_name (column_properties)
```

For example, if you want to add a telephone number column to a table, you might use the following syntax:

```
ALTER TABLE customer
ADD telephone varchar(12)
```

Modifying a Column

If you want to modify a column with the `ALTER TABLE` statement, use this syntax:

```
ALTER TABLE table_name
ALTER COLUMN column_name (column_properties)
```

If you change the name of a column, you must rebuild all objects that refer to that column, including all indexes, views, stored procedures, and triggers.

If you set a column's properties such that it doesn't permit nulls, the ALTER TABLE *statement requires that you specify a default value for the column.*

Dropping a Column

If you want to drop a column, you must first drop all indexes and constraints that reference the column. When you're ready, here's the syntax for dropping a column:

```
ALTER TABLE table_name
DROP COLUMN column_name
```

APPLY YOUR KNOWLEDGE 4-4

Suggested time:
20 minutes

Modifying Table Structure

Objective: To use the ALTER TABLE statement to modify the structure of the practice table.

Setup: You created a table named practice in the pubs database.

1. In the space below, write a SQL statement for adding a column named phone with a data type of varchar(15) to the practice table.

2. In SQL Query Analyzer, select pubs from the Database drop-down list. Execute the query you wrote in step 1.

3. Execute a query to verify the structure of the table.

4. Write a query to add a column named description with a data type of varchar(20) to the practice table. Don't permit null values in this column.

5. Execute this query in SQL Query Analyzer. What must you do to fix this query so that it will run properly?

6. Revise the query you wrote in step 4 so that it will run properly. If necessary, refer to Books Online to find the correct syntax. Write the revised query in the space below.

7. Execute this query in SQL Query Analyzer to verify that you can add the new column.

8. Write a SQL statement for dropping the column named phone from the practice table.

9. Execute this query in SQL Query Analyzer.

10. Execute a query to verify that your table no longer contains a phone column.

11. Clear the Query window.

Dropping a Table

If you find that you no longer need a table, you can use the DROP TABLE statement to delete it. Use the following syntax: DROP TABLE *table_name*.

In this syntax, replace *table_name* with the appropriate table. Before you execute this statement, make sure you use the correct database first.

APPLY YOUR KNOWLEDGE 4-5

Suggested time:
5 minutes

Dropping a Table

Objective: To use the DROP TABLE statement to delete the practice table from the pubs database.

1. Write a query for deleting the practice table.

2. In SQL Query Analyzer, verify that you're using the pubs database. Execute the query you wrote in step 1.

3. Verify that you no longer see the practice table by using the sp_help stored procedure.

4. Close SQL Query Analyzer.

Scripting Tables

After you've created your tables, you can use utilities such as SQL Server Enterprise Manager to generate scripts for the tables. You can use scripts as a backup for re-creating your database and its tables. In addition, you can use scripts to transfer a database's structure (but not its data) to another SQL server. You might also use scripts while you are developing a database.

You can generate a script for an entire database, a specific table or several tables, or script files for separate types of objects. Use the following steps to generate a script in SQL Server Enterprise Manager:

1. In your server's Databases folder, right-click on the database (or object) for which you want to create a script. From the shortcut menu, choose All Tasks→Generate SQL Script.

2. In the Generate SQL Scripts dialog box, select the objects you want to include in your script.

3. Use the Preview button to preview the script.

4. Save your script.

You can also right-click on an object and choose Copy; then open a text editor such as Notepad, right-click, and choose Paste to create a script for that object.

TASK 4B-1:

Using SQL Server Enterprise Manager to Generate a Script

Objective: To create a script for creating all of the tables in the movies database.

1. From the Microsoft SQL Server program group, **start SQL Server Enterprise Manager.**

2. Below your server, **expand the Databases folder.**

3. **Right-click on the movies database and choose All Tasks→Generate SQL Script** to open the Generate SQL Scripts dialog box.

4. On the General page, **click Show All** to display all of the objects in the movies database.

5. **Look at the General page.** By default, SQL Server Enterprise Manager doesn't configure the script for any of the database's objects.

6. Below Objects To Script, **check All Tables** to configure SQL Server Enterprise Manager to generate a script to re-create all of the user-defined tables within the movies database.

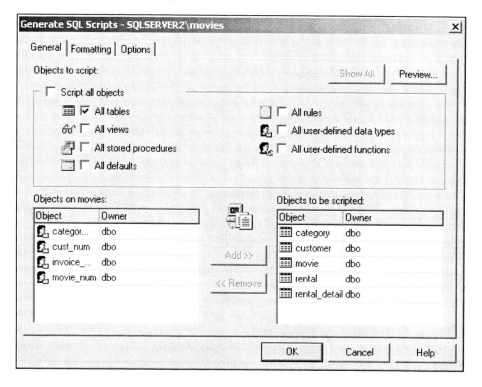

7. **Select the Formatting tab.** SQL Server Enterprise Manager automatically includes lines in your script to drop the objects if they exist and then create the object whenever you run the script.

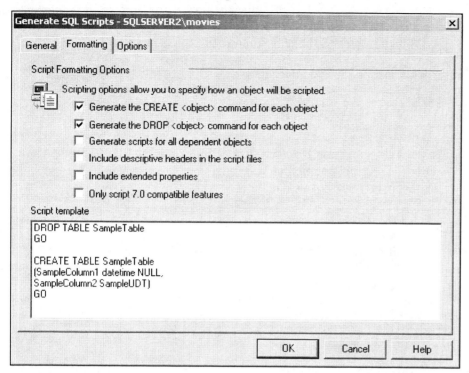

8. **Select the Options tab.** You can use the Options page to specify whether you want to include your server's logins, database users, and their permissions in the script, as well as indexes and constraints.

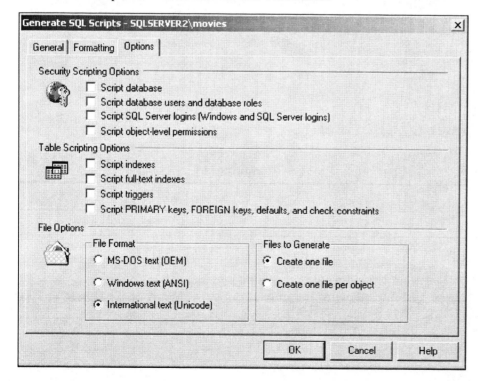

9. **Select the General tab.**

10. **Click Preview** to display a preview of your script. You can add comments as well as other SQL statements to your script.

11. **Look at your script.** The first lines of your script contain the statements for dropping the category, customer, movie, rental, and rental_detail tables. Your script then re-creates the tables and their structures.

12. **Click Close** to close the Generate SQL Script Preview dialog box.

13. **Click OK** to close the Generate SQL Scripts dialog box, and to display the Save As dialog box.

14. In the File Name text box, **type *tables* and then click Save** to save the script file. At this point, your script file contains instructions for re-creating the tables in your movies database.

15. **Click OK** to close the Scripting message box.

16. **Close all open windows.**

Summary

In this lesson, you learned how to go about designing a database's tables, from normalizing their design to choosing each column's data type. You learned how to create your own user-defined data types, and how to create a table using both system- and user-defined data types. You also explored the techniques you can use to manage a table, including how to add, modify, or drop a column. Finally, you learned how to use SQL Server Enterprise Manager's scripting capabilities to generate a script for creating a database's objects.

LESSON 4 REVIEW

4A List the parameters you must configure when you add a column to a table.

4B You want to add a column named comments with a data type of text to the customer table in the movies database. What query should you use?

Designing and Implementing Data Integrity

Data Files:
pk_movie.sql
pk_constraints.sql
fk_movie.sql
fk_constraints.sql
df_movie.sql
df_constraints.sql
ck_movie.sql
disable_constraint.sql
category.txt
movie.txt
customer.txt
rental.txt
rental_detail.txt

Lesson Time:
2 hours, 30 minutes

Overview

In a relational database system, you use constraints to ensure the integrity of a database's data and to construct the relationships between tables. In this lesson, we explain how you go about designing constraints. We also show you how to create and manage each type of constraint.

Objectives

To enforce data integrity, you will:

5A **Describe the techniques you can use to enforce data integrity.**

SQL Server supports two types of data integrity techniques: procedural and declarative. In this topic, we explore the difference between both types and explain how to select a technique for ensuring the integrity of a database.

5B **Implement constraints on tables.**

After you've decided on the types of constraints you want to implement, your next task is to define them. In this topic, we show you how to create each type of constraint both when you're creating a table and by modifying an existing table. We also show you how to disable constraint checking to improve performance of your server during bulk load operations.

TOPIC 5A

Understanding Data Integrity

In SQL Server 2000, you can enforce *data integrity* by using a variety of methods. These methods enable you to make sure that the data users add or modify in your databases is valid. You can enforce data integrity by using either of two methods: declarative or procedural. With *declarative data integrity*, you enforce integrity as part of the object itself; the integrity becomes part of the database and table definitions. You use constraints, defaults, and rules to enforce declarative data integrity. You enforce *procedural data integrity* through the use of programming. You can use triggers and stored procedures to implement procedural integrity.

Because programming can add considerable overhead to your server's workload, Microsoft recommends that you primarily implement data integrity through declarative methods wherever possible instead of through procedural methods. For this reason, we focus on declarative data integrity in this lesson.

Declarative Data Integrity

You'll find that you have a lot of choices when it comes to enforcing declarative data integrity. First of all, SQL Server supports three types of declarative data integrity:

- Domain (Column) Integrity—enables you to specify a set of values that are valid for a column and whether or not the column can permit null values.

- Entity (Row) Integrity—requires that you configure all rows in a table with a unique identifier (the primary key).

- Referential Integrity—enables you to establish relationships between the primary key table (also known as the *referenced* table) and a foreign key table (the *referencing* table). By default, you can't delete a row in the primary key table, nor change the primary key of a row, if any rows in the foreign key table refer to it.

You implement the thee types of declarative data integrity through the use of constraints. These constraints include: default, check, referential, primary key, unique, and foreign key. The following table describes each type of constraint, the type of data integrity each enforces, and why you might use the constraint.

Type of Data Integrity	Constraint	Enables You to
Domain	CHECK	Define the valid values for a column.
	DEFAULT	Set a default value for a column if one isn't specified during data entry.
	REFERENTIAL	Define valid values for a column based on values in a column from another table.
Entity	PRIMARY KEY	Define a unique value for each row to make sure that users don't duplicate records. In addition, SQL Server automatically creates an index based on the primary key. You can't configure the primary key column to permit nulls.

Type of Data Integrity	Constraint	Enables You to
	UNIQUE	Define a column that must be unique (other than the primary key). SQL Server automatically creates an index based on this column. You can configure a unique column to permit nulls.
Referential	CHECK	Define the valid values for a column based on values in other columns in the same table.
	FOREIGN KEY	Specify that this column must match the primary key of the same table or another table within the same database.

Selecting Data Integrity Techniques

Some of the factors you should consider when choosing a data integrity technique include functionality, overhead, and whether the technique prevents problems from occurring before or after a transaction. Constraints provide you with a mid-range of functionality and prevent problems from occurring before a transaction is saved. They also offer you the advantage of very little processing overhead. Defaults and rules have a low level of functionality and also prevent problems from occurring before a transaction is saved, but both defaults and rules have more processing overhead because they're separate database objects.

Triggers provide you with a very high level of functionality for implementing data integrity, but they also have the highest processing overhead and prevent problems from occurring after the transaction, not before. The disadvantage to detecting problems after a transaction completes is that it means that SQL Server must do all the work associated with the transaction, and then it must undo that work when the trigger detects a problem. So, SQL Server has essentially done the work associated with the transaction twice without any results to show for it.

APPLY YOUR KNOWLEDGE 5-1

Suggested time:
20 minutes

Designing Data Integrity for the Movies Database

Objective: In this lab, you're going to design the data integrity for the movies database. (Hint: You can use the GETDATE( ) function within a default constraint to set date columns to the current date on your server.)

1. Given the structure of the movie table, what types of constraints do you think you should use on the movie table?

Column Name	Data Type	Permit Nulls?
movie_num	movie_num IDENTITY(100,1)	No
title	varchar(40)	No
category_num	category_num	No
rating	varchar(5)	No
date_purch	smalldatetime	Yes
rental_price	smallmoney	No

2. What types of constraints do you think you should use on the customer table?

Column Name	Data Type	Permit Nulls?
cust_num	cust_num IDENTITY(300,1)	No
lname	varchar(20)	No
fname	varchar(20)	No
address1	varchar(20)	Yes
address2	varchar(20)	Yes
city	varchar(20)	Yes
state	char(2)	Yes
zip	char(10)	Yes
phone	varchar(10)	No
join_date	smalldatetime	No

3. What types of constraints do you think you should configure on the category table?

Column Name	Data Type	Permit Nulls?
category_num	category_num IDENTITY(1,1)	No
description	varchar(20)	No

4. What types of constraints do you think you should configure on the rental table?

Column Name	Data Type	Permit Nulls?
invoice_num	invoice_num IDENTITY(1,1)	No
cust_num	cust_num	No
rental_date	smalldatetime	No
due_date	smalldatetime	No

5. What types of constraints do you think you should configure on the rental detail table?

Column Name	Data Type	Permit Nulls?
invoice_num	invoice_num	No
line_num	int	No
movie_num	movie_num	No
rental_price	smallmoney	No

TOPIC 5B

Implementing Constraints

Now that we've looked at the types of constraints you can define, let's get into how you create each type of constraint. You can define constraints when you create a table by specifying them as part of the CREATE TABLE statement, or you can add constraints later by using the ALTER TABLE statement. You can create, change, and delete constraints without having to drop and re-create a table. Keep in mind that SQL Server does check your existing data when you add a constraint to a table to make sure that your data doesn't violate the constraint. If your data violates the constraint you're attempting to define, SQL Server won't create the constraint.

You should be aware that if you have an existing table with data for which you add a primary key or unique constraint with a clustered index, SQL Server must completely re-order the rows in the table based on the primary key value. In addition, because the locations of the rows have changed, SQL Server must also re-create all nonclustered indexes. So, it's important that you realize that defining a clustered index on a populated table can take an additional 1.2 times the size of the table during the creation of the index. For example, if your table is currently 100 MB in size, SQL Server will use an additional 120 MB (over the 100 MB currently in use by the table) during the creation of the clustered index. We're going to talk more about the space requirements and how you go about re-creating indexes in the "Implementing Indexes" lesson.

Viewing Constraints

Before we get into how you define constraints, let's take a look at how you can determine what constraints are already defined on the table. You can view the constraints on a table by using the sp_helpconstraint, sp_helpdb, and sp_help stored procedures. The sp_helpconstraint stored procedure shows you all of the constraints you've defined for a particular table. Use the following syntax with sp_helpconstraint:

```
sp_helpconstraint 'table_name'
```

To view information about only a particular constraint, use the following syntax:

```
sp_help 'constraint_name'
```

When you use sp_help, you see a lot of additional information about the table including the table structure, any columns for which you've configured to use the identity property, and a list of constraints. Use the following syntax with sp_helpdb:

```
sp_helpdb 'table_name'
```

Defining Primary Key Constraints

primary key:
One or more columns that you use to uniquely identify each row in a table.

You can define a *primary key* that consists of one or more columns in a table; you use the primary key to uniquely identify each row in a table. Because you use a table's primary key to search for records, SQL Server requires that each row's primary key be unique throughout the table. For example, if you create a customer table with the account number column as its primary key, each row's account number must be unique throughout the table. So, by using a primary key, you can protect the integrity of the data in a table. In addition, by specifying a primary key when you create a table, you create an index for the table that's based on the primary key. Because the primary key is used for indexing the table, SQL Server requires that you configure the columns in the primary key to not accept null values. SQL Server doesn't permit duplicate entries in the primary key column(s) for a table.

SQL Server automatically creates a clustered index based on the primary key if you don't specify the type of index you want to create.

Use the following syntax to add a primary key constraint when you create a table:

```
CREATE TABLE table_name
(column_name data_type CONSTRAINT constraint_name PRIMARY KEY
[CLUSTERED | NONCLUSTERED], ... )
```

But what if you want to add a primary key constraint to an existing table? To do so, use the following syntax:

```
ALTER TABLE table_name
ADD CONSTRAINT constraint_name PRIMARY KEY (column_name)
[CLUSTERED| NONCLUSTERED]
```

By convention, you typically use PK_ plus the name of the table for the name of the primary key constraint. For example, to configure the movie_num column as the primary key for the movie table and to create a nonclustered index based on the primary key, use the following syntax:

```
ALTER TABLE movie
ADD CONSTRAINT PK_movie PRIMARY KEY (movie_num)
NONCLUSTERED
```

You should consider the following factors when choosing your primary key:

- You can define only one primary key per table.

- The column or columns you select for the primary key can't permit nulls.

- If you don't specify the index type, SQL Server automatically creates a clustered index based on the primary key (as long as you haven't already defined a clustered index for the table).

Defining Unique Constraints

In many cases, you'll find that you want to enforce uniqueness in a column other than the primary key column. In these cases, you can configure a unique constraint on a column to ensure that all values users enter for that column are unique within the table. You should use the unique constraint on any non-primary key column for which you want the values to be unique. For example, let's say that you're creating a table for storing employee information. You plan to use the social security number column as the table's primary key. You also plan to store each employee's security code in the table. If you want to prevent duplicate entries in the security code column, you should configure it with a unique constraint.

You can define a unique constraint when you create a table by using the following syntax:

```
CREATE TABLE table_name
(column_name data_type CONSTRAINT constraint_name
UNIQUE CLUSTERED | NONCLUSTERED (column_name),
...)
```

You typically name unique constraints UK_*table_name*. You can also specify whether you want to create a clustered or nonclustered index on this column.

You can add a unique constraint to an existing table by using the following syntax:

```
ALTER TABLE table_name
ADD CONSTRAINT constraint_name
UNIQUE CLUSTERED | NONCLUSTERED (column_name)
```

You should consider the following factors when configuring a unique constraint:

- Unique columns do permit nulls, but only one row's column can be null. (You can't have two columns with null values because they aren't unique.)

- You can configure more than one unique constraint on a table.

- SQL Server enforces a unique constraint through a unique index.

TASK 5B-1:

Adding a Primary Key Constraint

Objective: To add a primary key to the movie table.

Setup: You're logged on to Windows 2000 as student#. You've created a database named movies and tables within it named movie, category, customer, rental, and rental_detail.

Below the movies database, right-click on Diagrams and choose New Database Diagram.

1. In SQL Server Enterprise Manager, **create a database diagram for the movies database.** When prompted, **include the category, customer, movie, rental, and rental_detail tables in your diagram.**

2. **Look at the database diagram.** (If necessary, drag the tables so that it's easier for you to view all of the tables on one screen.) If you've defined any primary keys on your tables, SQL Server Enterprise Manager identifies them with a key icon as part of each table in the database diagram view. None of your tables currently have primary keys.

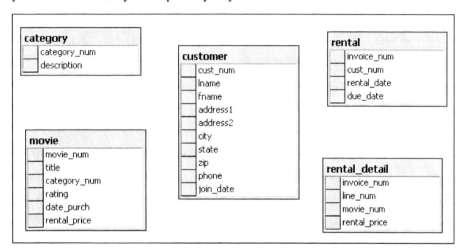

3. **Save your database diagram as** *movies*. **Close the Database Diagram window.**

4. **Open SQL Query Analyzer and log in with Windows Authentication. Select the movies database.**

5. **Execute the following query:**

```
ALTER TABLE movie
ADD CONSTRAINT PK_movie
PRIMARY KEY NONCLUSTERED (movie_num)
```

This query adds a primary key constraint to the movie table. By adding the keyword NONCLUSTERED, you configure SQL Server to create a nonclustered index based on the primary key.

6. **Execute a new query:**

```
sp_helpconstraint 'movie'
```

This query enables you to view the constraints on the movie table.

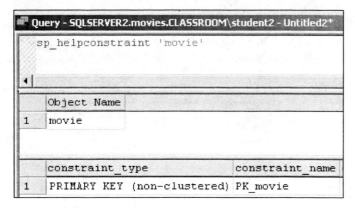

```
Query - SQLSERVER2.movies.CLASSROOM\student2 - Untitled2*
sp_helpconstraint 'movie'
```

	Object Name
1	movie

	constraint_type	constraint_name
1	PRIMARY KEY (non-clustered)	PK_movie

7. **Clear the Query window.**

APPLY YOUR KNOWLEDGE 5-2

Suggested time:
15 minutes

Defining Primary Key Constraints

Objective: To use queries in SQL Query Analyzer to define primary key constraints for the customer, category, and rental tables.

1. In SQL Query Analyzer, add a primary key constraint on the cust_num column of the customer table. Use PK_customer for the constraint name and create a nonclustered index.

   Record the query you used in the space below.

2. Add a primary key constraint on the category_num column of the category table. Use PK_category for the constraint name.

   Record your query below.

3. Add a primary key constraint on the invoice_num column of the rental table. Use PK_rental for the constraint name.

   Record your query below.

4. Use `sp_helpconstraint` along with each table name to verify your tables' primary keys.

5. Clear the Query window.

6. In SQL Server Enterprise Manager, open the movies database diagram. Look at the primary key columns you've defined. (You should see a primary key icon on each of the category, customer, movie, and rental tables.)

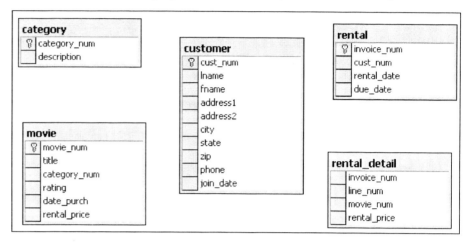

7. Close the movies database diagram.

Defining Foreign Key Constraints

foreign key:
The column or group of columns in one table that match the primary key column or columns of another table.

Earlier in the course we talked about normalizing your tables in order to avoid duplicating data across multiple database. After you split up your tables, you use relationships between those tables to link them together. For example, in the Northwind sample database, you find both an Orders and an Order Details table. Both tables contain an OrderID column, which means that the tables are linked together by this column. In the Orders table, the OrderID column is the primary key, and in the Order Details table, it's a *foreign key*. If you create one or more columns in one table that are identical to the primary key for another table, you can link these columns by defining a foreign key constraint.

You can temporarily disable the checking of foreign key constraints if necessary. We're going to cover how you do this later on in the lesson.

You must define the primary key before you can link a foreign key to it. After you've defined the foreign key constraint, data integrity prevents you from changing the value of a primary key if you have any matching rows in the foreign key table. Likewise, you can't delete a row from the primary key table if it has matching rows in the foreign key table (and vice versa). You can define a foreign key constraint when you create a table by using the following syntax:

```
CREATE TABLE table_name
(column_name data_type CONSTRAINT constraint_name
FOREIGN KEY REFERENCES ref_table(ref_column)
... )
```

In this syntax, you replace *ref_table* with the name of the referenced table that contains the primary key. Replace *ref_column* with the name of the primary key column in the referenced table. You'll typically name foreign key constraints FK_*table_name*.

You can add a foreign key constraint to an existing table by using the following syntax:

```
ALTER TABLE table_name
ADD CONSTRAINT constraint_name FOREIGN KEY
(column_name) REFERENCES ref_table(ref_column)
```

You should be aware that SQL Server doesn't automatically create indexes based on the foreign keys you define. Because you'll typically join tables together based on this primary key – foreign key relationship, you should consider creating an index on the foreign key column in order to enhance the performance of table joins. We're going to talk about optimizing indexes in detail in the "Implementing Indexes" lesson.

Another factor to keep in mind is that if you give users the necessary permissions to update the data in the foreign key table, you must also give those users either the SELECT or REFERENCES permission on the primary key table as well. Otherwise, your users won't be able to make changes to the table containing the foreign key constraint.

Let's take a look at how you view the primary key – foreign key relationship within a database diagram. In Figure 5-1, we show you the database diagram for the Orders and Order Details tables from the Northwind database. The line connecting the two tables enables you to see that these two tables have a primary key – foreign key relationship. Furthermore, the key symbol on the line identifies which table contains the primary key (the Orders table in this case), and the infinity symbol identifies the foreign key table (Order Details). Having these two symbols on the line connecting the tables also tells you that the relationship between the two tables is one to many. This means that you can have one row in the Orders table that's linked to one or more rows in the Order Details table.

Even though the relationship between the Orders and Order Details tables is called "one to many," you should be aware that you can have rows in the Orders table without any corresponding rows in the Order Details table. On the other hand, you can't have a row in the Order Details table unless a corresponding row exists in the Orders table.

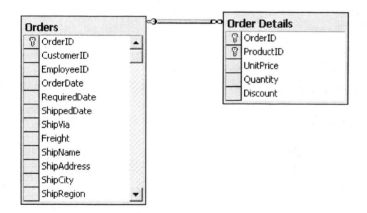

Figure 5-1: *Identifying a primary key – foreign key relationship in a database diagram.*

Cascading Integrity

By default, SQL Server configures the primary key – foreign key relationship such that you can't make changes to the primary key table if there are corresponding rows within the foreign key table. Likewise, you can't delete a row in the primary key table if it has linked rows in the foreign key table. One of the new changes in SQL Server 2000 is that you can define a CASCADE option for a foreign key constraint that enables you to have changes or deletions you make in the primary key table cascade down to the foreign key table. For example, if you enable cascading updates and then modify the primary key for a row, SQL Server will automatically update the information in the associated foreign key rows.

You can specify both update and delete cascading settings for a foreign key constraint. Here's the syntax:

```
CREATE TABLE table_name
(column_name data_type CONSTRAINT constraint_name
FOREIGN KEY REFERENCES ref_table(ref_column)
[ON DELETE {CASCADE | NO ACTION)]
[ON UPDATE {CASCADE | NO ACTION)]
```

Keep in mind that both the ON DELETE and ON UPDATE clauses are optional when you're defining a constraint. If you don't specify these clauses, SQL Server creates the constraint with NO ACTION as the cascade setting, which means you won't be able to update or delete the primary key row if it has corresponding foreign key rows. Use the CASCADE option to enable cascading integrity for updates or deletes.

TASK 5B-2:

Adding a Foreign Key Constraint to the Movie Table

1. In SQL Query Analyzer, **execute the following query:**

```
ALTER TABLE movie
ADD CONSTRAINT FK_movie
FOREIGN KEY (category_num)
REFERENCES category(category_num)
```

This query adds a foreign key constraint to link the category_num column in the movie table to the category_num column in the category table. The foreign key will enable SQL Server to prevent users from assigning invalid category numbers to movies.

2. **How will SQL Server handle cascading updates and deletes for the FK_movie constraint?**

3. **Execute a new query:**

```
EXEC sp_helpconstraint 'movie'
```

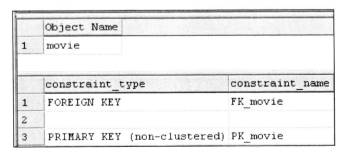

4. **Clear the Query window.**

APPLY YOUR KNOWLEDGE 5-3

Suggested time:
15 minutes

Defining Foreign Key Constraints

Objective: To use queries in SQL Query Analyzer to define foreign key constraints for the rental and rental_detail tables.

1. Add a foreign key constraint between the cust_num column of the rental table and the cust_num column of the customer table. Use FK_rental for the constraint name.

    Write the query you use in the space below.

2. Add a foreign key constraint between the invoice_num column of the rental_detail table and the invoice_num column of the rental table. Use FK_detail_invoice for the constraint name. You would like to be able to perform cascading deletes of invoices from both the rental and rental detail tables. Make sure you include the appropriate syntax for supporting cascading deletes.

    Write your query in the space below.

3. Add a foreign key constraint between the movie_num column of the rental_detail table and the movie_num column of the movie table. Use FK_detail_movie for the constraint name.

    Write your query below.

4. Use `sp_helpconstraint` to verify your tables' foreign keys.

5. Clear the Query window.

6. In SQL Server Enterprise Manager, open the movies database diagram. Look at the primary key to foreign key relationships between your tables. You should see the following relationships:

Primary Key Table	Foreign Key Table
category	movie
customer	rental
rental	rental_detail
movie	rental_detail

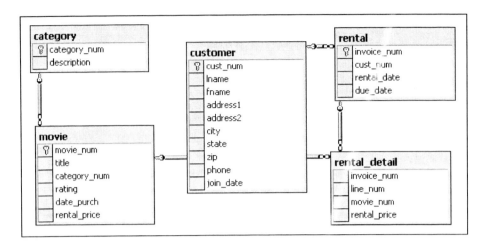

7. Close the movies database diagram.

Default Constraints

default constraint:
A value that you assign to a column. SQL Server automatically fills in the column with this value during data entry. You can always override the default value by entering another value into the column.

If you want to configure a default value for a column to make data entry easier on your users, you can create a *default constraint* for each column in your table. SQL Server automatically fills in a column with the value you specify in the default constraint. Of course, you can always change this default value for a given row. For example, if you're creating a table for storing customer address information, you might configure a default value for the state column if most of your customers are from the same state.

You define a default constraint when you create a table by using the following syntax:

```
CREATE TABLE table_name
(column_name data_type CONSTRAINT constraint_name
DEFAULT expression,
 ...)
```

In this syntax, you can replace *expression* with either a constant or a function (such as GETDATE( )). You'll typically name default constraints DF_*table_ name_column_name*.

You add a default constraint to an existing table by using the following syntax:

```
ALTER TABLE table_name
ADD CONSTRAINT constraint_name
DEFAULT expression FOR column_name
```

You should keep the following considerations in mind when defining default constraints:

- SQL Server applies the default constraint only when you insert data into a table (not when you modify data).
- You can't specify a default value on columns with either the IDENTITY property or the timestamp data type.
- You can use system-supplied values such as USER, CURRENT_USER, SESSION_USER, SYSTEM_USER, or functions such as GETDATE ( ) to define a default value.

Creating a Default Object

You can optionally create a default as a separate object so that you can use it for multiple columns. To create a default object, use the following syntax:

```
CREATE DEFAULT default_name
AS expression
```

After you've created a default object, you activate it for a column by using the `sp_bindefault` stored procedure. (The process of activating a default is called *binding* a default.) You can unbind the default from a column by using the `sp_unbindefault` stored procedure. Use the following syntax to bind a default object:

```
sp_bindefault default_name, 'table.column_name'
```

You can drop a default object by using the following syntax:

```
DROP DEFAULT default_name
```

TASK 5B-3:

Adding a Default Constraint to the Movie Table

1. In SQL Query Analyzer, **execute the following query:**

   ```
   ALTER TABLE movie
   ADD CONSTRAINT DF_movie_date_purch
   DEFAULT GETDATE() FOR date_purch
   ```

   Use this query to add a default constraint to the movie table. By using the GETDATE() functions, SQL Server will automatically fill in the column with the current system date when you add a row to the table. You can always override this value by typing in a date of your choice.

2. **Execute a new query:**

   ```
   EXEC sp_helpconstraint 'movie'
   ```

3. **Clear the Query window.**

APPLY YOUR KNOWLEDGE 5-4

Suggested time:
10 minutes

Defining Default Constraints

> **Objective:** To use queries in SQL Query Analyzer to define default constraints for the customer and rental tables.

1. Add a default constraint to the join_date column in the customer table. Use DF_customer_join_date for the constraint name and GETDATE() for the expression.

   Write your query below.

2. Add default constraints to the rental table on the rental_date and due_date columns. Use DF_rental_rental_date for the constraint on the rental_date column with GETDATE() for the expression. Use DF_rental_due_date for the constraint on the due_date column with GETDATE()+2 for the expression.

Write your queries in the following space.

3. Use `sp_helpconstraint` to verify your tables' default constraints.

4. Clear the Query window.

Check Constraints

check constraint:
A range of values that you define for a column to force users to enter only those values into the column.

If you want to force users to enter only specific values into a column, you should define a *check constraint*. You use a check constraint on a column to limit the range of values that users can enter. You can also use a check constraint to control the format users use to enter data in a column. For example, you might use a check constraint to require that users enter social security numbers using the format 999-99-9999.

You define a check constraint when you create a table by using the following syntax:

```
CREATE TABLE table_name
(column_name data_type CONSTRAINT constraint_name
CHECK (search_condition),
 ... )
```

You replace *search_condition* with a condition for controlling the data entered into the column. If you want the check constraint to require users to enter specific words, use a condition such as (rating IN ('G', 'PG', 'R', 'NC17', 'NR')). Check constraints aren't case-sensitive as long as you've configured your server to use a case-insensitive collation. So, if you used the previous constraint for the rating column, SQL Server will accept both 'G' and 'g' as valid values for that column. If you want the check constraint to evaluate numbers, you can use a search condition such as `salary >20000 AND salary <100000`. You typically name check constraints CK_table_name.

You can add a check constraint to an existing table by using the following syntax:

```
ALTER TABLE table_name
ADD CONSTRAINT constraint_name
CHECK (search_condition)
```

Consider the following factors when defining check constraints:

- SQL Server applies check constraints when you both insert and modify a table's data.

- You can create a check constraint that references another column within the same table.

- You can't define check constraints on columns with the IDENTITY property or the timestamp and uniqueidentifier data types.
- You can't use a subquery in a check constraint.

Creating Rules

You can create the equivalent to a check constraint by defining a rule. Similar to a default object, a rule is a separate object that you can then bind to columns in one or more tables. Use the following syntax to create a rule:

```
CREATE RULE rule_name
AS expression
```

You can then bind the rule to a column by using the syntax:

```
sp_bindrule rule_name, column_name
```

If necessary, you drop a rule by using this syntax:

```
DROP RULE rule_name
```

TASK 5B-4:

Adding a Check Constraint to the Movie Table

1. In SQL Query Analyzer, **execute the following query:**

   ```
   ALTER TABLE movie
   ADD CONSTRAINT CK_movie
   CHECK (rating IN ('G', 'PG', 'R', 'NC17', 'NR'))
   ```

   Use this query to set a check constraint so that users must enter either 'G', 'PG', 'R', 'NC17', or 'NR' when they add a movie to the movie table.

2. **Execute a new query:**

   ```
   EXEC sp_helpconstraint 'movie'
   ```

   You should see that you've defined primary key, foreign key, default, and check constraints on the movie table.

3. **In the space below, write a query for adding a check constraint to the rental table to make sure that the value in the due_date column is equal to or later than that of the rental_date column.**

4. **Execute the query you wrote in step 3.**

5. **Use sp_helpconstraint to verify the constraints on the rental table.**

6. **Clear the Query window.**

CHECK YOUR SKILLS 5-1

Creating a Script File

1. In SQL Server Enterprise Manager, generate a SQL script for creating the tables in the movies database and their constraints. Name the script file constraints.sql. (Right-click on the movie database and choose All Tasks→ Generate SQL Script. On the General page, click Show All and then check All Tables. On the Options page, check Script Primary Keys, Foreign Keys, Defaults, and Check Constraints.)

2. In Notepad, verify that SQL Server Enterprise Manager added the necessary commands to create the constraints on the tables as well as the structure of the tables.

3. Close Notepad.

Managing Constraints

You manage constraints by performing such tasks as deleting and disabling them. Let's take a look at how you go about deleting a constraint.

Deleting a Constraint

You can drop any constraint by using the following syntax:

```
ALTER TABLE table_name
DROP CONSTRAINT constraint_name
```

Disabling Constraint Checking of Existing Data

You can disable constraint checking of existing data when you add a constraint to a table. You should consider doing this when you know that your data already conforms to the constraint in order to improve performance. Otherwise, when you add a constraint to a table with existing data, SQL Server first checks all of the rows in the table to make sure that the existing data doesn't violate the constraint. After you've added the constraint, constraint checking becomes active.

You can disable only check and foreign key constraints; all others must be dropped and then re-added. You disable constraint checking when you create default and check constraints by adding the `WITH NOCHECK` option to the `ALTER TABLE` statement. For example, to add a foreign key constraint to a table with constraint checking disabled, use the following syntax:

```
ALTER TABLE table_name
WITH NOCHECK
ADD CONSTRAINT constraint_name
FOREIGN KEY (column_name)
REFERENCES ref_table(ref_column)
```

To add a check constraint to a table with constraint checking disabled, use the following syntax:

```
ALTER TABLE table_name
WITH NOCHECK
ADD CONSTRAINT constraint_name
CHECK (search_considiton)
```

Disabling Constraint Checking When Loading Data

You can also disable constraint checking on the CHECK and FOREIGN KEY constraints when you load new data (in order to improve performance) or update data. You might disable constraint checking if you plan to perform a bulk import of data into a table. Likewise, you might also disable constraint checking if you need to change the value of a primary key for which you've defined a foreign key relationship (and you haven't configured the foreign key for cascading updates). For example, consider the movies database: if you need to change a customer's account number in the customer table, and that customer has invoices in the rental table, SQL Server won't permit you to change the customer's account number. The only way you can change the customer's account number is to first disable the checking of the foreign key constraint, and then update the customer's account number in both the customer and rental tables.

Before you disable constraint checking, make sure that your data conforms to your constraints. To disable constraint checking, use the following syntax:

```
ALTER TABLE table_name
NOCHECK CONSTRAINT ALL | constraint_name
```

After you've completed your updates and inserts, you re-enable constraint checking by using the following syntax:

```
ALTER TABLE table_name
CHECK CONSTRAINT ALL | constraint_name
```

TASK 5B-5:

Disabling Constraint Checking

Objective: To disable constraint checking between two tables in the pubs database.

1. In SQL Server Enterprise Manager, **display the database diagram for the pubs database.**

2. **Point to the line linking the authors and titleauthor tables.** This line enables you to see that there is a primary key – foreign key relationship between the two tables. The authors table's primary key is the au_id column, and it's linked to the au_id column as a foreign key on the titleauthor table. SQL Server automatically generated a name for the foreign key of FK__ titleauthor__au_id__0519C6AF.

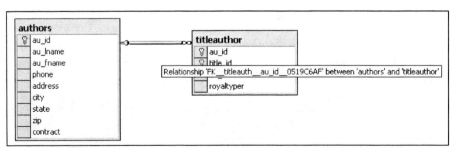

3. **Close the database diagram.**

4. In SQL Query Analyzer, **execute the following query:**

```
USE pubs
GO
SELECT au_id
FROM authors
WHERE au_lname = 'White'
```

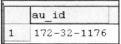

	au_id
1	172-32-1176

You should see that the author's ID number is 172-32-1176.

5. **Execute a new query:**

```
UPDATE authors
SET au_id = '172-32-1176'
WHERE au_lname = 'White'
```

6. **Look at the Results pane.** SQL Server won't permit you to change an author's ID number because of the foreign key constraint between the authors and titleauthor tables.

```
Server: Msg 547, Level 16, State 1, Line 1
UPDATE statement conflicted with COLUMN REFERENCE constraint 'FK__titleauth__au_id__0519C6AF'. The
The statement has been terminated.
```

7. **In the space below, write a SQL query for disabling checking of the primary key to foreign key relationship between the authors and titleauthor tables.**

8. **Execute the query you wrote in step 7.** (Hint: This foreign key's name uses two underscore characters (__) between each of the elements of the name except for "au_id." Use only one underscore character in au_id.)

9. **Execute a new query:**

```
UPDATE authors
SET au_id = '172-32-1177'
WHERE au_lname = 'White'
```

Because you've disabled constraint checking between the titleauthor and authors tables, SQL Server now permits you to change the author's ID.

10. **Now execute this query:**

```
SELECT *
FROM titleauthor
WHERE au_id = '172-32-1176'
```

You should see that although you changed the author's ID in the authors table, that change had no effect on the associated rows in the titleauthor table.

11. Execute a new query:

```
UPDATE titleauthor
SET au_id = '172-32-1177'
WHERE au_id = '172-32-1176'
```

By updating all of the rows in the titleauthor table with the new ID number for the author, you preserve the integrity of the data.

12. In the following space, write a query to enable constraint checking on the titleauthor table:

13. Execute the query you wrote in step 12 to re-enable constraint checking on the titleauthor table.

14. Attempt to change an author ID again by executing the following query:

```
UPDATE authors
SET au_id = '172-32-1178'
WHERE au_lname = 'White'
```

Use this query to verify that the foreign key constraint is active again.

Using Data Transformation Services

You can use the Data Transformation Services (DTS) included with SQL Server Enterprise Manager to transfer data between SQL Server and many different types of systems. For example, you can use DTS to import data from or export data to dBASE, Microsoft Access, Microsoft Excel, Oracle, Microsoft SQL Server, Visual FoxPro, Paradox, text files, and any ODBC data source.

Components of DTS

SQL Server's Data Transformation Services consists of the following key components:

- DTS Import/Export Wizard
- DTS Designer

You use the DTS Import/Export Wizard to configure your server to either import or export data. This wizard enables you to copy data between heterogeneous data sources, transfer the database structure (schema), copy a single database object or the results of a query, and transform data. When you run the wizard, you generate a DTS package. You run this package to start the import or export of data. You start the DTS Import/Export Wizard from within SQL Server Enterprise Manager.

If you have complex data transformations you want to perform, you can use the DTS Designer to create your DTS packages. You can also use the DTS Designer to modify existing packages. DTS Designer offers many advanced features that you can't configure when you use the DTS Import/Export Wizard. For example, you can define the workflow of the DTS package by using DTS Designer. After you've created a DTS package (by using either the Wizard or DTS Designer), you can use the dtsrun utility to open, run, delete, or overwrite the package.

You can use DTS to move only the database structure and data; you can't use it to transfer triggers, stored procedures, rules, defaults, constraints, and user-defined data types.

Using DTS to Import Data

You can use the DTS Import/Export Wizard, DTS Designer, or any programming language to create a DTS package for importing data. To use the Wizard in SQL Server Enterprise Manager, begin by selecting your server in the console tree. Choose Tools→Data Transformation Services, and then choose Import Data. SQL Server Enterprise Manager automatically launches the DTS Import/Export Wizard. On the Choose A Data Source page, select the appropriate data source from which you're importing the data. For example, if you want to import an ASCII delimited text file, choose Text File from the Source drop-down list. Next, depending on your data source, you might be prompted to provide additional information about that source. On the Choose a Destination page, select the database to which you want to import the data. Finally, you can specify the name of the destination table for the imported data.

Suggested time:
25 minutes

APPLY YOUR KNOWLEDGE 5-5

Importing Data into the Movies Database

Objective: To load data into the tables of the movies database.

Setup: Your instructor has copied the necessary files for importing data into the movies database to the path C:\data on your computer.

1. Given the constraints on the tables in the movies database, in what order do you think you should import data into those tables?

2. In SQL Server Enterprise Manager, in your server's Databases folder, expand the movies database. Choose Tools→Data Transformation Services→Import Data. In the DTS Import/Export Wizard, select the following options:

   • On the Choose A Data Source page, choose Text File as your source and specify a file name of C:\data\category.txt.

   • On the Select File Format page, accept the default settings. (You should see that the DTS Import/Export Wizard automatically chose the delimited file format, ANSI as the file type, {CR}{LF} as the row delimiter, and double quote as the text qualifier.)

   • On the Specify Column Delimiter page, accept the default settings. (You should see that the DTS Import/Export Wizard automatically chose the comma as the column delimiter.)

   • On the Choose A Destination page, verify that the DTS Import/Export Wizard has selected your server as the destination and that it will use Windows Authentication. If necessary, from the Database drop-down list, choose movies.

   • On the Select Source Tables page, click in the Destination column. From the Destination drop-down list, select the Category table.

Note: Even though the Category table is already selected, you must still use the drop-down list to select it again. There appears to be a bug with the DTS Import/Export Wizard that causes it to not work right if you don't select the table again from this list.

- On the Save, Schedule, and Replicate Package page, accept the default settings.

3. By using the same steps, import the data for the movie, customer, rental, and rental_detail tables. The file names are movie.txt, customer.txt, rental.txt, and rental_detail.txt.

Note: When you import the rental_detail.txt file, you must change the file format to the delimited file format on the Select File Format page.

---

4. In SQL Query Analyzer, examine the contents of each of the tables by using the SELECT statement.

5. Based on the data in the movie and category tables, write a query that will conflict with the foreign key constraint FK_movie. (If necessary, use sp_helpconstraint 'movie' to view the properties of this constraint.) Execute this query to verify that you receive an error. Write your query in the following space.

Try to insert a new movie with an invalid category number or update an existing row to give that movie an invalid category number.

6. Close all open windows.

Summary

In this lesson, you learned the types of data integrity techniques you can implement in SQL Server. You also explored the differences between each type of constraint, and how to create constraints on tables. Finally, you learned how you can disable constraints in order to modify or delete data, or to improve the performance of bulk operations.

LESSON 5 REVIEW

5A Explain the difference between declarative data integrity and procedural data integrity.

5B List two differences between the primary key and unique constraints.

Implementing Indexes

Overview

SQL Server uses indexes to speed up data retrievals when processing queries. In this lesson, we're going to begin by exploring the different types of indexes you can define, and why you might choose one type over the other. We then explore how you create indexes within Transact-SQL and configure their options. You also learn how to automate indexing by having SQL Server analyze the typical query workload on a database. Finally, we show you how to manage indexes by analyzing fragmentation, rebuilding the indexes, and managing the statistics used by the query optimizer.

Objectives

To understand how to implement indexes, you will:

6A **Design indexing for databases.**

SQL Server supports two types of indexes: clustered and nonclustered. In this topic, we explore how you go about selecting the type of indexes you should create for your tables.

6B **Implement indexing.**

After you've designed a database's indexes, your next task is to create them. In this topic, we teach you how to use the CREATE INDEX SQL statement to create both clustered and nonclustered indexes.

6C **Manage indexing.**

After you've created your indexes, you'll find that you need to maintain them. Management tasks include monitoring for fragmentation, and taking steps to correct it if necessary. In this topic, we teach you how you go about maintaining indexes by managing fragmentation and updating statistics.

Data Files:
cl_movie.sql
indexes.sql
dropindex.sql
sysindexes.sql
rebuild.sql
drop_existing.sql
queries.sql
ncindex.sql

Lesson Time:
2 hours, 30 minutes

TOPIC 6A

Designing Indexing

Your next task, after designing a database's tables and constraints, is to determine the indexes you should create. Let's start by looking at the role indexes play in optimizing query performance. When you query a table, SQL Server retrieves the results by using one of two methods: by scanning all of the pages in a table (this is called a table scan) or by using indexes. With a table scan, SQL Server scans the entire table (page by page) from the beginning to end. During the scan, it extracts the rows that meet the query condition. If SQL Server uses an index, it searches the index itself to find the rows that meet the query condition and then extracts the rows from the table.

When you execute a query (whether within a query tool such as SQL Query Analyzer or from within a custom program), SQL Server chooses between a table scan and searching an index by first determining whether an index exists. Next, the query optimizer identifies whether scanning the table or using the index to retrieve the data will be faster; this choice forms the foundation for the query execution plan.

keys:
The column (or columns) on which you've indexed a table.

As we've already discussed, you can create two types of indexes: clustered and nonclustered. When you define an index, you must identify one or more columns on which you want to base the index. This column (or columns) is referred to as the index's *keys*. A clustered index enables you to configure SQL Server to physically store the rows of a table in order by its keys. For example, if you create a clustered index on the lname column in the customer table of the movies database, SQL Server will write each row that you add to the table in order by last name. So, if your table has customers with last names of Smith, Jones, and Frey, SQL Server will store their rows in the following order: Frey, Jones, and Smith.

You can create a total of 250 indexes per table. Because a clustered index controls how SQL Server stores the rows of a table, and SQL Server can store the rows only in one order, you can define only one clustered index per table. You can create up to 249 nonclustered indexes.

In contrast to a clustered index, a nonclustered index is a separate database object. Similar to a clustered index, you create a nonclustered index by defining its keys, but SQL Server doesn't physically store the rows in the table based on the nonclustered index's keys. Instead, SQL Server stores information in the index, which enables it to find the actual data rows.

So how does SQL Server keep track of indexes? Well, first of all, it stores the information about each table's indexes within the sysindexes system table in each database. In addition, it uses an Index Allocation Map (IAM) page to keep track of the pages and extents allocated to an index—and actually each table as well. Each IAM page can keep track of up to 512,000 pages (roughly 4 GB of data). SQL Server can add more IAM pages as needed.

heap:
A table without a clustered index.

As you saw when we created the tables in the movies database, you can create a table without defining a clustered index. A table for which you haven't defined a clustered index is called a *heap*. A table and indexes can take any one of the following forms:

- A heap, which means you haven't defined a clustered index on the table.

- A clustered index, which means SQL Server will store the table's rows in order by the clustered index's key.

- A nonclustered index based on a heap.

- A nonclustered index based on a clustered index.

Before we look at each of these forms and how SQL Server uses them, let's look a little bit more at how SQL Server organizes an index.

Balanced Tree Architecture

For both clustered and nonclustered indexes, SQL Server uses the Balanced-tree (B-tree) architecture for storing the pages of the index, as shown in Figure 6-1. Keep in mind that, just like your data, SQL Server stores the index information in rows contained in 8 KB pages. The B-tree architecture consists of a root level page, one or more levels of non-leaf level pages (also called intermediate pages), and leaf-level pages. When you query a table and SQL Server uses the index, it navigates each level of the index—from the root level to the leaf-level pages—to retrieve the data.

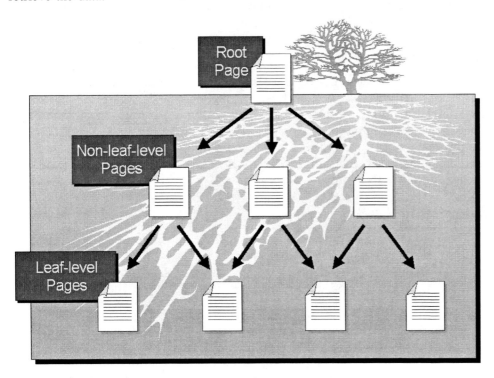

Figure 6-1: *Balanced-tree architecture.*

Here's an analogy for how SQL Server uses the B-tree architecture: think about how you search for a phone number in a phone book. For example, let's say you're looking for the phone number for someone named "Mike Johnson." You begin your search by looking in the Table of Contents to determine where the last names that begin with "J" are stored in the phone book—just as SQL Server starts its search for rows by starting at the root level page of your index. After you know where the "Js" are, you can turn your phone book to that section. Next, you use the range of names listed at the top of each page to narrow your search to a specific page in the phone book. For example, the top of one page might say "Jaworski - Johns, " the next "Johns - Johnson F," and the following page " Johnson G - Jones." This level of your search is analogous to how SQL Server uses the non-leaf level pages of an index. After you've found the phone book page containing the names "Johnson G - Jones," you can find Mike Johnson's phone number. Likewise, after SQL Server has identified the page containing the leaf-level of the index, it can proceed to the leaf-level of the index to retrieve the information you requested in your query.

The key to the B-tree architecture is that all of the levels of the index, from the root level to the leaf-level, are *balanced*. Balanced in this context means that all searches of the index require that SQL Server navigate the same number of index levels and pages. As you add or remove data from a table, SQL Server will automatically merge or split index pages in order to maintain this balance.

Heaps

SQL Server stores the rows within a heap based on the order they were entered. In other words, the rows within a heap aren't stored in any particular order (unless you happen to enter the table's rows in order—which is pretty unlikely). SQL Server uses IAM pages to keep track of the pages allocated to a heap. When you query a table that's a heap, SQL Server queries the sysindexes table to find the location of the first IAM page for the heap. Next, SQL Server queries the IAM page to find all of the pages for the heap.

If you query a table that's a heap and also doesn't have any nonclustered indexes, SQL Server performs a table scan. Keep in mind that the performance will be slow if SQL Server must search through a large number of rows. In addition, SQL Server returns the rows in the order they're stored in the table—which might or might not be the order in which you want them. Because retrieving data based on table scans can be very slow, you'll want to create either a clustered or nonclustered index to improve performance.

Clustered Indexes

In a clustered index, the leaf-level pages of the B-tree architecture contain the table data. So, when SQL Server navigates the levels of a clustered index from the root level to the leaf level, it has actually retrieved the data (instead of a pointer to the data). As you can see, a clustered index will provide you with fast access to a table's data.

It's important that you choose the clustered index's keys carefully. Because the leaf-level pages of the index are the data pages of the table itself, a clustered index is optimized for retrieving a range of rows (instead of only a single row). You should choose the key for your clustered index based on the most common query you will issue against the table to retrieve a range of rows. For example, consider the customer table in the movies database. Typical queries against this table might include retrieving a single customer's information or a list of all customers in alphabetical order or ZIP code order. In this scenario, your clustered index should be on either the lname or zip columns, not the customer number column, because these are the columns you'll typically query to retrieve a range of rows.

SQL Server requires that the values in the clustered index key for a table be unique. You can enforce uniqueness one of three ways: by using a table's primary key as the clustered index key, specifying the UNIQUE keyword when you create the index (which will force you to make all of the values in the clustered index key's column unique), or you can let SQL Server make each clustered index key's value unique. If you let SQL Server make the clustered index key values unique, it appends an internal number called a uniqueifier to each row's data in the clustered index key column. This four-byte number isn't visible to users.

Because creating a clustered index changes the order of a table's rows, you should create a table's clustered index before you create any nonclustered indexes. Otherwise, if you create a nonclustered index first, and then a clustered index, SQL Server must rebuild the nonclustered index.

Nonclustered Indexes

You can build a nonclustered index on top of a table that doesn't have a clustered index (a heap) or a table with a clustered index. The leaf-level pages of a nonclustered index contain *bookmarks*. If your nonclustered index is built on top of a heap, these bookmarks contain a row identifier (RID). An RID consists of the following information: the file number of the database file containing the table, the number of the page containing the data, and the number of the row (in the format file #:page #:row #). When SQL Server navigates the nonclustered index, it retrieves the RID from the leaf-level pages of the index and then retrieves the row itself from the table's pages by using the RID. SQL Server uses Index Allocation Map (IAM) pages to track information about heaps.

If your nonclustered index is built on top of a table with a clustered index, the bookmarks contain the row's clustered index key. When SQL Server navigates the nonclustered index, it retrieves the clustered index key from the leaf-level pages of the index and then navigates the clustered index (using the key) to find the actual data.

Retrieving data by using a nonclustered index requires extra workload than using a clustered index. In the case of a nonclustered index built on a heap, SQL Server must navigate the index first to find the RID, and then retrieve the data. In the case of a nonclustered index built on a clustered index, SQL Server must navigate both the nonclustered and clustered indexes to retrieve the data. If your query retrieves multiple rows, it's possible that SQL Server must read the nonclustered index, then retrieve the data, then read the nonclustered index again, retrieve more data, and so on. If your nonclustered index isn't highly selective (meaning the index doesn't eliminate most of the table's rows), it will be less efficient for SQL Server to retrieve the data using the index than by simply performing a table scan. For example, if you had an employee table containing employee information, a nonclustered index based on an employee's social security number is much more selective than a nonclustered index based on gender. As a rule of thumb, you should aim for your nonclustered indexes to eliminate more than 90 percent of the table; if the index can't eliminate that much of the table, you should simply let SQL Server perform a table scan instead.

SQL Server automatically rebuilds a clustered index whenever any of the following events occur:

- You create a new clustered index.

- You drop an existing clustered index.

- You use the DROP_EXISTING clause to change the columns used as the key for a clustered index.

Deciding Whether to Create an Index

You should consider both the advantages and disadvantages to indexes before you create them. Updating the information in nonclustered indexes adds extra workload for SQL Server; in addition, changing the order of the rows in a table based on your clustered index can also increase the workload. You should make sure that the performance you gain as a result of those indexes outweighs the cost of maintaining them.

Some of the advantages to implementing indexes include:

- Indexes typically make it faster for SQL Server to retrieve data (just as searching through a book without an index can be slow, so can searching through an un-indexed table).
- Indexes speed up queries that join tables and sort or group data.
- Indexes can enforce uniqueness.
- SQL Server maintains a specific sort order (ascending or descending) within the index that's based on the index's keys.

Some of the disadvantages to implementing indexes include:

- Indexes must be selective (result in only a few rows returned for a query) or they lose their value.
- Indexes increase your server's workload because SQL Server must update the indexes whenever you insert, update, or delete data from the table.

TASK 6A-1:

Understanding Index Architecture

1. Name two advantages to implementing a clustered index.

2. On what type of columns should you base a clustered index?

3. Explain the B-tree architecture for indexing.

Guidelines for Defining Indexes

There are several factors you should keep in mind when you are designing the indexes for a database. You should begin by zeroing in on the types of queries and reports you think you might need. Specifically, you should look closely at the WHERE clauses. For example, if you think you will frequently query the movie table by movie title, you should consider creating an index on the movie title column. You should also pay close attention to the order in which you specify columns in your WHERE clauses. For example, if you plan to query the customer table for a specific customer by name and you plan to use the format WHERE lname = 'value' AND fname = 'value', then your index should be based on the lname plus fname columns, not fname plus lname.

Evaluate Table Joins

Be aware of how you will use table joins when you're designing indexes. You typically use table joins (where you request data from more than one table) between tables for which you've defined a primary key to foreign key relationship. While SQL Server automatically creates an index based on a table's primary key, it doesn't create an index on foreign keys. For example, let's say you've configured the movies database so that the primary key column category_num from the category table is linked to the foreign key column category_num in the movie table. If you find that you frequently need a list of all movie titles sorted by category, and you want the result set to display a category's description rather than its number, you will need to use a table join in your query. To speed up the query, you should create an index on the category_num column in the movie table (which is the foreign key).

Identify the Role of Your Database

You should also keep in mind the role of the system for which you're defining indexes. If your database will be used as part of an online transaction processing system (OLTP), it will have frequent changes to its data (inserts, updates, and deletes). In this scenario, it would be better for you to create fewer indexes so that you can minimize your server's workload for updating those indexes. In contrast, if your database will be part of a decision support system, you will typically update it only in batches, and usually not very often. You would be better off in this environment creating more indexes.

Consider the Size and Selectivity of Index Keys

Keep in mind that smaller index keys are more efficient than larger keys. The smaller an index key is, the more index rows SQL Server can store on a page. Storing more index rows on a page improves SQL Server's performance because you decrease the number of I/O operations SQL Server must perform to retrieve information. In addition, you improve the likelihood that most of the index can be cached in RAM.

Another factor you should consider when designing an index is how selective the key is. Don't create an index based on keys that won't eliminate the majority of the rows in the table. If your index will result in SQL Server returning a large number of rows, SQL Server can retrieve those rows faster by using a table scan instead of an index. You can estimate the selectivity of an index by examining its keys and the number of possible unique values in those keys within a table. For example, let's say that you create a nonclustered index based on the customer account column that's also the primary key for the customers table. In this scenario, because the index key is also a primary key, each row must have a unique value in the customer account column. This means that an index based on the customer account column will be highly selective.

Determining the Order to Create Indexes

Remember, if you create a clustered index on a table for which you've already defined nonclustered indexes, SQL Server must rebuild all nonclustered indexes. Wherever possible, you should try to create a table's clustered index before its nonclustered indexes.

Suggested time:

15 minutes

APPLY YOUR KNOWLEDGE 6-1

Designing Indexing for the Movies Database

Objective: In this lab, you're going to analyze the movies database to see if you need any additional indexes. The following table lists the current indexes on your tables. (These indexes were created when you defined primary key constraints.) Use your database diagram for the movies database in SQL Server Enterprise Manager to review the tables and their columns. You can also refer to Appendix A.

Table	Index (Column)	Index Type
Movie	Primary key (movie_num)	Nonclustered
Category	Primary key (category_num)	Nonclustered
Customer	Primary key (cust_num)	Nonclustered
Rental	Primary key (invoice_num)	Nonclustered
Rental_detail	no indexes	

1. The movies database and its associated programs will be used for online transaction processing. What types of reports do you think you will generate from its tables? For example, you might want to print a report that lists all of the rented movies that are due back in today. When you list a report, indicate which table (or tables) you will use to generate that report.

2. Do you think you need any additional indexes? If so, list the table, the columns you will include in the index, indicate whether the index will be clustered or nonclustered, and explain why you need it. For example, you might want to create a clustered index on the title column of the movie table. This is because you might want to be able to retrieve a list of all movie numbers for a particular title—and clustered indexes are optimized for retrieving a group of rows.

TOPIC 6B

Implementing Indexes

Other than the indexes SQL Server automatically creates for the `PRIMARY KEY` and `UNIQUE` constraint columns, you create an index by using the `CREATE INDEX` statement. Use the following syntax:

```
USE database
CREATE index_type INDEX index_name
ON table_name (column_name)
```

When you create an index by using a primary key constraint, SQL Server typically assigns the name of the constraint to the index. You can assign names of your choice to other indexes you create. You should choose names that reflect the index keys so that it's easier for you to identify the purpose of the index. You might also choose to indicate whether the index is clustered or nonclustered by using a prefix such as CL or NC. For example, you might use the following statement to create a nonclustered index on the last name column (lname) in the customer table:

```
USE movies
CREATE NONCLUSTERED INDEX NC_lname
ON customer (lname)
```

You should keep the following factors in mind when creating indexes:

- If you don't specify the type of index, SQL Server automatically makes the index nonclustered.

- You must be the owner of the table in order to execute the CREATE TABLE statement.

- You can create an index based on a view.

- SQL Server tracks information about a database's indexes in the sysindexes table within the database itself.

- SQL Server automatically rebuilds all nonclustered indexes whenever you create a clustered index. When possible, you should try to create your clustered indexes before your nonclustered indexes.

- Make sure you have enough available disk space because building the clustered index can require approximately 1.2 times your table size as working space.

- Double-check that you don't already have an index on the column.

- Select the index's keys based on uniqueness and size.

Configuring the Fill Factor Option

You can use the FILLFACTOR option to configure how full SQL Server will fill an index's pages when it creates the index. Similar to tables, indexes store information in 8 KB pages. When an index page becomes full, SQL Server must split the index page and move some of its rows to a new page. This process of splitting an index page has an impact on your server's performance. By using a fill factor, you can configure how full SQL Server will make an index's leaf-level pages. If you build an index with a fill factor of 100 percent, SQL Server will fill each of the index's pages completely. As users add data to the table, SQL Server must update the index's information. If all pages of the index are completely full, SQL Server must split a page to accommodate the new data. By contrast, if you build an index with a lower fill factor, SQL Server will not fill each page of the index completely. So, as users add data, SQL Server won't have to split pages within the index as often. Using an index with a lower fill factor, such as 50 percent, improves SQL Server's performance when you're adding data to the table.

As an index is updated over time (as a result of users adding rows to a table), SQL Server doesn't maintain the fill factor percentage. It simply uses the fill factor percentage when it builds the index. If you want to re-establish the fill factor after you've added data to a table, you must rebuild the index.

You can specify a fill factor percentage with each index you create, or you can set the fill factor for your server by using the `sp_configure` stored procedure. By default, SQL Server configures your server with a fill factor of 0, which means it will fill all leaf-level index pages as full as possible and leave room for one non-leaf level entry. If you don't specify a fill factor percentage when you create an index, SQL Server uses the percentage set for your server. You should use a low fill factor for an OLTP environment. In contrast, you should use a high fill factor for indexes in decision support systems because the data in the tables won't change very often. You can use the guidelines in the following table to choose a fill factor for your indexes.

Remember, if you rebuild a clustered index, SQL Server automatically rebuilds the nonclustered indexes. For this reason, the easiest way to rebuild all indexes is to simply rebuild the clustered index, and SQL Server will do the rest.

Percentage	Pages	Type of Activity	Environment
0	Leaf-level: fill completely; Non-leaf-level: leave room for two index entries	Light	Mixed (OLTP and DSS)
1 – 99	Leaf-level: fill to specified percentage; Non-leaf-level: leave room for two index entries	Medium to heavy	OLTP
100	Leaf-level: fill completely; Non-leaf-level: leave room for two index entries	No changes	DSS

You use the following syntax to set the fill factor when you create an index:

```
USE database
CREATE index_type INDEX index_name
ON table_name (column_name)
WITH FILLFACTOR = percentage
```

If you change the fill factor percentage for your server, SQL Server will use this percentage for all new indexes you create unless you specify otherwise. Use the following syntax to set the fill factor for your server:

```
sp_configure 'fill factor', percentage
```

You can view your server's current fill factor setting by executing:

```
sp_configure 'fill factor'
```

Configuring the Pad Index Option

You use the pad index option to specify that SQL Server also leave free space in the non-leaf-level pages of your index in addition to leaving room in the leaf-level pages. Use the following syntax:

```
USE database
CREATE index_type INDEX index_name
ON table_name (column_name)
WITH PAD_INDEX, FILLFACTOR = percentage
```

SQL Server reserves room in the non-leaf-level pages based on the fill factor percentage you specify. If you don't include the PAD_INDEX option in the CREATE INDEX statement, SQL Server doesn't reserve room in the non-leaf-level pages (other than room for two new index entries). You should consider using the PAD_INDEX option on an OLTP system.

Viewing Index Information

Use the sp_helpindex and sp_help stored procedures to view information about a table's indexes. Use sp_helpindex 'table_name' to view only the indexes defined for a table. Use sp_help table_name to view all information about a table including its indexes.

TASK 6B-1:

Creating a Clustered Index on the Movie Table

Setup: You're logged on to Windows 2000 as student#. You've created a database named movies, and tables within it named movie, category, customer, rental, and rental_detail. You've defined primary key, foreign key, default, and check constraints on the tables, and created nonclustered indexes based on your primary keys. You've imported data into the tables.

1. **Start SQL Query Analyzer and select the movies database.**

2. **Execute the following query:**

```
CREATE CLUSTERED INDEX CL_title
ON movie (title)
```

Use this query to define a clustered index for the movie table based on the title column. This index will enable you to quickly find all tapes for a particular title.

3. **Execute a new query:**

```
sp_helpindex 'movie'
```

	index_name	index_description	index_keys
1	CL_title	clustered located on PRIMARY	title
2	PK_movie	nonclustered, unique, primary key located on PRIMARY	movie_num

You can use sp_helpindex to view a list of the indexes defined for the movie table. You should see that the movie table has two indexes: CL_title, a clustered index on the movie title, and PK_movie, a nonclustered index on the movie_num column. (You created the PK_movie index when you defined the primary key constraint on the movie table.)

4. **Clear the Query window.**

Creating Composite Indexes

If you want to search a table based on two or more columns, you can define a composite index. For example, if you plan to frequently use a query in which your WHERE clause includes two columns, you should create a composite index on those two columns. You can combine up to 16 columns in a composite index, but the total width of all columns that make up the index key can't exceed 900 bytes. You should put the most unique column first in the composite index. Also, put the column that you will use first in your WHERE clause first in the index. After you've created a composite index, make sure that your WHERE clause specifies the columns in the same order. If you don't use the columns in the same order, SQL Server can't use the index.

Use the following syntax to create a composite index:

```
USE database
CREATE index_type INDEX index_name
ON table_name (column_name_1, column_name_2)
```

You can use both the FILLFACTOR and PAD_INDEX options when you create a composite index.

APPLY YOUR KNOWLEDGE 6-2

Suggested time:
15 minutes

Creating Indexes

   Objective: To create the remaining indexes for the movies database.

1.   In SQL Query Analyzer, create a clustered index on the customer table based on the ZIP code column. Name the index CL_zip. Write your query in the following space.

2.   On the customer table, create a nonclustered composite index based on the lname and fname columns. Name the index NC_lname_fname. Write your query here.

3.   On the rental table, create a clustered index based on the cust_num column. Name the index CL_cust_num. Write your query in the following space.

4.   On the rental_detail table, create a clustered index on the invoice_num column. Name the index CL_invoice_num. Record your query here.

5.   On the rental_detail table, create a nonclustered index on the movie_num column. Name the index NC_movie_num. Write your query here.

6. On the movie table, create a nonclustered index on the category_num column. Name the index NC_category_num.

7. Use the `sp_helpindex` stored procedure to verify the indexes on all tables in the movies database.

8. Clear the Query window.

Creating a Unique Index

If you want to enforce uniqueness on a column, Microsoft recommends that instead of creating a unique index, you define a unique constraint on that column instead and SQL Server will automatically create a unique index for you.

As you know, when you define the primary key for a table, SQL Server automatically creates a unique index for that column. You can have only one primary key per table. If you have another column in which the data is inherently unique, you can create a unique index on that column. You can create unique indexes by using the syntax:

```
CREATE UNIQUE INDEX index_name
ON table_name (column_name)
```

You'll receive an error message when you run this statement if the column on which you want to create the index contains duplicate values. You can use the following query to determine if a column has duplicate values before you attempt to create a unique index:

```
SELECT column_name,
COUNT(column_name) AS [number of duplicates]
FROM table_name
GROUP BY column_name
HAVING COUNT(column_name) > 1
ORDER BY column_name
```

For example, if you want to determine if a customer has more than one rental invoice in the rental table, you could use the following query:

```
SELECT cust_num, COUNT(cust_num) AS [number of duplicates]
FROM rental
GROUP BY cust_num
HAVING COUNT(cust_num) > 1
ORDER BY cust_num
```

The results set for this query enables you to see each customer number that has more than one rental invoice in the table.

Dropping an Index

If you find that you no longer need an index, you should drop it so that your server won't have the overhead of maintaining it. Use the following syntax to drop an index:

```
USE database
DROP INDEX table_name.index_name
```

In order to drop an index, you must be the owner of the table; in addition, you must be using the database in order to drop one of its indexes. You can't use a fully qualified name to reference the index to drop it. SQL Server automatically reclaims the disk space whenever you drop an index. (If you drop a table, SQL

Server will automatically delete its indexes.) If you drop a clustered index, SQL Server automatically rebuilds the table's nonclustered indexes. You can't drop indexes created as a result of PRIMARY KEY or UNIQUE constraints. Instead, you must drop the constraints themselves.

APPLY YOUR KNOWLEDGE 6-3

Suggested time:
10 minutes

Dropping an Index

Objective: To drop and re-create an index.

1. In SQL Query Analyzer, attempt to drop the index named PK_movie from the movie table. Record the query you used and its results in the following space.

2. Drop the clustered index named CL_title from the movie table. Record your query here.

3. Re-create the index named CL_title. (This index is based on the title column of the movie table.)

4. Clear the Query window.

Using the Sysindexes Table

Now that we've looked at the different types of indexes you can create and how you create them, let's move on to how SQL Server keeps track of those indexes. SQL Server uses the sysindexes table as its "one-stop shop" for information about indexes. For example, SQL Server can use the sysindexes table to determine if a table is a heap or has a clustered index and whether any nonclustered indexes exist for the table. In addition, it uses the sysindexes table to find the IAM page for each table or index. You can use the columns within the sysindexes table to determine a lot of information about an object, including:

- Use the indid column to determine if the object is a heap, clustered index, or a nonclustered index. Use the following table as a guideline for identifying the type of object.

Indid Value	Type of Object
0	Heap.
1	Clustered index.
2 to 250	Nonclustered index.
255	Tracks the location of text, ntext, or image pages for a table. (You'll see this type of object only if you've defined a column within the table as using the text, ntext, or image data types.)

- Identify the location of the first IAM page by using the FirstIAM column.

- Determine the root page of a clustered or nonclustered index B-tree by using the root column.

SQL Server uses the id column in the sysindexes table to identify each object (table or index). Unfortunately, the sysindexes table doesn't contain the table names associated with an index. You can get around this drawback by joining the sysindexes table to the sysobjects table so that you can retrieve the name of the table. Here's the syntax:

```
SELECT o.name AS [Table Name], i.name AS [Index Name],
i.indid AS [Index ID], i.FirstIAM
FROM sysobjects AS o JOIN sysindexes AS i
ON o.id = i.id
WHERE o.id > 100
ORDER BY o.name
```

In this syntax, we're joining the sysindexes table to the sysobjects table to retrieve the table name, and then finding information about that object in the sysindexes table. (We use the phrase "object" because we can look at either a table that's a heap or an index using this query.) Using the WHERE o.id > 100 clause enables us to select only those objects that aren't system objects from the sysobjects table. In addition, we're using an inner join so our results set shows only those objects with associated rows in the sysindexes table.

TASK 6B-2:

Viewing the Information in Sysindexes

1. In SQL Query Analyzer, **execute the following query:**

```
SELECT o.name AS [Table Name], i.name AS [Index Name],
i.indid AS [Index ID], i.FirstIAM
FROM sysobjects AS o JOIN sysindexes AS i
ON o.id = i.id
WHERE o.id > 100
ORDER BY o.name
```

2. **Look at the results set.** You can see the name of the table and each index you've defined for the table, along with the indid and First IAM columns for each index. Your values in the FirstIAM column might be different from what you see in the following graphic.

	Table Name	Index Name	indid	firstiam
1	category	category	0	0x690000000100
2	category	PK_category	2	0x6B0000000100
3	category	_WA_Sys_description_77BFCB91	3	0x000000000000
4	customer	CL_zip	1	0x6F0000000100
5	customer	PK_customer	2	0x880000000100
6	customer	NC_lname_fname	3	0x730000000100

3. **Look at the indid column for the category table. What types of indexes have you defined on the category table? How can you tell?**

4. **What types of indexes have you defined on the movie table? What are the names of the indexes?**

5. **Clear the Query window.**

TOPIC 6C

Maintaining Indexes

One of the problems you can encounter with indexes is that they can become fragmented over time. Fragmentation occurs when you make changes to the data in a table. These changes include adding or deleting rows from a table as well as updating the value stored in an index's key column. As you make changes to a table's data, the index pages can end up spread across many pages, and each might have a very low *row density*. Depending on your database environment, this fragmentation can be either good or bad. In an online transaction processing environment, a low row density on your index pages can be beneficial because SQL Server won't have to split the pages to accommodate new data. In this case, fragmentation works very similar to a fill factor. In contrast, fragmentation of indexes in a decision support system (DSS) environment can be detrimental to your server's performance because SQL Server will have to retrieve more index pages in order to scan the index.

row density:
A measure of the number of rows stored on a data page. A high row density means that you have a greater number of rows per page. In contrast, a low row density means that you have only a few rows per page.

If you rebuild a clustered index, SQL Server automatically rebuilds the table's nonclustered indexes, but it uses the default fill factor configured for your server for those indexes.

You can use three methods to manage index fragmentation: you can drop and re-create a table's clustered index (and specify a new fill factor percentage); you can rebuild a specific index and specify a fill factor percentage; or you can use the DBCC INDEXDEFRAG statement to defragment the leaf level pages of both clustered and nonclustered indexes. Before we look at how you go about defragmenting an index, let's look at how you can determine if in fact an index is fragmented.

Displaying Fragmentation Statistics

You can use the DBCC SHOWCONTIG statement to view fragmentation information about the indexes on a specific table or view. The results set enables you to determine whether a table or index is heavily fragmented, as well as how full a table or index's pages are (row density). You can use the table name or ID, view name or ID, or index name or ID with the DBCC SHOWCONTIG statement. You can find a table or view's ID number by querying the sysobjects table, and an index's ID number by querying the sysindexes table, as follows:

```
USE database
SELECT id FROM sysindexes
WHERE name = 'index_name'
```

If you want to view additional information about an index, you should include other columns such as origfillfactor, reserved, and used in your SELECT statement. For example, the origfillfactor column enables you to view the fill factor percentage for the index. The reserved and used columns enable you to view how much space in the database is reserved for the index, and of that space, how much is currently in use.

When you're ready to analyze a table or index, use the following syntax:

```
DBCC SHOWCONTIG (table_id | table_name | view_name | view_id[,
index_name | index_id)
[WITH options]
```

In this syntax, you can specify only the table or view information, which means that SQL Server will display information about all indexes on the table or view, or you can identify a specific index for the table or view. If you specify only a table or view name, SQL Server checks the fragmentation of the table or view. For example, you use the following query to have SQL Server check the fragmentation for the movie table:

```
DBCC SHOWCONTIG (movie)
```

In contrast, you use this query if you want to check the fragmentation of the movie table's PK_movie index:

```
DBCC SHOWCONTIG (movie, PK_movie)
```

The DBCC SHOWCONTIG statement supports several different options. For example, you can use the WITH ALL_INDEXES option to have SQL Server check the fragmentation on all indexes for a specific table or view. We describe some of the options you can use with DBCC SHOWCONTIG in the following table.

Option Clause	Configures SQL Server to	Example
[WITH ALL_INDEXES]	Check fragmentation statistics for all indexes on a particular table or view.	DBCC SHOWCONTIG (movie)WITH ALL_INDEXES
[WITH FAST] [, ALL_INDEXES]	Perform a fast check of indexes, which means that SQL Server scans only the non-leaf level pages of the index. If you use WITH FAST, SQL Server scans only the index you specify. Using WITH FAST, ALL_INDEXES enables SQL Server to perform a fast check of all of a table or view's indexes.	DBCC SHOWCONTIG (movie)WITH FAST, ALL_INDEXES

```
DBCC SHOWCONTIG scanning 'movie' table...
Table: 'movie' (1977058079); index ID: 1, database ID: 7
TABLE level scan performed.
- Pages Scanned...........................: 1
- Extents Scanned..........................: 1
- Extent Switches..........................: 0
- Avg. Pages per Extent....................: 1.0
- Scan Density [Best Count:Actual Count].......: 100.00% [1:1]
- Logical Scan Fragmentation ................: 0.00%
- Extent Scan Fragmentation ...................: 0.00%
- Avg. Bytes Free per Page...................: 193.0
- Avg. Page Density (full)..................: 97.62%
DBCC execution completed. If DBCC printed error messages, contact your system administrator.
```

Figure 6-2: *Sample output of the* DBCC SHOWCONTIG *command.*

When you run the DBCC SHOWCONTIG command, SQL Server displays a lot of information that you use to analyze an object's fragmentation. You can see what the output from DBCC SHOWCONTIG looks like in Figure 6-2. The following table describes the information you see in the results set from running DBCC SHOWCONTIG and how you can use this information.

Remember, a fragmented index might or might not be a bad thing. In an OLTP environment, fragmentation can improve performance because SQL Server won't have to split pages as you add rows to the index or table.

Statistic	Enables You to Determine
Pages Scanned	The total number of pages that make up the table or index.
Extents Scanned	The total number of extents that make up the table or index.
Extent Switches	How often DBCC had to change extents when it was scanning the table or index.
Average Pages Per Extent	How many pages are in the extent chain that makes up the table or index.
Scan Density [Best Count: Actual Count]	The ideal number of extent changes SQL Server would have to make if the table or index is contiguous (Best Count), and the actual number of extent changes SQL Server had to make to analyze the table or index (Actual Count). This number is represented as a percentage, and it's calculated by dividing the Best Count by the Actual Count. You use this percentage to determine how contiguous an index or table is. A value of 100 percent indicates the object is 100 percent contiguous. A lower value indicates that the object is fragmented.

Statistic	Enables You to Determine
Logical Scan Fragmentation	What percentage of an index's pages are out-of-order, which means that the next page pointer in the IAM page contains a different value than that of the next page pointer in the index itself. This number doesn't mean anything if you're analyzing a table that's a heap or a text index.
Extent Scan Fragmentation	What percentage of an index's extents are out-of-order. This means that given a current extent, the next extent for the index is not physically next (contiguous) to the current extent. This number doesn't mean anything if you're analyzing a heap.
Average Bytes Free Per Page	The number of free bytes per page in the index or table. This statistic doesn't take into account row size. A higher number indicates higher page fragmentation. A lower number of free bytes per page indicates greater row density and less fragmentation.
Average Page Density (Full)	How full the index or table's pages are. This calculation does take into account the size of a row, unlike Average Bytes Free Per Page. For this reason, this number is a more accurate indication of page density. A higher percentage indicates fuller pages and lower fragmentation; a lower percentage indicates that the index pages are less full and have higher fragmentation.

Rebuilding an Index

As we've said, one of the ways you can counteract fragmentation is to rebuild an index with the DBCC DBREINDEX statement. Here's the syntax:

```
DBCC DBREINDEX ('database.owner.table', index_name, fillfactor)
```

In this syntax, you can replace *fillfactor* with the percentage to which you want SQL Server to fill the index's pages. If you specify a fill factor percentage of 0, SQL Server rebuilds the index with the fill factor you previously used when you created the index. Specifying a different percentage overrides the index's previous fill factor setting.

TASK 6C-1:

Rebuilding an Index

Objective: To rebuild the movie table's clustered index on the title column with a fill factor of 50 percent.

1. In SQL Query Analyzer, **execute the following query:**

    ```
    SELECT id, indid, reserved, used, origfillfactor, name
    FROM sysindexes
    WHERE name = 'CL_title'
    ```

This query enables you to view statistics about the clustered index you defined on the movie table.

2. **Look at the index's fill factor.** Because you didn't specify a fill factor percentage when you created the index, SQL Server automatically used the fill factor set for your server. By default, SQL Setup configures your server with a fill factor of 0, which means that your server will fill the index pages as full as possible.

	Updated	Rows	Rows Sampled	Steps	Density	Average key length
1	May 23 2001 8:41AM	156	156	37	6.4102565E-3	19.685898

3. **Execute the query:**

```
DBCC SHOWCONTIG (movie, CL_title)
```

```
DBCC SHOWCONTIG scanning 'movie' table...
Table: 'movie' (1977058079); index ID: 1, database ID: 7
TABLE level scan performed.
- Pages Scanned..............................: 1
- Extents Scanned............................: 1
- Extent Switches............................: 0
- Avg. Pages per Extent......................: 1.0
- Scan Density [Best Count:Actual Count].....: 100.00% [1:1]
- Logical Scan Fragmentation ................: 0.00%
- Extent Scan Fragmentation .................: 0.00%
- Avg. Bytes Free per Page...................: 193.0
- Avg. Page Density (full)...................: 97.62%
DBCC execution completed. If DBCC printed error messages, contact your system administrator.
```

You use this query to view the statistics for the CL_title index. The Scan Density indicates how contiguous the index is, so a value of 100 percent means the index is contiguous (no fragmentation). A number below 100 percent would indicate fragmentation. The numbers after the Scan Density Percentage, [Best Count: Actual Count], indicate the ideal number of extent changes that would be present if everything were contiguously linked (Best Count) and the actual number of extent changes (Actual Count). Based on the amount of data in the movie table, SQL Server is using one 8 KB page to store the clustered index (and thus the table itself).

4. **How full are the CL_title index's pages? What statistic do you use to find this information?**

5. **Execute a new query:**

```
DBCC DBREINDEX ('movies.dbo.movie', CL_title, 30)
```

This query rebuilds the clustered index on the movie table with a fill factor of 30 percent. You should see that SQL Server also automatically rebuilt the nonclustered indexes of the movie table. SQL Server also changes the fill factor percentage on the nonclustered indexes for the table to 30 percent. You can verify this by examining each index's properties in sysindexes.

6. **Execute the following query:**

```
SELECT id, indid, reserved, used, origfillfactor, name
FROM sysindexes
WHERE name = 'CL_title'
```

You can see that the fill factor has changed for the CL_title index.

7. **Execute the following query** to determine the fill factor for all of the movie table's indexes:

```
SELECT o.name AS [Table Name], i.name AS [Index Name],
i.origfillfactor AS [Fill Factor]
FROM sysobjects AS o JOIN sysindexes AS i
ON o.id = i.id
WHERE o.name = 'movie'
```

8. **Execute the following query:**

```
DBCC SHOWCONTIG (movie, CL_title)
```

You can see that the Average Page Density (Full) is 30 percent or less. Notice that the index now uses four pages to store its data.

```
DBCC SHOWCONTIG scanning 'movie' table...
Table: 'movie' (1977058079); index ID: 1, database ID: 7
TABLE level scan performed.
- Pages Scanned.............................: 4
- Extents Scanned...........................: 2
- Extent Switches...........................: 1
- Avg. Pages per Extent.....................: 2.0
- Scan Density [Best Count:Actual Count].......: 50.00% [1:2]
- Logical Scan Fragmentation ................: 0.00%
- Extent Scan Fragmentation .................: 50.00%
- Avg. Bytes Free per Page...................: 6120.3
- Avg. Page Density (full)...................: 24.39%
DBCC execution completed. If DBCC printed error messages, contact your system administrator.
```

9. **The Scan Density [Best Count: Actual Count] for the CL_title index (and thus the movie table) is now 50 percent. Is this a problem?**

Using DROP_EXISTING to Change an Index

You can use the `DROP_EXISTING` keyword with the `CREATE INDEX` statement to change an index's characteristics—without having to first drop the index and then re-create it. You can use `DROP_EXISTING` clause to change the following index characteristics:

- Change the index's key to a different column.
- Add or remove columns from a composite index.
- Configure the index to be unique or not unique.
- Change the `FILLFACTOR` and `PAD_INDEX` options. Use this option to correct problems with fragmentation.

You can also use the `DROP_EXISTING` keyword to change a nonclustered index to a clustered index, but not a clustered index to nonclustered. If you want to change a clustered index to a nonclustered index, you must drop the index and re-create it. Remember, if you change a nonclustered index to a clustered index, SQL Server can use up to 1.2 times the size of your table during the rebuilding process.

Here's the syntax:

```
CREATE index_type INDEX index_name
ON table_name (column_name)
WITH DROP_EXISTING[, FILLFACTOR = percent]
```

For example, if you want to re-create the PK_movie nonclustered index (based on the primary key column movie_num) and configure it with a fill factor of 60 percent, you can use the following query:

```
CREATE NONCLUSTERED INDEX pk_movie
ON movie (movie_num)
WITH DROP_EXISTING, FILLFACTOR = 60
```

Using DBCC INDEXDEFRAG to Defragment an Index

The third technique you can use to defragment an index is the DBCC INDEXDEFRAG statement. You use this statement to defragment the leaf-level pages of clustered and nonclustered indexes. In this scenario, SQL Server defragments the index by re-arranging the order of the pages that make up the leaf-level of the index. This re-arranging enables SQL Server to order the pages in sequence from left to right, which is the order in which it scans the index information. You can use DBCC INDEXDEFRAG to perform the following tasks:

If your index is very fragmented, it's often faster for you to rebuild the index instead of defragmenting it.

- Perform defragmentation with a minimum of locking. This makes it easier for your users to continue working while SQL Server defragments the index.

- Defragment indexes that span multiple files. Note: This command can't move an index's pages from one file to another.

- Determine the percentage of completion during defragmentation.

- Compact the pages of an index based on the fill factor you specified when you created the index.

Here's the syntax:

```
DBCC INDEXDEFRAG ({database_name | database_id | 0
, {table_name | table_id | 'view_name' | view_id}
, {index_name | index_id})
[WITH NO_INFOMSGS]
```

In this syntax, you can use 0 for the database and SQL Server will look for the table and index you specify in the current database. In the following example, we're defragmenting the CL_title index associated with the movie table:

```
DBCC INDEXDEFRAG (movies, movie, CL_title)
```

TASK 6C-2:

Using DROP_EXISTING to Re-create an Index Based on a Primary Key

1. In SQL Query Analyzer, **execute the following query:**

   ```
   CREATE UNIQUE NONCLUSTERED INDEX PK_movie
   ON movie (movie_num)
   WITH DROP_EXISTING, FILLFACTOR = 60
   ```

   You must use the UNIQUE keyword because the PK_movie index is based on the primary key constraint.

2. **Execute a new query:**

```
SELECT name, origfillfactor
FROM sysindexes
WHERE name = 'PK_movie'
```

You use this query to verify that the PK_movie index now has a fill factor of 60 percent.

3. **Clear the Query window.**

Using SQL Profiler

One of the handiest utilities in SQL Server 2000 is the Index Tuning Wizard. You can use this wizard to analyze the typical queries you perform on your server, and have it make recommendations on indexes you should create to improve the performance of those queries. This wizard can also make recommendations as to when an indexed view will improve performance. You'll need to capture the queries in SQL Profiler before you can analyze them with the Index Tuning Wizard. Let's start this process by looking at SQL Profiler first. You can use SQL Profiler to monitor your server and its databases, including user logins, user activity, and application activity. The information you obtain in SQL Profiler is sometimes called a trace. Before you begin using SQL Profiler, you should determine what you want to monitor on your server. The following table describes some of the information you can monitor within SQL Profiler.

Information to Monitor	Enables You to
Queries	Analyze the performance of a query and to identify queries that perform full table scans (and thus reduce the performance of the server).
Users	Monitor the activities performed by specific users or applications. You can also monitor login attempts, login failures, connections, and disconnections.
Hard Disk	Monitor disk reads and writes.
CPU	Monitor CPU utilization at the Transact-SQL statement level.
Locks	Identify any deadlock problems.
Errors	Monitor any errors that occur on your server.

You can capture the information in SQL Profiler to a table, file, or SQL script to analyze it later. You can analyze information in SQL Profiler as it's recorded. If you capture the information to a file, you can then replay the trace on the same server or a different server. You might want to replay a trace on a different server to test different hardware combinations. You can also use this trace file with the Index Tuning Wizard to analyze the indexes associated with a particular database. Finally, you can use the trace file to analyze SQL statements and stored procedures to debug an application.

TASK 6C-3:

Generating a Workload File in SQL Profiler

Objective: To prepare a file for analysis in the Index Tuning Wizard.

1. From the Microsoft SQL Server menu, **choose Profiler** to start SQL Profiler.

2. **Choose File→New→Trace.** When prompted, **log on to your server with Windows Authentication** to open the Trace Properties dialog box.

3. In the Trace Name text box, **type** *workload* to define a name for your trace file.

4. **Look at the Template Name.** By default, SQL Profiler configures your trace to use the Standard template for capturing server information. This template tracks logins and logouts, user connections, execution of stored procedures, and execution of SQL statements. This information is all you need for analyzing indexing with the Index Tuning Wizard.

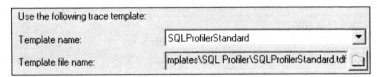

5. **Check Save To File** to specify that you want to capture the workload on your server to a file. SQL Profiler automatically displays the Save As dialog box and gives the file the name of workload.trc.

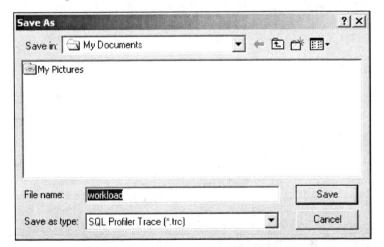

6. **Look at the default path for trace files.** SQL Profiler automatically saves your file to your user's My Documents folder.

7. **Click Save** to create the trace file.

8. **Click Run** to close the Trace Properties dialog box and begin capturing your server's workload to a file. You should see that SQL Profiler begins to capture information to the trace file.

9. **Switch to SQL Query Analyzer.** You're going to use SQL Query Analyzer to execute queries against the movies database so that you can analyze its indexes.

10. **Load the SQL script C:\Data\queries.sql.** This file contains three typical queries you might execute against the movies database. (Each query is preceded by a comment statement.) You can use these queries to generate a sample workload for your server.

```
Query - SQLSERVER2.movies.CLASSROOM\student2 - E:\Data\Queries.sql                    _|□|x|
/*These queries generate a sample workload on your server. */

USE movies

/*Query to list all movies in a specific category. */
SELECT *
FROM movie
WHERE category_num = '1'
ORDER BY title

/*Query to list each invoice, the customer number, the movie they rented, and the title.*/
SELECT r.invoice_num, r.cust_num, rd.movie_num, m.title
FROM rental AS r, rental_detail AS rd, movie AS m
WHERE rd.invoice_num = r.invoice_num AND rd.movie_num = m.movie_num

/*Query to list each invoice, the date of the rental, the date the movies were due, and the movie number.*/
SELECT r.invoice_num, r.rental_date, r.due_date, rd.line_num, rd.movie_num
FROM rental AS r INNER JOIN rental_detail AS rd
ON r.invoice_num = rd.invoice_num
ORDER BY r.invoice_num
```

11. **Run each query individually by highlighting it with your mouse.** (After you've highlighted a query, you can execute it by pressing [Ctrl]E or by clicking the Execute Query button on the toolbar.) We're using these queries to generate a workload on your server. You can also execute other queries of your own choice.

12. In SQL Query Analyzer, **open a new Query window, and then close the window containing the queries.sql script file.**

13. **Switch to SQL Profiler.**

14. **Choose File→Stop Trace** to stop capturing the workload in SQL Profiler.

15. **Close SQL Profiler.**

Using the Index Tuning Wizard

After you've generated a workload file in SQL Profiler, you can use the Index Tuning Wizard to analyze the workload and the tables in a database to identify any additional indexes you might need. The Index Tuning Wizard works by analyzing the cost of various methods of retrieving the data for your queries, including both table scans and indexes. In addition, the wizard will also tell you the cost of implementing its recommendations.

Use the following steps to analyze your indexes with the Index Tuning Wizard:

1. Generate a workload file. This workload file must represent typical database activity such as queries against the database. A workload file can be either a SQL script or captured information from SQL Profiler.

2. Analyze the workload file by using the Index Tuning Wizard.

3. Implement recommendations. You can implement the recommendations immediately, or specify a date (SQL Server Agent then runs these tasks), or save them as a script file.

The Index Tuning Wizard doesn't provide recommendations for the following scenarios:

- You've distributed database queries that access tables that don't exist in the local database.

- Indexes for system tables.

- Columns with `PRIMARY KEY` and `UNIQUE` constraints defined.

- Queries that use quoted identifiers instead of square brackets.

- Tables without enough data.

- If the Index Tuning Wizard's suggested indexes don't offer enough projected improvement in query performance, it won't provide you with any recommendations.

APPLY YOUR KNOWLEDGE 6-4

Suggested time:
15 minutes

Using the Index Tuning Wizard

Objective: To use the Index Tuning Wizard to analyze the workload.trc file you created in SQL Profiler.

1. Start SQL Server Enterprise Manager. In the console tree, select your server. Run the Index Tuning Wizard. (Choose Tools→Wizards. In the Select Wizard dialog box, expand the Management category; then select Index Tuning Wizard.) Use the following information as you go through the wizard:

    - On the Select Server And Database page, choose the movies database. Leave Keep All Existing Indexes and Add Indexed Views checked. Set the Tuning Mode to Thorough. (Because the movies database is small, it won't take long for SQL Server to perform a thorough analysis.)

    - On the Specify Workload page, select My Workload File, and then select the workload.trc file.

    - On the Select Tables To Tune page, click Select All Tables so that the wizard can analyze all tables.

2. When the Index Tuning Wizard is done, observe the recommended indexes for the movies database. Did the wizard recommend any new indexes? If so, what performance increase can you expect as a result?

3. On the Index Recommendations page, click Analysis to view a report of the indexes used in your queries. This report enables you to see what percentage each index was used to retrieve the data in your queries. You can also see the size of each index. Don't save this report.

4. On the Index Recommendations page, click Next. If the Index Tuning Wizard had suggested any new indexes, you would see the Schedule Index Update Job page. You use this page to schedule jobs or create a script file. Click Finish to close the wizard, and then click OK.

5. Close SQL Server Enterprise Manager.

Managing Index Statistics

SQL Server stores statistics in the statblob column within the sysindexes table.

SQL Server automatically creates and maintains statistics about index columns and their data for use by the query optimizer. You should be aware that SQL Server maintains statistics only on the first column of a composite index. The query optimizer uses this statistical information to identify whether performing a table scan or using an index will be more efficient when it retrieves data. SQL Server automatically updates statistics as you insert or modify data into columns.

Creating Statistics

By default, SQL Server enables the Auto Create Statistics option on any new databases you create. This option enables SQL Server to automatically create statistics for any indexed columns that contain data. In addition, SQL Server automatically creates statistics for any non-indexed columns you use in table joins or a WHERE clause. SQL Server creates these statistics when it attempts to optimize a query for which there aren't any statistics.

You can manually force SQL Server to create index statistics by using the CREATE STATISTICS statement. You use this statement to define additional statistics for non-indexed columns or for columns other than the first column within a composite index by using the following syntax:

```
CREATE STATISTICS statistics_name
ON {table_name | view_name} (column_name,...)
```

You typically name your statistics STATS_*column_name*. You can drop statistics by using the syntax DROP STATISTICS *statistics_name*.

Updating Statistics

By default, SQL Server also enables the Auto Update Statistics option for any new database you create. SQL Server automatically updates the statistics for a table and its indexes whenever they become outdated. Statistics become outdated when you make a large number of updates to a table relative to its size. If necessary, you can manually force SQL Server to update its statistics by using the UPDATE STATISTICS statement. You might want to force an update of statistics if you create an index on an empty table and then populate it later or execute the TRUNCATE TABLE statement to delete all rows from a table. To update the statistics of all indexes for a table, use the following query:

```
UPDATE STATISTICS table_name | view_name [index_name |
(statistics_name[, ...])]
```

To update statistics for a specific index, use this query:

```
UPDATE STATISTICS table_name index_name
```

When you run the UPDATE STATISTICS statement, SQL Server selects a sample of the rows on which to base the statistics. SQL Server selects the size of the sample based on the size of the table. If you want SQL Server to base the statistics on all rows in the table or on a specific percentage of rows, you can use either the FULLSCAN or SAMPLE options. The FULLSCAN option specifies that you want SQL Server to calculate the statistics based on all rows in the table. Use the SAMPLE option to specify a percentage or number of rows. You can use the following syntax with the FULLSCAN or SAMPLE options:

```
UPDATE STATISTICS table_name
WITH [FULLSCAN | SAMPLE number {PERCENT | ROWS}]
```

When you use SAMPLE, specify a number followed by either PERCENT (if the number is a percentage) or ROWS (if the number identifies a specific row count). If the sample size you specify is too small to generate accurate statistics, SQL Server will automatically adjust your sample size.

You can also use the sp_updatestats stored procedure to update the statistics for all tables within a particular database. Use the following syntax:

```
USE database_name
EXEC sp_updatestats
```

Determining When Statistics Were Last Updated

You can use the DBCC SHOW_STATISTICS or STATS_DATE statements to determine when SQL Server last updated an index's statistics. Here's the syntax for DBCC SHOW_STATISTICS:

```
DBCC SHOW_STATISTICS (table_name, index_name)
```

Some of the information the DBCC SHOW_STATISTICS statement enables you to view includes:

- The date and time SQL Server last updated statistics.

- The total number of rows in the table.

- The total number of rows SQL Server sampled to update the table's statistics.

- How many rows SQL Server skipped over when sampling data (called distribution steps).

- The average length of an index's key.

Use the following syntax for the STATS_DATE statement:

```
STATS_DATE (table_id, index_id)
```

Remember, you can obtain the table index ID numbers by querying the sysobjects and sysindexes tables.

Turning Off Statistics

SQL Server automatically updates index statistics whenever the query optimizer detects that the statistics are no longer current. Although Microsoft recommends that you not turn off these automatic updates, you can turn them off by using the UPDATE STATISTICS statement with the WITH NORECOMPUTE option. The only plausible scenario where you might consider turning off automatic statistics would be if your data is relatively static (meaning you make very few inserts, updates, and deletes to the tables) and you need to reduce your server's overhead.

To turn off automatic statistics with the UPDATE STATISTICS statement, use the following syntax:

```
UPDATE STATISTICS table_name
WITH NORECOMPUTE
```

This statement will turn off automatic statistics updates for all indexes for the table you specify. You can also turn off automatic statistics for a single index.

TASK 6C-4:

Observing Index Statistics

1. In SQL Query Analyzer, **execute the following query:**

   ```
   DBCC SHOW_STATISTICS (movie, PK_movie)
   ```

   This query enables you to view the statistics information SQL Server has created for the PK_movie index.

2. **Look at the first set of information in the results set.** Some of the information you can find in this results set includes when the statistics were last updated (by examining the Updated column), the total number of rows in the table (Rows column), how many rows SQL Server sampled to generate the statistics (Rows Sampled column), how selective the index is (Density), and the average length in bytes of the index's key (Average Key Length column). The number of steps you see will vary—the closer a value in the Density column is to zero, the more selective the index.

	Updated	Rows	Rows Sampled	Steps	Density	Average key length
1	May 6 2001 1:41PM	156	156	156	0.0	19.621796

3. **Look at the next set of information in the results set.** (The section that has the column headings of All Density, Average Length, and Columns.)

	All density	Average Length	Columns
1	6.4102565E-3	4.0	movie_num
2	6.4102565E-3	19.621796	movie_num, title

   The first row enables you to view the statistics created for the movie_num key column. SQL Server calculates the All Density value by dividing 1 by the number of unique values in the movie table. Because the movie_num column is the table's primary key, each row must have a unique value, which means that if we have 156 rows in the table, we must have 156 unique movie_num values. So, SQL Server calculated the number you see in the All Density by dividing 1 by 156, or .0064. (By default, SQL Server displays this number in scientific notation.) The second row tells you that SQL Server also created statistics on the combination of the movie_num and title columns. Again, because the value in each row's movie_num column must be unique, the movie table has 156 unique combinations of the movie_num and title columns. As a result, the All Density value for the movie_num and title columns is the same as that of the movie_num column.

   So what does all of this mean? The lower the number you see in the All Density column, the more selective the index is. The more selective an index is, the greater its efficiency for retrieving data as compared to a table scan. The values you see in this column can be anywhere from 0 to 1. You can consider an index as highly-selective if it has a density value of 0.10 or lower.

4. Execute a new query:

```
DBCC SHOW_STATISTICS (movie, CL_title)
```

5. Use the results set you see for the CL_title index to complete the following table.

Statistic	Value
Total Number of Rows in Table	
Total Number of Rows Sampled	
Density	
All Density	

Given the information you recorded in the table, how selective is this index? Is it more or less selective then the PK_movie index?

6. In SQL Query Analyzer, **choose File→Open.** When you're prompted to save your current query, **click No.**

7. Open the C:\Data\ncindex.sql script file. You're going to use this script to create a nonclustered index based on the state column in the pubs..authors table.

8. Highlight and execute the first four lines of the script to create the new nonclustered index.

9. Highlight and execute the DBCC SHOW_STATISTICS statement to view the index's statistics.

10. Use the results set you see for the NC_state index to complete the following table.

Statistic	Value
Total Number of Rows in Table	
Total Number of Rows Sampled	
Density	
All Density for State column	

Given the information you recorded in the table, how selective is this index? Should you keep this index? Why or why not?

11. Close all open windows.

Summary

In this lesson, you learned the factors you should consider when designing indexing. For example, you should use a clustered index to optimize queries that retrieve a range of rows, and a nonclustered index to optimize queries that are more selective. You also explored the techniques you can use to create and configure an index's options. Finally, you learned how to manage an index by analyzing fragmentation, updating its statistics, and using the Index Tuning Wizard to make recommendations for a database's indexes.

LESSON 6 REVIEW

6A In what scenario should you choose to implement a nonclustered index? How about a clustered index?

6B What is the role of the fill factor in an index? How should you configure the fill factor for OLTP and DSS environments?

6C What is the easiest way for you to create and maintain the index statistics for all of a database's indexes?

Joining Tables

Overview

In the "Creating and Managing Tables" lesson, we talked about how you should normalize tables so that you can avoid having redundant data in those tables. But after you split data into multiple tables, your next problem becomes how do you query multiple tables at the same time. In this lesson, we will show you how you go about retrieving data from multiple tables simultaneously by using table joins. We will explore the different types of table joins you can use and how you go about querying two or more tables with join statements.

Objectives

To learn how to join tables, you will:

7A   Use Transact-SQL to query multiple tables.

In this topic, we will define the different types of joins you can implement (inner, outer, and cross). We also provide you with the syntax for each type of join, along with hands-on activities for implementing joins.

7B   Implement advanced table joins.

In this topic, we will show you how to join three or more tables together. You'll explore how to combine multiple SELECT statements in order to generate a single results set. Finally, you'll learn how to create a table based on a results set by using the SELECT INTO statement.

Data Files:

inner_joins.sql
outer_joins.sql
cross_joins.sql
multiple.sql
multi_table.sql
self_joins.sql
union.sql
select_into.sql
temp_tables.sql

Lesson Time:
3 hours

TOPIC 7A

Querying Multiple Tables

You use table joins to produce a results set that contains columns from two or more tables. For performance reasons, you should limit the number of tables you reference in a join; the more tables you use in a join, the longer it will take SQL Server to process your query. You join tables together based on a column (or columns) that both tables have in common. You'll frequently base your joins on the primary key to foreign key relationship between tables. For example, you can use a join to display data from both the Rental and rental_detail tables based on the invoice_num column. In this example, the invoice_num column is the primary key of the Rental table and the foreign key of the rental_detail table.

SQL Server supports three types of joins: inner, outer, and cross. We describe each type of join in the following table.

Join	Description
Inner	Use an inner join to link two tables that have common values in one or more columns. For example, you might want to use an inner join to link the Invoice Number column in the Rental table to the Invoice Number column in the rental_detail table. The results set from an inner join contains only the rows that have matching values in the linked column from both tables
Outer	Use an outer join whenever you want to join two tables together, but you want your results set to contain not only the rows that match the join condition, but also any unmatched rows from one or the other of the tables. For example, you can use an outer join to link the Customers table to the Rental table so that you can view a list of all customers even if they've never rented a movie.
Cross	Use a cross join whenever you want to join every row in one table with every row in the other table. For example, you might use a cross join if you want a quick way to populate a new table with a lot of data. This type of join is also called a Cartesian product.

You join tables together by using the SELECT statement. The syntax consists of a SELECT statement that includes a list of columns from both tables, a FROM clause that identifies which tables you want to join, and an ON clause that specifies which column you're using to join the two tables. Here's the basic syntax:

```
SELECT column list
FROM table1 join_type JOIN table2
ON table1.column = table2.column
```

If your SELECT statement contains columns that have the same name in both tables, you must explicitly specify the table from which you want to retrieve the column. For example, the following query lists each movie's title (from the Movie table) and the description of its category (from the Category table). Because you must join the Movie table to the Category table by using the category_num column in both tables, you must qualify the column names by using the table names:

```
SELECT movie.title, category.description
FROM movie INNER JOIN category
ON movie.category_num = category.category_num
```

Likewise, if the columns you include in the SELECT statement are common to both tables, you must also precede each column with the name of the table. Although it isn't required, you should precede each column in the SELECT statement with the name of the table from which you want to retrieve it—even if the columns are unique to each table. To reduce the amount of typing, SQL Server enables you to define short aliases for your table names by using an AS clause. For example, consider the following query:

```
SELECT m.title,  c.description
FROM movie AS m INNER JOIN category AS c
ON m.category_num = c.category_num
```

As you can see by this example, instead of using the table name movie before each of its columns, you can define an alias of "m" and use it to identify the movie table's columns. Likewise, you can use an alias of "c" to identify the category table's columns.

Defining an Inner Join

As we've said, you use an inner join when you want to display matching rows in two or more tables. If you don't specify a type of join when you define your JOIN statement, by default, SQL Server assumes that you're using an inner join. You can use a WHERE clause to restrict the rows returned in your query, and you can also use an ORDER BY clause to specify an order for the rows.

You can't use a column that could contain null values in the join condition.

For example, the following query enables you to display a list of employees from the pubs database and the publishers they work with:

```
USE pubs
SELECT e.fname, e.lname, p.pub_name
FROM employee AS e INNER JOIN publishers AS p
ON e.pub_id = p.pub_id
ORDER BY e.lname, e.fname
```

You can optionally use the DISTINCT keyword to restrict the rows returned in the results set. For example, if you want to see a list of customers who have ever rented a movie, but not see a customer listed more than once, you could use the following query:

```
USE movies
SELECT DISTINCT r.cust_num, c.fname, c.lname
FROM rental AS r INNER JOIN customer AS c
ON r.cust_num = c.cust_num
ORDER by c.lname, c.fname
```

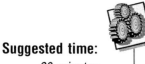

APPLY YOUR KNOWLEDGE 7-1

Working with Inner Joins

Objective: To use inner joins to display information from the tables in the movies and pubs databases.

Setup: You're logged on to Windows 2000 as student#. You've created a database named movies and tables within it named movie, category, customer, rental, and rental_detail. You've defined primary key, foreign key, default, and check constraints on the tables, and you've created nonclustered indexes based on your primary keys. You have imported data into the tables. You have created database diagrams for both the movies and pubs databases.

1. Start SQL Server Enterprise Manager and display your database diagram for the movies database. You can use the diagram to review the columns in your tables when you construct the following joins.

You can use the CONVERT function to convert a date column to character format and optionally enable you to specify a format for the date. Other formats include 102 (yyyy.mm.dd) and 103 (dd/mm/yy).

2. In SQL Query Analyzer, select the movies database. Design and execute a query to display the invoice number, rental date, and the customer's first and last names for all of the movie rentals. Sort the results by the rental date column. Hint: You can use CONVERT(CHAR(10), rental_date, 101) to display the rental date in the format month/day/year. You can also concatenate the customer's first and last name columns. Record your query in the following space.

3. Design and execute a query to list invoice numbers, rental date, invoice line item numbers, and movie numbers (join the rental table to the rental_detail table). Sort the results by the invoice number column.

What query did you use?

4. Design and execute a query to list the titles and the category descriptions for all movies with a rating of PG. List each movie only once, and sort the list of titles in alphabetical order. Record your query below.

How many PG titles does your store have?

5. Refer to the database diagram for the pubs database. Design and execute a query to display the store name and their discount percentage. Sort the results by the store name column. (Note: This query returns only one row in the results set.) What query did you use?

6. Based on the tables in the pubs database, design and execute a query to display a list of titles for which authors have a royalty percentage greater than 20 percent. (Join the titles table to the roysched table.) Display the title name and royalty percentage in the results set; sort the results in descending order by royalty percentage.

Record your query below.

How many titles have royalty percentages greater than 20 percent?

7. Clear the Query window in SQL Query Analyzer. Minimize SQL Server Enterprise Manager.

Defining an Outer Join

Because outer joins enable you to list all of the rows from one table, but only the matching rows from the other table, you must identify the table from which you want to display all rows. Use the keywords LEFT OUTER JOIN when you want to list all rows from the first table in your join statement and only the matching rows from the second table. Use RIGHT OUTER JOIN when you want to list all rows from the second table and only the matching rows from the first table. For example, to display a list of all customers regardless of whether they have rented any movies, use the following syntax:

You can use LEFT JOIN *instead of* LEFT OUTER JOIN *and* RIGHT JOIN *instead of* RIGHT OUTER JOIN.

```
SELECT c.fname+' '+c.lname, r.invoice_num, r.rental_date
FROM customer AS c LEFT OUTER JOIN rental AS r
ON c.cust_num = r.cust_num
```

In this example, your results set will list all customers in the customer table whether or not they have ever rented a movie. If the customer has rented a movie, you will see the invoice number and the date of the rental.

Suggested time:

30 minutes

APPLY YOUR KNOWLEDGE 7-2

Working with Outer Joins

Objective: To use outer joins to display information from the tables in the movies and pubs databases.

1. In SQL Query Analyzer, select the movies database. Design and execute a query to display category, description, and movie title. Include all categories whether the store has movies in a category or not. Sort the results by category description. What query did you use?

   For which movie categories do you not find any movies in stock?

2. Design and execute a query to display a list of all movies and the invoices (if any) on which they have been rented. Include the movie's title and the invoice number in the results set. Sort the results by movie title. Write your query below.

3. Based on the pubs database, design and execute a query to list publishers' names and titles of books. Display all publishers in the results set whether they have published a book or not. Sort the results by publisher name. (Use a right outer join.) What query did you use?

   How many publishers do not have any published titles yet?

4. Using the pubs database, design and execute a query to display a list of all stores and any discounts on file. Include the store name and their discount (if any) in the results. Sort the results by store name. What query did you use?

5. Clear the Query window.

Designing a Cross Join

You'll often hear cross joins referred to as Cartesian products, because the number of rows in the results set they generate is equal to the total number of rows in one table multiplied by the total number of rows in the second table. For example, if you cross join the customers table (91 rows) and orders table (830 rows) from the Northwind database, you'll get a total of 75,530 rows in your results set. You typically shouldn't run cross joins because they can put a tremendous workload on your server.

Use the following syntax to implement a cross join:

```
USE database
SELECT column list
FROM table1 CROSS JOIN table2
```

Notice that you don't need to include the ON clause in your statement because a cross join simply combines every row in the products table with every row in the categories table. Be careful with cross joins as you can overload your server.

TASK 7A-1:

Working with Cross Joins

1. In SQL Query Analyzer, from the Database drop-down list, **select the movies database.**

2. **Execute the following query:**

    ```
    SELECT m.title, c.description
    FROM movie AS m CROSS JOIN category AS c
    ```

    This query generates a cross join between the movie and category tables.

3. **How many rows are in the results set?**

4. **When would you use a cross join?**

5. **Clear the Query window.**

TOPIC 7B

Implementing Advanced Table Joins

Up until this point in the lesson, we've focused on using joins between only two tables. Let's move on to how you go about using joins with more than two tables. In order to do so, you must have at least one table with a primary key to foreign key relationship with the other tables you want to include in the join statement. You must also have a JOIN clause with references to each of the tables. For example, think about the movies database. If you want to display a list of invoice numbers, the date of the rental, and the movies rented by title instead of movie number, you'll need to join the rental table to the rental_detail table by using the invoice_num column and the rental_detail table to the movie table by using the movie_num column. The following query shows you how to join these three tables:

```
USE movies
GO
SELECT r.invoice_num,r.rental_date, rd.line_num, m.title
FROM rental AS r INNER JOIN rental_detail AS rd
ON r.invoice_num = rd.invoice_num
INNER JOIN movie AS m
ON rd.movie_num = m.movie_num
```

Notice that the FROM clause begins the join of the three tables. First, the example joins the rental table to the rental_detail table. Next, the example joins the rental_detail table to the movie table. In general, a three table join uses the following syntax:

```
USE database_name
SELECT column_list
FROM table1 INNER JOIN table2
ON join_condition_tables_1_&_2
INNER JOIN table3
ON join_condition_tables_2_&_3
```

The first join condition joins table1 to table2, and the second join condition joins table2 to table3. If necessary, you can use a WHERE clause in multiple table joins to limit the number of rows returned by the query.

TASK 7B-1:

Joining Multiple Tables

1. In SQL Query Analyzer, **verify that the movies database is your current database.**

2. **Open the script file C:\Data\multiple.sql.**

3. **Look at the script file.** This statement enables you to join the rental table to the rental_detail table by invoice number and the rental_detail table to the movie table by movie number.

4. Execute the script file.

5. Open a new Query window, and then close the window containing the multiple.sql script file.

APPLY YOUR KNOWLEDGE 7-3

Suggested time:
30 minutes

Designing Multiple Table Joins

Objective: To design multiple table joins to display information from the tables in the movies and pubs databases.

1. In SQL Query Analyzer, design and execute a query to display movie rentals by category. Include the title and category description in the results. Sort the results by the category description. (You should see 525 rows in the results set.) What query did you use?

2. Design and execute a query to display a list of movies rented by each customer. Include the customer's first and last names and the movie titles in the results. Sort the results by customer name. (Hint: This query requires that you join four tables together. You should see 525 rows in the results set.) What query did you use?

3. Based on the pubs database, design and execute a query to display a list of titles and their authors. Include each author's first and last names and the book titles in the results. Sort the results by name. (You should see 25 rows in the results set.) What query did you use?

4. Clear the Query window.

Implementing Self Joins

You use a self join when you want to join a table to itself in order to reference one column in a table to another. You must define aliases for the tables in this scenario. If you have duplicate rows, use a WHERE clause to eliminate duplicates. For example, consider the following scenario of when you would use a self join: You have a table that lists all employees by ID number, as well as each employee's manager by that ID number. If you want to display each employee's name as well as his/her manager's name, you must use a self join.

TASK 7B-2:

Working with Self Joins

1. In SQL Query Analyzer, **use the Northwind database.**

2. **Execute the following query:**

```
SELECT e.firstname+' '+e.lastname AS 'Employee',
       m.firstname+' '+m.lastname AS 'Manager'
FROM employees AS e JOIN employees AS m
ON e.reportsto = m.employeeid
ORDER BY e.lastname, e.firstname
```

Use this query to list each employee's name and his/her manager's name. You're joining the Northwind database's Employees table to itself by joining the reportsto column with the employeeid column.

	Employee	Manager
1	Steven Buchanan	Andrew Fuller
2	Laura Callahan	Andrew Fuller
3	Nancy Davolio	Andrew Fuller
4	Anne Dodsworth	Steven Buchanan
5	Robert King	Steven Buchanan
6	Janet Leverling	Andrew Fuller
7	Margaret Peacock	Andrew Fuller
8	Michael Suyama	Steven Buchanan

3. **Clear the Query window.**

Combining the Results of Multiple SELECT Statements

You can use the UNION operator to join the results set of multiple SELECT statements together. Use UNION when the data you want to retrieve is in different tables and can't be retrieved by using a single query statement. If you're trying to execute a complex query, you might find that you get better performance from SQL Server if you break the queries into multiple SELECT statements and then use UNION to display the results. In order to use the UNION operator, the referenced tables must have similar data types, the same number of columns, and the same column order in the select line of each query. SQL Server automatically discards any duplicate rows from the results set.

Use the following syntax with the UNION operator:

```
select_statement UNION [ALL] select_statement
```

Replace the two *select_statement* variables with the SELECT statements for which you want to merge the results sets. If you use the ALL keyword as part of this statement, SQL Server won't eliminate any duplicate rows from the results set.

For example, you could use the following query to retrieve the name and telephone number from the employees and customers tables in the Northwind database:

```
USE northwind
SELECT name = (firstname+' '+lastname), homephone
FROM employees
UNION
SELECT companyname,phone
FROM customers
```

Note that you must combine the first and last name columns into a single column for the first SELECT statement in order for this query to work. This is because the UNION operator requires that each SELECT statement select the same number of columns. The following query won't work:

```
USE northwind
SELECT firstname, lastname, homephone
FROM employees
UNION
SELECT companyname, phone
FROM customers
```

TASK 7B-3:

Combining SELECT Statements

1. In SQL Query Analyzer, **select the pubs database.**

2. **Execute the following query:**

    ```
    SELECT name = (au_fname+' '+au_lname), address, city+',
    '+state+' '+zip
    FROM authors
    UNION
    SELECT stor_name, stor_address, city+', '+state+' '+zip
    FROM stores
    ```

    This query enables you to display a list of authors' names and addresses along with store names and addresses. You might use such a list to generate mailing labels. You should see a total of 29 rows.

3. **Clear the Query window.**

Creating a Table Based on a Results Set

You can use the `SELECT INTO` statement to create a table based on a `SELECT` statement. This means that you can use this statement to populate new tables in a database. For example, you might use the `SELECT INTO` statement to create a new table with only selected columns from another table. You can then query these new tables (whether temporary or permanent). By using `SELECT INTO`, you can create narrower tables to break up complex queries.

Use the `SELECT INTO` statement to create either temporary or permanent tables. Whether the table is temporary or permanent, you must specify a unique table name when you create the table. Any temporary tables you create can be either local or global. A local temporary table is available only in your current session. In contrast, a global temporary table is available to all users with current sessions on your server. You identify a local temporary table by preceding its name with # and global temporary tables by preceding them with ##. SQL Server will automatically reclaim the space used by temporary tables. For local temporary tables, SQL Server reclaims the table's space when you close your current session. For global temporary tables, SQL Server reclaims their space when none of the users are using the tables.

You must use aliases for the columns you choose as part of your `SELECT` statement. SQL Server uses these aliases as the column names for the new table. You define an alias for a column when you use the syntax: `SELECT column_name AS alias_name`. In this example, whatever name you specify as the alias name will be the column's name in the new table. (You must enclose the alias name in quotes if the name contains a space.) Use the following syntax to create a new table with the `SELECT INTO` statement:

```
SELECT statement
INTO new_table_name
FROM existing_table_name
```

For example, if you want to create a table which contains the fname, lname, and phone number columns from the customer table, you could use the following query:

```
USE movies
GO
SELECT fname AS first, lname AS last, phone AS phone
INTO #temp_customer
FROM customer
```

Using Table Joins in the SELECT INTO Statement

You can also use table joins as part of your `SELECT INTO` statement. By using joins, you can build a single table that consists of columns from more than one table. For example, you could use the following query to build a table that contains authors' names and the titles of their books (using the tables in the pubs sample database):

```
USE pubs
GO
SELECT a.au_fname+' '+a.au_lname AS author, t.title AS title
INTO auth_title
FROM authors AS a INNER JOIN titleauthor AS ta
ON a.au_id = ta.au_id
INNER JOIN titles AS t
ON ta.title_id = t.title_id
```

Creating Tables From Data in Other Databases

You can also use the SELECT INTO statement to create a table in a database by using data from a table in another database. To do so, you must use a fully qualified name for the table in your FROM statement. For example, if you want to copy the author names and ID numbers from the authors table in the pubs database into a table named test in the movies database, use the following syntax:

```
USE movies
SELECT a.au_fname+' '+a.au_lname AS 'author', a.au_id AS 'id'
INTO test
FROM pubs.dbo.author AS a
```

TASK 7B-4:

Creating a New Table Based on a SELECT INTO Statement

1. In SQL Query Analyzer, **select the movies database.**

2. **Execute the following query:**

   ```
   SELECT title AS title, rental_price AS rental_price
   INTO G_movie
   FROM movie
   WHERE rating = 'G'
   ```

   You use this query to create a new table named G_movie, which contains only the movies with a "G" rating.

3. **Execute a new query:**

   ```
   EXEC sp_help 'g_movie'
   ```

   This query enables you to view the structure of the G_movie table. You should see that it has two columns, title and price.

	Name	Owner	Type	Created_datetime	
1	G_movie	dbo	user table	2001-05-07 13:33:11.970	

	Column_name	Type	Computed	Length	Prec	Scale	Nullable
1	title	varchar	no	40			no
2	rental_price	smallmoney	no	4	10	4	no

4. **Execute a new query:**

   ```
   SELECT *
   FROM g_movie
   ```

5. **How many rows do you have in the G_movie table?**

6. **Clear the Query window.**

APPLY YOUR KNOWLEDGE 7-4

Creating Temporary Tables

Objective: In this lab, you're going to create temporary tables by using the SELECT INTO statement.

1. Design and execute a query for creating a local temporary table for storing all movies with a rating of PG. Use an appropriate name for a local temporary table. Include the Title and Movie Number columns in the table. What query did you use?

2. Write a query to view all rows of your new table. Execute this query in SQL Query Analyzer.

3. In SQL Query Analyzer, open a second connection to your server. (Click the New Query button on the toolbar.)

4. Can you query your new table in this second connection? (Execute `SELECT * FROM #PG_movie`.) Why or why not?

5. Close your new Query window without saving your changes.

6. Design and execute a query for creating a global temporary table for storing all movies with a rating of "R." Use an appropriate name for a global temporary table. Include the title and movie number columns in the table. Execute this query. What query did you use?

7. Write a query to view all rows of your new table. Execute this query in SQL Query Analyzer. Record your query below.

8. Open a second connection to your server. Can you query your new table? Why or why not?

9. Close all open windows.

Summary

In this lesson, you learned just about everything there is to know about table joins: what types of joins you can implement (inner, outer, and cross), and the syntax for each type of join statement. Lastly, you saw how you can use the `SELECT INTO` statement to create a new table, and that this new table can contain data from multiple tables if you use a join condition.

LESSON 7 REVIEW

7A What types of joins can you use to query multiple tables? When would you use each type?

7B Why might you use the `UNION` keyword in a query? What are some of the restrictions to using the `UNION` keyword?

Designing Advanced Queries LESSON

8

Data Files:
single_value.sql
subqueries.sql
correlated.sql
insert_data.sql
delete_rows.sql
update_queries.sql

Lesson Time:
1 hour, 30 minutes

Overview

In Transact-SQL, you can use a nested query within a SELECT, INSERT, UPDATE, or DELETE query. You use a nested query (also called a subquery) to perform tasks such as inserting rows into one table based on another table's rows. In this lesson, you're going to learn how to implement subqueries to view, insert, update, and delete data.

Objectives

To design advanced queries, you will:

8A   Define the role of subqueries.

In this topic, you're going to learn the different types of subqueries you can implement and how to implement them. Types of subqueries you can implement include using a subquery to return a single value or a list of values and using a subquery to return matching rows from a second table.

8B   Use queries to change data.

In this topic, you will learn how to make changes to data based on a subquery. For example, you can use the INSERT...SELECT statement to insert rows into one table based on the values in the second table. You also learn how to delete rows based on a subquery.

TOPIC 8A

Designing Subqueries

A subquery is simply a nested `SELECT` statement within another query. You can use subqueries to break down complex queries into smaller (less complex) queries. You'll typically use subqueries when a query uses the results set from a subquery to retrieve its results set. For example, if you want to retrieve a list of books with prices greater than the average book price, you must use a subquery first to find the average book price, as follows:

```
USE pubs
SELECT title, price
FROM titles
WHERE price > (SELECT AVG(price)
                FROM titles)
```

You should evaluate your subqueries carefully. In some cases, you might find that you can rewrite a subquery as a table join instead. If so, you should use a join rather than a subquery because the query optimizer can retrieve data more efficiently when you use a join instead of a subquery.

SQL Server requires that you enclose a subquery in parentheses. Your subquery can contain only one column or expression, but you can have as many subqueries as necessary.

Using a Subquery to Return a Single Value

You typically use a single value subquery as part of a `WHERE` clause. For example, the following query enables you to list the book title and price of the highest priced book in the titles table:

```
USE pubs
SELECT title, price
FROM titles
WHERE price = (SELECT MAX(price)
                FROM titles)
```

Notice that the subquery must be enclosed in parentheses. In this example, you use the subquery to return a single value that SQL Server can then use in your `WHERE` clause to evaluate the rows in a table. Because you have the subquery returning only a single value, you'll typically use aggregate functions in the subquery such as `MAX( )`, `MIN( )`, and `AVG( )`.

If your subquery returns more than one value and your `WHERE` clause doesn't support multiple values, you'll get an error message. In other words, in the statement `WHERE price = (subquery)`, if the subquery returns multiple values, SQL Server will display an error. For example, a `WHERE` clause of `WHERE price = (SELECT price FROM titles)` returns more than one value.

You can also use subqueries as part of your `SELECT` statement. For example, if you want to see a list of all movie titles with a G rating, their rental price, and the average rental price for movies with a G rating, you can use the following query:

```
USE movies
GO
SELECT title, rental_price,
    (SELECT AVG(rental_price)
     FROM movie
     WHERE rating = 'G') AS 'avg. price'
FROM movie
```

TASK 8A-1:

Designing Single Value Subqueries

Setup: You're logged on to Windows 2000 as student#. You've created a database named movies and tables within it named movie, category, customer, rental, and rental_detail. You've defined primary key, foreign key, default, and check constraints on the tables, and you've created nonclustered indexes based on your primary keys. You have imported data into the tables. You have created database diagrams for both the movies and pubs databases.

1. **Start SQL Query Analyzer and select the movies database as your current database.**

2. **Execute the following query:**

    ```
    SELECT AVG(rental_price)
    FROM movie
    ```

    This query enables you to display the average price of a movie in the movie table.

(No column name)
1	2.8746

3. **Execute a new query:**

    ```
    SELECT title, rental_price
    FROM movie
    WHERE rental_price < (SELECT AVG(rental_price)
                          FROM movie)
    ```

    Use this query to list all movies with a rental fee of less than the average rental fee.

    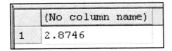

	title	rental_price
1	12 Angry Men	1.9900
2	2001: A Space Odyssey	1.9900
3	African Queen The	1.9900
4	All Quiet on the Western Front	1.9900

4. How many movies have prices that are less than the average price?

5. Clear the Query window.

Using a Subquery to Return a List of Values

You can also use a subquery to return a list of values for use with comparison operators such as IN. The IN operator enables you to provide SQL Server with a list of values in the WHERE clause instead of a single value. For example, you used the IN operator to configure a check constraint on the movie table's rating column in the "Designing Data Integrity" lesson. The check constraint consists of the following: rating IN 'G', 'PG', 'R', 'NC17', 'NR'. You should use the IN operator when you want to use subqueries that will return multiple rows. Consider the following example:

```
USE movies
GO
SELECT fname, lname
FROM customer
WHERE cust_num IN (SELECT cust_num
                   FROM rental
                   WHERE rental_date > '8/1/99')
```

In this example, SQL Query Analyzer returns a list of customer numbers from the rental table based on the WHERE clause. After SQL Query Analyzer evaluates the subquery to obtain a list of customer numbers, it can then display a list of customers who have rented movies after 8/1/99.

You can also use NOT IN as a comparison operator. NOT IN enables you to find all rows in the main query that don't have matching rows in the subquery. For example, if you wanted to view a list of customers' names who haven't rented any movies, you could use the following query:

```
USE movies
GO
SELECT fname, lname
FROM customer
WHERE cust_num NOT IN (SELECT cust_num
                       FROM rental)
```

APPLY YOUR KNOWLEDGE 8-1

Suggested time:
30 minutes

Using Subqueries

Objective: To use the tables in the pubs database to design and execute subqueries. If necessary, use the database diagram for the pubs database in SQL Server Enterprise Manager to review the structure of the tables.

1. By using the pubs database, design and execute a query to list the title and royalty percentage of the book(s) with the highest royalty percentage. What query did you use?

   How many books are in your results set?

2. Based on the pubs database, design and execute a query to list all books with sales in the sales table. Record your query in the following space.

   How many books have sales on file?

3. What query could you use to achieve the same results as step 2 by using a `JOIN` statement instead of a nested subquery? Execute this query in SQL Query Analyzer to verify that you get the same results. Write your query in the following space.

4. Why should you consider using a table join instead of a subquery when they both generate the same results set?

5. Clear the Query window.

Designing Correlated Subqueries

Use a correlated subquery to specify that you want to compare rows from the main query to matching rows in the subquery. SQL Server evaluates the subquery once for each row in the main query. So, you might think of a correlated subquery as being very similar to the do-while and for loops you typically use in programming. For example, you can use the following query to list all movies from the movie table with a rental price of $2.99 or less that haven't been rented (by checking the rental_detail table):

```
USE movies
GO
SELECT DISTINCT m.title
FROM movie AS m
WHERE m.rental_price <= 2.99
    AND m.movie_num NOT IN (SELECT rd.movie_num
                            FROM rental_detail AS rd)
```

You could restate this query in English as, "Select the first movie in the movie table with a rental price of $2.99 or less, then check the rental_detail table to see if this movie has ever been rented, then go back to find the next movie with a rental price of $2.99 or less and see if it has ever been rented, and so on." Notice that the syntax requires that you use aliases to identify the tables you use in correlated subqueries.

As another example, you can use a correlated subquery to list all of the titles from the title table in the pubs database with a price of 5.99 or less that have generated more than one hundred dollars in sales. Use the following query to accomplish this task:

```
USE pubs
GO
SELECT t.title_id, t.title
FROM titles AS t
WHERE price <= 5.99
    AND t.title_id IN (SELECT s.title_id
                       FROM sales AS s
                       WHERE s.qty * t.price > 100)
```

You can begin to build your correlated queries by first creating and testing the subquery and then using it with your main query. Keep in mind that you can highlight some or all of a query to execute only that portion. (So you can test a subquery simply by highlighting it with your mouse and then executing that portion.)

Using EXISTS and NOT EXISTS

Use the EXISTS and NOT EXISTS operators whenever you want to correlate more than one column from the main query to the subquery. The EXISTS operator simply checks to see if any rows are returned by the subquery. If the subquery returns rows, the EXISTS operator returns a value of true; otherwise, it returns a value of not true. Similarly, the NOT EXISTS operator checks to see if the subquery didn't return any rows (in this case, NOT EXISTS returns a value of true) or if it did return rows (in this case, NOT EXISTS returns a value of not true).

For example, you might use the following query to find the titles of books for which none of the stores in the pubs database have any sales:

```
USE pubs
GO
SELECT t.title_id, t.title
FROM titles AS t
WHERE NOT EXISTS (SELECT *
                 FROM titles AS t2 JOIN sales AS s
                 ON t2.title_id = s.title_id
                 WHERE t2.title_id = t.title_id)
```

In English, this query says, "Select all titles and their ID numbers from the titles table that aren't included in a list of all titles with sales on file."

APPLY YOUR KNOWLEDGE 8-2

Suggested time:
15 minutes

Designing Correlated Subqueries

Objective: To design and execute a correlated subquery in SQL Query Analyzer.

1.   In SQL Query Analyzer, design and execute a correlated subquery with the EXISTS keyword. By using the movies database, write a query that displays a list of customer names and numbers if they have rented any movies. Sort the results by customer name. What query did you use?

How many customers have rented movies?

2.   Design and execute a correlated subquery to display a list of all customers who rented movies between 8/1/99 and 8/31/99. What query did you use?

How many customers are on the list?

3.   Clear the Query window.

TOPIC 8B

Changing Data Through Queries

You can use the combination of the INSERT...SELECT statement to add rows to a table based on a SELECT statement. To do so, use the following syntax:

```
INSERT table_name
SELECT columns
FROM table
WHERE condition
```

SQL Server inserts the data into the table name you specify in the INSERT statement. For example, if you wanted to add all of the authors in the pubs database as customers in the customer table of the movies database, you could use the following query:

```
USE movies
GO
INSERT customer
SELECT au_lname, au_fname, address, ' ', city, state, zip,
phone, getdate()
FROM pubs.dbo.authors
```

Notice that in the FROM clause you must use a fully qualified name if the table from which you're inserting the rows is in another database. You can optionally use the WHERE clause to restrict the rows inserted into the table. In the previous example, you could have used WHERE state = 'CA' to limit the rows inserted into the customer table to only those authors who live in California.

When you use the INSERT...SELECT statement, all rows that meet the SELECT statement are inserted into the table you specify. You must make sure that the columns you select have data types and formats that are compatible with the columns in the table into which you want to insert the data.

TASK 8B-1:

Inserting Data Based on a Query

Objective: To add names from the authors table in the pubs database to the customer table in the movies database.

1. In SQL Query Analyzer, **verify that movies is your current database.**

2. **Execute the following query:**

```
SELECT au_id, au_lname
FROM pubs.dbo.authors
```

Use this query to obtain a list of all rows in the authors table. You should see that the table has 23 rows.

3. **Execute a new query:**

```
INSERT customer
SELECT au_lname, au_fname, address, ' ', city, state, zip,
phone, getdate()
FROM pubs.dbo.authors
```

This query attempts to add all of the rows in the authors table in the pubs database to the customer table in the movies database. You receive an error because the phone column in the authors table has a width of 12 characters, where the phone column in the customer table has a width of 10 characters. The data in the phone column in the authors table consists of a space after the area code and a hyphen after the prefix of the phone number. If you want to copy each author's phone number to the customer table, you can extract just the numeric portion of the phone number by using the SUBSTRING function.

```
Server: Msg 8152, Level 16, State 9, Line 1
String or binary data would be truncated.
The statement has been terminated.
```

4. **Execute a new query:**

```
INSERT customer
SELECT au_lname, au_fname, address, ' ', city, state, zip,
       SUBSTRING(phone,1,3)+SUBSTRING(phone,5,3)
+SUBSTRING(phone,9,4), getdate()
FROM pubs.dbo.authors
```

This query inserts all rows from the authors table into the customer table in the movies database. You should see a message stating that 23 rows were affected. This message means that SQL Server inserted 23 new rows into the customer table.

5. **Execute a new query:**

```
SELECT *
FROM customer
```

Use this query to view a list of customers on file. You should see that you now have 228 customers in the customer table.

6. **Clear the Query window.**

Deleting Rows Based on a Query

You can use the DELETE FROM statement to delete rows based on a table join or a subquery. Use the following syntax to delete the rows:

```
DELETE FROM table_name
[FROM table_source]
WHERE condition
```

Use the second FROM clause to specify a table join if necessary. You use the WHERE clause to select specific rows or to specify a subquery. For example, to delete rows by using a subquery, use the following syntax:

```
USE movies
GO
DELETE FROM movie
WHERE movie_num NOT IN (SELECT rd.movie_num
                                FROM rental_detail AS rd)
```

In this example, SQL Server will delete all movies from the movie table if the movie hasn't been rented. In another example, you can use the following query to delete rows based on a table join:

```
USE movies
GO
DELETE FROM rental_detail
FROM rental_detail AS rd JOIN rental AS r
ON rd.invoice_num = r.invoice_num
WHERE r.rental_date <= '3/1/99'
```

This query enables you to delete the line item rows from the rental_detail table for all invoices prior to 3/1/99. You must use a join to delete these rows because the rental date is stored in the rental table, not the rental_detail table.

TASK 8B-2:

Deleting Rows Based on a Query

1. In SQL Query Analyzer, **execute the following query:**

    ```
    DELETE FROM customer
    WHERE lname+fname IN (SELECT au_lname+au_fname
                            FROM pubs.dbo.authors)
    ```

    Use this query to delete all rows added to the customer table in the movies database from the authors table in the pubs database. (You must use both the lname and fname columns to delete these rows.)

2. **How many rows does this query delete?**

3. **Verify that you no longer have any of the authors in your customer table by executing the query:**

    ```
    SELECT *
    FROM customer
    ```

    You should now have 205 rows in the customer table.

4. **Clear the Query window.**

Updating Rows Based on a Query

You can use the UPDATE statement to update rows in tables based on a WHERE clause, table join, or both. SQL Server permits only a single update of a row in an UPDATE statement. You use the SET keyword to specify the column and the value you want to update. Use the following syntax to update rows based on a query:

```
UPDATE table_name
SET column_name = expression | value
[FROM table [JOIN table2]
ON join_condition]
[WHERE condition]
```

For example, you could use the UPDATE statement to increase the price of the books in the pubs database with total sales of more than $250. To increase the books' prices by 10 percent, use the following query:

```
USE pubs
GO
UPDATE titles
SET price = price * 1.1
FROM titles AS t
WHERE t.title_id IN (SELECT s.title_id
                     FROM sales AS s
                     WHERE s.qty * t.price > 250)
```

In this example, you're using a correlated subquery to list all book ID numbers for which the pubs database has sales of more than $250. After you have this list, you can use the main query to update the prices in the titles table.

APPLY YOUR KNOWLEDGE 8-3

Suggested time:
30 minutes

Working with Update Queries

Objective: To use the UPDATE statement to change the prices of movies in the movie table.

1. In SQL Query Analyzer, design and execute a query to list the titles and rental prices of any movies that haven't rented. Note: The movie table contains more than one copy of many of the movies. Write your query so that it will return a list of only those movies for which none of the copies have rented. (Hint: You'll need to use a subquery that contains an outer join between the movie and rental_detail tables.) You'll find that only one movie hasn't rented. What query did you use?

2. Design and execute a query to reduce the price of any movie by 20 percent if it hasn't rented. (Remember, you want to reduce the price only if all copies of a movie have not rented. Don't reduce the price of a movie if some of its copies have rented.) Note: Because the smallmoney data type supports four decimal places, SQL Server will calculate the decrease in the rental price column to four digits of precision. You can round the rental price to two digits of precision by using ROUND(rental_price * .8, 2) in your formula. What query did you use?

3. Repeat the query you wrote in step 1 to verify that you've lowered the prices.

4. Design and execute a query to list the titles of all movies that have rented and their rental price even if one of the copies of a specific title hasn't rented. What query did you use?

5. Design and execute a query to increase the price of all copies of movies that have rented by 10 percent. Record your query below.

6. Repeat the query you wrote in step 4 to verify that you've increased the prices of the movies that have rented.

7. Close all open windows.

Summary

In this lesson, you learned the different types of subqueries you can implement, including those that return a single value, a list of values, or correlate rows between tables. You also learned how to implement subqueries as part of the SELECT, INSERT, UPDATE, and DELETE statements.

LESSON 8 REVIEW

8A **What are some of the reasons why you might choose to use subqueries instead of table joins?**

8B **In what scenario might you use the INSERT...SELECT statement instead of only the INSERT statement?**

Designing Views

Overview

SQL Server enables you to create views as "windows" to some or all of one or more tables' columns. In this lesson, we're going to explore the advantages to creating views and the nuts and bolts of how you create them. We'll also examine two new features that you can implement in views in SQL Server 2000, indexed views and partitioned views.

Objectives

To design and implement views, you will:

9A Create and manage views.

SQL Server 2000 enables you to create views based on one or more tables as both a convenience for your users and a way to improve your server's performance. In this topic, we show you how you go about implementing the different types of views you can define by using the CREATE VIEW statement.

Data Files:

create_view.sql
join_views.sql
encrypted_views.sql
modify_view.sql
drop_view.sql
view_change.sql
partitioned_view.sql
indexed_view.sql

Lesson Time:
1 hour, 15 minutes

TOPIC 9A

Creating and Managing Views

You can use a view to save almost any SELECT statement as a separate database object. This SELECT statement enables you to create a results set that you can use just as you would any table. In a sense, you can think of a view as a virtual table. Traditional views don't actually contain data; they simply consist of SELECT statements for extracting data from the actual tables in your database. (You can create an indexed view so that SQL Server stores the view's data in a database to improve its performance. We're going to look at how you create indexed views later on in this lesson.)

The tables on which you base a view are referred to as base tables. You can use a view to create a subset of a base table by selecting only some of its columns, or you can use a view to display columns from multiple base tables by using a join statement.

Why Use Views?

One of the best advantages of views is that you need to give your users permissions to only the view itself and not the underlying table (or tables). So, a view provides you with additional security. You can also use views to enable users to see some but not all columns in a table, so if a table contains a column with sensitive information, you can use a view to prevent users from seeing that column. For example, if you have an employee table that contains employee names, addresses, and salaries, you can create a view to enable users to see the employee names and addresses, but not salaries.

You can also use views as a way to hide a complex database design. If you've normalized the design of your database such that data is spread out over multiple tables, it can be difficult for users to learn how to retrieve data from those tables. By using views, you can avoid users having to learn how to write SQL statements to join the tables.

Creating a View

You create a view by using the CREATE VIEW Transact-SQL statement. You can include a total of 1,024 columns in a view. You can't combine the CREATE VIEW with other SQL statements in the same batch. If you want to use other statements (such as USE *database*) with the CREATE VIEW statement, you must follow those statements with the GO keyword. Use the following syntax to create a view:

```
USE database
GO
CREATE VIEW view_name
AS
SELECT column_list
FROM table_name
```

In this syntax, you replace *view_name* with the name you want to assign to the view. You should come up with a naming convention for your views that makes it easier for you to differentiate between tables and views. For example, you might try using "view" as part of all of your view names. Replace *column_list* with the list of columns you want to include in the view and *table_name* with the name of the table on which you want to base the view.

For example, if you want to create a view that consists of each customer's name and phone number only, use the following syntax:

```
USE movies
GO
CREATE VIEW dbo.CustView
AS
SELECT lname, fname, phone
FROM customer
```

You can optionally specify a list of column names so that SQL Server will use these names for the columns in the view instead of the column names from the table in the SELECT portion of the statement. For example, in the following query, the (lname, fname) clause assigns these names to the columns in the view instead of the names au_lname, au_fname:

```
USE pubs
GO
CREATE VIEW dbo.PracticeView
(lname, fname)
AS
SELECT au_lname, au_fname
FROM authors
```

Restrictions

You can't include the ORDER BY, COMPUTE, or COMPUTE BY clauses in the SELECT statement you use to create a view. In addition, you can't use the SELECT INTO keywords. Your view can't refer to temporary tables. For example, the following SQL statement is invalid:

```
CREATE VIEW dbo.TestView
AS
SELECT col1, col2
FROM #temp_table
```

Permissions

If your users have permissions to the database in which you create the view, they will inherit permissions to the view itself. But, if your users don't inherit permissions to the view, you must assign them permissions or they won't be able to access the view. You don't have to give users permissions to the base tables on which you create a view; you just have to give users permissions to the view itself, provided you are both the owner of the table and the view.

Ownership

The views that you create depend on the base tables (or other views). SQL Server refers to objects that depend on other objects as dependent. Objects can have either the same or different owners. If the same owner owns both the view and the table, that owner (typically you) needs only to assign users permissions to the view. Likewise, when users access your view, SQL Server needs to check users permissions only for that view.

If you (or another user with sufficient permissions) create a view based on a table for which you aren't the owner, SQL Server considers the ownership chain to be broken. Each object's owner can change users' permissions; so, SQL Server must check users' permissions for the view and all objects on which the view depends. Checking users' permissions for each object hurts your server's performance. Microsoft recommends that you don't break the ownership chain (meaning, create views with different owners from the base tables) in order to avoid degrading the performance of your server.

To avoid breaking the ownership chain, you should explicitly specify the owner of the view when you create it. You should typically make the database owner (dbo) user the owner of all views, along with all of the other objects in a database. You make the dbo user the owner of a view by using the following syntax:

```
CREATE VIEW dbo.view_name
AS
SELECT column_list
FROM table_name
```

You can determine the objects on which a view depends along with their owners by using the sp_depends stored procedure. Here's the syntax:

```
sp_depends 'view_name'
```

Nested Views

SQL Server enables you to create a view based on another view (this is also called a nested view). Keep in mind, though, that nested views can be much more difficult to troubleshoot because you must search through multiple view definitions to find a problem. For this reason, Microsoft recommends that you create separate views instead.

TASK 9A-1:

Creating a View

Objective: To create a view based on the titles table in the pubs database.

Setup: You're logged on to Windows 2000 as student#. You've created a database named movies and tables within it named movie, category, customer, rental, and rental_detail. You've defined primary key, foreign key, default, and check constraints on the tables, and you've created nonclustered indexes based on your primary keys. You've imported data into the tables. You've created database diagrams for both the movies and pubs databases.

1. **Start SQL Query Analyzer and select the pubs database.**

2. **Choose File→Open. Open the C:\Data\create_view.sql file.**

3. **Highlight and execute the CREATE VIEW statement** to create a view containing the title, price, and ytd_sales columns for the books that have sold more than 5,000 copies this year. By creating the view and specifying dbo as the owner, you avoid breaking the ownership chain between the view and the underlying table.

4. **Highlight and execute the `SELECT * FROM MyTitleView` query** to display a list of rows in the view.

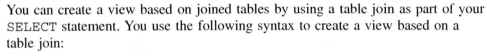

	title	price	ytd_sales
1	You Can Combat Computer Stress!	2.9900	18722
2	The Gourmet Microwave	2.9900	22246
3	But Is It User Friendly?	22.9500	8780
4	Fifty Years in Buckingham Palace Kitchens	11.9500	15096

5. **Open a new Query window.**

6. **Close the Query window containing the create_view.sql file.**

Creating a View Based on Joined Tables

You can create a view based on joined tables by using a table join as part of your SELECT statement. You use the following syntax to create a view based on a table join:

```
CREATE VIEW view_name (column_list)
AS
SELECT columns
FROM table1 JOIN table2
ON join_condition
```

For example, if you want to create a view that contains the title of each book in the pubs database, along with the author's royalty percentage for that book, you could use the following query:

```
USE pubs
GO
CREATE VIEW dbo.TitleRoyaltyView
AS
SELECT t.title, r.royalty
FROM titles AS t JOIN roysched AS r
ON t.title_id JOIN r.title_id
```

You should base views only on inner joins, not outer joins. While SQL Server enables you to specify an outer join in the SELECT statement, you'll get unpredictable results. For example, SQL Server frequently returns null values for the inner table in the outer join.

APPLY YOUR KNOWLEDGE 9-1

Creating Views From Joined Tables

Objective: To design and create views in SQL Query Analyzer. Some of the views will be based on joined tables.

1. In the movies database, create a view that contains the title and category number of each movie with an 'R' rating. Name the view R_MovieView. What query did you use?

2. Use the SELECT statement to display the rows in the view. Record your query here.

3. In the movies database, create a view that contains the movie_num, title, and category description columns. Name the view MovieCategoryView. What query did you use?

4. Use the SELECT statement to verify the view. Display the results in order by title. Display each title only once. Record your query here.

5. Create a view consisting of each customer's first name, last name, invoice number, and rental date. Name the view RentalsView. (Note: This view will create a row for every invoice. If you have a customer who has rented movies more than once, you'll see their name listed once for each rental invoice when you use this view.) What query did you use?

6. Use the SELECT statement to verify the RentalsView view. Display the customer's first and last names in a single column. Sort the results by customer name. (You should see multiple rows for customers who have rented movies more than once.) What query did you use?

7. Clear the Query window.

Displaying View Definitions

SQL Server includes several system-created schema views that you can use to find information about a database's views. We describe these views in the following table.

System View	Based on System Table	Enables You to View
information_schema.tables	sysobjects	View names.
information_schema.view_table_usage	sysdepends	Names of tables on which views have been defined. Note: SQL Server displays only the views for which the current user has permissions.
information_schema.views	syscomments	View definition.
information_schema.view_column_usage	syscolumns	Names of columns used in a view. Note: SQL Server displays only the views for which the current user has permissions.

For example, to view a list of views defined in a database, you can use the following syntax:

```
SELECT *
FROM information_schema.tables
WHERE table_type = 'view'
```

To view the SELECT statement that makes up a view, use the sp_helptext stored procedure. Use the following syntax:

```
sp_helptext view_name
```

Preventing Users From Displaying View Definitions

SQL Server stores a view's definition in the syscomments table; however, you shouldn't delete the definition from this table as a technique for hiding the view definition. Instead, you can encrypt the view. (Although you can delete the definition of the view and it will still work, Microsoft recommends that you not delete it from syscomments to avoid problems when you upgrade to future versions of SQL Server.)

To encrypt a view, add the WITH ENCRYPTION operator to prevent users from reading a view's definition. Here's the syntax:

```
CREATE VIEW view_name
WITH ENCRYPTION
AS select_statement
```

TASK 9A-2:

Displaying View Information

1. In SQL Query Analyzer, **open the C:\Data\encrypted_views.sql script.**

2. **Highlight and execute the `sp_helptext MovieCategoryView` statement** to display the `CREATE VIEW` statement you used to define the view.

	Text
1	CREATE VIEW dbo.MovieCategoryView
2	AS
3	SELECT m.movie_num, m.title, c.description
4	FROM movie AS m JOIN category AS c
5	ON m.category_num = c.category_num
6	

3. **Highlight and execute the query for creating the view named MovieEncryptView** to create a view with an encrypted definition.

4. **Highlight and execute the query `sp_helptext MovieEncryptView`** to view the message SQL Server generates when you attempt to display the definition of an encrypted view.

```
The object comments have been encrypted.
```

5. **Highlight and execute the `SELECT * FROM information_schema.views` query** to display a list of the views defined in the movies database. SQL Server displays both system-created views (copied from the model database) and user-created views such as the MovieCategoryView.

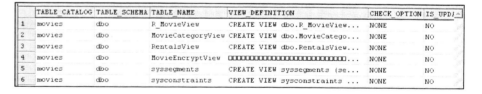

	TABLE_CATALOG	TABLE_SCHEMA	TABLE_NAME	VIEW_DEFINITION	CHECK_OPTION	IS_UPD.
1	movies	dbo	R_MovieView	CREATE VIEW dbo.R_MovieView...	NONE	NO
2	movies	dbo	MovieCategoryView	CREATE VIEW dbo.MovieCatego...	NONE	NO
3	movies	dbo	RentalsView	CREATE VIEW dbo.RentalsView...	NONE	NO
4	movies	dbo	MovieEncryptView	□□□□□□□□□□□□□□□□□□□□□□□□□□...	NONE	NO
5	movies	dbo	syssegments	CREATE VIEW syssegments (se...	NONE	NO
6	movies	dbo	sysconstraints	CREATE VIEW sysconstraints ...	NONE	NO

6. If necessary, in the results pane, **scroll down the window so that you can view the View_Definition column.** This column displays the `CREATE VIEW` statement you used to define the view. You can see the definitions of most of the views. Because you encrypted the MovieEncryptView, you see squares in the view_definition column.

7. **Open a new Query window.**

8. **Close the Query window containing the encrypted_views.sql script file.**

Modifying a View

You can alter a view by either dropping and re-creating it or by using the
ALTER VIEW statement. If you drop a view, you must re-create any permissions
assignments when you re-create the view. In contrast, if you change a view by
using the ALTER VIEW statement, the view retains whatever permissions you
had assigned to your users. You can use the following syntax to change an existing view:

```
ALTER VIEW view_name  (column_list)
AS
select_statement
```

Keep in mind that if you created the view with the WITH ENCRYPTION operator, you must include that option in the ALTER VIEW statement.

APPLY YOUR KNOWLEDGE 9-2

Suggested time:
10 minutes

Modifying a View

Objective: To write a query to modify the MovieCategoryView.

1. Write and execute a query for modifying the MovieCategoryView to add the
    rating column from the movie table. What query did you use?

2. Write and execute a query to verify that MovieCategoryView now contains
    the rating column. What query did you use?

3. What is an advantage to using ALTER VIEW instead of dropping and
    re-creating a view?

4. Clear the Query window.

Dropping a View

You drop a view by using the DROP VIEW statement. When you delete a view,
SQL Server automatically deletes the view definition and any permissions you've
assigned to users for it. If you delete a table that's referenced by a view, SQL
Server doesn't automatically drop the view. In this scenario, you must manually
drop the view. You can use the sp_depends stored procedure to determine if a
table has any dependent views by using the following syntax:

```
sp_depends object_name
```

You must be the owner of a view to delete it. But, if you're a member of the sysadmins server role or the database owner database role, you can drop a view that's owned by another user by specifying the owner's name in the DROP VIEW statement.

Use the following syntax to delete a view:

```
DROP VIEW [owner.] view_name
```

TASK 9A-3:

Dropping a View

1. **Write and execute a query for dropping the view named MyTitleView from the pubs database. Record your query in the following space.**

2. **Execute a new query:**

```
SELECT *
FROM information_schema.views
```

Verify that the MyTitleView view no longer exists in the pubs database.

3. **Clear the Query window.**

Using Views to Work With Data

You can insert, update, and delete rows from a table by using a view. Note that traditional views don't contain the actual data in a table; instead, views are simply windows to the data in the table. If you've configured any of the columns in the tables on which the view is based to not permit nulls, and these columns aren't contained in the view, you won't be able to insert rows into the table. Depending on the UPDATE statement, you might not be able to change the table either.

You can't modify the data in more than one table through a view. If a view is based on joined tables, you can modify the data in only one of the joined tables, not both. If you want to modify the data in both tables on which a view is based, you'll need to write separate statements for modifying the data in each table.

Because traditional views are essentially windows to your tables, you can't insert, update, or delete rows if your statements will violate data integrity. For example, the rental and rental_detail tables in the movies database are linked together in a primary key to foreign key relationship based on the invoice_num column. So, you can't change a value in the invoice_num column in either table, nor can you change it through a view.

Use the following syntax to insert data into a table by using a view:

```
INSERT INTO view_name
VALUES(value_list)
```

Replace the *value_list* with a list of values you want to insert into the columns contained in the view.

Use the following syntax to update data through a view:

```
UPDATE view_name
SET column_name = value
WHERE condition
```

Likewise, you can use the following syntax to delete rows through a view:

```
DELETE FROM view_name
WHERE condition
```

One of the problems you can encounter when users make changes to data through a view instead of modifying a table directly is that their changes can cause a row to disappear from the view. For example, let's say that you've created the following view:

```
USE pubs
GO
CREATE VIEW dbo.UtahAuthors
AS
SELECT au_id, au_lname, au_fname, state
FROM pubs
WHERE state = 'UT'
```

In this scenario, it's possible that a user could add a row to the pubs table using this view, but use a value other than "UT" in the state column. This means that as soon as the user adds the row, the row would disappear from the view. You can avoid this problem by creating the view and specifying WITH CHECK OPTION as part of the view's definition. This option forces users to enter data that conforms to the SELECT statement you specified in the view—including the condition you specified in the WHERE clause. If a user attempts to add or modify a row that doesn't conform to the SELECT statement, SQL Server displays an error message. Here's the syntax if you want to specify the WITH CHECK OPTION:

```
USE pubs
GO
CREATE VIEW dbo.UtahAuthors
AS
SELECT au_id, au_lname, au_fname, state
FROM pubs
WHERE state = 'UT'
WITH CHECK OPTION
```

APPLY YOUR KNOWLEDGE 9-3

Suggested time:

20 minutes

Using a View to Work With Data

Objective: To create a view containing all columns in the movie table except the movie_num and date_purch columns. You'll then use this view to work with the data in the movie table.

1. In SQL Query Analyzer, design and execute a query to create a view named MovieView. Configure dbo as the owner of the view. Include the title, category_num, rating, and rental_price columns in the view. What query did you use?

2. Can you use this view to insert data into the movie table? (Hint: You can review the structure of the movie table by looking at it in the movies database diagram or by executing the query `sp_help movie`.)

3. Design and execute a query to insert a new movie into the table by using the view. Use values of your choice. (To choose a movie category number before you add the row, you can use the query `SELECT * FROM` category to view a list of categories.)

4. Verify that your new movie was added to the table by using a `SELECT` statement against the MovieView. (Your new movie will appear in alphabetical order because you've defined a clustered index on the title column.) Write your query here.

5. Verify the movie number and date purchased assigned to the new movie by querying the movie table directly.

   What query did you use?

6. Clear the Query window.

Creating Indexed Views

One of the enhancements in SQL Server 2000 is that you can create an index that's based on a view. The advantage to creating such an index is that it forces SQL Server to store the view's results set as an object within the database. This means that when you select information from a view, SQL Server won't have to retrieve the data from the table or tables on which you've based the view—which can significantly improve the performance of the view. You create an indexed view by defining a unique clustered index on that view. (You can also create nonclustered indexes on a view, but you must create the clustered index first.) Notice that the clustered index must be unique, which means that you must base it on a column that contains unique values (such as the primary key).

After you create indexes on a view, SQL Server automatically updates them whenever you (or your users) make changes to the views' base tables. Of course, you should keep in mind that there's a cost associated with updating an index. So, you should make sure that the cost of updating the index is less than the cost SQL Server incurs when retrieving a view's results set. You'll typically find that an indexed view works best when you don't make changes to its base tables very often. You'll also see significant performance gains with an indexed view if your users frequently perform complex queries on the base tables.

So how do you go about creating an indexed view? Well, your first step is to create a regular old view, but you must create it with the WITH SCHEMABINDING option. This option binds the base table's schema to the view, which means that you can't drop or alter the base table unless you first drop the view (or modify the view to remove the SCHEMABINDING option). Using this option enables SQL Server to prevent indexed views from having schemas that are different from that of their base tables, and from having an indexed view for which its base table no longer exists. The SCHEMABINDING option requires that you use each table or user-defined function's two-part name, meaning you must include the owner name as part of the object name. Here's how you create the view:

```
USE database_name
GO
CREATE VIEW view_name
WITH SCHEMABINDING
AS
SELECT column_list
FROM owner.table_name
```

As you know, it's possible for you to create a view based on tables owned by another user. However, you can't create a view with the SCHEMABINDING option based on tables you don't own. That's because using the SCHEMABINDING option effectively prevents the tables' owner from making changes to their schema. If the tables' owner wants to permit you to create a view with the SCHEMABINDING option, the owner must grant you the REFERENCES permission for the table (or tables) on which you want to base your view.

Now that you've created your view, your next step is to create the unique clustered index based on the view. As a reminder, here's the basic syntax for creating a clustered index:

```
CREATE UNIQUE CLUSTERED INDEX index_name
ON view_name (column_name)
```

You can create an indexed view only on tables; you can't create an indexed view based on another view.

Only the SQL Server 2000 Enterprise Edition supports indexed views.

You can use the query SELECT
OBJECTPROPERTY(OBJECT_ID('view_name'), 'IsIndexable') to
determine whether or not you can create an index on a view. This query returns a
value of 1 if the view is indexable, and 0 if it isn't.

TASK 9A-4:

Creating an Indexed View

1. In SQL Query Analyzer, **open the C:\Data\indexed_view.sql script file.**

2. **Highlight and execute the query to view the definition of the view named MovieView.** This query enables you to see the SELECT statement that makes up the view.

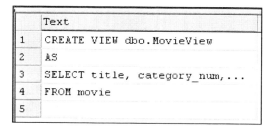

	Text
1	CREATE VIEW dbo.MovieView
2	AS
3	SELECT title, category_num,...
4	FROM movie
5	

3. **Can you create a clustered index based on this view? Why or why not?**

4. **Highlight and execute the SELECT OBJECTPROPERTY query.** You use this query to determine if you can define an index for a view. You should see that you can't index MovieView.

5. **Highlight and execute the query to alter the MovieView so that it's indexable.** This query adds the WITH SCHEMABINDING option to the view, and uses the two-part name for the movie table. In addition, it adds the movie_num column to the view so that it contains a unique column on which you can base the view's clustered index.

6. **Highlight and execute the query to create the unique clustered index on MovieView.**

7. **Highlight and execute the sp_helpindex query.** You use this query to verify that you successfully created the index based on MovieView.

8. **Open a new Query window, and then close the Query window containing the indexed_view.sql script file.**

Partitioned Views

Another technique you can use to improve your server's performance is to implement a partitioned view. Such a view can be based on data from multiple sources (such as multiple SQL servers or multiple instances of SQL Server) or even on data from heterogeneous sources (such as data on an Oracle server). One way that a partitioned view enhances performance is that SQL Server can scan all tables referenced by the view simultaneously if those tables are on separate servers or if the tables are on the same server as long as the server has multiple processors.

You create a partitioned view by specifying the UNION ALL keywords as part of the SELECT statement. If you recall, the UNION ALL keywords enable you to combine the rows generated by two or more SELECT statements into a single results set. For example, let's say that you have two tables in which you maintain the sales orders for two different retail stores. If you want to consolidate the data so that you can view both tables' data together, you could use the following syntax:

```
CREATE VIEW SalesTotalsView
AS
SELECT *
FROM store1
        UNION ALL
SELECT *
FROM store2
```

Before you attempt to create a partitioned view, keep the following factors in mind:

* All of the columns you reference in their relative positions within the SELECT statements must have the same data type and collation. In other words, if your first SELECT statement retrieves two columns, each with the varchar data type, the second SELECT statement must also retrieve two columns that use the varchar data type.

* You must include a column in both SELECT statements for which you've defined a CHECK constraint. In addition, you must reference this column in the same relative position in both SELECT statements. (This means that if you reference this column as the third column in one SELECT statement, you must also reference it as the third column in the other SELECT statement.) Microsoft refers to this column as the *partitioning column*, and you use it to make sure that the data stored in each table is mutually exclusive. For example, in the previous example where we have two tables containing each store's sales orders, you could define a check constraint on a column containing the store ID number in both tables.

* You can't base a table's partitioning column on a computed column. In addition, you can't base a partitioned view on a table for which you've defined an index based on a computed column.

* You can't reference a table more than once in the view definition.

* You can create a distributed partitioned view, which means that the view references a table on a remote server. In this scenario, you must first define the remote server as a linked server. We show you how to define a linked server in the "Implementing Distributed Queries" lesson.

partitioning column:
The column in each table you reference in a partitioned view that you use to ensure that each table's data is mutually exclusive.

Creating a partitioned view automatically implies the WITH CHECK OPTION on that view. This means that SQL Server will enforce the check constraints you defined on the underlying tables whenever you use this view to modify data. Let's take a look at how you create and use a partitioned view.

TASK 9A-5:

Creating a Partitioned View

1. In SQL Query Analyzer, **open the C:\Data\partitioned_view.sql script file.** You're going to use this script file to create tables, insert data into them, and then create a partitioned view based on the tables.

2. **Highlight and execute the two CREATE TABLE statements** to create the tables named store1 and store2 within the movies database. **Notice that the CREATE TABLE statements include a check constraint on the storeID column in both tables.**

```
Query - sqlserver2.movies.SQLSERVER2\Rozanne - F:\Data\partitioned_view.sql
--Step 2: Query to create each store's table.
USE movies
GO
CREATE TABLE store1
(orderID int,
total money,
storeID char(3) CHECK (storeID = '001'),
PRIMARY KEY (orderID, storeID))

CREATE TABLE store2
(orderID int,
total money,
storeID char(3) CHECK (storeID = '002'),
PRIMARY KEY (orderID, storeID))
```

3. **Highlight and execute the two INSERT statements** to insert a row into each table. **Notice that each INSERT statement doesn't violate the table's check constraint.**

4. **Highlight and execute the CREATE VIEW statement** to create the partitioned view named SalesTotalsView. Because both tables have the same structure, you don't have to worry about the order of the columns or their data types.

5. **Highlight and execute the SELECT statement.** You use this statement to access the partitioned view. You see the rows from both tables, store1, and store2.

	orderID	total	storeID
1	10123	3230.0000	001
2	20549	4379.0000	002

6. **Highlight and execute the INSERT INTO SalesTotalsView statement.** Because this statement doesn't violate the check constraint, SQL Server permits you to insert the row.

7. **Into which table do you think SQL Server inserted the row?**

8. **Highlight and execute the `SELECT` queries for the SalesTotalsView and store1 table.** You can see that SQL Server inserted the new row into the store1 table.

9. **Highlight and execute the last `INSERT` statement in the script file.** This query enables you to see the error message SQL Server displays when you violate a base table's check constraint.

10. **Close all open windows.**

Summary

Views offer you a powerful resource for providing easy access to data, securing your server (because users don't need access to the view's underlying tables), and enhanced performance (through indexed views and partitioned views). In this lesson, you learned how to create each type of view and access its data.

LESSON 9 REVIEW

9A You would like to prevent anyone from reading the statement you used to build a view. What should you do?

Creating Stored Procedures

Overview

In SQL Server, you create stored procedures as a way of automating any tasks that you perform on a regular basis. In addition, you use them to make programs more modular and to take advantage of the performance benefits stored procedures offer you. (For example, SQL Server automatically caches the execution plans of stored procedures the first time you run them, which means that you'll see enhanced performance each time you run them after that.) Many programming languages such as Visual Basic enable you to call stored procedures from within your programs. This means that you'll see enhanced performance with these programs as well. In this lesson, we're going to define all of the factors you should consider when designing stored procedures, and how you go about creating, executing, and managing them.

Data Files:
extended_proc.sql
create_proc.sql
createproc_lab.sql
input.sql
output.sql
return_codes.sql
custom_errors.sql
addnewmovie.sql

Lesson Time:
3 hours

Objectives

To design and implement stored procedures, you will:

10A **Identify the considerations for designing stored procedures.**

In this topic, we're going to explore the different types of stored procedures SQL Server supports, including system, extended, and user-defined. We also examine how SQL Server processes stored procedures the first time you run them.

10B **Create stored procedures.**

Here's where we get down to the details. In this topic, you're going to learn how to create stored procedures by using the CREATE PROCEDURE SQL statement. You'll learn how to execute stored procedures, and how to insert data using a stored procedure.

10C **Use parameters in stored procedures.**

In this topic, we're going to explore the techniques you can use to make your stored procedures more flexible. You can use input parameters to pass values to stored procedures, and you can use output parameters to retrieve the results of a stored procedure. You'll also learn how you can detect and manage errors within stored procedures.

10D **Manage stored procedures.**

SQL Server includes techniques that you can use to control when it compiles stored procedures. In this topic, you're going to learn how to manage the compilation of stored procedures. We'll also explore the techniques you can use to analyze stored procedure performance in System Monitor and SQL Profiler.

TOPIC 10A

Designing Stored Procedures

procedure cache:
*The memory in which SQL
Server stores compiled query
execution plans.*

Although at its core a stored procedure is simply a named series of SQL statements just like any other query, a stored procedure offers several distinct advantages over sending the equivalent statement (or statements) as a regular query. First, after SQL Server parses and compiles a stored procedure, it caches the execution plans in its *procedure cache*. When you run the same stored procedure again, SQL Server can re-use the cached execution plan instead. For this reason, stored procedures execute faster than if you execute their SQL statements individually. Second, if you call stored procedures from your applications instead of explicitly writing the queries into your applications, it is much easier for you to change a query within a stored procedure than it is to search for and change the code in an application.

Another advantage of stored procedures is that you typically batch your SQL statements within them. Batches offer you enhanced performance because SQL Server can process all of the statements together instead of individually. You can also see that executing a stored procedure that contains SQL batches will reduce your network traffic. This is because SQL Server can send the results set for all of the statements in the batch at the same time rather than individually.

Some of the features of stored procedures include:

- Can contain virtually any SQL statement, including commands to execute other stored procedures.

- Can accept input parameters and generate output parameters.

- Capable of returning a status code to indicate what happened during the execution of the stored procedure.

SQL Server supports three types of stored procedures. The first two types of stored procedures, system and extended, are built-in, which means they're installed automatically when you install SQL Server itself. The third type of stored procedure is user-defined: you create these yourself. User-defined stored procedures can be local, temporary, or remote.

System and Extended Stored Procedures

Microsoft has written many system stored procedures to perform a wide variety of administration tasks. The system stored procedures are stored in the master database. All of the system stored procedures have names that begin with *sp_* . Even though these stored procedures are stored in the master database, you can execute them from within any database on your server without having to use a fully qualified object name. For example, the `sp_helptext` stored procedure enables you to view the definition of a view or stored procedure, and you can execute this stored procedure simply by executing `sp_helptext` regardless of your current database. (In other words, you don't have to use `master.dbo.sp_helptext` if your current database isn't the master database.)

SQL Server also includes extended stored procedures. These are implemented as dynamic link libraries (DLLs). Extended stored procedures primarily have names that begin with *xp_*. For example, the `xp_cmdshell` extended stored procedure enables you to shell out to the operating system (typically Windows 2000) to run an operating system command. Another extended stored procedure, xp_sendmail, enables SQL Server to send email messages. You must execute extended stored procedures either from within the master database or by using a fully qualified name (such as master.dbo.xp_cmdshell).

User-defined Stored Procedures

You can create several types of user-defined stored procedures: local, temporary, and remote. If you create a stored procedure as a database object within a database, this type of stored procedure is referred to as local. These types of stored procedures are considered permanent. That is, they're always available for execution unless you delete them. You can create user-defined stored procedures in any database including the master database.

You can create two types of temporary stored procedures: local or global. You identify a temporary stored procedure as either local or global by preceding its name with a # if it's local, and ## if it's global. A local stored procedure is available only to you during your current session. A global stored procedure is available to all current sessions on your server.

SQL Server 2000 includes support for remote stored procedures to support legacy applications. These types of stored procedures have been replaced in SQL Server 2000 by distributed queries.

TASK 10A-1:

Using Books Online to Research System Stored Procedures

Setup: You're logged on to Windows 2000 as student#. You've created a database named movies and tables within it named movie, category, customer, rental, and rental_detail. You've defined primary key, foreign key, default, and check constraints on the tables, and created nonclustered indexes based on your primary keys. You've imported data into the tables. You've created database diagrams for both the movies and pubs databases.

1. **Start SQL Server Books Online.**

2. On the Contents page, **expand Transact-SQL Reference.**

3. **Expand System Stored Procedures** to view a list of system stored procedures included with SQL Server 2000. (You'll need to scroll several screens down the Contents page to find system stored procedures.)

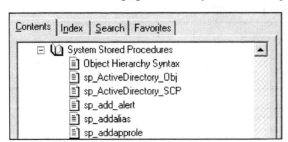

4.   On the Contents page, **select the stored procedure `sp_helptext`** to display the help screen for this stored procedure.

> ### sp_helptext
> Prints the text of a rule, a default, or an unencrypted stored procedure, user-defined function, trigger, or view.
>
> **Syntax**
> **sp_helptext** [**@objname** =] '*name*'
>
> **Arguments**
> [**@objname** =] '*name*'
>   Is the name of the object for which to display definition information. The object must be in the current database. *name* is **nvarchar(776)**, with no default.

5.   **In what scenario would you use the `sp_helptext` stored procedure?**

6.   **Close SQL Server Books Online.**

Executing Extended Stored Procedures

If you want to run an extended stored procedure, you must either run it from within the master database, or identify the master database as part of the name as follows:

```
master.owner.extended_procedure_name.
```

You can leave out the owner name if you're the owner of the procedure. You can view the name of the DLL file that makes up an extended, stored procedure by executing the following query:

```
sp_helptext extended_procedure_name
```

You can create your own extended stored procedures but you must store them within the master database. You can use extended stored procedures to call your own external programs in programming languages such as C++ and Visual Basic. You can include functions within an extended stored procedure.

TASK 10A-2:

Running Extended Stored Procedures

1.   **Start SQL Query Analyzer and log on with Windows Authentication.**

2.   **Open the C:\Data\extended_proc.sql script file.**

3. **Highlight and execute the `master..xp_logininfo` query.** This query enables you to view a list of Windows login accounts on your server. If this statement wasn't the first line of the query, you would have had to precede it with the EXEC keyword.

	account name	type	privilege	mapped login name	permission path
1	BUILTIN\Administrators	group	admin	BUILTIN\Administrators	NULL
2	CLASSROOM\sqlservice	user	admin	CLASSROOM\sqlservice	NULL
3	CLASSROOM\Rozanne	user	user	CLASSROOM\Rozanne	NULL

4. **Highlight and execute the query `master..xp_cmdshell 'dir'`.** This stored procedure enables you to run an external operating system command and return its results to SQL Query Analyzer's results pane.

	output
1	Volume in drive C has no label.
2	Volume Serial Number is 580E-F491
3	NULL
4	Directory of C:\WINNT\system32
5	NULL
6	05/06/2001 10:24a \<DIR\> .

5. **Highlight and execute the query `sp_helptext xp_cmdshell`** to view the name of the DLL file associated with the extended stored procedure.

	Text
1	xplog70.dll

6. **Open a new Query window, and then close the Query window containing the extended_proc.sql script file.**

Running Stored Procedures the First Time

When you run a stored procedure for the first time, SQL Server must begin by parsing the stored procedure. Next, it compiles your stored procedure. Finally, SQL Server executes the procedure. Let's take a look at each of these steps in more detail.

Parse

When you run a stored procedure for the first time, SQL Server parses the SQL statements to test their accuracy. SQL Server does support delayed name resolution, which enables your stored procedures to reference objects that don't already exist (this scenario typically occurs when you create objects when the stored procedure executes). It then translates the SQL statements into an internal format for processing; this format is called the query tree or sequence tree. Finally, SQL Server updates the sysobjects system table with the name of your stored procedure. It also writes a row to the syscomments system table with the text of the stored procedure.

Compile

After SQL Server has the sequence tree for your stored procedure, it can compile an execution plan. SQL Server checks your security as well as determines how to optimize the query as part of creating the execution plan. The execution plan contains step-by-step instructions on how SQL Server will process the query. For example, the execution plan includes the steps for checking any constraints you might have on referenced tables.

Execute

SQL Server can process the stored procedure after it completes creating the execution plan. SQL Server sends statements within the stored procedure to the appropriate manager for those statements. For example, if your stored procedure contains Data Definition Language (DDL) statements for creating objects such as tables, SQL Server sends those statements to the DDL manager.

Running Stored Procedures a Second Time

After you run a stored procedure for the first time, SQL Server caches the execution plan in its procedure cache. All subsequent executions of the same stored procedure can then use this cached execution plan unless one of the following conditions occurs:

- You restart your server (which clears the procedure cache).

- You make changes to the structure of any table or view referenced in your stored procedure.

- You generate new index statistics for a table by using the UPDATE STATISTICS statement.

- You drop an index that was used by the stored procedure's execution plan.

- You make considerable changes to the index keys in the table referenced in the stored procedure.

- You force SQL Server to recompile the stored procedure's execution plan.

If any of these conditions occurs, SQL Server must retrieve your stored procedure's definition from the syscomments table, recompile its execution plan, and then cache it again in the procedure cache. The advantage to a stored procedure is that after the execution plan is cached, SQL Server can simply retrieve it from RAM, rather than parsing and recompiling the stored procedure each time you run it. This means that you'll see the performance benefits of stored procedures the second time you run them (but not the first time).

Notice that if you restart your server, SQL Server clears the procedure cache. SQL Server must parse and recompile the execution plans of stored procedures whenever you reboot. If you have stored procedures that you use frequently, you can create a stored procedure to execute them, and then configure this stored procedure to run automatically when you start up your server.

TASK 10A-3:

Understanding How SQL Server Processes Stored Procedures

1. How does a stored procedure differ from a SQL script file?

2. What scenarios will cause SQL Server to automatically parse and recompile a stored procedure?

TOPIC 10B

Creating Stored Procedures

Now that we've looked at the role of stored procedures, let's move on to how you go about creating them. You create a stored procedure by using the CREATE PROCEDURE Transact-SQL statement in SQL Query Analyzer. (You can also create a stored procedure by right-clicking on the Stored Procedure object within a database in SQL Server Enterprise Manager. You then type the SQL statements into your stored procedure just as you would within the SQL Query Analyzer.) You might find it a little easier to develop your stored procedure within SQL Query Analyzer because you can test your SQL statements as you write them. Then after you've debugged your statements, simply add the CREATE PROCEDURE statement to them.

Use the following syntax to create a stored procedure:

```
CREATE PROCEDURE procedure_name
[WITH option]
AS
        sql_statement [...n]
GO
```

Replace *procedure_name* with the name you want to assign to your stored procedure. You can abbreviate CREATE PROCEDURE as CREATE PROC. You can't use the CREATE PROCEDURE statement along with other statements in a batch; you must follow it with the GO keyword. For example, you might create the following stored procedure to list all of the rented movies that are due today:

In this stored procedure, you must convert the due_date and getdate() values to character strings because both contain not just a date but also a time. You must strip out the month, day, and year information from the time information in order for this WHERE condition to work. Otherwise, you would be able to see a list of movies due only if they happened to be due today and at the exact current time.

```
USE movies
GO
CREATE PROC dbo.MoviesDue
AS
  SELECT m.title, m.movie_num, rd.invoice_num, r.due_date
  FROM rental AS r JOIN rental_detail AS rd
  ON r.invoice_num = rd.invoice_num
  JOIN movie AS m
  ON rd.movie_num = m.movie_num
  WHERE convert(char(10), r.due_date, 101)
      = convert(char(10), getdate(), 101)
GO
```

Because you can't include the CREATE PROC statement with other statements, you must end it with the GO keyword. As you can see in the previous example, the GO keyword comes after the SQL statements that make up your stored procedure.

Your stored procedure can refer to just about anything in a database, including tables, user-defined functions, views, other stored procedures, and temporary tables. Keep in mind that if you design your stored procedure to create a temporary table, that table's available to you only while the stored procedure is executing.

Permissions

To create a stored procedure, you must be either a member of the sysadmins server role or a member of the db_owner or ddl_admin database roles for the database in which you're attempting to create the procedure. If you have users who you want to create stored procedures, but you don't want them to be a member of either the server or database roles, you can explicitly grant these users the CREATE PROCEDURE statement permission.

You should try to avoid breaking the ownership chain between a stored procedure and the tables or views on which it is based. Microsoft recommends that you make the dbo user the owner of all objects in the database (including stored procedures) to avoid this problem.

Limitations

Your stored procedures can be up to 128 MB in size, but can be further limited by the amount of available RAM in your server. You can nest up to 32 levels of stored procedures. You nest stored procedures when one stored procedure calls another.

You can't include the following statements in a stored procedure:

- CREATE DEFAULT
- CREATE PROCEDURE
- CREATE RULE
- CREATE TRIGGER
- CREATE VIEW

Recommendations

After you've debugged your stored procedure on the SQL server, you should always test it from a client computer. This test will enable you to detect any communication problems between the client and the server. You should also test it logged on as a typical user, not as a system administrator so that you can verify that you've given users sufficient permissions.

Viewing the Text of Stored Procedures

You can view the text of a stored procedure by using the `sp_helptext` system stored procedure. For example, to view the text of the MoviesDue stored procedure, use the following syntax:

```
sp_helptext MoviesDue
```

You can also use the `sp_help` stored procedure to view information about who owns a stored procedure, as well as when the stored procedure was created. Use the following syntax:

```
sp_help procedure_name
```

The `sp_depends` stored procedure enables you to see a list of objects on which a stored procedure depends. For example, you can use `sp_depends` to determine which tables a stored procedure references. Use the following syntax with `sp_depends`:

```
sp_depends procedure_name
```

Finally, you can use the `sp_stored_procedures` procedure to list all of the defined stored procedures in your current database. Use the following syntax:

```
sp_stored_procedures
```

TASK 10B-1:

Creating a Stored Procedure

Objective: To create a stored procedure for displaying a list of movies sorted by category.

1.   In SQL Query Analyzer, **open the C:\Data\create_proc.sql stored procedure.**

2.   **Highlight and execute the first query in the script file.** You can use this query to verify that it works and that it provides you with the desired results set. This query lists each movie on file along with the category of that movie. (The DISTINCT keyword prevents SQL Server from displaying multiple copies of the movies.)

	title	description
1	African Queen The	Adventure
2	Indiana Jones and the Last ...	Adventure
3	Raiders of the Lost Ark	Adventure
4	Tarzan	Adventure
5	Fish Called Wanda A	Comedy

3. **Highlight and execute the query to create the MovieByCategory stored procedure.**

4. **Highlight and execute the `sp_helptext` query.** You can use the `sp_helptext` stored procedure to view an unencrypted stored procedure's definition.

	Text
1	CREATE PROC dbo.MovieByCategory
2	AS
3	SELECT DISTINCT m.title, c.description
4	FROM movie AS m JOIN category AS c
5	ON m.category_num = c.category_num
6	ORDER BY c.description, m.title

5. **Open a new Query window, and then close the Query window containing the create_proc.sql script.**

Executing Stored Procedures

SQL Server requires that you run a stored procedure either as the first line of a query or that you precede it with the EXECUTE (or EXEC) keyword. For example, you'll get an error message if you execute the following query:

```
USE movies
GO
SELECT *
FROM movie
sp_help movie
```

This query won't work because the `sp_help` stored procedure isn't the first line of the query, and you haven't preceded it with the EXECUTE keyword. You can rewrite this query so that it will run successfully by using the following syntax:

```
USE movies
GO
SELECT *
FROM movie
EXEC sp_help movie
```

If you choose to run a stored procedure simply by typing its name (and not the EXECUTE or EXEC keywords), you must make it the first statement in a batch. You must use a fully qualified name to run a stored procedure that's stored in a database other than your current database. For example, if you want to run the MoviesDue example stored procedure, but your current database is pubs, you can use the name `movies.dbo.MoviesDue` to run it.

Using Stored Procedures to Insert Data

You can use a stored procedure to insert data into a table based on the results set. For this to work, the results set returned by the stored procedure must supply the appropriate values and data types for the table's columns. For example, you might use a stored procedure to extract data from one table, modify its format, and then insert it into another table. To insert the results set of a stored procedure into a table, use the following syntax:

```
USE database
INSERT INTO table_name
EXEC procedure_name
```

TASK 10B-2:

Executing a Stored Procedure

1. In SQL Query Analyzer, **execute the following query:**

    ```
    EXEC MovieByCategory
    ```

    (You can also use EXECUTE MovieByCategory or MovieByCategory to run this stored procedure.)

2. **Look at the Results pane.** You should see a list of movies sorted by category (Adventure, Comedy, Drama, etc.).

3. **Clear the Query window.**

Preventing Users From Reading the Text of a Stored Procedure

You can use the WITH ENCRYPTION keywords in the CREATE PROCEDURE statement to encrypt the definition of a stored procedure. You can't read the contents of an encrypted stored procedure. Use the following syntax to encrypt a stored procedure:

```
CREATE PROCEDURE procedure_name
WITH ENCRYPTION
AS
        sql_statement [...n]
GO
```

Just as in views, SQL Server stores the definition of your stored procedure in the syscomments system table. You should never edit this table directly, especially if you want to hide the definition of a stored procedure. Instead, you should encrypt the stored procedure.

APPLY YOUR KNOWLEDGE 10-1

Creating and Running Stored Procedures

Objective: To create stored procedures for producing some of the reports you would like to retrieve from the movies database. If necessary, refer to your database diagram for the movies database in SQL Server Enterprise Manager.

1. By using the movies database, design a query for listing the customer name, invoice number, and rental date. (You can use CONVERT(CHAR(10), rental_date, 101) to format the date.) Sort the results by customer name and rental date. After you've tested the query, create a stored procedure based on this query and name it RentalsByCustomer. What query did you use?

2. Save the statements you use to create the stored procedure in a script file. (Choose File→Save As.) Name the script file rentals.sql, and save it in your My Documents folder.

3. Open a new Query window, and then close the Query window that contains the rentals.sql script.

4. Check the statements in your stored procedure by using `sp_helptext`. What query did you use?

5. Verify that the stored procedure you created in step 1 works by running it. What command did you use to run the stored procedure?

6. Clear the Query window.

7. By using the movies database, design a query for listing the category description, title, and rating for all movies that have rented. Sort the results by category description and title. After you've tested the query, create an encrypted stored procedure based on this query and name it RentalsByCategory. (Hint: You must use a three-table join in your SELECT statement.) What query did you use?

8. Save the statements you use to create the stored procedure in a script file. Name the script file category.sql.

9. Open a new Query window, and then close the query window that contains the category.sql script.

10. Verify that you can't read the stored procedure's definition by using sp_helptext. (You should see a message stating that the object's comments are encrypted.) What query did you use?

11. Verify that your stored procedure works by running it.

12. Clear the Query window.

Modifying a Stored Procedure

You can change a stored procedure by using the ALTER PROCEDURE statement. (You can also use ALTER PROC.) When you change a stored procedure, SQL Server replaces its previous definition with the new definition (SQL statements) you specify. Modifying a stored procedure instead of dropping and re-creating it enables you to retain the permissions you've assigned to users for the stored procedure. If you want to modify an encrypted stored procedure, you must include the WITH ENCRYPTION option in the ALTER PROCEDURE statement.

You must be the owner of the stored procedure, a member of the sysadmins server role, or a member of either the db_owner or db_ddladmin database roles in order to modify a stored procedure. You can't assign the permission for editing a stored procedure.

You can use ALTER PROCEDURE to modify only one stored procedure at a time. If you want to modify several nested stored procedures, you must modify each one individually.

Use the following syntax to edit a stored procedure:

```
ALTER PROCEDURE procedure_name
[WITH option]
AS
        sql_statement [...n]
GO
```

Microsoft strongly recommends that you don't modify any of the system stored procedures that come with SQL Server. If you want to modify them, you should copy their definitions to a new stored procedure, and then make the necessary changes.

Dropping a Stored Procedure

You can drop a stored procedure by using the DROP PROCEDURE statement. You should always run the sp_depends stored procedure to check for objects that depend on a stored procedure before you drop it. After you've checked its dependencies, you can drop the procedure by using the following syntax:

```
DROP PROC owner.stored_procedure_name
```

APPLY YOUR KNOWLEDGE 10-2

Suggested time:
10 minutes

Modifying a Stored Procedure

> **Objective:** To modify the RentalsByCategory stored procedure.

1. In SQL Query Analyzer, open the script file named category.sql. This script file contains the commands for creating the RentalsByCategory stored procedure.

2. Add the necessary commands to your script file to modify the RentalsByCategory stored procedure to add the date you purchased the movie to the results set. Save your changes to a new script file named newcategory.sql. Record your new query in the following space.

3. Open a new Query window, and then close your old Query window.

4. Verify that your stored procedure works by running it.

5. Clear the Query window.

TOPIC 10C

Using Parameters in Stored Procedures

You can use *parameters* in stored procedures to make them more interactive. You can use both input and output parameters. *Input parameters* enable you to pass a value to a variable within the stored procedure. In contrast, *output parameters* return a value after you run a stored procedure. You can use output parameters to return information to a calling stored procedure. You can define a total of 1,024 parameters in a stored procedure.

Input Parameters

You begin implementing input parameters in stored procedures by first defining the name of the parameter as well as its data type. You can optionally assign a default value to the parameter. For example, you might want to create a stored procedure that enables you to list all customers who live in a specific ZIP code. Instead of hard-coding a specific ZIP code into the stored procedure, you can define an input parameter as part of the stored procedure, and then specify a ZIP code whenever you execute the stored procedure.

Use the following syntax to define an input parameter:

```
CREATE PROCEDURE procedure_name
[@parameter_name data_type] [= default_value]
[WITH option]
AS
sql_statement [...n]
```

In this syntax, you replace *@parameter_name* with the name you want to assign to the parameter, and *data_type* with the data type (such as char, varchar, and so on). You should typically define a default value for the parameter so that the stored procedure will run successfully in the event its user doesn't supply a value. You can use either constants (character strings or numeric values) or null for the default value.

The following example shows you how to define an input parameter. This parameter, *@rating*, enables you to pass a particular movie rating to the stored procedure. The SELECT statement then displays all movies in the movie table that have a rating equal to the rating you supply using the parameter.

```
CREATE PROCEDURE dbo.MovieByRating
@rating varchar(5) = null
AS
        SELECT rating, title
        FROM movie
        WHERE rating = @rating
        ORDER BY title
GO
```

In this example, we're using a default value of null for the @rating input parameter. This means that if you run this stored procedure without providing a value for the @rating parameter, you won't see any rows in the results set.

parameter:
A programming entity that enables you to send information to or retrieve information from a stored procedure.

input parameter:
A value that you pass into a stored procedure.

output parameter:
A value SQL Server passes out of a stored procedure. This value is typically generated by a statement within the stored procedure.

You can use an input parameter only within the stored procedure where you define it.

Executing a Stored Procedure With Input Parameters

You can pass values for parameters to a stored procedure either by reference or by position. If you pass a value by reference, you explicitly identify the name of the parameter followed by the value you want to use. Use the following syntax to pass a value by reference:

```
EXEC procedure_name @parameter_name = value
```

For example, to pass a value to the @rating parameter by reference, you could use this syntax:

```
EXEC MovieByRating @rating = 'G'
```

Notice that you must specify the parameter's value by using the appropriate syntax for its data type. In other words, values for character-based parameters must be enclosed in quotes.

You can also pass a value to a parameter simply by position. This means that SQL Server uses the first value you specify after the stored procedure name as the value for the first parameter in the stored procedure. If your stored procedure has multiple parameters, specify the values for each parameter separated by commas. You can skip a value for a parameter if you have specified a default value. Use the following syntax to specify a value for a parameter by position:

```
EXEC stored_procedure_name value [, value...]
```

For example, to use the MovieByRating stored procedure to list all movies with a G rating, and to specify a value for the input parameter by using position, you could also use this syntax:

```
EXEC MovieByRating 'G'
```

TASK 10C-1:

Creating a Stored Procedure With an Input Parameter

1. In SQL Query Analyzer, **open the C:\Data\input.sql script file.**

2. **Highlight and execute the query to create the MovieByRating stored procedure** to create a stored procedure for listing movies by rating. This procedure won't list any movies unless you run it with a parameter.

3. **Open a new Query window, and then close the old Query window containing the input.sql script file.**

4. **Write and execute a query to run the stored procedure; specify a value of your choice for the @rating parameter by reference. What query did you use?**

5. **Write and execute a query to execute the stored procedure; specify a value for the @rating parameter by position. What query did you use?**

6. **Clear the Query window.**

Checking for Valid Input Parameter Values

If your stored procedure uses parameters, you should include code for making sure that those parameters have values. You can do your error checking by using the IF statement. You can use the RETURN keyword to break out of the stored procedure if a parameter doesn't have an appropriate value. For example, you can use the following syntax to check the values for your input parameters:

```
CREATE PROCEDURE stored_procedure_name
@parameter data_type = value
AS
        IF @parameter IS NULL
                BEGIN
                        PRINT 'Message Line 1'
                        PRINT 'Message Line 2'
                RETURN -- Ends running the stored procedure
        END
        SELECT statement
GO
```

APPLY YOUR KNOWLEDGE 10-3

Suggested time:
15 minutes

Adding Syntax For Checking Parameters

Objective: To modify the MovieByRating stored procedure to check for parameters before it runs.

1.   In SQL Query Analyzer, open the input.sql script file. Modify the script so that it alters the stored procedure. Add an IF statement to check to see if the @rating parameter is null or if it isn't G, PG, R, NC17, or NR. (Hint: Use the NOT IN keywords.) Have the stored procedure display a message if the @rating parameter isn't set correctly, and then exit the stored procedure. Save the changes to a file named newmovierating.sql (choose File→Save As). Record your changes here.

2.   Execute your query to modify the MovieByRating stored procedures.

3.   Open a new Query window, and then close your previous Query window.

4. Test your `IF` statement by running the MovieByRating stored procedure without specifying any values. Test it again by using an incorrect rating such as 'Q'.

5. Clear the Query window.

Output Parameters

You can use output parameters to return a value from a stored procedure. This value can then be used by whatever method you used to call the stored procedure. For example, you might have two stored procedures: the first stored procedure calls the second, and the second procedure then returns a value to the first procedure. You might also simply call a stored procedure from a SQL statement, and then use the value in the output parameter in a subsequent SQL statement.

You'll typically use the values assigned to output parameters in other stored procedures. Output parameters thus enable you to use the results of one stored procedure in another stored procedure.

Identify an output parameter by adding the `OUTPUT` keyword to its definition within the stored procedure. In addition, you must also identify the output parameter as part of the `EXECUTE` statement you use to call its stored procedure. Use the following syntax to define an output parameter:

```
CREATE PROCEDURE procedure_name
[@parameter_name data_type] [= default_value] OUTPUT
[WITH option]
AS
        SQL statement [...n]
```

For example, the following stored procedure uses five output parameters to store the row counts of each of the tables in the movies database:

```
CREATE PROC count_rows
@movie_count int OUTPUT, @cust_count int OUTPUT, @cat_count int
OUTPUT,
@rental_count int OUTPUT, @rd_count int OUTPUT
AS
        SELECT @movie_count = COUNT(*) FROM movie
        SELECT @cust_count = COUNT(*) FROM customer
        SELECT @cat_count = COUNT(*) FROM category
        SELECT @rental_count = COUNT(*) FROM rental
        SELECT @rd_count = COUNT(*) FROM rental_detail
GO
```

Executing a Stored Procedure With Output Parameters

When you call a stored procedure that contains output parameters, you must declare the variables in which you want to store the output parameters. These variables can use the same names as the output parameters or different names. In addition, you must specify the names of the output parameters along with the `OUTPUT` keyword when you execute the stored procedure.

For example, to call the `count_rows` stored procedure from the previous example, you should use the following syntax:

```
DECLARE @movie_count int, @cust_count int,
  @cat_count int, @rental_count int, @rd_count int
EXEC count_rows @movie_count OUTPUT, @cust_count OUTPUT,
  @cat_count OUTPUT, @rental_count OUTPUT, @rd_count OUTPUT
SELECT @movie_count AS movie, @cust_count AS customer,
  @cat_count AS category,@rental_count AS rental,
  @rd_count AS rental_detail
```

In this example, using the same names for both the output parameters and the variables simplifies the information. When you run the stored procedure (as shown in the line that begins with EXEC), you specify the variables in which you want to store the output parameters' values. Finally, the SELECT line displays the contents of the variables. You can see the output from this example in Figure 10-1. The DECLARE line in this example simply declares the variables in which you want to store the values from the output parameters.

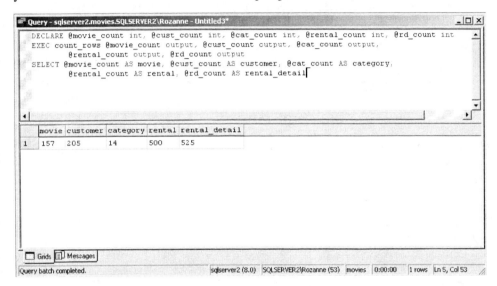

Figure 10-1: *The* `count_rows` *stored procedure lists each table in the movies database and the number of rows in each table.*

TASK 10C-2:

Creating and Executing a Stored Procedure With Output Parameters

1. In SQL Query Analyzer, **open the script file named C:\Data\output.sql.**

2. **To create the SimpleMath stored procedure, highlight and execute the following query:**

```
USE movies
GO
CREATE PROC dbo.SimpleMath
@x smallint,
@y smallint,
@calculation smallint OUTPUT
AS
        SET @calculation = @x + @y
GO
```

3. **In the above query, what type of parameters are @x and @y? How do they get values?**

4. **Highlight and execute the next query (the one that begins with the DECLARE statement)** to run the SimpleMath stored procedure. Notice that you supplied the values for the input parameters @x and @y by reference. Because @x is the first parameter defined in the stored procedure, when you execute SimpleMath, the first value you specify is stored in @x (in this example, 8).

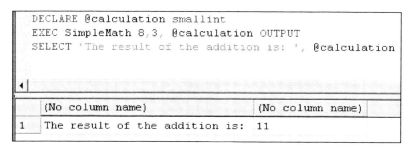

```
DECLARE @calculation smallint
EXEC SimpleMath 8,3, @calculation OUTPUT
SELECT 'The result of the addition is: ', @calculation
```

(No column name)	(No column name)
1	The result of the addition is:	11

5. **Open a new Query window, and then close the window containing the output.sql script.**

Managing Errors

SQL Server provides you with several tools you can use to manage errors in your stored procedures. These tools include the RETURN SQL statement, sp_addmessage stored procedure, the RAISERROR statement, and the @@ERROR function. Let's start by looking at the RETURN statement.

The RETURN Statement

You use the RETURN statement to force an unconditional exit from a stored procedure. You can use the RETURN statement by itself, or you can use it to return status codes to a calling stored procedure, SQL statement batch, or application. For example, by default, a return value of zero (0) indicates that the stored procedure ran successfully. SQL Server currently uses return values 0 to -14 and has reserved the values -15 to -99. You can specify your own status codes as well. Any user-defined status codes take precedence over the SQL Server status codes. In the following example, we're using the RETURN statement simply to exit the stored procedure.

```
USE pubs
GO
CREATE PROCEDURE dbo.ListAuthors
@author_id varchar(10) = null
AS
        IF @author_id IS NULL
                BEGIN
                    PRINT 'Please enter a valid author ID number.'
                    PRINT 'Use the format 999-99-9999.'
                    RETURN -- Ends running the stored procedure
        END
        SELECT au_lname, au_fname, au_id
        FROM authors
        WHERE au_id = @author_id
GO
```

If you have the RETURN keyword return a status code, then these return codes actually function as output parameters. You must save the return code into a variable in order to use it for further processing. For example, the following stored procedure returns the total number of rows in the results set as a RETURN status code:

```
CREATE PROCEDURE dbo.NumRentals
@cust_num cust_num = null
AS
  SELECT CONVERT(CHAR(10),rental_date,101) AS 'rental date',
    invoice_num, cust_num
  FROM rental
  WHERE cust_num = @cust_num
  RETURN (@@rowcount)
GO
```

Just as you must declare a variable for SQL Server to store the values of output parameters, so must you declare a variable for return status codes. Continuing with the previous example, you could use the following query to run the NumRentals stored procedure, store the return status code in the variable named @answer, and then display it on the screen:

```
DECLARE @answer smallint
EXEC @answer = NumRentals 74
SELECT 'Total number of rentals is: ', @answer
```

In this example, the DECLARE statement initializes the variable @answer. Next, the EXEC @answer = NumRentals 74 statement runs the NumRentals stored procedure with an input parameter of 74 (a customer's account number) and stores the return status code to the @answer variable. Finally, the SELECT statement simply displays the return status code (in this case, the number of rows in the results set). The results of this query are shown in Figure 10-2.

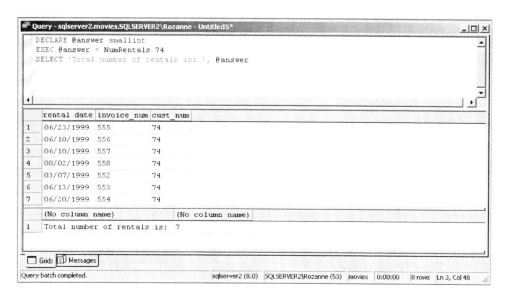

```
DECLARE @answer smallint
EXEC @answer = NumRentals 74
SELECT 'Total number of rentals is: ', @answer
```

	rental date	invoice_num	cust_num
1	06/23/1999	555	74
2	06/10/1999	556	74
3	06/10/1999	557	74
4	08/02/1999	558	74
5	03/07/1999	552	74
6	06/13/1999	553	74
7	06/20/1999	554	74

	(No column name)	(No column name)
1	Total number of rentals is:	7

Grid | Messages

Query batch completed.   sqlserver2 (8.0) | SQLSERVER2\Rozanne (53) | movies | 0:00:00 | 8 rows | Ln 3, Col 48

Figure 10-2: *You can use the* RETURN *status code to return a status code to a calling stored procedure.*

Suggested time:

25 minutes

APPLY YOUR KNOWLEDGE 10-4

Using Return Status Codes

Objective: To write a stored procedure to count the number of times a specific movie has been rented. You will return this count by using a return status code.

1. In SQL Query Analyzer, by using the movies database, design a stored procedure for listing the invoice number, title, and the date rented for a specific movie number. Sort the results by the rental date. Name your stored procedure MoviesRented. Include an input parameter in the stored procedure so that you can input the movie number when you run it. Have your stored procedure return the number of rows in the results set as a return status code. (Hint: You'll need to join the movie, rental, and rental_detail tables.) What query did you use?

2. Design and execute a new query to call the MoviesRented stored procedure, display all of the movie rentals for a specific movie number (such as 155), and display the number of rows returned by the RETURN statement. What query did you use?

3. Clear the Query window.

Creating and Using Custom Error Messages

In order to provide you with greater flexibility in programming, SQL Server enables you to create and call your own error messages. You typically use these messages when the data a user enters violates your program's business logic. You use the sp_addmessage stored procedure to create your own custom error messages. SQL Server stores all error messages, including both system and user-defined, in the sysmessages table within the master database. You can then call these messages by using the RAISERROR statement.

Creating Custom Error Messages

Let's start by examining how you go about defining your own error messages. Use the following syntax to add custom error messages with the sp_addmessage stored procedure:

```
EXEC sp_addmessage
@msgnum = number,
@severity = severity_level,
@msgtext = 'Text of error message.',
@with_log = 'true' or 'false'
```

You can use message numbers 50000 and higher, and set the severity level from 0 to 25. Use the @with_log option to control whether or not SQL Server records the error in the Windows 2000 Application log. Be aware that only system administrators can create error messages with a severity level greater than 19. The following table explains the differences between the various severity levels.

Severity Level	Used to Indicate
0 or 10	Errors in information entered by the user. These messages are considered informational.
11 through 16	Errors that can be corrected by the user.
17	Insufficient resources (such as locks or disk space).
18	Nonfatal internal errors. These errors usually indicate an internal software problem.
19	That an internal non-configurable limit in SQL Server was exceeded.
20 through 25	Fatal errors.

As a general rule, you should use either 0 or 10 for informational messages. SQL Server considers error messages with a severity greater than 20 as fatal and terminates the client's connection to the server. Use 15 as the severity level for warning messages and 16 and higher as the severity level for errors.

In the following example, we're creating a custom error message that we can use whenever a user searches for a movie by number that isn't in the table:

```
EXEC sp_addmessage
@msgnum = 50001,
@severity = 10,
@msgtext = 'Movie number cannot be found.',
@with_log = 'true'
```

You can view a list of existing error messages by executing the following query:

```
USE master
GO
SELECT *
FROM sysmessages
```

This query displays each message's error number in the error column, the severity level in the severity column, and the text of the error message in the description column.

Deleting Custom Error Messages

You can drop a custom error message by using the `sp_dropmessage` stored procedure. Use the following syntax to drop a message:

```
EXEC sp_dropmessage message_number
```

Replace *message_number* with the number of the custom error message you want to delete from the sysmessages table.

Using Custom Error Messages

After you've set up custom error messages, you can call them from within a stored procedure by using the RAISERROR SQL statement. Use the following syntax:

```
RAISERROR (msg_id|msg_txt, severity_level, state) [WITH LOG]
```

Replace *msg_id* with the ID number of the custom error message you've already created and stored in the sysmessages table. You can optionally have RAISERROR display a new message by specifying a message text instead. If you specify a message text, SQL Server doesn't store this message for later use—it simply displays it if the error occurs. Because you can display a new error message by using the RAISERROR statement, you must also specify the severity level and state. The *state* is an arbitrary number from 1 to 127 that you can use to provide information about what actions invoked the error. The syntax for the RAISERROR statement requires that you specify the severity level and state parameters even if you're calling a custom error message you've stored in the sysmessages table.

You can optionally use the WITH LOG keywords with the RAISERROR statement to force SQL Server to write the error message to the Windows Application log. You can view these messages by using Event Viewer. If you set the @with_log option equal to true when you defined the error message by using the sp_addmessage stored procedure, SQL Server will automatically write the message to the Application log regardless of whether you specify the WITH LOG keywords with the RAISERROR statement or not.

Let's walk though a complete example from creating the error message to calling it from a stored procedure. In the following example, we start by creating a custom error message by using the `sp_addmessage` stored procedure:

```
sp_addmessage @msgnum = 50001,
@severity = 10,
@msgtext = 'Cannot delete customer. Customer has rentals on
file.'
@with_log = 'true'
```

So how do you call this error message from your stored procedure? You call it by using the following syntax:

```
RAISERROR (50001, 10, 1)
```

Next, you incorporate the RAISERROR statement into your stored procedure. For example, you might use the following stored procedure to delete a customer from the customer table in the movies database. You can use the RAISERROR statement to display an error if you attempt to delete a customer if that customer has rented any movies.

```
CREATE PROC dbo.DeleteCust
@cust_num cust_num = null
AS
IF EXISTS (SELECT cust_num FROM rental WHERE cust_num =
@cust_num)
        BEGIN
           RAISERROR(50001, 10, 1)
           RETURN
        END
DELETE FROM customer
WHERE cust_num = @cust_num
GO
```

Finally, you can run this stored procedure by using the following syntax (where 101 represents a customer number for the input parameter):

```
EXEC DeleteCust 101
```

Let's take a look at another example. In this scenario, you could configure your message to identify the user who performed the action. To do so, you must add the parameter %s to your error message as follows:

```
sp_addmessage
@msgnum = 50002,
@severity = 10,
@msgtext = 'Customer record deleted by %s.' ,
@with_log = 'true'
```

Next, you must populate %s with the user's name by declaring a variable and then storing the user name in it. You can then reference the variable as part of the RAISERROR statement by using the following syntax:

```
DECLARE @username char(30)
SELECT @username = suser_sname()
RAISERROR(50002, 10, 1, @username)
```

APPLY YOUR KNOWLEDGE 10-5

Creating and Calling Custom Error Messages

Objective: To create a custom error message. You will then create a stored procedure to delete a movie from the movie file. If an error occurs, you will have the stored procedure call the custom error message.

1. In SQL Query Analyzer, use the `sp_addmessage` stored procedure to create a custom error message. You will use this error message to notify users if they attempt to delete a movie for which there are rentals on file. Assign the error message a message number of 50001, a severity level of 10, and configure it to write a message to the Application log. Use a message text of your choice. What query did you use?

2. Use the `sp_addmessage` stored procedure to create another custom error message. You will use this error message to record the name of the user who deletes a movie from the movie table. Assign the error message a message number of 50002, a severity level of 10, and configure it to write a message to the Application log. Use a message text of your choice, but include a variable to display the user name. What query did you use?

3. Execute a query to view only your new custom messages in the sysmessages table. Record your query below.

4. Create a stored procedure named DeleteMovie to delete a movie from the movie database. Configure the stored procedure to accept an input parameter for the movie number. Have your stored procedure generate an error if you try to delete a movie for which there are rentals on file; generate the second error message if you successfully delete a movie from the file. What query did you use?

5. Execute the DeleteMovie stored procedure. Use 105 as the value for the input parameter. Record the results below.

6. Retrieve a list of movies that haven't rented by executing the following query:

```
SELECT movie_num, title
FROM movie
WHERE movie_num NOT IN (SELECT movie_num FROM rental_detail)
```

7. Execute the DeleteMovie stored procedure for a movie that has not rented. Record the results below.

8. Clear the Query window.

9. Open the Event Viewer (from Administrative Tools). Select the Application log. Verify that SQL Server recorded a message stating that you deleted a movie record.

10. Close Event Viewer.

Using @@Error

Another technique you can use to detect errors within a stored procedure is to check the value of the @@ERROR system function. SQL Server automatically stores a value to this function each time you execute a SQL statement. It uses a value of 0 if the statement executes successfully, and a value that corresponds to an error message in the sysmessages table if the statement is unsuccessful. You can use the IF statement in conjunction with @@ERROR to control what SQL Server does when an error occurs.

We're going to create the AddNewMovie stored procedure later on in this lesson.

For example, let's say that you want to create a procedure for inserting a new movie into the movie table. You want to make sure that SQL Server doesn't add the new row if any errors occur. You can use the @@ERROR function, along with the ROLLBACK TRANSACTION statement, to abort the transaction if an error occurs. Let's take a look at the code:

```
USE movies
GO
CREATE PROCEDURE dbo.AddNewMovie
@title varchar(40) = null,
@category_num category_num = null,
@rating varchar(5) = null,
@date_purch smalldatetime = null,
@rental_price smallmoney = null
AS
BEGIN TRANSACTION
  INSERT INTO movie
  (title, category_num, rating, date_purch, rental_price)
  VALUES (@title, @category_num, @rating, @date_purch,
    @rental_price)
  IF @@error <> 0
    BEGIN
    ROLLBACK TRAN
    RETURN
  END
COMMIT TRANSACTION
GO
```

In this syntax, if SQL Server detects an error, it will roll back the transaction without inserting the new row into the movie table. For example, the following statement generates an error because the rating violates the table's check constraint and thus causes SQL Server to roll back the transaction:

```
EXEC AddNewMovie 'Meet Joe Black',  '3','Q', '05-08-01', 1.99
```

TOPIC 10D

Managing Stored Procedures

You might find that you need to force SQL Server to recompile a stored procedure whenever you run it. For example, it's possible for you to have an index that, depending on your input parameter, varies widely in its selectivity. As a result, when you run the stored procedure, some of the time it will be more efficient if SQL Server performs a table scan rather than using an index. In this scenario, you should create the stored procedure so that SQL Server will recompile it each time you run it. Here's the syntax:

```
CREATE PROCEDURE name
WITH RECOMPILE
AS SQL Statements
```

By adding the `WITH RECOMPILE` option, you prevent SQL Server from caching a plan for the stored procedure. SQL Server must recompile it every time you run the stored procedure.

If you don't want to force SQL Server to recompile a stored procedure every time you run it, but you have had enough changes to your data that the stored procedure's execution plan might be inefficient, you can have SQL Server recompile it by using the following syntax:

```
EXECUTE procedure_name
WITH RECOMPILE
```

By adding the `WITH RECOMPILE` option when you run the stored procedure, SQL Server generates a new execution plan, caches it, and then executes the stored procedure.

You can also mark a stored procedure to be recompiled without running it by using the following syntax:

```
EXEC sp_recompile procedure_name | table_name
```

SQL Server doesn't recompile the stored procedure when you run this command. Instead, it marks it for recompiling the next time you run it. If you use `sp_recompile` with a table name instead of a stored procedure name, SQL Server automatically marks all stored procedures that reference the table for recompiling.

TASK 10D-1:

Recompiling a Stored Procedure

1. In SQL Query Analyzer, **execute the following query:**

   ```
   EXEC sp_recompile MovieByRating
   ```

   This marks the MovieByRating stored procedure for recompiling the next time you run it.

   ```
   Object 'MovieByRating' was successfully marked for recompilation.
   ```

2. Execute a new query:

```
EXEC MovieByRating 'PG'
```

By running the stored procedure, you force SQL Server to recompile it.

3. Clear the Query window.

Managing the Performance of Stored Procedures

You can take advantage of Windows 2000's System Monitor to analyze the performance of stored procedures. The following table describes the objects and counters you should monitor.

Object	Counter	Enables You to View
SQL Server: Cache Manager	Cache Hit-Ratio	The percentage of pages SQL Server retrieves from cache rather than hard disk. The higher this value, the better your server's performance.
	Cache Object Counts	The number of objects cached in RAM. After your server is up and running, this number does not change much over time.
	Cache Pages	The total number of pages in use in the cache by objects. Once your server is up and running, this number does not change much over time.
	Cache Use Count/sec	The number of times per second each object that is cached has been used. The higher this value, the better your server's performance.
SQL Statistics	SQL Re-compilations/sec	The number of recompiles per second your server is performing. In general, unless you've just restarted your server, this number should be low.

You can also use SQL Profiler to analyze stored procedures. For example, you can create a trace in SQL Profiler to capture events such as the start time for a stored procedure, whether it completed, and what happened for each of the statements that make up the stored procedure.

APPLY YOUR KNOWLEDGE 10-6

Suggested time:
15 minutes

Objective: To create a trace in SQL Profiler, execute a stored procedure, and then review the information you see within SQL Profiler.

1. Open SQL Profiler and create a new trace using the following settings:
   - Choose File→New Trace.
   - Log in to your server with Windows Authentication.
   - In the Trace Properties dialog box, select the Events tab.
   - Below Available Event Classes, select the Stored Procedures event class and click Add. This adds all of the events you can capture for stored procedures to the trace. Select the TSQL event class and click Add again.
   - Click Run to begin capturing the trace information.

2. In SQL Query Analyzer, open the C:\Data\addnewmovie.sql script file.

3. Highlight and execute the query to create the AddNewMovie stored procedure.

4. Highlight and execute the query to test the AddNewMovie stored procedure. This query generates an error.

5. Switch to SQL Profiler and stop the trace. (Choose File→Stop Trace.)

6. Review the trace information. You'll see a row for both the start and completion of each statement in the stored procedure. You can also see which steps SQL Server performed after processing the IF @@ERROR <> 0 statement. As a developer, this information can come in quite handy if you're trying to figure out what SQL Server does when it encounters conditional logic in your program.

7. Close all open windows.

Summary

In this lesson, you learned how to create a stored procedure by using the CREATE PROCEDURE SQL statement. You also learned how to execute your stored procedures, and how to encrypt their contents to prevent users from reading their definitions. To make stored procedures more flexible, you implemented both input and output parameters. Finally, you added statements to detect and report errors to your stored procedures.

LESSON 10 REVIEW

10A List and describe the three types of stored procedures supported in SQL Server.

10B How can you view the definition of a stored procedure? How can you determine on which objects a stored procedure depends?

10C What's the difference between an input parameter and an output parameter? Give an example of when you might use each.

10D You would like SQL Server to recompile a stored procedure the next time you run it. What should you do?

Using Functions

Overview

SQL Server 2000 includes many different system functions that you can use to perform a variety of tasks. For example, you can use the AVG( ) function to find the average value in a column. In addition, you can now create your own user-defined functions in SQL Server 2000. In this lesson, we will explore how you use both system and user-defined functions to query your server.

Objectives

To use functions in queries, you will:

11A   Implement aggregate functions in queries.

Of the system functions, the ones you'll use most often when querying tables are the aggregate functions. These functions enable you to summarize data. In this topic, you will learn how to use the aggregate functions. You'll also learn how to group the results sets by using the GROUP BY clause.

11B   Design and create user-defined functions.

In SQL Server 2000, you can create your own user-defined functions. In this topic, you will learn how to design, create, and manage three types of user-defined functions: scalar, multi-statement table-valued, and inline table-valued functions.

Data Files:
functions.sql
agg_functions_lab.sql
groupby.sql
groupbylab.sql
topvalues.sql
scalar.sql
multi-statement.sql
in-line.sql

Lesson Time:
3 hours

TOPIC 11A

Working with Aggregate Functions

aggregate functions:
Functions that enable you to summarize data. The result of these functions is a single value.

The SQL language includes many functions that you can use to summarize data from a column within a table. Collectively, the functions that enable you to summarize data are referred to as *aggregate functions*. You might also hear aggregate functions referred to as group functions because they operate on groups of rows to provide you with a single result. The following table describes the aggregate functions supported by SQL Server and the types of calculations you can use them to perform.

Function	Enables You to Calculate the
AVG ( )	Average of an expression (such as all values in a column).
COUNT ( )	Number of values in an expression.
COUNT (*)	Number of selected rows.
MAX ( )	Maximum value of an expression.
MIN ( )	Minimum value of an expression.
SUM ( )	Total of all values in an expression.
STDEV ( )	Statistical deviation of all values.
STDEVP ( )	Statistical deviation of a population.
VAR ( )	Statistical variance of all values.
VARP ( )	Statistical variance of all values of a population.

You use the following basic syntax with aggregate functions:

```
USE database
SELECT FUNCTION(expression)
FROM table
```

In this syntax, you replace *expression* with a column name. You can optionally include an AS clause after the function so that SQL Server can display a heading for the column in the results set. If you don't specify an alias when you use a function, SQL Server doesn't display a column heading. When you use an aggregate function in your SELECT statement, you can't include other columns in the SELECT clause unless you use a GROUP BY clause. We show you how to use the GROUP BY clause later in this lesson.

Let's take a look at an example. The following query shows you how to find the highest rental price for a movie in the movie table:

```
USE movies
GO
SELECT MAX(rental_price) AS 'Highest Rental Fee'
FROM movie
```

The following example enables you to count the number of rows in the customer table in order to determine the total number of customers:

```
USE movies
GO
SELECT COUNT(*)
FROM customer
```

Aggregate Functions and Data Types

You'll most often use the aggregate functions on numeric data, but you can use some of these functions against character data. For example, you can use the MAX() function against character-based columns as follows:

```
USE movies
GO
SELECT MAX(title)
FROM movie
```

In this example, SQL Server returns the movie title of "Young Frankenstein" because alphabetically, it's the last movie title in the table. You can't use the MIN() and MAX() functions against the bit data type. Some of the other considerations for aggregate functions and data types include:

- You can use the COUNT function against all data types. COUNT is the only aggregate function you can use against text, ntext, and image data types.

- You can use only the int, smallint, decimal, numeric, float, real, money, and smallmoney data types in the SUM() and AVG() functions.

Null Values

Other than the COUNT function, the aggregate functions ignore null values in columns. All of the aggregate functions base their calculations on the premise that the values in columns are significant only if those values aren't null. If you count the number of rows based on a column with null values (such as COUNT (zip)), SQL Server skips any rows that have null values in that column. If you use COUNT (*), you'll get the actual row count—even if a row has nothing but null values in all columns.

TASK 11A-1:

Using Aggregate Functions to Summarize Data

Setup: You're logged on to Windows 2000 as student#. You've created a database named movies and tables within it named movie, category, customer, rental, and rental_detail. You've defined primary key, foreign key, default, and check constraints on the tables, and you've created nonclustered indexes based on your primary keys. You have imported data into the tables. You have created database diagrams for both the movies and pubs databases.

1. **Start SQL Query Analyzer and log in with Windows Authentication.**

2. **Open the C:\Data\functions.sql script file.**

3. **Highlight and execute the first query.** You can use this query to find the highest-priced movie in the movie table. Notice that because this query doesn't specify a column alias, you don't see a column heading in the results set.

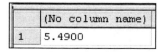

(No column name)
1   5.4900

4. **Highlight and execute the second query.** You receive an error message because you can't include both a column and an aggregate function in your SELECT statement unless you add a GROUP BY clause.

```
Server: Msg 8118, Level 16, State 1, Line 1
Column 'movie.title' is invalid in the select list because it is not contained in an aggregate function
```

5. **Open a new Query window, and then close the window containing the functions.sql script file.**

APPLY YOUR KNOWLEDGE 11-1

Using Aggregate Functions in Queries

Objective: To use aggregate functions to query the movies and pubs databases. Design and execute your queries in SQL Query Analyzer. If necessary, refer to your database diagrams for both tables in SQL Server Enterprise Manager.

1. What is the average price of movies with a G rating? What query did you use?

2. What's the title and price of the highest-priced movie? (Hint: You must use a subquery to find this information.) What query did you use?

3. How many authors live in Utah? (Use the pubs database.) What query did you use?

4. What is the highest royalty percentage paid to an author? (Hint: Query the roysched table.) What query did you use?

5. What's the total year-to-date sales for all titles in the Pubs database? What query did you use?

6. Clear the Query window.

Using GROUP BY to Group the Results of Aggregate Functions

You use the GROUP BY clause to divide the rows of a table into groups and then display summary results for a specific column. You shouldn't use the GROUP BY clause on a column in which multiple rows have null values because SQL Server will treat all of the rows with null values in that column as a group.

For example, you might want to count the number of movies you have in stock for each rating (G, PG, etc.). To find this information, you must use a GROUP BY clause to group the movies by rating—and then count the number of movies in each group. Use the following syntax:

```
USE movies
GO
SELECT rating, COUNT(movie_num)
FROM movie
GROUP BY rating
```

In this example, you can use COUNT(movie_num), because the structure of the movie table doesn't permit null values in the movie_num column.

The GROUP BY clause requires a one-to-one relationship between the columns you specify in the SELECT statement (other than the aggregate function) and the GROUP BY clause. For example, the following query is invalid because the rating column isn't included in the SELECT clause:

```
USE movies
GO
SELECT COUNT(movie_num)
FROM movie
GROUP BY rating
```

This query is also invalid because the rating column isn't referenced in a GROUP BY clause:

```
USE movies
GO
SELECT rating, COUNT(movie_num)
FROM movie
```

In this next example, you can use a GROUP BY clause to enable you to calculate the total rental fee collected for each invoice in the rental_detail table:

```
USE movies
GO
SELECT invoice_num, SUM(rental_price)
FROM rental_detail
GROUP BY invoice_num
```

Using a WHERE Clause

You can also add a WHERE clause to a query that contains an aggregate function in order to restrict the groups on which the aggregate function performs its calculations. If you use a WHERE clause, SQL Server groups only the rows that meet the condition you specify. For example, if you want to see the average price of movies with a PG or R rating, you could use the following query:

```
USE movies
GO
SELECT rating, AVG(rental_price)
FROM movie
WHERE rating = 'PG' OR rating = 'R'
GROUP BY rating
```

Notice that the WHERE clause must precede the GROUP BY clause. If you reverse the order of these clauses, you will get a syntax error.

TASK 11A-2:

Designing GROUP BY Queries

1. In SQL Query Analyzer, **open the C:\Data\groupby.sql script file.**

2. **Execute the query** to observe the error displayed by SQL Query Analyzer when you attempt to include both a column and a group function in the SELECT statement without a GROUP BY clause.

3. **How can you fix this query?**

4. **Add `GROUP BY rating` to the query, and then execute it again** to display the average rental price for movies by rating.

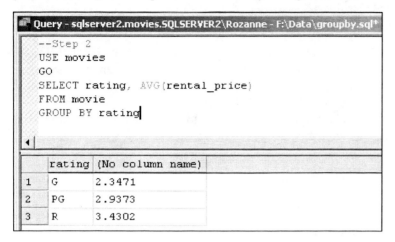

```
--Step 2
USE movies
GO
SELECT rating, AVG(rental_price)
FROM movie
GROUP BY rating
```

	rating	(No column name)
1	G	2.3471
2	PG	2.9373
3	R	3.4302

5. **Save your changes to the groupby.sql script.**

6. **Open a new Query window, and then close the window containing the groupby.sql script.**

Using GROUP BY With HAVING

If you want to restrict the rows returned by a query in which you're using an aggregate function and a GROUP BY clause, you can use a HAVING clause instead of a WHERE clause. The HAVING clause offers you a distinct advantage over a WHERE clause because it enables you to use aggregate functions to restrict the rows returned in the results set.

For example, you could use the following query to display the rating and average price of all movies for each rating as long as the average price of those movies is greater than 2.50:

```
USE movies
GO
SELECT rating, AVG(rental_price)
FROM movie
GROUP BY rating
HAVING AVG(rental_price) >= 2.50
```

One other difference between a WHERE clause and a HAVING clause is that the WHERE clause restricts the groups of rows on which the aggregate function calculates its results; in contrast, the aggregate function calculates values for all groups of rows but displays only those that meet the HAVING clause's criteria in the results set.

APPLY YOUR KNOWLEDGE 11-2

Designing Queries Using GROUP BY and HAVING Clauses

Objective: To design and execute queries that use the GROUP BY and HAVING clauses. Use SQL Query Analyzer to execute each query.

1. Design and execute a query based on the movies database that shows the total rental price collected for each invoice in the rental_detail table. What query did you use?

2. Design and execute a query on the movies database that shows all invoices and their total rental price where the total price was more than $4.00. (You should get 22 rows in the results set.) What query did you use?

3. Design and execute a query that lists the category and average rental price of movies in the Comedy category. (The category_num for Comedy is 1.) What query did you use?

4. Design and execute a query that lists the average rental price of movies by category. Include the category description in the results set and sort the results by the description. (Hint: You must join two tables in this query.) What query did you use?

5. Design and execute a query that shows all customer names who have rented movies, and the total price of each customer's rentals. Sort the results in order by last name and then first name. (Hint: You must join three tables in this query.) What query did you use?

6. Clear the Query window.

Displaying the TOP n Rows in a Results Set

You can use the TOP *n* or TOP *n* PERCENT keywords to specify that you want SQL Server to return only a specific number of rows in the results set. You must include an ORDER BY clause so that SQL Server can determine the top rows.

TASK 11A-3:

Using TOP in a Query

1. In SQL Query Analyzer, **select the Northwind database and execute the following query:**

   ```
   SELECT TOP 5 orderid, productid, quantity
   FROM [order details]
   ORDER BY quantity DESC
   ```

   This query returns the top five orders based on quantity.

2. **Look at the results.** SQL Query Analyzer displays the orders and product IDs with the largest quantity ordered.

3. **Clear the Query window.**

Suggested time:

20 minutes

APPLY YOUR KNOWLEDGE 11-3

Determining the Top Values

Objective: In this lab, you're going to use SQL Query Analyzer to design and execute queries that return the top values in the results set.

1. By using the movies database, write and execute a query to list the titles of the top three movies based on rental price. What are they? (Hint: Make sure you use the DISTINCT keyword so that you get three unique titles.) What query did you use?

2. Use the movies database to write and execute a query listing the top three invoice numbers based on total money spent renting movies. Which invoices are they? What query did you use?

3. Use the pubs database to write and execute a query listing the titles and prices of the top five most expensive books. What is the title and price of the most expensive book? What query did you use?

4. Clear the Query window.

TOPIC 11B

Designing and Creating User-defined Functions

One of the new features in SQL Server 2000 is that you can now create your own user-defined functions. These functions enable you to create programs that return either a single value or a table. At first glance, you might think that a function and a stored procedure are the same thing. They do have several features in common: SQL Server does parse, compile, and cache both stored procedures and functions. In addition, you can use control-of-flow statements (such as IF) and variables in both stored procedures and functions. But the key difference between stored procedures and user-defined functions is that you can use user-defined functions as part of a SQL statement, whereas you simply execute stored procedures. For example, let's say that you create a user-defined function named AverageRental to calculate the average rental price for a specific category of movie. You can then include that function within a WHERE clause, as follows:

```
SELECT title, rating
FROM movie
WHERE rental_price < dbo.AverageRental(1)
```

Notice that although you can create a stored procedure to calculate the average rental price for a specific movie category, you can't execute that procedure as part of the WHERE clause.

SQL Server supports three types of user-defined functions, as described in the following table.

SQL Server requires that you include the owner name whenever you execute a user-defined function.

Function	Enables You to Create a Function that
Scalar	Accepts a single value and returns a single value. You can create these functions to not accept any input parameters, or you can design them to accept up to 1,024 input parameters. Scalar functions are most similar to system functions (such as MAX( )).
Multi-statement Table-valued	Uses multiple SQL statements to return multiple rows. This type of function is similar to a view in that you can reference it in the FROM clause of a SELECT statement. Microsoft refers to these functions as "multi-statement," because you use multiple statements to generate the results set for the function. In this sense, a multi-statement table-valued function is very similar to a stored procedure.
Inline Table-valued	Uses a single SELECT statement to return multiple rows. Like the multi-statement table-valued function, the inline table-valued function is also very similar to a view. (Remember, you create a view by defining a single SELECT statement.) One key difference, though: an inline table-valued function accepts parameters—which makes the function much more flexible than a view.

Before we get into how you go about creating functions, let's look at the permissions you need to create them. You must have the CREATE FUNCTION permission in order to create, modify, or delete user-defined functions. You must give any user you want to execute a user-defined function the EXECUTE permission for that function. If you plan to use a user-defined function within a check or default constraint when you create or modify a table, the owner of the function and the table must be the same user.

Creating a Scalar User-defined Function

Because how you go about creating each type of user-defined function is a little different, let's look at each one individually. You create all user-defined functions by using the CREATE FUNCTION SQL statement. Here's the basic syntax for creating a scalar function:

```
CREATE FUNCTION [owner_name.]function_name
([@parameter_name scalar_parameter_data_type [=default_value]}
[,...n]])
RETURNS scalar_return_data_type
[WITH option [...n]]
AS
BEGIN
        function_statements
        RETURN scalar_expression
END
```

For example, here's how you might create a function to calculate the average rental price for a specific movie category:

```
CREATE FUNCTION dbo.fn_AverageRental
(@movie_category category_num)
RETURNS smallmoney
AS
BEGIN
        DECLARE @avg smallmoney
        SELECT @avg = avg(rd.rental_price)
        FROM rental_detail as rd join movie as m
        ON rd.movie_num = m.movie_num
        WHERE m.category_num = @movie_category
        RETURN @avg
END
```

Let's break this function down so that you can figure out what's going on. Here's what each line means:

- In the first line, we're assigning the name of fn_AverageRental to our function, and specifying that the dbo user is the owner.

- We're using the next line, (@movie_category category_num), to specify a name for an input parameter. In this example, the name of the input parameter's variable is @movie_category, and its data type is the user-defined data type of category_num. This means that we want our function to accept an input value and to assign it to the @movie_category variable.

- In the next line, RETURNS smallmoney, we're identifying the data type of the value our function returns. We want our function to return the average rental price, so the data type we're using is smallmoney. (We chose this data type because the rental_price column also uses the smallmoney data type.) You can use any data type for the return data type except text, ntext, image, cursor, or timestamp.

- We use the AS statement to mark the beginning of the actual definition of the function.

- Next, SQL Server requires that we use BEGIN and END to delineate the start and end of the work we want the function to perform.

- We use the DECLARE @avg smallmoney line to identify the variable in which we want to store the function's results.

- Next, we use the SELECT statement to store a value into the @avg variable. In this example, we're using a table join between the movie and rental_detail tables to find the average rental price for all movies in a specific category. Notice that the WHERE m.category_num = @movie_category clause enables us to select all movies based on the category we specify. (Remember, we're using @movie_category as an input parameter for the function.

- The RETURN @avg line enables us to return the value calculated by the function.

- The END line marks the end of the function's definition.

When you're ready to use a function, you must use the function's two-part name. In other words, you must specify the function's name as *owner.function_name*. You can use the function simply with the SELECT statement, as follows:

```
SELECT dbo.fn_AverageRentals(1)
```

You can also use a function as part of a WHERE clause:

```
SELECT title, rental_price
FROM movie
WHERE rental_price > dbo.fn_AverageRentals(1)
```

There are several system functions that you can't include in a user-defined function's definition. That's because these system functions are considered non-deterministic, which means that they give you different values each time you execute them—even if you're using the same set of input values. These system functions include those found in the following table.

System Functions	System Functions Continued
@@ERROR	@@IDENTITY
@@ROWCOUNT	@@TRANCOUNT
APP_NAME	CURRENT_TIMESTAMP
CURRENT_USER	DATENAME
FORMATMESSAGE	GETANSINULL
GETDATE	GetUTCDate
HOST_ID	HOST_NAME
IDENT_INCR	IDENT_SEED
IDENTITY	NEWID
PERMISSIONS	SESSION_USER
STATS_DATE	SYSTEM_USER
TEXTPTR	TEXTVALID

Setting the SCHEMABINDING Option

One of the options you can specify for all types of functions is WITH SCHEMABINDING. As you saw with views, this option enables you to prevent a user from changing or dropping an object (such as a table) on which a function is based. In order for the schemabinding option to work, the following conditions must be valid:

- Any user-defined functions or views referenced by the user-defined function you're attempting to create must also use the WITH SCHEMABINDING option.

- You don't reference any objects within the function definition using their two-part names.

- You create the function and any objects on which it depends in the same database.

- You have the REFERENCES permission on all of the objects on which your function depends.

Suggested time:

20 minutes

APPLY YOUR KNOWLEDGE 11-4

Designing and Creating a Scalar Function

Objective: To create a scalar function to calculate the average price of a book for a specific type (such as business or psychology).

1. In the pubs database, create a function named fn_AvgPrice to calculate the average price of books for a specific book type. Define the function so that you can use the book type as an input parameter. Base the function on the titles table. If necessary, use the Object Browser window or SQL Server Enterprise Manager to review the structure of the titles table. What query did you use?

2. Execute a query to find out what types of books are in the titles table. What query did you use?

3. Execute a SELECT query to view the average price for a book type. What query did you use?

4. Execute a query that uses the fn_AvgPrice in a WHERE clause. Design the query to display the title, type, and price columns for titles with a price greater than the average price for a book type. What query did you use?

5. Design and execute a query that enables you to display the title, type, and price columns for titles with a price greater than the average price for a book type. Include only those titles that have the same book type as that of the function. Record your query in the space below.

6. Clear the Query window.

Creating a Multi-statement Table-valued Function

Let's move on to looking at a multi-statement table-valued function. These functions enable you to retrieve multiple rows from a table. In a sense, a multi-statement table-valued function is the combination of a stored procedure and a view. Here's the syntax:

```
CREATE FUNCTION [owner_name.]function_name
([@parameter_name parameter_data_type [=default_value]} [,...n]])
RETURNS @return_variable TABLE
        (table_definition)
[WITH option [...n]]
AS
BEGIN
        function_statements
        RETURN
END
```

Notice that, like the scalar user-defined functions, you also define the heart of a multi-statement table-valued function by enclosing it within the BEGIN and END statements. Let's take a look at an example. In the following function, we retrieve a list of movie titles and their ratings for a given category of movie:

```
CREATE FUNCTION fn_TitleRatings
(@category category_num)
RETURNS @fn_TitleRatings TABLE
(title varchar(40) NOT NULL,
rating varchar(5) NOT NULL)
AS
BEGIN
        INSERT @fn_TitleRatings
                SELECT title, rating
                FROM movie
                WHERE category_num = @category
        RETURN
END
```

Let's look at some of the differences you see when you create a table-valued function instead of a scalar function:

- You use the RETURNS line to specify the name of the function and that its data type is TABLE.

- After you specify the name of the function, you must provide information about the columns you want the table the function returns to contain. In this example, we're specifying that we want the function to return two columns: title and rating.

You can use other types of statements within the BEGIN and END statements, including statements such as IF and CASE.

- Use the statements between BEGIN and END to insert data into the table you're creating.

After you've created your multi-line table-valued function, you retrieve its data just as you would retrieve data from a table or view, by using the SELECT statement. So, here's how you can view the rows in the fn_TitleRatings function:

```
SELECT *
FROM dbo.fn_TitleRatings(1)
```

Because we designed this function to accept an input parameter, we must specify a value when we retrieve the data from the function. We're using the category of 1 in our example, which means we're retrieving all science fiction movies.

Suggested time:
10 minutes

APPLY YOUR KNOWLEDGE 11-5

Creating and Testing a Multi-statement Table-valued Function

Objective: To create a user-defined function that displays each author's name, phone number, and state. As part of the function, you're going to have SQL Server display the complete state name instead of its two-letter abbreviation.

1. In SQL Query Analyzer, open the C:\Data\multi-statement script file.

2. Highlight and execute the query to create the fn_AuthorState function.

3. Design and execute a query to test this function. What query did you use?

4. Design and execute a query that uses a value for the state abbreviation that doesn't exist in the authors table. What happens when you execute this query?

5. Open a new Query window, and then close the window containing the C:\Data\multi-statement script file.

Creating an Inline Table-valued Function

Now let's look at how you use an inline table-valued function. While both a multi-statement table function and an inline table function enable you to retrieve a table, with an inline table function, you can specify only a SELECT statement to retrieve the table. Another difference you'll notice is that you use simply RETURNS TABLE to return the results of the function. You don't have to specify a return variable and data type because SQL Server automatically formats the values based on the results set of the SELECT statement. Here's the basic syntax:

```
CREATE FUNCTION [owner_name.]function_name
([@parameter_name parameter_data_type [=default_value]} [,...n]])
RETURNS TABLE
[WITH option [...n]]
AS
        RETURN (SELECT statement)
END
```

As an example, let's restate our previous multi-statement table-valued function as an inline table-valued function. Here's what it looks like:

```
CREATE FUNCTION fn_TitleRatings2
(@category category_num)
RETURNS TABLE
AS
RETURN (SELECT title, rating
        FROM movie
        WHERE category_num = @category)
```

Notice that we can't use a BEGIN and END statement with an inline function. Instead, we use the RETURN (SELECT ...) statement to specify the rows we want to retrieve in the function.

You use this function by specifying its name in the FROM clause of a SELECT statement. Here's the syntax:

```
SELECT *
FROM dbo.fn_TitleRatings2(1)
```

APPLY YOUR KNOWLEDGE 11-6

Suggested time:
20 minutes

Creating and Testing an Inline Table-valued Function

Objective: To create an inline table-valued function that enables you to list rental invoices that have a total price greater than a value you specify.

1. Design and execute a query to create an inline table-valued function named fn_Rentals. Design this query so that you can use it to find all rental invoices with a total value greater than a dollar value you specify. Include the invoice_num and the total value of the rentals. (Hint: You'll need to use SUM(rental_price) to find the total value of the rentals.) What query did you use?

2.   Design and execute a query to test the fn_Rentals function. What query did you use?

3.   Clear the Query window.

Managing User-defined Functions

You can make changes to a user-defined function by using the ALTER FUNCTION statement. As you saw with stored procedures and views, modifying a function enables you to retain whatever permissions you have assigned to users for the function. In contrast, if you drop and re-create the function, you must re-assign users' permissions. Here's the syntax for the ALTER FUNCTION statement:

```
ALTER FUNCTION owner.function_name
New function definition
```

You can also delete a function by using the DROP FUNCTION statement. Here's the syntax:

```
DROP FUNCTION owner.function_name
```

TASK 11B-1:

Dropping a User-defined Function

1.   In SQL Query Analyzer, **select the pubs database.**

2.   **Execute the following query:**

```
DROP FUNCTION dbo.fn_AuthorState
```

This query deletes the fn_AuthorState function from the Pubs database.

3.   **Close all open windows.**

Summary

In this lesson, you explored how to use the aggregate system functions within queries. You learned how to summarize results by groups using the GROUP BY clause and how to restrict the results displayed by using the HAVING clause. You also learned how you can create your own user-defined functions by using the CREATE FUNCTION statement.

LESSON 11 REVIEW

11A In what scenario must you include a GROUP BY clause when you use an aggregate function? Give an example of a query that includes a GROUP BY clause.

11B In what scenario should you create a multi-statement table-valued function instead of an inline table-valued function?

YOUR NOTES:

Creating Triggers

LESSON
12

Data Files:

insert-trigger.sql
insert-trigger-lab.sql
delete-trigger.sql
update-trigger.sql
instead-trigger.sql
manage-triggers.sql
updatemovie.sql

Lesson Time:
1 hour, 30 minutes

Overview

You use triggers in SQL Server to have your server perform specific actions whenever a user inserts, updates, or deletes from a table. In SQL Server 2000, you can also define INSTEAD OF triggers on views and tables. In this lesson, we're going to examine the different types of triggers you can create and then show you how to create them by using the CREATE TRIGGER statement.

Objectives

To design and implement triggers, you will:

12A   **Identify the issues for designing triggers, and create each type of trigger.**

SQL Server supports FOR, AFTER, and INSTEAD OF triggers that you can base on the INSERT, UPDATE, and DELETE actions. In this topic, we show you the why and how you go about creating each type of trigger.

TOPIC 12A

Designing and Implementing Triggers

You can define triggers on tables in your SQL databases so that SQL Server will automatically perform tasks such as verifying data, tracking changes to a table, or enforcing business rules. The table on which a trigger is based is referred to as the trigger table. Although a trigger is very similar to a stored procedure, you can't execute a trigger directly. Instead, you base triggers on the INSERT, UPDATE, and DELETE SQL statements, and SQL Server automatically executes the triggers for you whenever a user executes one of these SQL statements. For example, if you create an INSERT trigger on a table, SQL Server automatically calls the trigger whenever you insert a new row into the table.

SQL Server treats a trigger and the statement that calls it as a single transaction. You don't have to explicitly mark the beginning of the transaction by using the BEGIN TRANSACTION statement. You can roll back the entire transaction from anywhere within the trigger. For example, you can include error checking within your trigger and call the ROLLBACK TRANSACTION statement if an error occurs. Keep in mind that if a user transaction calls a trigger, and the trigger executes the ROLLBACK TRANSACTION statement, SQL Server rolls back both the trigger's steps along with the steps in the user transaction. It's important that you be aware that rolling back transactions can degrade the performance of your server. When you roll back a transaction, SQL Server will have performed all of the steps up to the ROLLBACK TRANSACTION statement, and then it must undo those steps. It's much better for you to check your data prior to beginning the transaction rather than within the transaction itself.

Why Use Triggers?

You use triggers for a couple of reasons: to enforce data integrity and to enforce business rules. You should use triggers to enforce data integrity on your tables, not for returning query results. Keep in mind that triggers are typically fired when you change the data in a table. For example, you might use a trigger to perform cascading deletes. You can use a trigger to delete a customer by first deleting the customer's invoices (from both the rental_detail and rental tables), and then the customer themselves. Likewise, you can use a trigger to perform cascading updates of rows in multiple tables.

You can also use triggers to enforce business rules that are too complex for constraints. For example, you might not want to rent new movies to a customer if that customer has any overdue movies. You can use a trigger to verify that the customer doesn't have overdue movies before permitting the customer to rent a new movie.

Another use for triggers is to generate computed values. For example, you might use a trigger to create each customer's account number in the customer table by using a portion of their last name plus a portion of their phone number instead of using the IDENTITY property to auto-generate account numbers.

Here's one last use for triggers: you can use them to keep track of changes (updates) to a table. For example, you can use an update trigger to detect whenever users change the data in a sensitive table such as one that contains employee salary information. The update trigger can then record the changed information not only to the user table, but also to an audit trail table.

Considerations

You should keep in mind that triggers are essentially reactive, whereas constraints are proactive. For example, SQL Server fires an UPDATE trigger only after you've updated the data in a table. In contrast, table constraints are proactive. SQL Server checks a table's constraints before it will let you perform an action. For example, if you attempt to add a new movie to the movie table with a duplicate movie number (the primary key for this table), the primary key constraint, not the trigger, will prevent you from adding the new row.

You can configure more than one trigger for an action. If you're the owner of a table with multiple triggers for an action (such as updates), you can specify which of the triggers must fire first and last. However, you can't specify the order in which SQL Server calls the in-between triggers (if you have that many!). For example, you can configure four update triggers on a table and specify which of the triggers you want to be first and which one you want to be last, but SQL Server will call the remaining two triggers in random order, and the order will vary from one UPDATE statement to the next. If you want the steps in the triggers to be performed in a specific order, you should combine them into a single trigger.

TASK 12A-1:

Designing Triggers

1. **What's the difference between a constraint and a trigger?**

2. **What are two triggers you might use in the movies database?**

Creating a Trigger

You create a trigger by using the CREATE TRIGGER SQL statement in SQL Query Analyzer. You must be a member of the sysadmins server role, db_owner or db_ddladmin database roles, or the owner of the trigger table before you can create, alter, or drop a trigger. Obviously, if you want a trigger to perform such tasks as updating another table, you must have the necessary permissions for that table.

You can't create FOR *or* AFTER *triggers on views—only on tables. In contrast, you can create* INSTEAD OF *triggers on both views and tables.*

Microsoft added the support
for the AFTER and
INSTEAD OF keywords
in SQL Server 2000. Prior
versions of SQL Server supported only the FOR
keyword.

SQL Server supports three types of triggers: INSERT, UPDATE, and DELETE. You can precede each type of trigger with FOR, AFTER, or INSTEAD OF. The FOR and AFTER keywords are functionally equivalent. In both cases, you use FOR or AFTER to create a traditional trigger. For example, you create a traditional insert trigger by specifying FOR INSERT. SQL Server fires this type of trigger whenever you perform the specified action (INSERT in this example). In contrast, you use an INSTEAD OF trigger to have SQL Server perform a specific action instead of any other triggers you've defined on a table or view for that same action. For example, you might define an INSTEAD OF INSERT trigger on a view so that SQL Server performs the steps of this trigger instead of the INSERT trigger you've defined on the view's base table. (By default, SQL Server fires any triggers on the table even when you're working with a view based on that table.)

You identify whether the trigger is an INSERT, UPDATE, or DELETE trigger as part of the CREATE TRIGGER statement. Here's the syntax:

```
CREATE TRIGGER owner.trigger_name
ON owner.table_name
[WITH ENCRYPTION]
{FOR | AFTER | INSTEAD OF} {INSERT | UPDATE | DELETE}
AS
SQL statements
```

As you've seen with objects such as views, stored procedures, and functions, SQL Server stores each trigger's definition in the syscomments system table. In addition, SQL Server updates the sysobjects table with information about the trigger. You can optionally use the WITH ENCRYPTION keywords to create an encrypted trigger. This prevents users from viewing a trigger's definition.

You can include almost all SQL statements in your trigger definition. For example, you can use the IF statement to define conditional logic for the trigger. You can also use any of the error-checking techniques we covered in the "Creating Stored Procedures" lesson. There are a few statements you can't use in a trigger, though. Here's the list:

- ALTER DATABASE
- CREATE DATABASE
- DROP DATABASE
- DISK INIT
- DISK RESIZE
- LOAD DATABASE
- LOAD LOG
- RECONFIGURE
- RESTORE DATABASE
- RESTORE LOG

You should always specify the dbo user as the owner of any triggers you create. Microsoft recommends that you configure the dbo user as the owner of all objects within a database to avoid a broken ownership chain.

Viewing Information About Triggers

As we've said, SQL Server stores information about triggers in the sysobjects and syscomments tables. Unless the trigger is encrypted, you can view a trigger's definition by executing the sp_helptext stored procedure as follows:

```
sp_helptext trigger_name
```

The `sp_helptrigger` stored procedure enables you to view a list of the triggers defined for a table. Use the following syntax with `sp_helptrigger`:

```
sp_helptrigger table_name
```

Finally, you can use the `sp_depends` stored procedure to identify which tables have triggers. Use the following syntax:

```
sp_depends table_name
```

Creating an INSERT Trigger

You create an `INSERT` trigger to fire whenever a new row is inserted into the trigger table. When you add a new row to a table on which you've defined an `INSERT` trigger, SQL Server not only inserts the row into the trigger table, but also into a logical table named *inserted*. The inserted table contains a copy of the row (or rows) you've just inserted into the trigger table; so, the inserted and trigger tables have these rows in common. You can optionally reference the inserted table to perform some of the trigger's actions. SQL Server creates the inserted table by using information from the transaction log. For this reason, if you perform a non-logged operation, the trigger won't fire.

You might create `INSERT` triggers to perform several actions. For example, you might use an `INSERT` trigger to insert information into the same table or another table's columns whenever you add a new row. Or, you could use an `INSERT` trigger to write a copy of the inserted row to an audit table.

The following example creates a trigger on the roysched table in the pubs database. (This table contains a list of titles published by authors along with the author's royalty percentage.) Because of the sensitive nature of this information, you can use an `INSERT` trigger to write a copy of any rows added to the roysched table to another table named audit_trail. This table must have the same column names and data types as the roysched table if you want to write a copy of all of the row's information. You could optionally create the audit_trail table to contain only the title_id and royalty columns. Use the following syntax to create the trigger:

```
CREATE TRIGGER dbo.audit_changes
ON roysched
FOR INSERT
AS
INSERT audit_trail (title_id, royalty)
SELECT title_id, royalty
FROM inserted
```

We could use either FOR INSERT *or* AFTER INSERT *to create the audit_changes trigger.*

In this example, we're using the row (or rows) that SQL Server stores in the inserted table to update the rows in the audit_trail table. After you've created this trigger, SQL Server will automatically invoke it whenever you insert a new row into the roysched table.

TASK 12A-2:

Creating an INSERT Trigger

Setup: You're logged on to Windows 2000 as student#. You've created a database named movies and tables within it named movie, category, customer, rental, and rental_detail. You've defined primary key, foreign key, default, and check constraints on the tables, and created nonclustered indexes based on your primary keys. You have imported data into the tables. You have created database diagrams for both the movies and pubs databases.

1. In SQL Query Analyzer, **open the C:\Data\insert-trigger.sql script file.**

2. **Highlight and execute the first query** to view the structure of the roysched table. You should see that this table consists of four columns: title_id, lorange, hirange, and royalty.

	Column_name	Type	Computed	Length	Prec	Scale	Nullable
1	title_id	tid	no	6			no
2	lorange	int	no	4	10	0	yes
3	hirange	int	no	4	10	0	yes
4	royalty	int	no	4	10	0	yes

3. **Highlight and execute the next query** to create a new table named audit-trail. You're going to use this table to store a copy of all new rows inserted into the roysched table. By specifying a default value of getdate() for the date_add column, SQL Server will automatically record the date and time a user inserted a new row into the roysched table. By specifying a default value of suser_sname() for the user_add column, SQL Server will record the Windows login account of the user who inserted the row into the roysched table.

4. **Highlight and execute the query to create the audit_inserts trigger.** This query creates an INSERT trigger on the roysched table. The audit_inserts trigger will automatically add a row to the audit_trail table whenever you add a new row to the roysched table.

5. **Highlight and execute the query that inserts a row into the roysched table.** You're inserting royalty information for a book with a title_id of PC9999. This statement assigns a lorange value of 0, hirange of 5000, and a royalty percentage of 10 percent. This INSERT statement causes SQL Server to fire your audit_inserts trigger.

6. **Highlight and execute the query that displays all rows in the audit_trail table** to verify that your INSERT trigger copied the new row into the audit_trail table. You should see that because you set default values for the date_add and user_add columns, SQL Server automatically recorded that information for you.

	title_id	royalty	date_add	user_add
1	PC9999	10	2001-05-11 19:12:00	SQLSERVER2\Student2

7. **Add a query to the insert-trigger.sql script file to view the definition of the audit_inserts trigger. What query did you use?**

8. **Save your changes to the insert-trigger.sql script file.**

9. **Open a new Query window, and then close the Query window containing the insert-trigger.sql script file.**

APPLY YOUR KNOWLEDGE 12-1

Suggested time:
20 minutes

Defining an INSERT Trigger on the Rental_detail Table

Objective: To run a SQL script to add a new column named "rented" to the movie table. You will then create an INSERT trigger on the rental_detail table. This trigger will mark a movie in the movie table as rented when you create the customer's invoice by using the rental and rental_detail tables.

1. In SQL Query Analyzer, open and execute the script file C:\Data\ updatemovie.sql. This script file contains the SQL statements for adding a new column to the movie table. The name of the column is "rented" and its data type is char(1). The script also defines a default value of N to the rented column. Finally, the script inserts a value of either Y or N for this column for all movies on file.

2. Open a new query window. Close the query window containing the updatemovie.sql.script file.

3. Create an `INSERT` trigger on the rental_detail table that will set the rented column to Y for a movie whenever a customer rents it. Name the `INSERT` trigger movie_rental. (Hint: Your `INSERT` trigger should use an `UPDATE` statement to update the movie table. You will need to join the movie table to the inserted table on the movie_num column as part of the `UPDATE` statement.) What query did you use?

4. Before you can test your trigger, you must first add a new invoice to the rental table. This is because you have defined a primary key to foreign key relationship between the rental and rental_detail tables. Execute the following SQL statement to insert a new invoice into the rental table:

```
INSERT INTO rental(cust_num)
VALUES (1)
```

5. Execute the following query to find the invoice number assigned to the row you just added (record the invoice number below):

```
SELECT *
FROM rental
WHERE cust_num = 1
```

Invoice number: _____

6. Now test the movie_rental trigger by executing the following query to add a line item containing the rented movie's movie number into the rental_detail table (replace invoice_number with the number you recorded in step 5):

```
INSERT INTO rental_detail
(invoice_num, line_num, movie_num, rental_price)
VALUES (invoice_number, 1, 105, 3.99)
```

(This statement adds a line item row for the invoice you added to the rental table specifying that the movie rented was movie number 105.)

7. Design and execute a query to check to see if your INSERT into the rental_ detail table caused your trigger to fire. What query did you use?

8. Clear the Query window.

Creating a DELETE Trigger

You use a DELETE trigger to perform specific functions whenever a row is deleted from the trigger table. Similar to an INSERT trigger, SQL Server also creates a logical table containing the rows deleted by the DELETE statement. This table is referred to as *deleted*. You can make calls to the deleted table as part of your DELETE trigger. Unlike the inserted table, the deleted table doesn't have any rows in common with the trigger table. This is because you have deleted the original rows from the trigger table, but SQL Server stores those rows in the deleted table. SQL Server builds the deleted table by using entries in the transaction log. If you execute a non-logged operation such as the TRUNCATE TABLE statement, SQL Server doesn't write the deleted rows to the deleted table.

You might use a DELETE trigger to cascade deletes. For example, if you want to delete a customer and all of their associated rental invoices, you must delete all of the customer's rows from both the rental and rental_detail tables before you can delete the customer. Keep in mind that one of the new features in SQL Server 2000 is support for the ON DELETE CASCADE option for foreign key constraints. This option enables you to delete a row in the primary key table— and have SQL Server automatically delete the associated rows in the foreign key table. If you recall, we defined such a foreign key on the invoice_num column in the rental_detail table in the "Designing and Implementing Data Integrity" lesson. So, we don't need to define a trigger to perform cascade deletes between the rental and rental_detail tables.

TASK 12A-3:

Creating a DELETE Trigger

1. In SQL Server Enterprise Manager, **display the database diagram for the movies database.**

2. **Look at the link between the rental and rental_detail tables.** You configured the invoice_num column in the rental table as the primary key. In the rental_detail table, you configure the invoice_num column as a foreign key that references the same column in the rental table.

3. **Right-click on the link between the rental and rental_detail tables and choose Properties** to view the properties of the primary key to foreign key relationship between the two tables.

4. **Look at the Cascade options** (at the bottom of the page). You can see that you configured the FK_detail_invoice foreign key constraint to support cascading deletes.

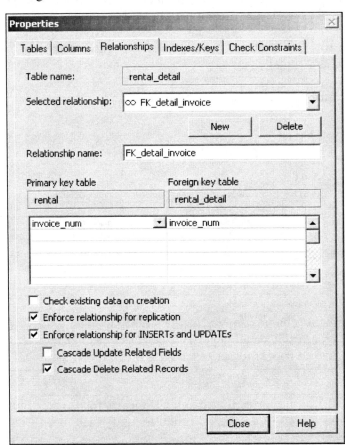

5. **Uncheck Cascade Delete Related Records** to change the foreign key constraint to not support cascading deletes. We're going to create a trigger to perform cascading deletes instead.

6. **Click Close** to close the Properties dialog box.

7. On the toolbar, **click the Save button** to save your changes to the foreign key constraint.

8. **Click Yes** to confirm that you want to save your changes.

9. **You want to delete an invoice. Given that to delete an invoice you must delete it from both the rental and the rental_detail tables, from which table must you delete the invoice first?**

10. **You've decided to define a DELETE trigger to delete an invoice from both the rental and rental_detail tables. On which table must you define the DELETE trigger?**

11. In SQL Query Analyzer, **open the C:\Data\delete-trigger.sql script file.**

12. **Highlight and execute the query that creates the delete_invoice trigger** to create a trigger that will delete an invoice from the rental table whenever you delete that invoice's line items from the rental_detail table.

13. In the script file, **highlight and execute the next two queries** to view the rows in the rental and rental_detail tables for invoice number 243. You will delete this invoice to test your DELETE trigger.

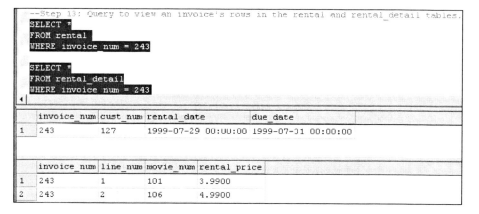

```
--Step 13: Query to view an invoice's rows in the rental and rental_detail tables.
SELECT *
FROM rental
WHERE invoice_num = 243

SELECT *
FROM rental_detail
WHERE invoice_num = 243
```

	invoice_num	cust_num	rental_date	due_date	
1	243	127	1999-07-29 00:00:00	1999-07-31 00:00:00	

	invoice_num	line_num	movie_num	rental_price
1	243	1	101	3.9900
2	243	2	106	4.9900

14. **Highlight and execute the next query in the script file** to delete invoice number 243 from the rental_detail table. This delete causes SQL Server to fire your delete_invoice trigger to delete the related invoice in the rental table.

15. **Re-execute the SELECT queries that display the rows for invoice number 243 in the rental and rental_detail tables** to verify that your DELETE trigger fired properly.

16. **Open a new Query window, and then close the Query window containing the delete-trigger.sql script file.**

Creating an UPDATE Trigger

You can use an UPDATE trigger to perform specific actions whenever you update the data in a table. SQL Server records a copy of the data before your change in the deleted logical table, and a copy of the data after your change in the inserted logical table. You can use your trigger to work with both the deleted and inserted tables in addition to performing almost any SQL statement.

If you plan to maintain an audit trail of changes to a table, you must create an UPDATE trigger in addition to the INSERT trigger. You might also use an UPDATE trigger to cascade updates to a column to multiple tables within a database. For example, you might use an UPDATE trigger to cascade a change to a customer's account number to both the customer and rental tables.

SQL Server fires an UPDATE trigger whenever you update a row in a table, regardless of the information you change in that row. You can focus your UPDATE trigger more tightly by using the IF UPDATE statement. This statement enables you to specify a column to monitor for updates—and if that column is modified, SQL Server fires the UPDATE trigger. Use the following syntax:

```
CREATE TRIGGER trigger_name
ON table_name
FOR UPDATE
AS
IF UPDATE (column_name)
BEGIN SQL statement(s)
END
```

You can use the IF UPDATE statement to specify an action you want SQL Server to perform if the column is modified (such as recording information in your audit trail table), or you can simply use the RAISERROR( ) function to display an error message to your users. For example, you might use the following trigger to prevent users from changing a customer's account number in the customer table:

```
CREATE TRIGGER no_update_cust_num
ON customer
FOR UPDATE
AS
IF UPDATE (cust_num)
BEGIN
 RAISERROR ('You cannot change a customer's account number.',
10, 1)
 ROLLBACK TRANSACTION
END
```

In this example, if you attempt to change a customer's number, SQL Server will display the text of the error message in the RAISERROR statement and then undo the transaction. So, this trigger will prevent you from changing the customer's account number.

APPLY YOUR KNOWLEDGE 12-2

Defining an UPDATE Trigger on the Roysched Table

Objective: To design and create an UPDATE trigger to audit changes to the roysched table.

1. In SQL Query Analyzer, use the pubs database.

2. You're planning to create an UPDATE trigger on the roysched table to record changes to the audit_trail table. Which logical table should you use to copy the data into the audit_trail table?

3. Design and execute a query to create an UPDATE trigger on the roysched table. Configure the trigger so that SQL Server will fire it only if a user changes the royalty column. Have the trigger add a row to the audit_trail table to record the changes. Name your trigger dbo.audit_updates. What query did you use?

4. Write and execute a query that will cause SQL Server to fire your UPDATE trigger. (Hint: Use the title_id you inserted in Task 12A-2, step 5.) What query did you use?

5. Verify that your UPDATE trigger recorded a row in the audit_trail table. What query did you use?

6. Clear the Query window.

Creating an INSTEAD OF Trigger

You create an INSTEAD OF trigger to have SQL Server perform only this trigger's actions. You can create INSTEAD OF INSERT, INSTEAD OF UPDATE, and INSTEAD OF DELETE triggers. You can create only one INSTEAD OF trigger for each action (INSERT, UPDATE, and DELETE for each table or view).

In all cases, SQL Server ignores any `FOR` or `AFTER` triggers you've defined for an action if you create an `INSTEAD OF` trigger. For example, let's say that you've defined a `FOR UPDATE` trigger on the customer table. If you now create an `INSTEAD OF UPDATE` trigger on the customer table, SQL Server executes this trigger instead.

Here's the basic syntax for creating an `INSTEAD OF` trigger:

```
CREATE TRIGGER trigger_name
ON table_name | view_name
INSTEAD OF {INSERT | UPDATE | DELETE}
AS
SQL statement(s)
```

While we've been using tables as an example, you'll find that you most commonly create `INSTEAD OF` triggers on views, not tables. That's because you can use these triggers to update views that you can't typically update. For example, let's say that you've created a view based on a table join. In this scenario, you can't `DELETE` rows using the view. But, you can use an `INSTEAD OF DELETE` trigger to enable you to delete rows. Here's an example of how an `INSTEAD OF` trigger works. We start by creating the following view to enable you to see a list of invoices from the rental table, and each invoice's line items from the rental_ detail table:

```
CREATE VIEW dbo.vw_Invoices
AS
SELECT r.invoice_num, r.rental_date, rd.line_num, rd.movie_num,
rd.rental_price
FROM rental AS r LEFT OUTER JOIN rental_detail AS rd
ON r.invoice_num = rd.invoice_num
```

Next, attempt to delete an invoice using the view, as follows:

```
DELETE FROM dbo.vw_Invoices
WHERE invoice_num = 244
```

When we execute this query, SQL Server displays the error message you see in Figure 12-1. You can get around this problem by creating an `INSTEAD OF DELETE` trigger. Here's what it should look like:

```
CREATE TRIGGER dbo.DeleteInvoices
ON dbo.vw_Invoices
INSTEAD OF DELETE
AS
     DELETE FROM rental_detail
     WHERE invoice_num IN (SELECT invoice_num
                           FROM deleted)
     DELETE FROM rental
     WHERE invoice_num IN ((SELECT invoice_num
                            FROM deleted)
```

This trigger enables us to delete an invoice from both the rental and rental_detail tables using the vw_Invoices view. Let's create this view and `INSTEAD OF` trigger so that you can try them out.

You can't create an `INSTEAD OF` *trigger on a view for which you've* configured the `WITH CHECK OPTION`.

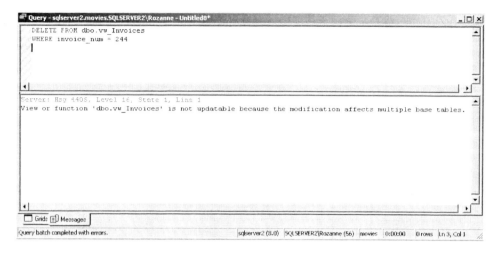

Figure 12-1: *Without an* `INSTEAD OF` *trigger, you can't delete rows using a view.*

TASK 12A-4:

Creating an INSTEAD OF Trigger

1. In SQL Query Analyzer, **open the C:\Data\instead-trigger.sql script file.**

2. **Highlight and execute the query to create the vw_Invoices view.** This query lists the invoice_num, rental_date, line_num, movie_num, and rental_price columns.

3. In the script file, **highlight and execute the query to display all rows using the vw_Invoices view.** Depending on what you've done in earlier tasks in this course, you might see different invoice numbers than the ones in the screen shot below.

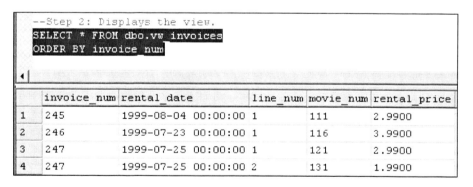

4. Now, let's try to delete an invoice using the view. In the script file, **highlight and execute the DELETE query** to attempt to delete all invoices in the rental and rental_detail tables with an invoice_num of 250 by using the view.

5. **Highlight and execute the query to create the DeleteInvoices** `INSTEAD OF` **trigger.** This trigger will allow you to delete rows using a view.

6. Now that you've created the `INSTEAD OF` trigger, **highlight and execute the query to delete invoice number 250.** You should see that SQL Server successfully deleted the rows. Note: You'll see several messages stating that rows were deleted. This is because SQL Server must first delete the rows from the view and place them in the deleted table, and then delete the associated rows in both the rental and rental_detail tables.

7. **Open a new Query window, and then close the window containing the instead-trigger.sql script.**

Managing Triggers

SQL Server includes commands that you can use to modify, delete, or temporarily disable triggers. You can modify a trigger by using the `ALTER TRIGGER` statement. You can use the `ALTER TRIGGER` statement to change an `UPDATE` trigger to a `DELETE` trigger. Use the following syntax to modify a trigger:

```
ALTER TRIGGER owner.trigger_name
ON owner.table_name
[WITH ENCRYPTION]
FOR {INSERT | UPDATE | DELETE}
AS
SQL statements
```

Deleting a Trigger

You can use the `DROP TRIGGER` statement to permanently remove a trigger. You must either be the owner of the table on which a trigger is defined or a member of either the sysadmin or db_owner roles in order to delete the trigger. SQL Server automatically deletes a table's triggers whenever you delete the table itself. Use the following syntax to delete a trigger:

```
DROP TRIGGER trigger_name
```

Disabling and Enabling Triggers

You can temporarily disable a trigger (or all of a table's triggers) by using the `ALTER TABLE` statement along with `DISABLE TRIGGER`. You might want to disable a trigger if you want to speed up the import of a large amount of data into a table and you've already validated the data so the triggers aren't necessary during the import process.

Use the following syntax to disable a trigger:

```
ALTER TABLE table_name
DISABLE TRIGGER {ALL | trigger_name}
```

In this syntax, you replace *trigger_name* with the name of the trigger you want to disable. If you want to disable all triggers, use the `ALL` keyword instead.

When you're ready to re-enable a trigger, use the following syntax:

```
ALTER TABLE table_name
ENABLE TRIGGER {ALL | trigger_name}
```

APPLY YOUR KNOWLEDGE 12-3

Managing Triggers

Objective: To disable and enable the audit_updates trigger in the pubs database.

1. In SQL Query Analyzer, use the pubs database. Design and execute a query to temporarily disable the audit_updates trigger. What query did you use?

2. Design and execute a query to verify that SQL Server doesn't fire your UPDATE trigger. Record your query below.

3. Verify that SQL Server didn't add a row in the audit_trail table. What query did you use?

4. Design and execute a query to re-enable the audit_updates trigger. What query did you use?

5. Re-run your queries in steps 2 and 3 to verify that SQL Server fires your UPDATE trigger.

6. Close all open windows.

Implementing Complex Triggers

SQL Server enables you to create triggers that by their actions call other triggers. These types of triggers are referred to as nested triggers. You can also have a trigger call itself. This type of trigger is referred to as a recursive trigger.

Nested Triggers

You can design a trigger to INSERT, UPDATE, or DELETE from another table whenever SQL Server fires your trigger. For example, the audit_updates trigger inserts a new row into the audit_trail table whenever you make a change to the roysched table. In addition to the trigger on the roysched table, you could create an INSERT trigger on the audit_trail table. In this scenario, whenever you make a change to a royalty in the roysched table, SQL Server will fire your audit_ updates trigger. Because the audit_updates trigger inserts a row into the audit_ trail table, SQL Server could then fire an INSERT trigger on the audit_trail table.

When one trigger's action causes another trigger to fire, these triggers are called nested triggers. You can define up to 32 levels of nested triggers. You can use the @@NESTLEVEL function to identify the number of levels in nested triggers. SQL Server considers a trigger a transaction; so, if you have nested triggers and any single trigger fails, SQL Server will roll back all of the actions performed by all of the nested triggers.

By default, SQL Server enables nested triggers, but you can disable support for them by using the sp_configure stored procedure. You might find it necessary to turn off nested triggers in order to debug errors. Use the following syntax to disable nested triggers:

```
sp_configure 'nested triggers', 0
```

Recursive Triggers

A recursive trigger is one that contains an INSERT, UPDATE, or DELETE statement as its action, yet the trigger is called by that same action. For example, you might create an UPDATE trigger on a table to update a specific column in the table that called the trigger. Yet, the action your trigger performs (in this case, an UPDATE) can cause the same trigger to fire again. To avoid exceeding the 32-level nesting limit, your trigger must include a variable for checking the number of times the trigger has fired, along with statements to break out of the trigger.

By default, SQL Server doesn't enable the recursive trigger option. You can enable it for your server by using the sp_dboption stored procedure as follows:

```
sp_dboption database_name, 'recursive triggers', True
```

Summary

In this lesson, you learned why you might create triggers: to ensure the integrity of your data, perform cascading deletes and updates, and to keep track of changes to a table. You also learned how to create each type of trigger (INSERT, UPDATE, and DELETE) by using the CREATE TABLE statement.

LESSON 12 REVIEW

12A In what scenario would you choose to implement a check constraint instead of a trigger? In what scenario would you choose to implement a trigger instead of a check constraint?

YOUR NOTES:

Understanding Transactions and Locks

Data Files:

transactions.sql
transaction-lab.sql
locking.sql
customer.sql
lock1.sql
lock2.sql
tablock.sql
tablock2.sql

Lesson Time:
1 hour, 45 minutes

Overview

In SQL Server, you use transactions to control how SQL Server processes a query. SQL Server must be able to process all of the statements within the transaction successfully, or all of the statements fail. In this lesson, you will explore the types of transactions SQL Server supports and how to implement them. You'll also learn how SQL Server protects resources in a multi-user environment by using locks. Finally, you will see how to reduce contention by modifying locking and the potential drawbacks to these techniques.

Objectives

To manage transactions and locks, you will:

13A   Work with transactions.

SQL Server supports two types of transactions: explicit and implicit. In this topic, we will explore how you implement both types of transactions.

13B   Work with locks.

SQL Server uses locks to protect against such problems as lost updates, nonrepeatable reads, phantoms, and dirty reads. In this topic, you'll learn how the different levels of locking you can implement protect (or don't protect) against these problems, and why you might change your session's default locking settings. In addition, you'll learn how to monitor locking by using the `sp_lock` stored procedure.

TOPIC 13A

Designing and Implementing Transactions

You can use transactions to specify that you want SQL Server to process a series of SQL statements as a single unit rather than individually. When SQL Server processes the statements as a single unit, all of them must be completed successfully, or they will all fail. This capability is referred to as *atomicity*.

atomicity:
A state in which SQL Server either performs all of a transaction's modifications or none of them.

A banking application is a common example of implementing transactions in SQL Server. Consider the scenario where a customer transfers money from a savings account to a checking account. In this example, you would want the banking application to implement both actions as a single transaction: a debit to the savings account, and a credit to the checking account. If either action fails, you want the entire transaction to fail.

Types of Transactions

SQL Server supports two types of transactions: explicit and implicit. An explicit transaction is a group of one or more Transact-SQL statements that begin with a `BEGIN TRANSACTION` statement and end with the `COMMIT TRANSACTION` statement. SQL Server doesn't commit the changes made in an explicit transaction's SQL statement until it processes the `COMMIT TRANSACTION` statement. For this reason, you can roll back the transaction at any time prior to the `COMMIT TRANSACTION` statement. Remember, however, that you must always use `COMMIT TRANSACTION` after you use `BEGIN TRANSACTION`. If you enter the `BEGIN TRANSACTION` before an `INSERT` statement, for example, SQL Server won't commit the `INSERT` transaction to the table without the `COMMIT TRANSACTION` statement.

You use an implicit transaction when you use Transact-SQL statements by themselves without the `BEGIN TRANSACTION` statement. SQL Server considers all statements you execute part of a transaction until you issue either a `COMMIT TRAN`, `COMMIT WORK`, or `ROLLBACK TRAN` statement. SQL Server doesn't enable implicit transactions by default.

What SQL Server does enable by default is the autocommit transaction mode. This mode configures SQL Server to treat each individual SQL statement (along with its parameters) as a separate transaction. For example, if you execute a query and you don't use the `BEGIN TRAN` and `COMMIT TRAN` statements, nor do you turn on implicit transactions, SQL Server autocommits the transaction.

You can optionally set a savepoint within a transaction. This savepoint acts sort of like a bookmark in that it enables SQL Server to return to this point if you conditionally cancel part of a transaction. By "conditionally," we mean that you might have an `IF` statement to cancel some of the transaction steps. When SQL Server returns to the savepoint, it can either complete the transaction or roll it back (based on your programming). You define a savepoint by using the following syntax:

```
BEGIN TRANSACTION
SQL statements
SAVE TRANSACTION savepoint_name
...
```

If you later want to roll back the transaction to the savepoint, you use the statement `ROLLBACK TRANSACTION savepoint_name`.

How Transactions Work

When you change a database, the first thing SQL Server does is to copy the pages of the database that you're changing into a portion of RAM called the buffer cache. (Depending on what's happening on your server, these pages might already be cached in RAM.) Next, SQL Server records your change to both the data pages and the transaction log in RAM. It then writes the change to the database's transaction log on your server's hard disk. At this point, SQL Server considers your change committed. Only after writing the change to the transaction log can SQL Server then write the changed data pages in RAM out to the database on your server's hard disk. What's most important for you to understand is that SQL Server *always* writes the change to the transaction log on the hard disk before it writes that same change to the database. It's this strategy of writing to the transaction log before writing to the database that makes it possible for you to recover a failed transaction (or to undo a transaction, for that matter). Because SQL Server writes to the transaction log before it writes to your database, you'll sometimes hear a database's transaction log referred to as a write-ahead log.

SQL Server temporarily caches committed transactions. When the cache fills up, it then writes the information to your server's hard disk. The copies of your database on the server's hard drive and in RAM are identical at this point. To prevent database corruption, don't use a write-caching hard drive controller on a SQL server. With this type of controller, it's possible that SQL Server will think it has written information to the hard disk when in fact the information is still cached on the hard drive controller. If you have a power failure at this point, SQL Server will not be able to roll back or roll forward the necessary transactions to repair your database.

Designing Transactions

You should try to keep your transactions short to minimize the amount of work SQL Server must do to roll back the transaction in the event of a problem. In addition, SQL Server locks resources whenever a transaction is open. When a resource (such as an entire table) is locked, other users can't access it. To keep your transaction short, try not to use control-of-flow statements such as WHILE. You also should not use Data Definition Language statements such as CREATE TABLE within a transaction. Don't require user input from within a transaction (again, to minimize locking). Instead, gather all of the necessary information from user data entry first, write the statements to begin the transaction, perform whatever task is necessary, and then end the transaction.

You should also try to avoid nesting transactions. In other words, don't begin a transaction and then begin a second transaction within the first. If you do, SQL Server ignores the innermost BEGIN TRANSACTION and COMMIT TRANSACTION statements. One of the most common situations that leads to nested transactions is when you have nested triggers or stored procedures. You can use the @@trancount function or the DBCC OPENTRAN statement to view a count of open transactions. This information helps you to determine if you have nested transactions. The @@trancount system function is set to zero when you don't have any open transactions. When SQL Server processes the first BEGIN TRANSACTION statement, it increases @@trancount by one; if SQL Server processes a ROLLBACK TRANSACTION statement, it sets @@trancount to zero.

Creating Explicit Transactions

You begin an explicit transaction by using the `BEGIN TRANSACTION` statement. You can optionally name a transaction; you can then use this name when you either commit or roll back the transaction. Use the following syntax to begin an explicit transaction:

`BEGIN TRANSACTION [transaction_name]`

Because you use a transaction when you're making changes to data, you will most commonly use the `INSERT`, `UPDATE`, and `DELETE` statements within a transaction. You can't include the following statements within an explicit transaction:

- Any system stored procedure that creates a temporary table (such as `sp_dboption`)
- `ALTER DATABASE`
- `BACKUP LOG`
- `CREATE DATABASE`
- `RECONFIGURE`
- `RESTORE DATABASE`
- `RESTORE LOG`
- `UPDATE STATISTICS`

You end a transaction by using the `COMMIT TRANSACTION` statement as follows:

`COMMIT TRANSACTION [transaction_name]`

If you want to abort a transaction, use the `ROLLBACK TRANSACTION` statement as follows:

`ROLLBACK TRANSACTION [transaction_name]`

In all of these statements, you can abbreviate `TRANSACTION` as `TRAN`. For example, you can use `BEGIN TRAN` instead of `BEGIN TRANSACTION`.

TASK 13A-1:

Working with Explicit Transactions

Setup: You're logged on to Windows 2000 as student#. You've created a database named movies and tables within it named movie, category, customer, rental, and rental_detail. You've defined primary key, foreign key, default, and check constraints on the tables, and you've created nonclustered indexes based on your primary keys. You have imported data into the tables. You have created database diagrams for both the movies and pubs databases.

1. **Start SQL Query Analyzer and use the movies database.**

2. **Open the script file C:\Data\transactions.sql.** This script changes the title of movie 105 from "Godfather The" to "Godfather, The".

3. **Look at the script file.** This script file begins a transaction and then displays the current value for the @@trancount system function. Next, it displays the current title of movie number 105. It then sends an update to the movie table to change the title of movie number 105 and displays the title of the movie after the UPDATE statement. Finally, it displays the value of the @@trancount system function again.

4. **What do you think the value of the @@trancount system function will be at the end of this script?**

5. **Execute the script file and look at the results.** You should see that the current number of open transactions on your server is still 1 when SQL Server finishes processing your script.

(No column name)		(No column name)	
1	The current number of open transactions is:	1	

(No column name)		title	
1	The current title of movie number 105 is:	Godfather The	

(No column name)			title
1	After the UPDATE statement, the title of movie number 105 is:		Godfather, The

(No column name)		(No column name)	
1	The current number of open transactions is:	1	

6. **Open a second Query window.**

7. **Execute a new query:**

```
SELECT title, movie_num
FROM movie
WHERE movie_num = 105
```

This query attempts to view the title of the movie with movie number 105.

8. **Why is SQL Server unable to process your query?**

9. **What do you think the current title of movie number 105 is?**

10. **Choose Query→Cancel Executing Query** to stop the current query to view the title of movie number 105.

11. **Switch to your first Query window.** (This is the window that contains the transactions.sql script.)

12. At the end of the script, **add the following line:**

```
COMMIT TRAN
```

13. **Highlight and execute the COMMIT TRAN statement** to execute just this statement. You don't need to re-run the entire script to complete the transaction.

14. **Switch back to your other Query window.** (The window that contains the SELECT statement for viewing the title of movie number 105.)

15. **Execute this query** to view the title of movie number 105. You should see that the title for movie number 105 is now "Godfather, The".

16. **Close the Query window containing the transactions.sql script. Don't save your changes to the script.**

17. **Clear the Query window.**

Suggested time:

15 minutes

APPLY YOUR KNOWLEDGE 13-1

Rolling Back a Transaction

Objective: To write the SQL statements to begin a transaction, update the data, and then roll back the change.

1. In SQL Query Analyzer, make sure that you're using the movies database.

2. Design and execute a query to perform the following steps:
   - Begin a transaction.
   - Display the current value of the @@trancount system function.
   - Display the current value of the lname column for customer number 2.
   - Change the last name of customer 2 to Johnson.
   - Display the current value of the lname column for customer number 2 after the update.
   - Roll back the transaction.
   - Display the current value of the lname column for customer number 2 after the roll back.
   - Display the current value of the @@trancount system function after the roll back.

   What query did you use?

3. Clear the Query window.

Enabling Implicit Transactions

Microsoft recommends that you explicitly define transactions wherever possible; however, you might run into situations, such as when you migrate an application from another environment into the SQL Server environment, where you must maintain implicit transactions. To use implicit transactions, you must first configure SQL Server to support them by using the following syntax: SET IMPLICIT_TRANSACTIONS ON.

After you've enabled implicit transactions, you start a transaction whenever you issue a query that begins with any of the following SQL statements:

- ALTER TABLE
- CREATE
- DELETE
- DROP
- FETCH
- GRANT
- INSERT
- OPEN
- REVOKE
- SELECT
- TRUNCATE TABLE
- UPDATE

Remember, after you've begun an implicit transaction, SQL Server doesn't commit the transaction's changes until you execute one of the following statements: COMMIT TRAN, COMMIT WORK, or ROLLBACK TRAN.

TOPIC 13B

Managing Locks

lost updates:
An update that gets lost when one user's update overwrites another user's update.

inconsistent analysis (nonrepeatable read):
Occurs when a transaction reads a row multiple times and retrieves different values.

phantom:
Occurs when one transaction adds a new row while another transaction is in the midst of updating several rows.

dirty read:
Occurs when one transaction reads another transaction's uncommitted changes. As you'll see in this lesson, you can configure SQL Server's locking such that it's possible for this scenario to occur.

To avoid conflicts, SQL Server uses locks to protect the integrity of your databases during transactions. For example, locks prevent *lost updates*, which is a scenario in which two users update the same row at the same time. Without locks, one user's change would overwrite the other user's change. Locks also prevent inconsistent analysis. *Inconsistent analysis (nonrepeatable read)* occurs when a transaction in SQL Server reads the same row twice, yet the values in the row change between each read. SQL Server uses locks to prevent phantoms as well. A *phantom* can occur when two transactions are executed at the same time. For example, you might have one user updating the rows in the customer table to reflect a ZIP code change, while at the same time another user inserts a new row into the customer table. If these two transactions occur simultaneously, the transaction for changing the ZIP codes might change the necessary customer rows, but then find a new row when the other user's transaction is completed. This new row is referred to as a phantom. Finally, locks can be used to prevent *dirty reads*. A dirty read occurs when a transaction attempts to read uncommitted data.

SQL Server locks resources based on the type of action you're performing. SQL Server tries to implement locking that affects the smallest amount of a resource while still maintaining the integrity of your data. For example, SQL Server 2000 includes the ability to lock a table at the row level rather than at the page level. SQL Server can place locks on the following resources:

- A single row in a table by using the Row IDentifier (RID).
- A single row in an index by using the index key.
- An 8 KB page of a table or index.
- An extent (eight 8 KB pages).
- An entire table (including its indexes).
- An entire database.

SQL Server implements several different types of locks. These locks can be divided into two categories: basic and special use. Let's take a look at both types.

Basic Locks

SQL Server implements two types of basic locks: shared and exclusive. SQL Server uses shared locks during read transactions, and exclusive locks during write transactions. SQL Server uses shared locks (S) only if your transaction doesn't modify data. This lock is referred to as *shared* because other transactions can also place a shared lock on the same resource as well. So, multiple transactions can use the resource at the same time. SQL Server releases a shared lock on a row as soon as it reads the next row in a table. If you issue a query that returns multiple rows, SQL Server maintains the shared lock until it has retrieved all rows that satisfy the query.

SQL Server uses exclusive locks (X) whenever you issue transactions that change data. For example, SQL Server uses an exclusive lock if your transaction contains an `INSERT`, `UPDATE`, or `DELETE` statement. This lock is referred to as *exclusive* because only one transaction can use the resource. In addition, other transactions can't place a shared lock on a resource that has an exclusive lock on it. Likewise, your transaction can't place an exclusive lock on a resource if it has shared locks on it.

Special Use Locks

SQL Server also uses special locks for other types of situations. For example, it uses an intent lock to minimize conflicts between locks. An *intent lock* creates a locking hierarchy such that other transactions and locks can't conflict with each other. For example, let's say you're updating a row in a table. In this scenario, your transaction results in an exclusive lock on that row. An intent lock prevents another user from attempting to perform an action that would require an exclusive lock on the table that contains this row. An intent lock can be *shared (IS)*, *exclusive (IX)*, or *shared with intent exclusive (SIX)*. SQL Server uses an intent shared lock when your transaction simply reads some of the data in the resource. In contrast, SQL Server uses an intent exclusive lock if your transaction will change data. SQL Server uses a shared with intent exclusive lock when your transaction will read all of the data in the resource and change some of that data.

SQL Server uses an *update lock (U)* on a table when it plans to modify one of the table's pages. SQL Server places an update lock on a page when it first reads the page. It then changes the update lock to an exclusive lock when it writes the changes to the page. An update lock on a page prevents user transactions from obtaining exclusive locks on rows within the same page; however, user transactions can still place shared locks on the page.

If a table or index is in use, SQL Server places a *schema lock* on that table or index. A *schema stability lock (Sch-S)* prevents the table or index from being dropped while it's currently in use. A *schema modification lock (Sch-M)* prevents users from accessing a table or index while you're modifying its structure.

Finally, SQL Server uses *bulk update locks* to prevent other transactions from accessing a table when you're importing data into the table. SQL server places a bulk update lock on a table whenever you configure a table to use the Table Lock On Bulk Load option. You can configure this option by using the `sp_tableoption` stored procedure.

Coexistence of Locks

Some locks can't be placed on the same resource at the same time. The following table shows you which locks can coexist with each other.

Requested Lock	Existing Lock					
	S	X	IS	IX	SIX	U
S (shared)	Yes	No	Yes	No	No	Yes
X (exclusive)	No	No	No	No	No	No
IS (intent shared)	Yes	No	Yes	Yes	Yes	Yes
IX (intent exclusive)	No	No	Yes	Yes	No	No
SIX (shared with intent exclusive)	No	No	Yes	No	No	No
U (update)	Yes	No	Yes	No	No	No
Sch-M (schema modification)	No	No	No	No	No	No
Sch-S (schema stability)	Yes	Yes	Yes	Yes	Yes	Yes

[1]The Sch-M lock is incompatible with all other locks.

[2]The Sch-S lock is compatible with all other locks except Sch-M.

Viewing Current Locks

You can use the `sp_lock` stored procedure to view information about locks on your server. The `sp_lock` stored procedure lists the locks on your server, the ID number of the database, the type of resource, and the type of lock. `Sp_lock` also identifies the transaction that has placed the lock on the resource by process ID number. You can view information about the process ID numbers in use on your server by using the `sp_who` stored procedure. If you want to find the ID number SQL Server assigned to a database, execute the query `sp_helpdb` *database_name.*

You can also use the Current Activity object in SQL Server Enterprise Manager to view information about locks held by a process or user, as well as any locks that are currently being blocked (due to an exclusive lock) and locks that are blocking other processes or users. SQL Server Enterprise Manager enables you to view locks by process ID or by object. Of the different types of locks, you should be most concerned about exclusive locks as these locks can block other processes from performing their tasks. When you view the locks within SQL Server Enterprise Manager, you can determine whether a lock is blocking other processes or not.

Other utilities you can use to monitor locks include SQL Profiler and the Windows 2000 System Monitor. You can use SQL Profiler to monitor server events within a trace file. For example, you can use SQL Profiler to monitor login attempts and connections and to troubleshoot deadlocks. You use System Monitor to analyze locks by using the SQL Server: Lock Manager and SQL Server: Locks objects and their counters.

TASK 13B-1:

Observing the Current Locks on Your Server

1. In SQL Query Analyzer, **execute the following query:**

```
EXEC sp_lock
```

The numbers you see for spid, dbid, ObjID, and IndID in this task will vary depending on what resources you have open. You should focus on the Mode and Status columns for this task.

This query enables you to view a list of the current locks on your server. The Type column enables you to determine the type of resource on which the lock was placed: row (RID), key (KEY), page (PAG), table (TAB), database (DB), or extent (EXT). The Mode column enables you to view the type of lock in use: S, X, IS, IX, SIX, or U. Use the status column to determine the status of the lock. If SQL Server has granted the lock, you will see a status of GRANT. If SQL Server can't grant the lock because another process currently has a lock on the resource, you'll see the status of WAIT. When the blocking process releases its lock, SQL Server converts the lock from WAIT to GRANT. During the conversion process, SQL Server displays the lock's status as CNVRT.

	spid	dbid	ObjId	IndId	Type	Resource	Mode	Status
1	51	7	0	0	DB		S	GRANT
2	53	6	0	0	DB		S	GRANT
3	54	1	85575343	0	TAB		IS	GRANT

2. Open a second Query window and verify that you're using the movies database.

3. Execute the following query:

```
BEGIN TRAN
UPDATE customer
SET fname = 'Joan'
WHERE cust_num = 100
```

Use this query to begin a transaction that will place a lock on the Customers table.

4. Switch back to the first Query window.

5. Execute the `sp_lock` query again. You should see that SQL Server has placed several new locks on your server's resources. For example, SQL Server has placed exclusive locks on index key rows. This is because the customer table has a nonclustered index on the lname column. In addition, you should see several intent exclusive locks on pages and the table because the UPDATE statement requires an exclusive lock.

	spid	dbid	ObjId	IndId	Type	Resource	Mode	Status
1	51	7	0	0	DB		S	GRANT
2	51	7	741577680	3	KEY	(b601d97d25f0)	X	GRANT
3	51	7	741577680	1	PAG	1:110	IX	GRANT
4	51	7	741577680	1	PAG	1:111	IX	GRANT
5	51	7	741577680	3	KEY	(b60107735e2d)	X	GRANT
6	51	7	741577680	0	TAB		IX	GRANT
7	51	7	741577680	1	KEY	(b100acad0b53)	X	GRANT
8	53	6	0	0	DB		S	GRANT
9	54	1	85575343	0	TAB		IS	GRANT

6. Open a third Query window.

7. Execute the query:

```
SELECT lname
FROM customer
WHERE cust_num = 100
```

Use this query to attempt to access the customer's row in the table. SQL Server can't process this query until the exclusive lock on this customer is released.

8. In the first Query window, **execute sp_lock again.** You should see a new shared lock listed among the last rows of the results set. This lock displays a status of WAIT because of the exclusive locks on the customer's information in the customer table.

	spid	dbid	ObjId	IndId	Type	Resource	Mode	Status
1	51	7	0	0	DB		S	GRANT
2	51	7	741577680	3	KEY	(b601d97d25f0)	X	GRANT
3	51	7	741577680	1	PAG	1:110	IX	GRANT
4	51	7	741577680	1	PAG	1:111	IX	GRANT
5	51	7	741577680	3	KEY	(b60107735e2d)	X	GRANT
6	51	7	741577680	0	TAB		IX	GRANT
7	51	7	741577680	1	KEY	(b100acad0b53)	X	GRANT
8	53	6	0	0	DB		S	GRANT
9	54	1	85575343	0	TAB		IS	GRANT
10	55	7	741577680	0	TAB		IS	GRANT
11	55	7	741577680	2	PAG	1:174	IS	GRANT
12	55	7	741577680	2	KEY	(6400b740ff6a)	S	GRANT
13	55	7	741577680	1	KEY	(b100acad0b53)	S	WAIT
14	55	7	0	0	DB		S	GRANT
15	55	7	741577680	1	PAG	1:111	IS	GRANT

9. **Switch to the second Query window.** (You might find it easier to choose Window and then choose the appropriate Query window from the list of open windows. You want to switch to the Query window that contains the BEGIN TRAN statement.)

10. At the end of the BEGIN TRAN query, **add the statement:**

    COMMIT TRAN

    This adds the necessary statement to commit the transaction.

11. **Highlight and execute the COMMIT TRAN statement** to commit the transaction.

```
BEGIN TRAN
        UPDATE customer
        SET fname = 'Joan'
        WHERE cust_num = 100
COMMIT TRAN
```

12. **Close all Query windows except for the one containing the EXEC sp_lock statement.**

13. **Re-run the EXEC sp_lock statement** to verify that your transactions no longer have any exclusive locks.

14. **Clear the Query window.**

Managing Locks

SQL Server includes options that enable you to control how it locks resources. These options are referred to as isolation levels. You can set the isolation level at either the session- or table-level. You use the isolation levels to configure how sensitive an application is to changes made by others. The isolation levels you set determine how a transaction holds a lock to protect your data. The longer a transaction holds a lock, the more likely that lock is to conflict with other users' actions.

Session-level Locking

You can control locking at the session level by setting the transaction isolation level. SQL Server uses the transaction isolation level to determine to what degree it will isolate a transaction. If you change the transaction isolation level, SQL Server applies this setting to all transactions in your current session. (You can later override these settings by specifying the transaction isolation level on a statement.)

Use the following syntax to set the transaction isolation level for your current session:

```
SET TRANSACTION ISOLATION LEVEL
{READ COMMITTED | READ UNCOMMITTED | REPEATABLE READ |
SERIALIZABLE}
```

You set the transaction isolation level by specifying one of the options in the list. By default, SQL Server configures your session's transaction isolation level as READ COMMITTED. The following table describes these options beginning with the least restrictive and progressing to the most restrictive.

Isolation Level Option	Enables You to Configure SQL Server to
READ UNCOMMITTED	Permit a transaction to read any data currently on a data page regardless of whether SQL Server has committed that data or not. If you set your isolation level to read uncommitted, your transaction doesn't use shared locks and it ignores any exclusive locks when reading data. So, it's possible that you might read a row's data while another user is modifying that row's data. You can use this setting to prevent users from locking each other out, but only if your application can tolerate inconsistencies. This option is the least restrictive of the transaction isolation levels.
READ COMMITTED	Use shared locks when a transaction reads rows to prevent you from reading rows on which a transaction has placed exclusive locks. This level of isolation prevents you from reading data that's uncommitted (dirty reads); however, another user might change the data before the end of your read transaction, so you might get nonrepeatable reads and phantom data. In addition, because you put a shared lock on the data, your transaction might prevent other users from using the data. This is the default transaction isolation level.

Isolation Level Option	Enables You to Configure SQL Server to
REPEATABLE READ	Use locks to prevent dirty reads and nonrepeatable reads. This level essentially incorporates the capabilities of READ COMMITTED to guarantee that your transaction won't use dirty reads and adds the mechanisms to prevent nonrepeatable reads; however, in order to guarantee this level of isolation, SQL Server must hold all shared locks until completion (such as with either a COMMIT TRAN or ROLLBACK TRAN statement) of the transaction. No other users will be able to modify the data as long as your transaction's locks are outstanding. For this reason, your server's performance can degrade when you set the transaction isolation level to REPEATABLE READ.
SERIALIZABLE	Lock the data to prevent other users from updating or inserting rows until your transaction is complete. This level of isolation guarantees that if you issue a query and then re-issue the same query within the same transaction, no users will have added rows in the interim. (In other words, you won't see any phantoms.) Transactions are the most isolated with this level; this level prevents the occurrence of dirty reads, nonrepeatable reads, and phantoms.

You can use the DBCC USEROPTIONS statement to view the current isolation level for your session.

TASK 13B-2:

Implementing Session Locking

1. In SQL Query Analyzer, **verify that you have one Query window open with the movies database as your current database.**

2. In the Query window, **open the C:\Data\locking.sql script file.** This script file contains a query that begins a transaction, issues an update statement, waits 10 seconds, and then rolls back the transaction. You will use this transaction to test the READ COMMITTED and READ UNCOMMITTED transaction isolation levels.

3. **Open a second Query window, and then open the C:\Data\customer.sql script file.** This file contains a query that enables you to view the current last name assigned to customer number 100.

4. **Highlight and execute the SELECT query** to view the last name of customer number 100.

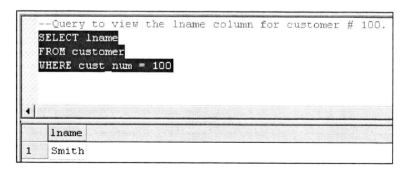

5. **What is your current transaction isolation level?**

6. In the first Query window, **highlight and execute the query** to begin the transaction for changing the customer's last name. (This is the Query window containing the BEGIN TRAN statement.)

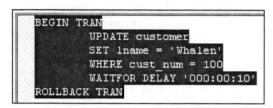

```
BEGIN TRAN
        UPDATE customer
        SET lname = 'Whalen'
        WHERE cust_num = 100
        WAITFOR DELAY '000:00:10'
ROLLBACK TRAN
```

7. In the second Query window (the Query window containing the SELECT lname statement), **highlight and execute the SELECT query** to verify that you can't read the row until the BEGIN TRAN transaction completes.

8. When the BEGIN TRAN query finishes, **look at the results set in the SELECT lname Query window.** After the BEGIN TRAN query waited 10 seconds, it then rolled back the change to the customer's last name and released its exclusive lock on the row. SQL Server could then process the SELECT lname query. You should see that the customer's last name is still Smith.

9. In the SELECT lname Query window, **highlight and execute the query that sets your transaction isolation level to READ UNCOMMITTED.** By setting your isolation level to READ UNCOMMITTED, you will be able to read the changes made to rows even though a user has placed an exclusive lock on the row.

```
--Query to view the lname column for customer # 100.
SELECT lname
FROM customer
WHERE cust_num = 100

--Query to set the transaction isolation level to READ UNCOMMITTED.
SET TRANSACTION ISOLATION LEVEL READ UNCOMMITTED
```

10. In the BEGIN TRAN Query window, **execute the query again** to begin an update to the customer table.

11. In the SELECT lname Query window, **highlight and execute the SELECT statement.** You'll see that while the transaction to change the customer's last name is running, your SELECT statement displays this customer's last name as Whalen. Even though SQL Server hasn't committed this change to the database, SQL Server enables you to view the uncommitted transaction because you set your isolation level to support reading uncommitted transactions.

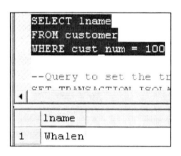

12. After the BEGIN TRAN statement finishes running, **re-execute the SELECT lname statement in the second Query window.** You can see that SQL Server rolled back the transaction to change the customer's name.

13. Close the second Query window. (This is the Query window containing the customer.sql script.)

14. Open a new Query window, and then close the window containing the locking.sql script.

15. Execute a new query:

```
SET TRANSACTION ISOLATION LEVEL SERIALIZABLE
DBCC USEROPTIONS
```

Use this query to set your session's transaction isolation level to SERIALIZABLE and then view the settings for your connection. When you change your transaction isolation level, you change it only for that session. You open multiple sessions with the server when you open multiple Query windows in SQL Query Analyzer.

	Set Option	Value
1	textsize	64512
2	language	us_english
3	dateformat	mdy
4	datefirst	7
5	quoted_identifier	SET
6	arithabort	SET
7	ansi_null_dflt_on	SET
8	ansi_defaults	SET
9	ansi_warnings	SET
10	ansi_padding	SET
11	ansi_nulls	SET
12	concat_null_yields_null	SET
13	isolation level	serializable

16. Open a new Query window and execute the following query:

```
DBCC USEROPTIONS
```

You should see that SQL Server doesn't display a value for this session's transaction isolation level, which means that SQL Server configured your session to use the default isolation level of READ COMMITTED.

17. **Open a new Query window, and close all other Query windows without saving your changes.**

Configuring a Lock Timeout

You can use the SET LOCK_TIMEOUT statement to specify how long a transaction can wait for the release of a blocked resource. You might use the lock timeout to prevent a transaction from waiting indefinitely for a resource to be released. If the timeout expires and the resource is still locked, SQL Server cancels the transaction. Use the following syntax to set the lock timeout:

```
SET LOCK_TIMEOUT time_in_milliseconds
```

By default, SQL Server sets the lock timeout to -1, which means it's disabled. Thus, a transaction will wait indefinitely for a blocking transaction to clear its lock. If you set the lock timeout to 0, SQL Server immediately cancels the transaction if the resource it needs to access is locked. You can view the value of the lock timeout for your session by executing the following query:

```
SELECT @@lock_timeout
```

TASK 13B-3:

Implementing a Lock Timeout

1. In SQL Query Analyzer, **open the C:\Data\lock1.sql script file. Highlight and execute the following query:**

```
BEGIN TRAN
        UPDATE customer
        SET zip = '70130'
        WHERE cust_num = 125
```

2. **Open a second Query window, and then open the C:\Data\lock2.sql script file.**

3. In the second Query window, **highlight and execute the following query:**

```
SET LOCK_TIMEOUT 5000
```

This query configures your session with a lock timeout of 5000 milliseconds (5 seconds). This means that your session will wait five seconds for a blocked resource to be released. If the resource is still locked after five seconds, SQL Server will abort your transaction.

4. **Highlight and execute this query:**

```
SELECT *
FROM customer
WHERE cust_num = 125
```

After five seconds, you should see that SQL Server aborted this transaction.

```
Server: Msg 1222, Level 16, State 50, Line 1
Lock request time out period exceeded.
```

5. **Close the second Query window.**

6. In the remaining Query window, **execute the following query:**

    ```
    ROLLBACK TRAN
    ```

    This query rolls back the changes in this transaction.

7. **Open a new Query window, and then close the Query window containing the lock1.sql script file.** Don't worry about saving your changes.

Table-level Locking

By default, SQL Server automatically tunes locking for your environment. If necessary, however, you can specify how you want SQL Server to lock resources by including table-level locking as part of your transaction. You specify table-locking by adding lock hints to SELECT and UPDATE queries. You must use lock hints as part of a transaction. For example, the following query contains a lock hint to make the transaction SERIALIZABLE:

```
BEGIN TRAN
        UPDATE movie (SERIALIZABLE)
        SET rented = 'Y'
        WHERE movie_num = 110
COMMIT TRAN
```

You can use the same options to set table locking that you can with session-level locking: READUNCOMMITTED, READCOMMITTED, REPEATABLEREAD, and SERIALIZABLE. In addition, you can use the following hints to specify how you want SQL Server to lock the resource:

*   HOLDLOCK. This option holds the resource lock until your transaction completes. The HOLDLOCK option is functionally equivalent to the SERIALIZABLE option.

*   NOLOCK. Configures SQL Server to not use any shared locks for the transaction, and to not honor any exclusive locks for the transaction either. You can use this option only on a SELECT statement query.

*   ROWLOCK. This option locks a row.

*   PAGLOCK. Use this option to lock a page.

*   TABLOCK. This option locks a table.

*   TABLOCKX. Use this option to place an exclusive lock on a table. When you use this option, it prevents other transactions from reading or updating the table.

*   READPAST. Use this option to skip locked rows.

*   UPDLOCK. Set this option if you want to use update locks instead of shared locks.

TASK 13B-4:

Implementing Table-level Locking

1. In SQL Query Analyzer, **open the C:\Data\tablock.sql script file. Highlight and execute the following query:**

```
BEGIN TRAN
        UPDATE customer
        SET phone = '5045552215'
        WHERE cust_num = 125.
```

   This query starts a transaction to update a customer's information. Because you don't have a COMMIT TRAN or ROLLBACK TRAN statement at the end of this query, SQL Server hasn't yet committed the changes

2. **Open a new Query window, and then open the C:\Data\tablock2.sql script file.**

3. In the second Query window, **highlight and execute the following query:**

```
BEGIN TRAN
        SELECT phone
        FROM customer (READUNCOMMITTED)
        WHERE cust_num = 125
        COMMIT TRAN
```

   Because you added the READUNCOMMITTED table-locking hint, SQL Server could read the change made by your first query even though it hasn't yet committed its change to the table.

```
--Query to use the READUNCOMMITTED locking hint
BEGIN TRAN
        SELECT phone
        FROM customer (READUNCOMMITTED)
        WHERE cust_num = 125
COMMIT TRAN
```

	phone	
1	5045552215	

4. **Close the second Query window.** (This is the window containing the tablock2.sql script file.)

5. **Roll back the transaction in the first Query window.**

6. **Close all open windows.**

Deadlocks

A deadlock occurs when two users or processes have locks on different objects and each needs to also place a lock on the other's object. In this situation, SQL Server will choose a deadlock victim and abort that user's process, thus allowing the other user or process to continue. The SQL server then informs the deadlock victim of the termination. SQL Server notifies the deadlock victim's application by using error message number 1205.

A deadlock can occur when you run several long transactions simultaneously in a database or when the query optimizer designs a query execution plan for a complex query. You can minimize deadlocks by designing your transactions such that they use resources in the same order. You should also try to keep your transactions as short as possible to avoid deadlocks. Another technique you should implement is to have transactions check to see if error 1205 occurred. (Remember, you can use the statement `IF @@error = 1205`.) If you find that this error has occurred, you should have your application attempt the transaction again.

Summary

In this lesson, you learned the ins and outs of implementing both transactions and locking. SQL Server uses both transactions and locks to help protect the integrity of your data. With transactions, you can force SQL Server to commit a series of SQL statements as a unit. With locking, you help to prevent the problems that can occur when multiple users access the same data at the same time. For example, you use locking to control what SQL Server does when one user modifies a row when another user attempts to view that same row.

LESSON 13 REVIEW

13A What is the difference between explicit and implicit transactions?

13B What techniques can you use to control resource locking?

Implementing Distributed Queries

Data Files:
linked.sql
distqueries.sql
linkedprocs.sql
modify.sql

Lesson Time:
1 hour, 45 minutes

Overview

You use distributed queries to enable you to retrieve data from not just your own local SQL server, but also from other SQL servers (and even non-SQL Server sources). In this lesson, we will explore how you go about executing distributed queries. We will begin by showing you how to create linked server definitions if you're going to be querying another server frequently. We will also demonstrate how you can control which server processes the query, and how to perform different types of distributed queries. Finally, we will discuss some ways to execute queries without defining a remote server as a linked server.

Objectives

To implement distributed queries, you will:

14A   Configure linked servers.

If you find that you're going to use distributed queries to access another server's data frequently, you'll save yourself some time by defining that server as a linked server. In this topic, we will show you how to define a linked server and configure its security.

14B   Create and manage distributed queries.

There are all kinds of ways you can access remote data sources through distributed queries. In this topic, we will start by executing a distributed query against a linked server. You'll also learn how to control which server processes the query (your local server or the linked server). Next, you'll learn how to query a remote server without adding it as a linked server. You'll also learn how to modify data through a distributed query.

 **TOPIC 14A**

Establishing Linked Servers

SQL Server 2000 enables you to create distributed queries. You use a distributed query to access data from not only SQL servers, but also from any heterogeneous data source that supports the OLE DB interface (such as Microsoft Access). Before you can use distributed queries, you must first define each OLE DB data source as a linked server. SQL Server stores the definitions of linked servers in order to make it easier and more efficient for you to access those servers' data.

You can define a linked server or a remote server in SQL Server 2000. A linked server enables you to connect to OLE DB data sources. A remote server enables you to connect to another SQL server for the purpose of running a stored procedure on that server. Support for remote servers is considered a legacy feature and is included in SQL Server 2000 for backwards-compatibility.

Defining Linked Servers

You begin defining a linked server by identifying information about how you want to connect to that server. You can define this information by using either SQL Server Enterprise Manager or the `sp_addlinkedserver` stored procedure. You add a linked server in SQL Server Enterprise Manager by right-clicking on the Linked Servers object and choosing New Linked Server. The Linked Servers object is stored in your server's Security folder.

Use the following syntax to add a linked server with the `sp_addlinkedserver` stored procedure:

```
EXEC sp_addlinkedserver
        @server = 'server',
        @srvproduct = 'product_name',
        @provider = 'provider_name',
        @datasrc = 'data_source',
        @location = 'location'',
        @provstr = 'provider_string'
```

We describe each of the parameters you use with the `sp_addlinkedserver` procedure in the following table.

Parameter	Enables You to Specify
server	The name you want to assign to the linked server. (This name doesn't have to be the same as the server's actual name.)
srvproduct	The product name of the OLE DB data source. For example, if you're adding a link to a SQL server, use "SQL Server" as the product name. Note: If you use "SQL Server" as your product name, you don't need to specify the provider_name, data_source, location, and provider_string parameters.
provider	The name of the OLE DB provider that will manage access to the data source.
datasrc	The name for the data source as used by the OLE DB provider.
location	The location of the database as used by the OLE DB provider.
provstr	OLE DB-specific connection strings for identifying the data source.

The following table identifies some of the common data sources and the associated values for the provider name, product name, data source, and other parameters.

Type of Data Source	OLE DB Provider	Product Name	Provider Name	Data Source
SQL Server	Microsoft OLE DB Provider for SQL Server	SQL Server	N'SQLOLEDB'	Not required to specify.
Oracle	Microsoft OLE DB Provider for Oracle	Anything	'MSDAORA'	SQL*Net alias for Oracle database
Access/Jet	Microsoft OLE DB Provider for Jet	Anything	'Microsoft.Jet.OLEDB.4.0'	Full path name of Access database file

For example, to define a SQL server as a linked server, use the following syntax:

```
EXEC sp_addlinkedserver
        @server = 'linked_server_name',
        @srvproduct = 'SQL Server'
```

In this syntax, you replace *server_name* with the name you want to assign to the linked server. You'll typically use the server's computer name as the linked server name.

In contrast, if you want to define a Microsoft Access database as a linked server, you use this syntax instead:

```
EXEC sp_addlinkedserver
        @server = 'linked_server_name',
        @srvproduct = 'Microsoft.Jet.OLEDB.4.0',
        @provider = 'OLE DB Provider for Jet',
        @datasrc = 'C:\Data\accounting.mdb'
```

Viewing Linked Servers

You can use the `sp_linkedservers` stored procedure to view a list of linked servers defined on your server. In addition, you can see the same list of linked servers by accessing the Linked Servers object in SQL Server Enterprise Manager. We define some of the other stored procedures you can use to view information about linked servers in the following table.

Stored Procedure	Enables You to View
sp_catalogs	Information about the catalogs on a linked server. For a linked SQL server, this stored procedure displays a list of databases on the linked server.

sp_indexes	A list of indexes on the linked server. Use this syntax:
	`sp_indexes 'linked_server',`
	`'table_name', 'table_owner', 'database'.`

sp_primarykeys	The primary key columns on a linked server's table.
sp_foreignkeys	The foreign keys on a linked server's table.
sp_tables_ex	Information about the tables on a linked server.

TASK 14A-1:

Defining a Linked Server

Setup: You're logged on to Windows 2000 as student#. You've created a database named movies and tables within it named movie, category, customer, rental, and rental_detail. You've defined primary key, foreign key, default, and check constraints on the tables, and created nonclustered indexes based on your primary keys. You have imported data into the tables. You have created database diagrams for both the movies and pubs databases.

1. **Record the name of your partner's SQL server:**

    _____.

2. **Start SQL Query Analyzer and open the C:\Data\linked.sql script file.**

3. **Edit the following query to use your partner's server name:**

    ```
    SELECT *
    FROM partner_server_name.pubs.dbo.authors
    ```

    (Replace partner_server_name with the name of your partner's server.)

4. **Highlight and execute this query** to attempt to execute a distributed query. This query uses a fully qualified name to query your partner's server. Because you haven't yet defined your partner's server as a linked server, you can't execute a distributed query.

    ```
    Server: Msg 7202, Level 11, State 2, Line 1
    Could not find server 'sqlserver1' in sysservers.
    ```

5. **Edit the next query to use your partner's server name. Highlight and execute the query:**

    ```
    sp_addlinkedserver
    @server = 'partner_server_name',
    @srvproduct = 'SQL Server'
    ```

    This query adds a linked server definition to your partner's server.

6. **Execute the next query:**

    ```
    EXEC sp_linkedservers
    ```

    This query displays a list of linked servers defined on your server. By default, SQL Server automatically includes your server in this list.

    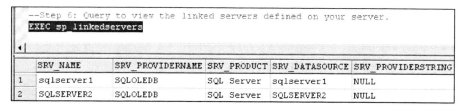

7. **Open a new Query window, and then close the Query window containing the linked.sql script without saving your changes.**

8. **Start SQL Server Enterprise Manager.**

9. Below your server, **expand the Security folder** to display the objects for configuring login accounts, server roles, linked servers, and remote servers.

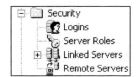

10. **Expand the Linked Servers object.** SQL Server displays a list of the servers you've linked to your server below the Linked Servers object.

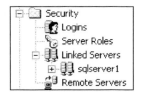

11. **Minimize SQL Server Enterprise Manager.**

Configuring Linked Server Security

After you've defined a linked server, your next step is to configure security. When a user logs in to your server and then runs a distributed query on the linked server, your SQL server must log in to the linked server in the background. One method your server can use to log in to the linked server is to use the login account and password of the user who ran the distributed query. This method is referred to as *security delegation*. In this scenario, you must define the user's login account and password on your SQL server as well as on the linked server. Remember, even if you use Windows Authentication to log users in to a SQL server, you must still define users' login accounts on the SQL server—and then map them to a Windows 2000 user or group account. This method of implementing linked server security is easiest to configure when both SQL servers are in the same Windows 2000 domain, and you're using Windows Authentication on those servers.

If you don't want to define a user's login account on both your local server and the linked server, another strategy you can use is to configure the user's local login account to use a specific login account and password on the linked server. You map local login accounts to a login account on the linked server by using the sp_addlinkedsrvlogin stored procedure. You can also use the sp_addlinkedsrvlogin stored procedure to enable your SQL server's users to access a linked server that doesn't support security delegation (such as Microsoft Access). Use the following syntax to map a user's local login account to a login account on the linked server:

You don't have to configure a linked server login for a user if you've defined the user's login account on both the local and linked servers.

```
sp_addlinkedsrvlogin
        @rmtsrvname = 'linked_server_name',
        @useself = 'false',
        @locallogin = 'local_login_account',
        @rmtuser = 'linked_server_login_account',
        @rmtpassword = 'linked_server_password'
```

The following table describes the parameters you use in the sp_addlinkedsrvlogin stored procedure.

Parameter	Enables You to Define
rmtsrvname	The name you've assigned to the linked server (typically the server's computer name).
useself	Whether or not you want this user to log in to the linked server by using his/her login account on the local server.
locallogin	The user's login account on the local server. If you don't specify a value for the locallogin parameter, SQL Server automatically maps all login accounts on the local server to the remote login account you specify with the rmtuser parameter.
rmtuser	The login account you want the user to use to log in to the linked server. You must specify this parameter when you set useself = false.
rmtpassword	The password for the login account you specify with the rmtuser parameter.

In summary, when one of your users executes a distributed query (a query that retrieves data from a linked server), your SQL server must log that user in to the linked server. Your server can use any of the following methods to log in:

- If the user's Windows account (or a Windows group of which the user is a member) has been mapped to a login account on both the local server and the linked server, and you haven't defined a linked server login for this user by using the `sp_addlinkedsrvlogin` stored procedure, your server will log the user in to the linked server by using the user's Windows account.

- If you've created a SQL login account for a user on both the local server and the linked server, and you haven't defined a linked server login for this user, your server will log the user in to the linked server by using the user's SQL login account.

- If you want a local user to log in to the linked server by using a specific login account on the linked server, you must define a linked server login for this user on your local server by using the `sp_addlinkedssrvlogin` stored procedure.

For example, if you want a user named Sally to log in to a linked server named *Accounting* as the login account named *Accountant* with a password of *password*, you add the linked server login by using the following statement:

```
sp_addlinkedsrvlogin
        @rmtsrvname = 'Accounting',
        @useself = 'false',
        @locallogin = 'Sally',
        @rmtuser = 'Accountant',
        @rmtpassword = 'password'
```

Permissions Considerations

Regardless of how you have a user log in to a linked server, you must configure the user with the appropriate permissions to the linked server's databases. For example, assume that you want the user named Susan to be able to query the pubs database on a linked server. You've configured Susan to log in to the linked server by using her Windows login account. (You've created Susan's Windows login account on both the local and linked servers.) Although Susan can log in to both the local and linked servers, she still can't execute a distributed query against the pubs database unless she has permissions to that database. At a minimum, you should assign her login account to the db_datareader database role to enable her to read information from the pubs database.

TASK 14A-2:

Logging in to Linked Servers

Setup: You're logged on to Windows 2000 as student#. You've created a SQL login account named sqluser#. You've added sqluser# to the public and db_owner database roles for the pubs database.

1. From the Administrative Tools program group, **start Active Directory Users And Computers.**

2. In the console tree, **select the Users folder. Double-click on your student# account** to display the User Properties dialog box for your user account.

3. **Select the Member Of tab. Look at your group memberships.** You should see that your user account, student#, is a member of the Domain Admins and Domain Users global groups.

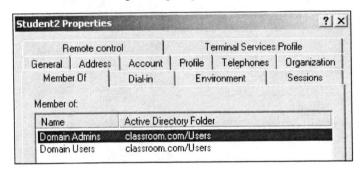

4. **Click Cancel** to close the Properties dialog box for your user account. **Close Active Directory Users And Computers.**

5. **Switch to SQL Server Enterprise Manager.**

6. Below your server's Security folder, **select the Logins object and look at the Details pane.** By default, SQL Server automatically maps members of the local Administrators group to login accounts. This means that if you log on to Windows 2000 as a user who's a member of the local Administrators group, you can log in to SQL Server by using Windows Authentication. Because your user account is a member of Domain Admins and thus the local Administrators group, you can log in to SQL Server by using your student# account.

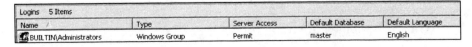

7. **Minimize SQL Server Enterprise Manager.**

8. In SQL Query Analyzer, **execute the following query:**

```
SELECT *
FROM partner_server_name.pubs.dbo.authors
```

This query executes a distributed query against your partner's server. You don't have to create a linked server login for your student# account because your account has a login account on both servers. That's because SQL Server Setup automatically creates a login for the built-in Windows 2000 Administrators group, and your student# user is a member of this group.

9. **Choose File→Connect** to display the Connect To SQL Server dialog box. You're going to log in to SQL Server by using your sqluser# login account.

10. Below Connection Information, **select Use SQL Server Authentication. In** the Login Name text box, **type *sqluser#*. (Replace # with your assigned number.) In the Password text box, **type *password*.**

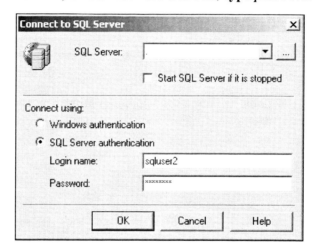

11. **Click OK** to log in to your SQL server with your SQL login account.

12. In the new Query window, **execute the following query:**

```
SELECT *
FROM partner_server_name.pubs.dbo.authors
```

This query enables you to attempt to execute a distributed query while logged in as sqluser#.

You can copy and paste this query from the first Query window into the second Query window.

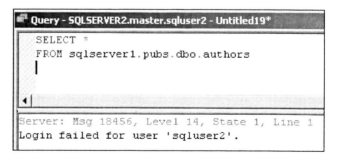

13. **Why does your login fail?**

14. How should you fix this problem?

15. In your first Query window, **execute a new query:**

```
sp_addlinkedsrvlogin
        @rmtsrvname = 'partner_server_name',
        @useself = 'false',
        @locallogin = 'your_sqluser#',
        @rmtuser = 'your_partner's_sqluser#',
        @rmtpassword = 'password'
```

This query maps your own sqluser# account on your server to your partner's sqluser# account on his or her server. By executing this query, you enable your sqluser# account to log on to your partner's linked server.

16. In the second Query window, **re-execute the following query:**

```
SELECT *
FROM partner_server_name.pubs.dbo.authors
```

(You're connected to your local server as sqluser# in this window, so you can test the linked server login in this window.) Use this query to verify that you can now execute a distributed query of the Pubs database on your linked server (your partner's server). You can access the Pubs database on your partner's server because your partner added sqluser# to the public and db_owner database roles for the Pubs database.

17. Close the second Query window.

18. Clear the first Query window.

Configuring Linked Server Settings

You can use the `sp_serveroption` stored procedure to configure settings for linked servers. These settings include Collation Compatible, Use Remote Collation, Collation Name, Data Access, and RPC and RPC Out. Use the following syntax to set server options:

```
USE master
GO
EXEC sp_serveroption 'linked_server_name', 'option', [true |
false]
```

Use the Collation Compatible option if the character set and collation (sort) order are the same on both the local and linked servers. By default, SQL Server sets the Collation Compatible option to false so that it evaluates differences between the character set and sort order between the local and linked servers. If both servers use the same character set and sort order, you should enable this option in order to reduce SQL Server's overhead when processing distributed queries. If the linked server uses a different collation, and you want your query to use that collation, you should set the Use Remote Collation option to true. If the linked server isn't a SQL server, and you set the Use Remote Collation option to true, you must specify the name of the collation by using the Collation Name option.

Use the Data Access option to configure a remote server used in replication to also act as a linked server so that you can access it through distributed queries. Use the RPC option to specify whether your local server can send out Remote Procedure Calls (RPCs); likewise, use the RPC Out option to enable support for RPCs to the linked server.

TOPIC 14B

Creating and Managing Distributed Queries

After you've defined linked servers, you can access the data on those servers through distributed queries. You must use an object's fully qualified name to access an object on a linked server. An object's fully qualified name consists of the following components:

linked_server_name.database_name.owner.object_name

For example, if you want to display all rows in the authors table of the pubs database on your partner's server, use the following name: `sqlserver#.pubs.dbo.authors`.

You can use the SELECT, INSERT, UPDATE, and DELETE statements in distributed queries. You can use a WHERE clause with your statements—and you can use table joins. You can even join tables between your local and linked servers.

You can't use the CREATE, ALTER, DROP, READTEXT, WRITETEXT, or UPDATETEXT statements in a distributed query. You also can't use the CREATE TABLE along with the SELECT INTO statement to create a table and fill it with data on the linked server, but you can use these statements to create a table and fill it with data on the local server. You also can't use an ORDER BY clause as part of your SELECT statement if your select list contains a large object column.

Which Server Processes the Query?

When you execute a distributed query, either your local server or the linked server can process the query. Unless you specify otherwise, your local server processes a distributed query. For example, if you execute the query SELECT * FROM sqlserver1.pubs.dbo.authors and your local server is sqlserver2, SQL Server processes the query on your local server (sqlserver2).

You can use the OPENQUERY function to specify that you want the linked server to process your query instead of your local server. This type of query is referred to as a *pass-through query*. The OPENQUERY function enables you to force the linked server to process a distributed query. You use the OPENQUERY function with the following syntax:

OPENQUERY (*linked_server_name*, '*query*')

You can use the OPENQUERY function in place of a table name. For example, the following query enables you to select all movies from the movie table with a rating of G and specifies that the linked server must process the query:

```
SELECT *
FROM OPENQUERY(sqlserver1,'SELECT * FROM movies.dbo.movie WHERE
rating = "G"')
```

You can use the results of an OPENQUERY function in a SELECT, INSERT, UPDATE, or DELETE statement.

APPLY YOUR KNOWLEDGE 14-1

Suggested time:
25 minutes

Working with Distributed Queries

Objective: To design and execute distributed queries against your partner's SQL server.

Setup: You have defined your partner's server as a linked server.

1. In SQL Query Analyzer, design and execute a query to list all movies on your partner's server with a category number of 4 (comedy). Don't use a pass-through query. What query did you use?

2. Design and execute a query to list all customers in alphabetical order on your partner's server. Use a pass-through query. What query did you use?

3. Design and execute a query to join the movie table on your partner's server with the category table on your server. Include the movie title and the category description in the results set. Sort the results by category description and then movie title. Don't use a pass-through query. What query did you use?

4. Design and execute a query to create a new local table named partner_movie in your movies database. Use the `SELECT INTO` statement to populate this table with movies that have a rating of G from your partner's movie table. Verify the contents of the partner_movie table when you are done. What queries did you use?

5. Clear the Query window.

Executing Stored Procedures

In addition to queries, you can also execute stored procedures on a linked server. After you define a linked server, your users can execute stored procedures on that server without having to establish a connection to that server first. The linked server actually processes the stored procedure and then returns the results to you.

You must use a fully qualified name to execute a stored procedure on a linked server. For example, you could use the following query to display information about the movies database on a linked server:

```
EXEC linked_server_name.master.dbo.sp_helpdb movies
```

Suggested time:
10 minutes

APPLY YOUR KNOWLEDGE 14-2

Executing Stored Procedures on Linked Servers

Objective: To run stored procedures on your partner's server.

Setup: You have created user-defined stored procedures in the movies database.

1. In SQL Query Analyzer, design and execute a query to list all stored procedures on your partner's server. What query did you use?

2. Design and execute a query to list the definition of one of the stored procedures. What query did you use?

3. Run one of your partner's stored procedures. If necessary, provide the appropriate values for any input parameters. (Use the appropriate stored procedure to view the definition of the stored procedure to determine if you need any input parameters.) What query did you use?

4. Clear the Query window.

Modifying Data Through Distributed Queries

You can modify data on a linked server by using a distributed transaction. You begin a distributed transaction by first enabling the XACT_ABORT session option. This option enables SQL Server to roll back the entire distributed transaction in the event that any of the SQL statements fail. If you don't set this option, SQL Server can roll back only a failed statement, not the entire transaction. Begin a distributed transaction by using the BEGIN DISTRIBUTED TRANSACTION statement. You end a distributed transaction by using either the COMMIT TRAN or ROLLBACK TRAN statements.

You can't nest distributed transactions.

You can use distributed transactions to work with data in tables on the linked server just as you would on your local server (provided you have the necessary permissions). You can use the INSERT, UPDATE, and DELETE statements within a distributed transaction. For example, you can use the following query to insert a row into the movie table:

```
SET XACT_ABORT ON
BEGIN DISTRIBUTED TRAN
        INSERT INTO linked_server_name.movies.dbo.movie
        (title, category_num, rating, rental_price, rented)
        VALUES ('Mr. Smith goes to Washington', 4, 'G',1.99, 'N')
COMMIT TRAN
```

Microsoft Distributed Transaction Coordinator

SQL Server uses the Microsoft Distributed Transaction Coordinator (MSDTC) service to manage the integrity of distributed transactions. SQL Server uses the MSDTC service whenever you execute a BEGIN DISTRIBUTED TRANSACTION statement. MSDTC is responsible for making sure that if you execute a distributed transaction across multiple linked servers, those transactions occur at the same time. MSDTC's primary goal is to ensure consistency between data on multiple servers. So, if you have multiple linked servers and you want to maintain a copy of a database on those servers, you can use MSDTC to update those databases.

By default, SQL Server Setup configures the MSDTC service to start automatically, but it configures the MSDTC service to log on to Windows 2000 by using the Local System account. If you want to use MSDTC to support distributed transactions across multiple servers, you must configure the MSDTC service to log on by using the same user account on all servers. You can change the configuration of any service by using the Services snap-in within a Microsoft Management Console (MMC).

TASK 14B-1:

Configuring the MSDTC Service

1. From the Administrative Tools menu, **select Services** to open an MMC with the Services snap-in loaded. You see a list of all of the services available on your server.

2. In the details pane, **look at the Distributed Transaction Coordinator service.** You see that it's configured to start automatically, and to log on using the Local System account.

3. **Double-click on the Distributed Transaction Coordinator service** to display its Properties dialog box.

4. On the General tab, **verify that the Startup Type is Automatic.**

5. **Select the Log On tab.** You use this page to configure the service to log on as a specific domain user account.

6. Below Log On As, **select This Account.** In the text box, **type** *SQLService@classroom.com.* In the Password and Confirm Password text boxes, **type** *password.*

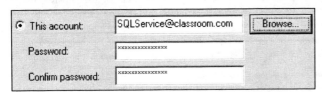

7. **Click OK** to save your changes.

8. **Click OK** to confirm the message stating that the new logon name won't take effect until you stop and restart the MSDTC service.

9. **Right-click on the Distributed Transaction Coordinator service and choose Stop** to stop the service.

10. **Right-click on the Distributed Transaction Coordinator service and choose Start** to start the service.

11. When the service is started, **close the Services MMC.**

Suggested time:
10 minutes

APPLY YOUR KNOWLEDGE 14-3

Modifying Data on a Linked Server

Objective: To write a query to insert data into your partner's customer table.

1. In SQL Query Analyzer, design and execute a query to insert yourself as a customer in your partner's customer table. (Hint: You don't need to provide values for the cust_num and join_date columns.) What query did you use?

2. When your partner has completed step 1, verify that you can see your partner's name in your own customer table. What query did you use?

3. Clear the Query window.

Using Ad Hoc Queries

If you don't plan to access a remote server very frequently, you can use an ad hoc query to retrieve data from that server instead of defining it as a linked server. You use the OPENROWSET function to connect to a server that you haven't defined as a linked server. The remote server can be any data source that supports the OLE DB provider for ODBC, such as computers running SQL Server, Access, or Oracle.

You use the OPENROWSET function in place of a table name. For example, you can use the OPENROWSET function in the SELECT statement as follows:

```
SELECT *
FROM OPENROWSET(remote server information)
```

Use the following syntax to define a remote server with the OPENROWSET function:

```
OPENROWSET ('provider_name' 'datasource';
'user_name'; 'password' | 'provider_string',
 catalog.schema.object 'query')
```

We use the following table to describe the parameters you use with the OPENROWSET function.

Parameter	Enables You to Specify the
provider	Name of the OLE DB provider that will manage access to the data source.
data source	Name for the data source as used by the OLE DB provider.
user_name	User name you want to use to log in to the OLE DB provider.
password	Password for the user name you specify.
provider_string	OLE DB-specific connection strings for identifying the data source.
catalog	Catalog (or database) in which the object is stored.
schema	Schema name or owner of the object.
object	Object name you want to access.
query	Query you want to run against the remote data source.

The name of the OLE DB provider is specific to the type of data source you want to access. The following table defines the provider and data source names for various data sources.

Data Source	Provider Name	Data Source Name
SQL Server	'SQLOLEDB'	Not required
Microsoft OLE DB Provider for Access (Jet)	'Microsoft.Jet.OLEDB.4.0'	Full path name of Access database file
Microsoft OLE DB Provider for Oracle	'MSDAORA'	SQL*Net alias for Oracle database
OLE DB Provider for ODBC	'MSDASQL'	'LocalServer'

For example, the following query returns all rows from the category table on the instructor's SQL server:

```
SELECT *
FROM OPENROWSET('SQLOLEDB', 'instructor';
'sa'; 'password',
'SELECT * FROM movies.dbo.category')
```

Notice that you must provide a user name and password. This user name and password must be a SQL login account, not a Windows login account and password.

The following example enables you to query a Microsoft Access database to retrieve data from the products table in the Northwind database (this database is also included as a sample in Microsoft Access):

```
SELECT *
FROM OPENROWSET('Microsoft.Jet.OLEDB.4.0'
'C:\MSOffice\Access\Samples\Northwind.mdb';
 'user_name'; 'password', Customers)
```

TASK 14B-2:

Using Ad Hoc Queries to Retrieve Data From Remote Servers

1. **Record the name of a server that you haven't defined as a linked server on your server:** _____. (You can also query the instructor's server.)

2. In SQL Query Analyzer, **execute the following query:**

```
SELECT *
FROM OPENROWSET('SQLOLEDB', 'server_name';
'sa'; '', 'SELECT * FROM movies.dbo.customer WHERE cust_num >
175')
```

This query executes an ad hoc query on a remote server. You log on to that server by using the sa login account without a password.

3. **Clear the Query window.**

Implementing Distributed Partitioned Views

As you saw in the "Designing Views" lesson, you create partitioned views based on data from multiple sources (such as multiple SQL servers or multiple instances of SQL Server), or even on data from heterogeneous sources (such as data on an Oracle server). A partitioned view enhances performance by enabling SQL Server to scan all tables referenced by the view simultaneously if those tables are on separate servers, or if the tables are on the same server as long as the server has multiple processors.

If you want your partitioned view to access databases on multiple servers, you must define those servers as linked servers. Here are the steps you should complete:

1. Create the databases on each server.

2. Horizontally partition the tables within each database on the servers. This means that you must define a column in all tables that you can use to uniquely identify each server's data. You must define a check constraint on this column.

3. Create linked server definitions on each server.

4. Create the partitioned view on each server by using the UNION ALL keywords. Use the same name for the view on each server so that you can access the view from any server.

Summary

In this lesson, we showed you how to define a linked server and configure its security. You also learned how to query a server by using a distributed query against a linked server and by using the OPENROWSET function to execute an ad hoc query.

LESSON 14 REVIEW

14A How do you define an SQL server as a linked server?

14B How can you configure a distributed query to be processed by the linked server instead of your local server?

Optimizing Queries

Overview

One of the most critical components of SQL Server's database engine is the query optimizer. Its job is to analyze the possible methods SQL Server can use to execute a query and then select the best method. In this lesson, we will explain how the query optimizer selects the best execution plan. In addition, we will show you how you can determine what execution plan SQL Server is using for a given query. Finally, we will show you how you can optimize queries through indexing.

Objectives

To optimize queries, you will:

15A **Identify the steps the query optimizer performs to optimize a query and analyze query execution plans.**

SQL Server 2000 includes several utilities that you can use to observe and analyze the execution plan selected by the query optimizer. In this topic, we will show you how you can analyze execution plans by using commands such as SET SHOWPLAN_ALL and the graphical execution plan in SQL Query Analyzer.

15B **Design indexes to improve query performance.**

In this topic, you will learn how to create an index that covers a query. Such an index can significantly improve your server's response time for a given query. You'll also learn how you can override the query processor's index selection by using table hints.

Data Files:
newcustomer.sql
statslab.sql
querygovernor.sql
showplan.sql
graphplan.sql
cleanindex.sql
indexcovers.sql
hints.sql

Lesson Time:
2 hours

TOPIC 15A

Exploring the Query Optimizer

One of the most important components of the SQL Server database engine is the query optimizer. (Actually, the query optimizer is one of several components that make up the query processor; the query processor is responsible for processing queries.) SQL Server uses the query optimizer to come up with a plan for how it should process your query. This plan includes all steps your server must carry out, plus information about any index (or indexes) your server should use when accessing the table or tables on which you've based your query. It also includes plans for performing steps such as sorting the data and grouping the data based on a GROUP BY clause, and for how it should retrieve data from joined tables.

The query optimizer's main job is to look at a whole bunch of factors and come up with the best plan. So how does it go about determining the best plan? The query optimizer evaluates the different plans it can use to retrieve the data based on cost and the speed with which they return the data. The query optimizer then selects the plan that retrieves the data the fastest with the lowest reasonable cost on your server's resources. We want to emphasize that the query optimizer considers both an execution plan's cost in resources along with how fast it retrieves the data, mostly because we don't want you to think that it chooses an execution plan strictly based on the lowest cost in server resources. For example, let's say that you're using a server with multiple processors. In this scenario, an execution plan that uses more than one processor has a higher resource cost, but your server will also be able to process the query much faster. For this reason, the query optimizer will select the execution plan that uses all of your server's processors (provided the query won't overwork your server).

Let's take a look at the calculations the query optimizer performs when choosing an execution plan:

- Identifying what indexes you have and whether or not they reduce the processing time for your query.

- Determining the indexes and columns the query optimizer can use to limit the number of rows SQL Server must examine to process your query. Limiting the number of rows SQL Server must examine reduces the amount of I/O your server must perform, which improves the overall performance of your server.

- Creating any necessary column statistics to improve your query's performance.

- Selecting the most efficient method for processing a table join. This calculation involves choosing the order in which it will join tables.

The query optimizer does put a limit on the number of execution plans it calculates for a given query. Obviously, generating an endless number of execution plans before executing a query can degrade your server's performance.

Understanding How the Query Optimizer Works

Now that you've seen the basics of what the query optimizer does for queries, let's take a look at what goes on behind the scenes whenever you execute a query. Here's what happens when SQL Server receives your query:

1. SQL Server begins by checking the syntax of the query. After it checks your syntax, SQL Server breaks your query into smaller components for the database engine to process. This step is called parsing, and the end result of parsing is called a parsed query tree.

2. Next, SQL Server verifies the names of objects you use in the query and checks whether you have the necessary permissions for those objects. It also checks for any redundant syntax clauses and removes them, and standardizes any subqueries. This step is called the standardization step, and the end result is a standardized query tree.

3. SQL Server next analyzes your query to determine which indexes, if any, it should use to speed up the query and how it will join tables if necessary. This is the query optimization step (and the focus of this lesson).

4. SQL Server now converts the query into executable language and includes identifiers as to which tables and indexes it will use to retrieve the data. This step is called the compiling step.

5. Finally, SQL Server sends the compiled requests for processing. We call this the executing step of query processing.

Because there are so many steps necessary to process a query, SQL Server saves a query's compiled execution plan in the procedure cache within its pool of available memory. In earlier versions of SQL Server, the procedure cache was a reserved area within your server's memory pool. In SQL Server 2000, the procedure cache isn't reserved in memory because SQL Server dynamically allocates and de-allocates memory as needed. Caching the execution plan for a query improves the performance of repetitive queries. When SQL Server executes a compiled query, it need only retrieve the execution plan from cache and execute it; it doesn't need to perform the steps of parsing, standardizing, optimizing, and compiling the query.

There are certain conditions that trigger SQL Server to recompile a query's cached execution plan. For example, SQL Server will automatically recompile a query's execution plan if you make a structural change to a table or view on which the query's based. Other situations which cause SQL Server to recompile a query's execution plan include:

- SQL Server updates the distribution statistics, either automatically because you've configured the database with the auto-update statistics option, or because you execute the UPDATE STATISTICS statement.

- You drop an index that's used by the query's execution plan.

- You make a large number of changes to the index keys (such as by using the INSERT or DELETE statements).

- You force SQL Server to recompile a stored procedure or trigger by using the sp_recompile stored procedure.

- You make a large number of changes to a table on which you've defined triggers.

Displaying Query Statistics

SQL Server includes a number of techniques that you can use to find out information about the execution plan selected by the query optimizer. You can begin by displaying statistics information. For example, you can use the command SET STATISTICS TIME ON to have SQL Query Analyzer display the amount of time in milliseconds SQL Server uses to parse, compile, and execute each statement in your query. We show you an example of the statistics you can view for a query in Figure 15-1. In this example, the first parse and compile statistics you see tell you the amount of time SQL Server used to parse and compile the query. The second parse and compile statistics enable you to see the amount of time SQL Server used to cache the query's execution plan. (If you execute this same query again, you won't see the second set of parse and compile statistics because SQL Server will have already cached the execution plan.) Use the execution times statistics to gain an idea of how long it takes SQL Server to execute your query.

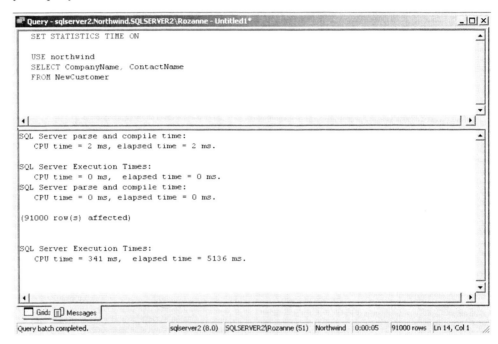

Figure 15-1: *Output generated with* SET STATISTICS TIME ON.

Another statement you can use to analyze a query's statistics is SET STATISTICS PROFILE ON. This command enables you to view both the output from the SET SHOWPLAN_ALL ON statement (which we'll look at in just a moment) plus two additional columns. The first column contains the total number of rows processed by SQL Server for each step in the query plan, and the second column indicates how many times SQL Server executed this step. You can see the output of this command in Figure 15-2.

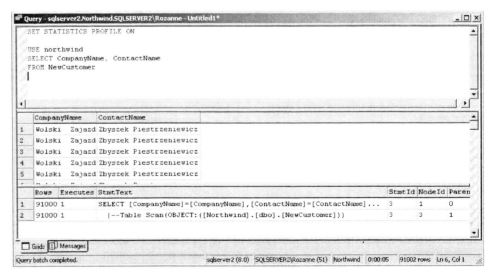

Figure 15-2: *Output generated with* SET STATISTICS PROFILE ON.

A third statement you can use to figure out the amount of disk activity generated by a SQL query is SET STATISTICS IO ON. This query enables you to determine exactly how much of your query SQL Server retrieved by accessing your server's hard disk. Before we look at the sample output for this command, let's take a look at the statistics it gives you. We describe each of these statistics in the following table.

Statistic	Enables You to Determine
Table	The name of the table on which your query is based.
Scan Count	How many times SQL Server had to access the table on which your query is based.
Logical Reads	How many pages SQL Server could retrieve from the data cache to satisfy your query instead of having to access the server's hard disk.
Physical Reads	How many pages SQL Server had to retrieve from the server's hard disk to satisfy your query.
Read-Ahead Reads	How many pages SQL Server placed into the data cache for your query.

You can calculate what percentage of time SQL Server was able to retrieve a query's data from cache by using the following formula: (Logical Reads - Physical Reads)/Logical Reads. This value tells you the Cache Hit Ratio for the query.

Given these statistics, let's take a look at the STATISTICS IO for a given query. In Figure 15-3, we show you the output generated when you enable the STATISTICS IO option. Notice that in this example, you see that the total number of logical reads was 1476 (meaning SQL Server read 1476 pages from the data cache to satisfy the query)—but that the total number of physical reads was 0. This means that SQL Server was able to retrieve all of the data for this query from cache without having to access the server's hard disk.

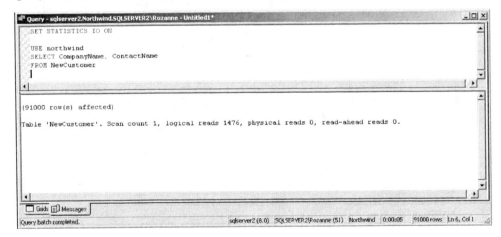

Figure 15-3: *Output generated with* SET STATISTICS IO ON.

Each of these SET STATISTICS statements stays active for your current session until you turn them off. You turn off the statistics by executing the statement SET STATISTICS *statistics_type* OFF. SQL Server also turns off the statistics when you close your current session.

Suggested time:
10 minutes

APPLY YOUR KNOWLEDGE 15-1

Analyzing Query Statistics

Objective: To execute an SQL script to create a very large table named NewCustomers in the Northwind database. You'll then analyze the statistics generated when you query this table.

Setup: You're logged on to Windows 2000 as student#. You've created a database named movies and tables within it named movie, category, customer, rental, and rental_detail. You've defined primary key, foreign key, default, and check constraints on the tables, and created nonclustered indexes based on your primary keys. You have imported data into the tables. You have created database diagrams for both the movies and pubs databases.

1. In SQL Query Analyzer, open the C:\Data\newcustomer.sql script file.

2. Take a look at this script file. We begin this script by creating a new table named NewCustomer. Next, we use a counter (@counter) to have SQL Server insert a copy of the rows in the Customers table into the NewCustomer table. We're also using a second counter (@counter2) to help generate values for the CustomerID column so that we have no more than five rows in the table that have the same value for the CustomerID.

3. Execute the newcustomer.sql script file.

4. Open the statslab.sql script file.

5. Execute the query to turn on STATISTICS IO and query the NewCustomer table. When you see the results set, select the Messages tab in the Results pane. You use this pane to view the statistics returned by the query optimizer.

6. How many times did SQL Server access this table? How can you tell?

7. What is the Cache Hit Ratio for this query? How do you calculate this value?

8. Open a new Query window, and then close the Query window containing the statslab.sql script file.

Limiting Long-running Queries

It's possible that you or your users can execute queries that use a huge amount of your server's resources. In some cases, such queries are accidental, but they nonetheless degrade your server's performance. You can help prevent such queries from executing by configuring the query governor. This setting enables you to specify a cost limit so that you can help prevent your server from executing high cost queries. You specify a value for the query governor in seconds, but this value doesn't actually correlate directly to the elapsed time when you execute the query; instead, it correlates to the estimated cost of the query.

By default, SQL Server Setup sets the query governor's value to zero, which disables the query governor. You can specify a value of up to 2,147,483,647 seconds for the query governor by using any of the following methods:

- Modifying the properties of your server in SQL Server Enterprise Manager. (Use the Server Settings tab in the Properties dialog box for your server.)

- Using the `sp_configure` stored procedure to set the query governor cost limit server option.

- Executing the `SET QUERY_GOVERNOR_COST_LIMIT` statement. You use this statement if you want to set the query governor for a specific connection instead of for all connections.

TASK 15A-1:

Configuring the Query Governor

1. In SQL Query Analyzer, **open the C:\Data\querygovernor.sql script file.**

2. **Highlight and execute the following query:**

   ```
   USE Northwind
   SET STATISTICS TIME ON
   SELECT CompanyName, ContactName
   FROM NewCustomer
   ORDER BY CompanyName
   ```

3. **Select the Messages tab** so that you can see how long it took SQL Server to execute this query.

4. **What value do you see for the CPU time? (Look at the SQL Server Execution Times at the end of the results set.)**

5. **Given the value you see for the CPU time, what value should you use if you want the query governor to prevent this query from executing? (Notice that SET STATISTICS TIME ON displays the value for CPU time in milliseconds, but you specify the value for the query governor in seconds.)**

6.	**Edit the querygovernor.sql script file. Add the** `SET` `QUERY_GOVERNOR_COST_LIMIT` **statement and specify a value that will prevent the** `SELECT` **query from running.**

```
Query - sqlserver2.Northwind.SQLSERVER2\Rozanne - C:\Documents and Settings\rozanne\My Documents\SQL Data\querygovernor.sql
  -Step 2: Query to display the amount of time SQL Server uses to parse, compile, and execute a query.
SET STATISTICS TIME ON
SET QUERY_GOVERNOR_COST_LIMIT 2
SELECT CompanyName, ContactName
FROM NewCustomer
ORDER BY CompanyName
```

7.	**Execute the script file again.** You should see that the query governor prevents your query from running. (Look at the end of the results set.)

8.	**Open a new Query window, and then close the window containing the querygovernor.sql script file. Don't save your changes to this file.**

Using SHOWPLAN_ALL and SHOWPLAN_TEXT

To view the execution plan the query optimizer chose for executing your query, execute the `SET SHOWPLAN_ALL ON` statement followed by a query. By viewing the execution plan, you can see whether or not the query optimizer uses a specific index when processing the query. For example, you can execute the following query to determine what (if any) indexes the query optimizer uses to return the results set:

```
USE movies
SET SHOWPLAN_ALL ON
GO
SELECT movie_num, title
FROM movie WHERE category_num = '1'
```

Use the `SHOWPLAN_ALL` statement to have SQL Server display detailed information about the query's execution plan, including information about the estimated number of rows your query will retrieve, the I/O generated by the query, CPU time, and the average row size of your query. For less detailed information, you can use the `SET SHOWPLAN_TEXT ON` statement instead.

When you use one of the `SET SHOWPLAN` statements, SQL Server displays information about the order in which it accesses your tables (if your query is against multiple tables), and which indexes it uses or which tables it scans. The following table describes the messages you will see when you run a query with `SHOWPLAN` turned on.

Message	Indicates that the Query Optimizer will
Index Seek	Use a nonclustered index to retrieve the results set for your query.
Clustered Index Seek	Use the clustered index for the table to retrieve the results set for your query.
Clustered Index Scan	Scan the clustered index for the table because no other index enables it to retrieve the results set. Essentially, the query optimizer performs a table scan in this scenario, but it's called a "clustered index scan" because the data in the table is stored in order by the clustered index. The clustered index doesn't improve the performance of the query.
Table Scan	Scan the table to retrieve the results set. You'll see this message if the table doesn't have a clustered index and none of its nonclustered indexes will help improve the performance of the query.

One thing you should be aware of is that when you turn on one of the SHOWPLAN options, SQL Server Query Analyzer stops processing your queries and displays only their execution plans instead. You must turn off the SHOWPLAN option in order to have SQL Server Query Analyzer process your query.

TASK 15A-2:

Using SHOWPLAN to View the Query Execution Plan

1. In SQL Query Analyzer, **open the C:\Data\showplan.sql script file.**

2. **Highlight and execute the query that uses the movies database, turns on SHOWPLAN_ALL, and selects data from the movie table.**

3. **Look at the results set.** You can see the steps the query optimizer estimates SQL Server must perform to retrieve this query's results set.

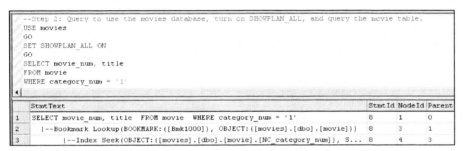

```
--Step 2: Query to use the movies database, turn on SHOWPLAN_ALL, and query the movie table.
USE movies
GO
SET SHOWPLAN_ALL ON
GO
SELECT movie_num, title
FROM movie
WHERE category_num = '1'
```

	StmtText	StmtId	NodeId	Parent
1	SELECT movie_num, title FROM movie WHERE category_num = '1'	8	1	0
2	|--Bookmark Lookup(BOOKMARK:([Bmk1000]), OBJECT:([movies].[dbo].[movie]))	8	3	1
3	|--Index Seek(OBJECT:([movies].[dbo].[movie].[NC_category_num]), S...	8	4	3

4. **How will SQL Server retrieve the results of this query?**

5. **Highlight and execute the next query** (the query that finds all movies with titles LIKE 's%').

	StmtText
1	SELECT movie_num, title FROM movie WHERE title LIKE 's%'
2	|--Clustered Index Seek(OBJECT:([movies].[dbo].[movie].[CL_title]...

6. **How will SQL Server retrieve the results of this query?**

7. **Highlight and execute the query to find all PG-rated movies.**

	StmtText
1	SELECT movie_num, title FROM movie WHERE rating = 'PG'
2	|--Filter(WHERE:(STARTUP EXPR(((([@1]='G' OR [@1]='NC17') OR [@1]='NR') ...
3	|--Clustered Index Scan(OBJECT:([movies].[dbo].[movie].[CL_title]),...

8. **How will SQL Server retrieve the results of this query?**

9. **Highlight and execute the last query** (the query that lists the description and category_num for all movie categories).

	StmtText
1	SELECT description, category_num FROM category ORDER BY description
2	|--Sort(ORDER BY:([category].[description] ASC))
3	|--Table Scan(OBJECT:([movies].[dbo].[category]))

10. **How will SQL Server retrieve the results of this query?**

11. **Open a new Query window, and then close the Query window containing the showplan.sql script file.**

Using the Graphical Execution Plan

Another technique you can use to analyze a query's execution plan is to configure SQL Query Analyzer to display a query's graphical execution plan. This option enables you to view graphically each step (in order) a query must perform, along with both the logical and physical operators SQL Server must use. The logical operators indicate the relational operations SQL Server uses to process the statement. For example, performing an aggregation represents a logical operation. The physical operators enable you to determine the physical steps SQL Server performs to retrieve the data. For example, the act of scanning a table represents a physical operator. In the following table, we describe some of the physical operators you can see in a query's graphical execution plan.

For an explanation of all of the icons you can see in SQL Query Analyzer, see the "Graphically Displaying the Execution Plan Using SQL Query Analyzer" topic in Books Online.

Physical Operator	Icon	Indicates that SQL Server
Bookmark Lookup		Used a bookmark row, either a row ID (if it's using the table's nonclustered index) or a clustering key (if it's using the table's clustered index) to look up the required row within the table or clustered index.
Clustered Index Scan		Executed a scan of a table's clustered index to select the necessary rows for your query.
Clustered Index Seek		Used a seek of the clustered index to select the rows for your query.

Physical Operator	Icon	Indicates that SQL Server
Filter		Implemented a filter to restrict the rows returned by the query. You typically see this step when your query includes a WHERE clause.
Index Scan		Used a scan of the nonclustered index to select the rows for your query.
Index Seek		Performed a seek of the nonclustered index to retrieve the rows for your query.
Merge Join		Performed all types of joins to generate the query's results set. This includes inner and outer joins, plus any SELECT statements that use the UNION keyword. SQL Server doesn't use a merge join for self and cross joins.
Nested Loops		Executed a search of an inner table for each row in the outer table; SQL Server typically uses an index for this type of search. SQL Server uses nested loops to process inner join and left outer join statements.
Table Scan		Performed a scan of the table to retrieve the rows for the results set.
Sort		Sorted all rows in the results set.

You display a query's graphical execution plan in SQL Query Analyzer by choosing Query→Show Execution Plan. After you select this option, SQL Server adds an Execution Plan tab to the Results pane for any query you execute, as shown in Figure 15-4. You read this graphical execution plan from right to left, and from top to bottom. Microsoft refers to each step in the execution plan as a node. So in this figure, you can see that the first step SQL Server performed is an index seek of the nonclustered index NC_category_num. (We can tell this by looking at the icons.) Next, SQL Server used the row IDs it retrieved from the nonclustered index to perform a bookmark lookup on the actual data pages. It then displayed the results set (that's what the Select icon means).

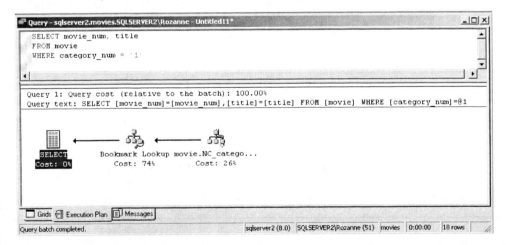

Figure 15-4: *A graphical query execution plan.*

You can point to each node in the graphical query execution plan to have SQL Server display additional information about that node, as shown in Figure 15-5. You can use this additional information to find out detailed statistics about this particular step in the query execution plan. We describe the statistics you see in the following table.

Statistic	Enables You to Determine
Physical Operations	The physical operation performed by the step (index seek in this example).
Logical Operations	The logical operation performed by the step.
Row Count	The number of rows selected by the operation.
Estimated Row Size	The estimated size of each row returned.
I/O Cost	The cost of performing all of the I/O activity for this step.
CPU Cost	The CPU cost for performing this step.
Number of Executes	The number of times SQL Server performed this step while processing the query.
Cost	The cost for processing this step. You'll also see the percentage cost of this step relative to the whole query. (In our example, this step used 26 percent of the total cost of processing our query.)
Subtree Cost	The total cost for processing this step and all preceding steps.

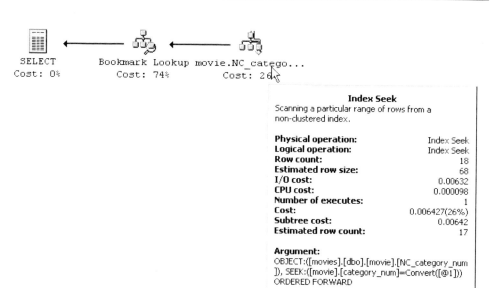

Figure 15-5: *Displaying additional information about a node.*

TASK 15A-3:

Analyzing a Graphical Execution Plan

1. In SQL Query Analyzer, **open the C:\Data\graphplan.sql script.** This script contains the same queries you used to view the output from SET SHOWPLAN_ALL ON. We're going to use it this time to display the graphical execution plan in SQL Query Analyzer.

2. **Choose Query→Show Execution Plan** to turn on the graphical execution plan in SQL Query Analyzer.

3. **Highlight and execute the first query in the script file.** This query enables you to list all movies with a category number of 1.

4. In the Results pane, **select the Execution Plan tab** to display the graphical execution plan for your query. You can see that SQL Server first used a seek of the nonclustered index NC_category_num to identify the rows it needs to retrieve the query's data. (You can determine whether SQL Server used an index seek or an index scan by pointing to the movie.NC_category_num node.) It then used a bookmark lookup on the table's clustered index to retrieve the query's rows.

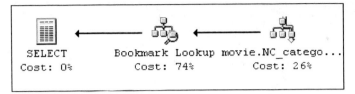

5. **Highlight and execute the next query** to find all movies with names that begin with "S."

6. **Select the Execution Plan tab.**

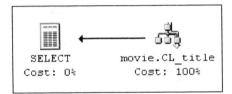

7. **How did SQL Server retrieve this query? (Hint: Point to the movie.CL_ title node to determine the action SQL Server performed with this object.)**

8. **Highlight and execute the query that retrieves all PG-rated movies. Look at the execution plan.**

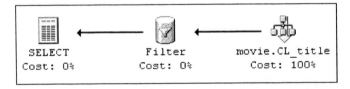

9. **What steps does SQL Server perform to retrieve this query's results set?**

10. **Highlight and execute the query that displays all category descriptions and their numbers. Look at the execution plan.**

11. How does SQL Server retrieve this query's results set?

12. Open a new Query window, and then close the window containing the graphplan.sql script.

TOPIC 15B

Using Indexes to Optimize Queries

Now that we've examined how SQL Server goes about selecting a query's execution plan, let's take a look at some of the techniques you can use to improve a query's performance. One technique you can use to improve a query's performance is to create a *covering index*. A covering index is a nonclustered index where the index key contains all of the columns necessary to satisfy a query.

covering index:
A nonclustered index where the index key consists of all of the values you select in a query. For example, if you execute the query SELECT movie_num, title, rating FROM movie, a covering index for this query must use the movie_num, title, and rating columns as its index key.

But why do we say that the covering index has to be nonclustered? Well, let's think about how SQL Server goes about retrieving data to satisfy a query. In this scenario, let's assume that you're querying the movie table and that you've defined the indexes we show you in Figure 15-6. This figure shows you that we have a clustered index on the movie table's title column, and nonclustered indexes on the category_num and movie_num columns respectively. If you execute a query where SQL Server retrieves data based on the clustered index, it accesses the data pages for the movie table directly—but it must retrieve all of a row's data and then filter out the columns that satisfy your query. On the other hand, let's say that you execute a query such as the following:

```
SELECT movie_num, title
FROM movie
WHERE category_num = 1
```

In this example, SQL Server uses the NC_category_num nonclustered index to first identify the rows it must retrieve, and then retrieves the rows by performing a bookmark lookup on the clustered index (which is the movie table itself). As you can see, SQL Server is performing more I/O operations, so this execution plan will take longer to process than one which uses only the clustered index.

But what if we created a nonclustered index that contained the movie_num, title, and category_num columns? In this scenario, the nonclustered index's keys would contain all of the necessary information to satisfy our query. This means that SQL Server would need to use only the nonclustered index to retrieve the query's results set and wouldn't have to access the movie table at all. And, because the nonclustered index key is smaller than the size of each row in the movie table, this means that more of the nonclustered index key rows can fit on a data page as compared to that of the movie table's rows. So, retrieving the data to satisfy a query from a nonclustered index's pages requires less I/O than retrieving the data from the table's actual data pages.

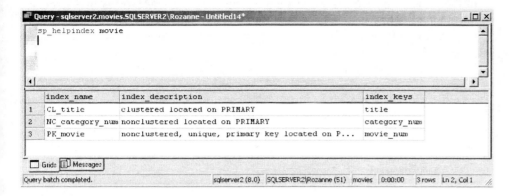

```
sp_helpindex movie
```

	index_name	index_description	index_keys
1	CL_title	clustered located on PRIMARY	title
2	NC_category_num	nonclustered located on PRIMARY	category_num
3	PK_movie	nonclustered, unique, primary key located on P...	movie_num

Grids Messages

Query batch completed.   sqlserver2 (8.0) SQLSERVER2\Rozanne (51) movies 0:00:00 3 rows Ln 2, Col 1

Figure 15-6: *The movie table's indexes.*

You can determine whether an index covers a query or not by analyzing both the execution plan for a query and the output generated by STATISTICS IO. If a nonclustered index covers a query, you'll see that SQL Server reads fewer pages as compared to other indexes. You should try to keep the index key for a nonclustered index that covers a query as small as possible in order to take advantage of the reduced I/O.

Let's take a look at some examples.

APPLY YOUR KNOWLEDGE 15-2

Suggested time:
30 minutes

Determining if an Index Covers a Query

Objective: To create indexes based on the NewCustomer table to determine the difference in performance with an index that covers a query.

Setup: You created the NewCustomer table.

1. In SQL Query Analyzer, open the C:\Data\cleanindex.sql script. This script creates a stored procedure named CleanIndex that you can use to drop all statistics and indexes for a given table in the Northwind database.

2. Execute the cleanindex.sql script file to create the CleanIndex stored procedure.

3. Open a new Query window, and then close the window containing the cleanindex.sql script file.

4. Open the C:\Data\indexcovers.sql script file.

5. Highlight and execute the query to delete the indexes and statistics for the NewCustomer table.

6. Configure SQL Query Analyzer to display the query execution plan. (Choose Query→Show Execution Plan.) Highlight and execute the query to create a clustered index on the NewCustomer table.

7. Highlight and execute the query to turn on STATISTICS IO.

8. Highlight and execute the query to retrieve all rows with the CustomerID of "ernsh1."

9. In the table below, use the information you see on the Messages and Execution Plan tabs in the Results pane to record the query's statistics. This information tells you how SQL Server executed the query by using the clustered index.

Statistic	Value
Scan Count	
Logical Reads	
Index or Table Scan	
Type of Index Operation	

10. Highlight and execute the next query to delete all statistics and indexes for the NewCustomer table.

11. Now let's create a nonclustered index and execute the same query so that we can compare the statistics. Highlight and execute the query to create a nonclustered index on the CustomerID column of the NewCustomer table.

12. Next, execute the same query to retrieve all rows with the CustomerID of "ernsh1."

13. In the table below, use the information you see on the Messages and Execution Plan tabs in the Results pane to record the query's statistics. This information tells you how SQL Server executed the query using the nonclustered index.

Statistic	Value
Scan Count	
Logical Reads	
Index or Table Scan	
Type of Index Operation	

14. Given the statistics you see in steps 9 and 13, which index is more efficient for this query? Why?

15. Now let's try both a clustered and a nonclustered index with a different query. In SQL Query Analyzer, highlight and execute the query to remove the statistics and indexes from the NewCustomer table.

16. Next, execute the query to create the clustered index on the CustomerID column again.

17. Highlight and execute the query to retrieve only the CustomerID column for the CustomerID of "ernsh1."

18. In the table below, use the information you see on the Messages and Execution Plan tabs in the Results pane to record the query's statistics. This information tells you how SQL Server executed this new query using the clustered index.

Statistic	Value
Scan Count	
Logical Reads	
Index or Table Scan	
Type of Index Operation	

19. Let's generate the same statistics but by using a nonclustered index. Execute the query to delete the NewCustomer table's indexes and statistics and then re-create the nonclustered index.

20. Highlight and execute the query to retrieve only the CustomerID column for the CustomerID of "ernsh1."

21. In the table below, use the information you see on the Messages and Execution Plan tabs in the Results pane to record the query's statistics. This information tells you how SQL Server executed this new query using the nonclustered index.

Statistic	Value
Scan Count	
Logical Reads	
Index or Table Scan	
Type of Index Operation	

22. Given the statistics you see in steps 18 and 21, which index is more efficient for this query? Why?

23. Now let's see which index provides us with better performance when we retrieve a range of rows. In SQL Query Analyzer, execute the query to remove all statistics and indexes, and then re-create the clustered index.

24. Highlight and execute the query to retrieve all CustomerID columns for customers with IDs between "ernsh1" and "folig1."

25. In the table below, use the information you see on the Messages and Execution Plan tabs in the Results pane to record the query's statistics. This information tells you how SQL Server executed this third query using the clustered index.

Statistic	Value
Scan Count	
Logical Reads	
Index or Table Scan	
Type of Index Operation	

26. Let's generate the same statistics but by using the nonclustered index. Execute the query to delete the NewCustomer table's indexes and statistics and then re-create the nonclustered index.

27. Next, highlight and execute the query to retrieve all CustomerID columns for customers with IDs between "ernsh1" and "folig1."

28. In the table below, use the information you see on the Messages and Execution Plan tabs in the Results pane to record the query's statistics. This information tells you how SQL Server executed this third query using the nonclustered index.

Statistic	Value
Scan Count	
Logical Reads	
Index or Table Scan	
Type of Index Operation	

29. Given the statistics you see in steps 25 and 28, which index is more efficient for this query? Why?

30. Open a new Query window, and then close the Query window containing the indexcovers.sql script file.

Designing Indexing to Optimize Queries

If you've been given the task to design the indexing for a database, one of the first things you should do is to get as familiar with the data as possible— including the queries your users will execute, along with the priorities for each query. By reviewing the data and the queries, you can develop an idea of what types of indexes will help speed up those queries. Next, you should evaluate how selective the WHERE clauses are for the queries. WHERE clauses that are more selective are better candidates for indexing.

You should next decide whether or not you want to create an index. If you recall from the "Implementing Indexes" lesson, your server does incur a certain amount of overhead for maintaining each index. For this reason, you shouldn't create an index unless its benefits outweigh its overhead. Don't create an index on a column that isn't highly selective (meaning it contains very few unique values). You also shouldn't create indexes on columns that are very wide.

After you've decided to create an index, your next decision is to select the index's key column (or columns). You should create indexes on columns that you use in table joins (typically foreign keys). In addition, you should consider creating indexes on columns that your users query frequently. If you've decided to create a composite index (consisting of multiple columns), make sure that you index the columns in the order that you query them.

Your last task when designing indexing is to monitor the performance of your indexes and queries. It's possible that an index you thought would improve your server's performance doesn't, so it's important that you periodically analyze performance. You can analyze index performance by using commands such as SET SHOWPLAN_ALL ON, SET STATISTICS IO ON, and SET STATISTICS TIME ON.

TASK 15B-1:

Designing Indexing

1. After analyzing your users' queries, you've determined that the majority of the queries retrieve the Contact Name and Phone columns from the Customers table. You've defined a clustered index on the customers table's SalesRepID column. Should you create an index to improve the performance of these queries? If yes, what factors should you consider when selecting the index's key?

2. You have created an index to help improve the performance of a query. You'd like to determine whether SQL Server is using the index and its impact on performance. What should you do?

Overriding the Query Optimizer

If necessary, you can use hints to help the query optimizer choose the most efficient query execution plan. Although Microsoft refers to these tips as "hints," the query optimizer doesn't have much choice in the matter: it must use the index you specify in your hint. For example, if you use a hint to specify that you want SQL Server to use a specific index in a query, the query optimizer will always use that index—even if you later add a more efficient index that would make the query run faster.

Because of the improvements in the query optimizer in SQL Server 2000, Microsoft recommends that you limit the use of hints. Instead, let the query optimizer find the best possible execution plan for you. If you suspect that the query optimizer isn't selecting the best possible execution plan, you should double-check the following before you use hints to override the query optimizer:

- Are the index statistics current? You should either enable the auto-update statistics option for the database or manually force SQL Server to update the statistics.

- Recompile your stored procedures.

- Evaluate your indexes to determine if they're effective.

- Review your queries and rewrite them if necessary.

You use table hints to force SQL Server to perform a table scan, use a specific index, or use a specific locking method. For example, you can use the following syntax to specify an index hint:

```
USE database_name
GO
SELECT column_list
FROM table_name
WITH (INDEX(index_name or index_id))
WHERE condition
```

You can use either the index's name or ID number in the INDEX( ) clause. For example, you could use the following query to specify that you want SQL Server to use the CL_title index to retrieve the results set:

```
USE movies
GO
SELECT title, movie_num
FROM movie
WITH (INDEX(CL_title))
WHERE title LIKE 'S%'
```

APPLY YOUR KNOWLEDGE 15-3

Suggested time:
5 minutes

Using Query Hints

1. Design and execute a query to use the movies database and list each movie's title, rating, and category from the movie table in order by category. Include the SET SHOWPLAN_ALL ON statement so that you can see how SQL Server will process this query. What query did you use? How will SQL Server retrieve this query's results set?

2. Write a query to list each movie's title, rating, and category from the movie table in order by category; include a hint in your query. (You can use sp_helpindex movie to identify the name of the index you want to use.) What query did you use?

3. Turn off the display of the query execution plan.

4. Close all open windows.

Summary

In this lesson, you learned the role of the query optimizer in processing queries: it's responsible for selecting the lowest-cost query execution plan. You also learned how to analyze a query's execution plan, and how to design indexes to improve query performance.

LESSON 15 REVIEW

15A You would like to determine how many I/O operations SQL Server must perform to retrieve the results set for a complex query. What should you do?

15B What steps should you take before you resort to adding table hints to a query?

Analyzing Queries

LESSON
16

Data Files:
gen_labcustomer.sql
cleanindexmovie.sql
and_queries.sql
or_queries.sql
invoices.sql
gen_labinvoice
joinlab.sql

Lesson Time:
2 hours

Overview

In this lesson, you'll learn how to analyze in detail the queries that use the AND and OR keywords and how to optimize such queries. You'll also learn the steps SQL Server uses to perform table joins and how to optimize them.

Objectives

To analyze queries, you will:

16A **Analyze and optimize the steps performed by SQL Server in AND, OR, and table join queries.**

In this topic, you'll learn how the query optimizer selects an execution plan when you use complex search conditions with the AND and OR keywords. You'll also examine the strategies the query optimizer can use when joining tables.

TOPIC 16A

Analyzing the Performance of Queries

You'll sometimes hear the WHERE clause of a query referred to as a search condition because you use the WHERE clause of a query to search for only specific rows instead of all rows from a table. You can specify multiple search criteria in the WHERE clause by using the AND or OR keywords. In order for you to analyze and optimize the performance of AND queries, it's important that you understand the tasks the query optimizer performs when it encounters such queries. First of all, the query optimizer returns all of the rows that meet the criteria you specify in the WHERE clause. For example, if you execute the following query, the query optimizer selects all movies that have a rating of PG and a category_num of 1:

```
SELECT title, rating
FROM movie
WHERE rating = 'PG' AND category_num = 1
```

As the query optimizer selects the rows from the table, it progressively filters them based on the values in the WHERE clause. So in the preceding statement, the first thing the query optimizer does is to select all movies with a rating of PG. Then from this set of rows, it selects those movies that also have a category_num of 1.

In order to optimize the performance of processing a query with a WHERE clause consisting of multiple search conditions, the query optimizer can use an index for each search condition. In fact, if you have multiple indexes, the query optimizer can use those indexes to optimize retrieving the rows for each search condition. Depending on the search conditions, the query optimizer can use one index or multiple indexes to optimize retrieving the data. If the query optimizer uses multiple indexes, it will retrieve the results set by performing the following steps:

1. The query optimizer will search for the rows that meet each search condition by using the appropriate index for that column.

2. Next, the query optimizer sorts the index keys it retrieves for each search condition.

3. The query optimizer combines the index keys from each search condition.

4. Finally, the query uses the index keys to retrieve the data from the table by performing a bookmark lookup.

When it comes to optimizing queries that use multiple search conditions by using the AND keyword, your best bet is to try to use at least one search condition that's highly selective—and define an index on that column. Another strategy you can implement is to experiment with creating several different types of indexes and generating query statistics in each scenario. For example, you might first try creating several single-column indexes and record your query statistics. Then, try creating a single composite index and record your query statistics with only the one index. This strategy will enable you to determine which indexing strategy works best for your data.

You'll typically find that you get better performance by implementing multiple indexes if the search conditions you specify with the AND keyword aren't very selective.

APPLY YOUR KNOWLEDGE 16-1

Analyzing AND Queries

Suggested time:
30 minutes

Objective: To create a variety of indexes and then execute queries to determine which types of indexes improve each query's performance. You'll also see which types of queries use your indexes more efficiently.

Setup: You're logged on to Windows 2000 as student#. You've created a database named movies and tables within it named movie, category, customer, rental, and rental_detail. You've defined primary key, foreign key, default, and check constraints on the tables and created nonclustered indexes based on your primary keys. You have imported data into the tables. You have created database diagrams for both the movies and pubs databases.

1. In SQL Query Analyzer, open and execute each of the following script files:

   • C:\Data\gen_labcustomer.sql. This script file creates a new table within the movies database named LabCustomer. This table consists of 10,000 rows. Here's the structure of the LabCustomer table:

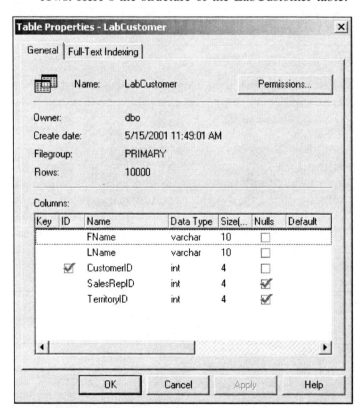

   • C:\Data\cleanindexmovie.sql. This script file creates the CleanIndex stored procedure in the movies database. (You will use the CleanIndex stored procedure to drop all statistics and indexes on the LabCustomer table.)

2. Open a new Query window, and close any Query windows you have open that contain script files.

3. Execute the following queries to delete all indexes and statistics and then create nonclustered indexes on the LabCustomer table:

```
EXEC CleanIndex LabCustomer
GO
CREATE NONCLUSTERED INDEX NC_Lname
        ON LabCustomer(LName)
CREATE NONCLUSTERED INDEX NC_SalesRepID
        ON LabCustomer(SalesRepID)
CREATE NONCLUSTERED INDEX NC_CustomerID
        ON LabCustomer(CustomerID)
GO
```

You're creating three single-columned indexes on the LabCustomer table.

4. Turn on STATISTICS IO by executing the following query:

```
SET STATISTICS IO ON
```

5. Configure SQL Query Analyzer to display the graphical execution plan for a query. (Choose Query→Show Execution Plan.)

6. Execute the following query:

```
SELECT *
FROM LabCustomer
WHERE LName LIKE 'e%'
AND SalesRepID > 350
AND CustomerID > 6500
```

You use this query to retrieve customers from the LabCustomer table with last names that begin with E, and whose SalesRepID is greater than 350, and whose CustomerID is greater than 6500.

7. Select the Execution Plan tab and take a look at your query's execution plan. This plan tells you that SQL Server used the NC_LName and NC_SalesRepID nonclustered indexes to retrieve the index key values. After retrieving the information from the two indexes, the query optimizer combined the index key values (this is the step performed by the Hash Match/ Inner Join node). Next, it used the index key values to perform a bookmark lookup on the LabCustomer table to retrieve the rows indicated by the index keys. Finally, it applied a filter to those rows to select only those rows with a CustomerID greater than 6500.

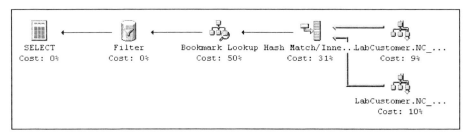

8. Record the information you see in the Results pane's Execution Plan and Messages tabs in the following table.

Statistic	Value
Number of Rows Retrieved	
Scan Count	
Logical Reads	
Number of Indexes Used (if any)	
Names of Indexes Used (if any)	

The number of rows your query retrieves will vary depending on the last names generated when you created the LabCustomer table. Your statistics should be similar to the ones you see in this table. This applies throughout the lab.

9. Now let's take a look at how SQL Server would process a query that uses only one of the search conditions instead of all three. Execute the following query:

```
SELECT LName
FROM LabCustomer
WHERE LName LIKE 'e%'
```

This query enables you to see how the query optimizer chooses to retrieve the data when your WHERE clause specifies only the Name column.

10. Record the information you see in the results pane's Execution Plan and Messages tabs for this new query in the following table.

Statistic	Value
Number of Rows Retrieved	
Scan Count	
Logical Reads	
Number of Indexes Used (if any)	
Names of Indexes Used (if any)	
Does this Index Cover the Query?	

11. Next, execute the following query to retrieve only those rows with a SalesRepID greater than 350:

```
SELECT SalesRepID
FROM LabCustomer
WHERE SalesRepID > 350
```

12. Record the information you see in the results pane's Execution Plan and Messages tabs for this new query in the following table.

Statistic	Value
Number of Rows Retrieved	
Scan Count	
Logical Reads	
Number of Indexes Used (if any)	
Names of Indexes Used (if any)	
Does this Index Cover the Query?	

13. Execute the following query to see how SQL Server retrieves the rows when you use a WHERE clause that's based on the CustomerID column:

```
SELECT CustomerID
FROM LabCustomer
WHERE CustomerID > 6500
```

14. Record the information you see in the results pane's Execution Plan and Messages tabs for this new query in the following table.

Statistic	Value
Number of Rows Retrieved	
Scan Count	
Logical Reads	
Number of Indexes Used (if any)	
Names of Indexes Used (if any)	
Does this Index Cover the Query?	

15. In the following table, summarize the results of each of the queries so that you can compare your results.

Statistic	Complete Query	LName Only	SalesRepID Only	CustomerID Only
Number of Rows Retrieved				
Scan Count				
Logical Reads				
Names of Indexes Used				
Number of Indexes Used				

Given these statistics, why do you think the query optimizer didn't use the NC_CustomerID index when it selected the execution plan for the complete query (the query consisting of three search conditions)?

Compare the number of logical reads SQL Server performs for the queries with only one search condition to the query with all three search conditions. Why is the I/O higher for the query with all three search conditions?

16. Now let's take a look at what happens when you execute a query that searches both the LName and SalesRepID columns. Execute the following query:

```
SELECT LName
FROM LabCustomer
WHERE LName LIKE 'e%'
AND SalesRepID > 350
```

17. In the following table, record the information you see in the results pane's Execution Plan and Messages tabs for this new query. In addition, record the information for the original three search condition query so that you can compare the results.

Statistic	Value for New Query	Value for Query with All Three Search Conditions
Number of Rows Retrieved		
Scan Count		
Logical Reads		
Number of Indexes Used (if any)		
Names of Indexes Used (if any)		

Why does this new query use less I/O than the original query?

18. Let's try a new query. Execute the following query:

```
SELECT *
FROM LabCustomer
WHERE LName LIKE 'e%'
AND SalesRepID > 350
AND CustomerID > 9500
```

19. Select the Execution Plan tab and take a look at this new query's execution plan. (You might want to compare it to the execution plan you see in step 7.) This plan tells you that it used all three nonclustered indexes to retrieve the query's results set.

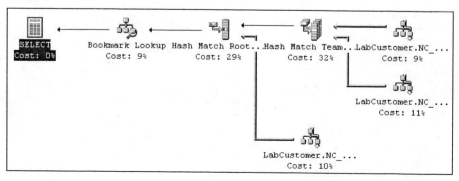

20. In the following table, record the information you see in the results pane's Execution Plan and Messages tabs for this new query.

Statistic	Value
Number of Rows Retrieved	
Scan Count	
Logical Reads	
Number of Indexes Used (if any)	
Names of Indexes Used (if any)	
Do the Indexes Cover the Query?	

Why does SQL Server use all three indexes to retrieve this query's results set?

21. Execute the following query to drop the NC_CustomerID index and replace it with a clustered index:

```
DROP INDEX LabCustomer.NC_CustomerID
GO
CREATE CLUSTERED INDEX CL_CustomerID
ON LabCustomer(CustomerID)
```

You now have three indexes on the LabCustomer table: a clustered index on the CustomerID column and nonclustered indexes on the SalesRepID and Name columns respectively.

22. Execute the following query so that you can analyze the execution plan with a clustered index:

```
SELECT *
FROM LabCustomer
WHERE LName LIKE 'e%'
AND SalesRepID > 350
AND CustomerID > 9500
```

23. In the following table, record the information you see in the results pane's Execution Plan and Messages tabs for this new query. In addition, record the information for the three search condition query from step 20 so that you can compare the results.

Statistic	Value for New Query	Value for Query with All Three Search Conditions
Number of Rows Retrieved		
Scan Count		
Logical Reads		
Number of Indexes Used (if any)		
Names of Indexes Used (if any)		

Did creating a clustered index improve the performance of this query? How can you tell?

24. Clear the Query window.

Analyzing OR Queries

In contrast to the AND keyword, the query optimizer returns the rows that meet any of the search conditions in the WHERE clause when you use the OR keyword. This means that the query optimizer progressively increases the number of rows it returns as it processes each search condition. For example, in the following query, the query optimizer will first select all movies that have a rating of PG and then select all movies that have a rating of G:

```
SELECT title, rating
FROM movie
WHERE rating = 'PG' OR rating = 'G'
```

You should be aware that with an OR query, the query optimizer will always per-form a table scan or a clustered index scan if you don't have an index for one of the search conditions (or if none of the indexes are useful). Depending on the search conditions, the query optimizer can use one index or multiple indexes to optimize retrieving the data. As you saw with the AND keyword, if the query optimizer uses multiple indexes, it will retrieve the results set by performing the following steps:

SQL Server's query optimizer automatically converts a query that uses the IN keyword into an OR query.

1. The query optimizer will search for the rows that meet each search condition by using the appropriate index for that column.

2. Next, the query optimizer sorts the index keys it retrieves for each search condition.

3. The query optimizer combines the index keys from each search condition.

4. Finally, the query uses the index keys to retrieve the data from the table by performing a bookmark lookup.

APPLY YOUR KNOWLEDGE 16-2

Analyzing OR Queries

Objective: To analyze the execution plans and statistics for queries that use the IN and OR keywords.

Setup: You've created the LabCustomer table and the CleanIndex stored procedure in the movies database.

1. In SQL Query Analyzer, execute the following query to delete all statistics and indexes on the LabCustomer table:

```
EXEC CleanIndex LabCustomer
```

2. Execute the following query to create a unique nonclustered index on the CustomerID column:

```
CREATE UNIQUE NONCLUSTERED INDEX NC_CustomerID
ON LabCustomer (CustomerID)
```

3. Turn on STATISTICS IO by executing the following query:

```
SET STATISTICS IO ON
```

4. If necessary, configure SQL Query Analyzer to display the graphical execution plan for a query. (Choose Query→Show Execution Plan.)

5. Execute the following query:

```
SELECT *
FROM LabCustomer
WHERE CustomerID = 1575
OR TerritoryID = 5
```

6. Look at the graphical execution plan. How did SQL Server retrieve this query's results set? Why does the query optimizer select this method?

7. Record the information you see in the results pane's Execution Plan and Messages tabs for this OR query in the following table.

The number of rows your query retrieves will vary depending on the last names generated when you created the LabCustomer table. Your statistics should be similar to the ones you see in this table. This applies throughout the lab.

Statistic	Value
Number of Rows Retrieved	
Scan Count	
Logical Reads	
Number of Indexes Used (if any)	
Names of Indexes Used (if any)	
Does the Index Cover the Query?	

8. Execute the following query:

```
SELECT *
FROM LabCustomer
WHERE CustomerID = 1575
OR SalesRepID = 22
```

9. Look at the graphical execution plan. How did SQL Server retrieve this query's results set? Why does the query optimizer select this method?

10. Record the information you see in the results pane's Execution Plan and Messages tabs for this OR query in the following table.

Statistic	Value
Number of Rows Retrieved	
Scan Count	
Logical Reads	
Number of Indexes Used (if any)	
Names of Indexes Used (if any)	
Does the Index Cover the Query?	

11. Compare the values you see in the tables in step 7 and step 10. Do you see any difference in these queries' execution plans? Why or why not?

12. Execute the following queries to drop the indexes on the LabCustomer table and then create new indexes:

```
SET STATISTICS IO OFF
GO
EXEC CleanIndex LabCustomer
CREATE UNIQUE NONCLUSTERED INDEX NC_CustomerID
ON LabCustomer(CustomerID)
CREATE CLUSTERED INDEX CL_SalesRepID
ON LabCustomer(SalesRepID)
```

13. Now execute a new query to see if SQL Server uses these indexes:

```
SET STATISTICS IO ON
GO
SELECT *
FROM LabCustomer
WHERE CustomerID = 1575
OR SalesRepID = 22
```

14. Look at the graphical execution plan. How did SQL Server retrieve this query's results set? Why does the query optimizer select this method?

15. In the following table, record the information you see in the results pane's Execution Plan and Messages tabs for this OR query.

Statistic	Value
Number of Rows Retrieved	
Scan Count	
Logical Reads	
Number of Indexes Used (if any)	
Names of Indexes Used (if any)	
Does the Index Cover the Query?	

16. Compare the values you see in the tables in step 10 and step 15. (These are the results for the same query but with different indexes.) Do you see any difference in these queries' execution plans? Why or why not?

17. Execute the following query to drop the existing indexes and create new ones:

```
EXEC CleanIndex LabCustomer
CREATE UNIQUE NONCLUSTERED INDEX NC_CustomerID
ON LabCustomer(CustomerID)
```

18. Now let's try a query that uses the IN keyword to see how the query optimizer processes it. Execute the following query:

```
SELECT *
FROM LabCustomer
WHERE CustomerID IN (1001,1002,1003,1004,1005,1101,1102,
                     1103,1104,1105,1106,1107,1108,1109,1110,
                     1200,1201,1202,1203,1204,1205,1206,1207,
                     1300,1301,1302,1303,1304,1305,1306,1307,
                     1308,1400,1401,1402)
```

19. Record the information you see in the results pane's Execution Plan and Messages tabs for this query in the following table.

Statistic	Value
Number of Rows Retrieved	
Scan Count	
Logical Reads	
Number of Indexes Used (if any)	
Names of Indexes Used (if any)	
Do the Indexes Cover the Query?	

20. Select the Execution Plan tab and take a look at the query execution plan.

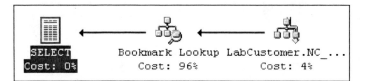

The values generated by STATISTICS IO indicate that SQL Server used a total of 105 logical reads to retrieve the data. What steps do you think generated this I/O on your server?

21. How would the execution plan change if you created an index that covered this query?

22. Clear the Query window.

Analyzing Table Join Queries

Now that we've looked at how you go about analyzing and optimizing AND and OR queries, let's move on to how you perform those same tasks on JOIN queries. The query optimizer evaluates the following when you execute a table join query:

- How selective is your join clause?
- What's the density of your join clause?
- Do you have any relevant indexes?
- What kind of search conditions (if any) are you using in a WHERE clause?

The query optimizer determines how selective your join clause is by analyzing what percentage of rows in one table are joined to a single row in the other table. The query optimizer considers a join clause highly selective if it returns only a few rows. Likewise, a join clause has low selectivity if it returns many rows. Next, the query optimizer identifies the density of your join clause by calculating the average percentage of duplicates in the joined tables. The query optimizer considers a join to have high density if there are a large number of duplicates in both tables (which also means that the join isn't highly selective). In contrast, a join has low density if there are few duplicates between the tables (which means that the join is highly selective). You can think of selectivity and join density as being inversely proportional: a join has high selectivity if it has a low join density, and it has low selectivity if it has a high join density.

So what does all this mean? If a query has a low join density, the query optimizer can retrieve the data by using either a clustered or a nonclustered index. On the other hand, if a query has a high join density, the query optimizer will typically use only a clustered index to retrieve the data.

When the query optimizer encounters a join in a query, it can use one of three strategies for joining the tables:

- A nested loop join
- A merge join
- A hash join

Let's take a look at each of these strategies in more detail.

Nested Loop Joins

With a nested loop join, SQL Server processes your query as a loop. This means that it takes one row from the first table (also called the outer table), and then uses that row to scan the second table (called the inner table) for matching rows. On the next iteration, SQL Server then takes the next row from the outer table and uses it to scan the inner table again for matching rows, and so on. Because SQL Server selects a row from one table and then finds the matching rows in the second table, you'll sometimes hear a nested loop join referred to as a one-to-many join. SQL Server doesn't necessarily perform a table scan to retrieve these rows—instead, it typically uses an index. In fact, if the query optimizer doesn't find a useful index, it typically uses a hash join strategy instead of the nested loop join strategy. In general, a nested loop join strategy provides you with the best performance as compared to the other join strategies if your query operates on a small number of rows. Figure 16-1 shows an example of the graphical query execution plan when SQL Server uses the nested loop join strategy.

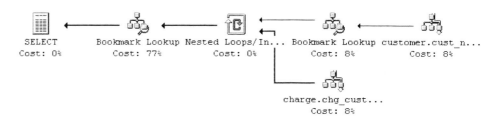

Figure 16-1: *The graphical execution plan for a query that uses the nested loop join strategy.*

You'll find that the query optimizer uses a nested loop join strategy when both of the following conditions are met: your outer table contains a small number of rows, and the inner table contains a larger number of rows and is indexed. Given the choice between the two tables in a join condition, the query optimizer will always use the table with fewer rows as the outer table.

Merge Joins

With a merge join, SQL Server retrieves a row from each table in the table join and evaluates whether or not the rows meet the join condition. For example, let's say that you execute the following query:

```
SELECT columns
FROM rental JOIN rental_detail
ON rental.invoice_num = rental_detail.invoice_num
```

If SQL Server uses a merge join strategy to process this join, it begins by selecting the first row from the rental table and the first row from the rental_detail table. Next, it checks to see if the rental table row's invoice_num column equals the rental_detail row's invoice_num column. If these columns are equal, SQL Server moves to the next row in both tables. But, if the rental table's invoice_num is less than the rental_detail table's invoice_num, SQL Server retrieves the

next row in the rental table. On the other hand, if the rental_detail table's invoice_num is less than the rental table's invoice_num, SQL Server retrieves the next row in the rental_detail table. SQL Server uses a temporary table to store the output of the merge join during processing. As you can see, for a merge join to work, both tables must be sorted in order by the column you specify in the join condition. (In our example, the join condition is
`ON rental.invoice_num = rental_detail.invoice_num`.) If the tables aren't sorted in order by the join condition, but the query optimizer determines that the merge join strategy will give the best performance, it will sort the tables first and then use a merge join.

Other than cross joins and full joins, the query optimizer can use a merge join for all types of join operations including those you specify with the UNION keyword. The query optimizer can select a merge join for one-to-one, one-to-many, and many-to-many joins. You'll find that you see very fast performance with a merge join. If the query optimizer must first sort the join tables, this performance can come at a high cost. The query optimizer typically uses a merge join when you have two tables with large amounts of data that are sorted by the column you specify in the join condition. We show you a query execution plan where SQL Server chose the merge join strategy in Figure 16-2.

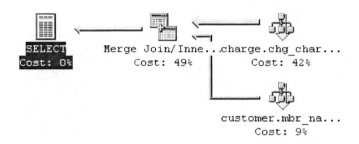

Figure 16-2: *The graphical execution plan for a query that uses the merge join strategy.*

Hash Joins

SQL Server uses a hash join for processing a table join whenever it doesn't find any useful indexes on either of the tables. The query optimizer will also choose a hash join, shown in Figure 16-3, if it determines that it's the most efficient table join strategy as compared to the nested loop and merge joins strategies. With a hash join, SQL Server designates the smaller of the tables as the *build input,* and the larger table as the *probe input.* SQL Server determines which table is smaller by analyzing column and index statistics for both tables. Next, it stores the build input table (the smaller table) into memory; at this point, the build input is called the hash table. SQL Server then stores the relevant columns from the build input table into a portion of the hash table called the hash bucket. SQL Server places these rows into the hash buckets based on a hash key value. This value enables SQL Server to essentially index the rows within the hash bucket.

built input:
The smaller of two tables in a hash join.

probe input:
The larger of two tables in a hash join.

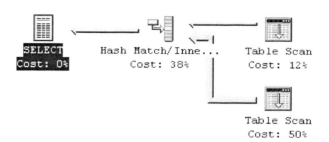

Figure 16-3: *The graphical execution plan for a query that uses the hash join strategy.*

After all of this prep work, SQL Server is now ready to process the table join. The first thing it does is to read a row from the probe input table (the larger of the tables). Next, it performs a hash algorithm against this row to generate a hash key value. SQL Server then uses this hash key value to find the appropriate hash bucket for that value and then looks to see if there is a matching row from the build input table within that hash bucket. Finally, it returns the row only if it finds a match between the row from the probe input table and a row in the hash bucket.

Just as you saw with merge joins, you'll find that you see very fast performance with a hash join. This is because it uses hash buckets along with hash keys to dynamically index the build input table's rows. Also like a merge join, SQL Server can use a hash join for all types of joins including those that use the UNION keyword, but not for cross and full joins. A hash join can also perform such tasks as grouping data and removing duplicates.

If both tables in your JOIN statement are similar in size, the performance of a hash join is equivalent to that of a merge join. On the other hand, if the size of the two tables are different, you'll see a significant performance improvement with a hash join as compared to a merge join. SQL Server uses hash joins to efficiently process large amounts of rows that aren't sorted and for which you haven't defined any indexes.

Forcing a Join Strategy with Hints

As you saw with table hints, you can force SQL Server to use a specific join strategy instead of letting the query optimizer select for you. You use the following syntax to force SQL Server to use a specific join strategy:

```
SELECT column list
FROM table1 join_type [MERGE | LOOP | HASH] JOIN table2
ON join condition
```

For example, you can use the following statement to force SQL Server to use the merge join strategy:

```
SELECT m.movie_num, c.description
FROM movie AS m INNER MERGE JOIN category AS c
ON m.category_num = c.category_num
```

If you use a join hint, you must specify the join type (such as INNER or OUTER). Microsoft recommends that you not specify join hints. Instead, you should let the query optimizer select the appropriate join strategy based on the volume of data in all tables, the available indexes, and the statistics SQL Server generates.

APPLY YOUR KNOWLEDGE 16-3

Suggested time:
15 minutes

Analyzing Table Joins

Objective: To analyze the join strategies the query optimizer selects for different table join queries.

1. In SQL Query Analyzer, open the C:\Data\invoices.sql script. This script creates a table named LabInvoice along with several stored procedures we use to automatically generate rows in this table. Execute this script.

2. Open the C:\Data\gen_labinvoice.sql script. This script creates 25,000 rows in the LabInvoice table. Execute the script file. Because this script file generates a large amount of data, it will take several minutes to complete. Wait until this script is done before continuing.

3. Open the C:\Data\joinlab.sql script. You're going to use this script file to perform the remaining steps of this lab.

4. Highlight and execute the lines in the script file to remove all statistics and indexes from the LabCustomer and LabInvoice tables. (These are the lines that begin with EXEC CleanIndex.)

5. You're going to build new indexes on both the LabCustomer and the LabInvoice tables. But before you do, you must increase the size of the movies database's transaction log file. (Otherwise, because the LabInvoice table is so big, you'll run out of transaction log space when you attempt to index the table.) Highlight and execute the query to configure the movies transaction log file to support unlimited file growth.

6. Highlight and execute the queries to create indexes on both the LabCustomer and the LabInvoice tables. This query enables you to create the following indexes:

   - A clustered index on the LName and FName columns in the LabCustomer table.

   - A nonclustered index on the CustomerID column in the LabCustomer table.

   - A clustered index on the CustomerID column in the LabInvoice table.

   - A nonclustered index on the Invoice_num column in the LabInvoice table.

   The last part of this query backs up the movies database's transaction log using the WITH TRUNCATE_ONLY option. This statement clears the inactive portion of the transaction log.

7. Highlight and execute the SET STATISTICS IO ON query to turn on the statistics information. Choose Query→Show Execution Plan to configure SQL Query Analyzer to display the graphical execution plan for your queries.

8. Highlight and execute the query to display the last name for the customer with a CustomerID of 4575. (The script you ran to create the LabCustomer table's data generates eight random characters for each customer's last name. For this reason, each time you run the gen_labcustomer.sql script you'll get a different last name for customer 4575.)

9. Highlight and execute the table join query. Make sure that you edit the query to insert a valid value for the customer's last name in the WHERE clause for this query. Don't worry if your query doesn't show any rows in the results set. The focus of this lab is on the query execution plan and statistics for table joins. The query execution plan is the same regardless of whether your query returns any rows.

10. Look at the execution plan for the table join query. What join strategy did the query optimizer select for this query? Why do you think it selected this strategy?

11. In the following table, record the statistics generated for this query.

The number of rows your query retrieves will vary depending on the invoices generated when you created the LabInvoice table. Your statistics should be similar to the ones you see in this table. This applies throughout the lab.

Statistic	Value
Join Strategy	
Scan Count for the LabInvoice Table	
Scan Count for the LabCustomer Table	
Logical Reads for LabInvoice Table	
Logical Reads for LabCustomer Table	
Total I/O Generated (add the values for all logical reads)	
Number of Indexes Used (if any)	
Names of Indexes Used (if any)	

12. Edit the table join query in the script file so that you can force SQL Server to use the merge join strategy. (Change the join clause to INNER MERGE JOIN.) Your query should look like the following:

```
SELECT LabCustomer.CustomerID, LabCustomer.LName,
LabInvoice.Invoice_num
FROM LabCustomer INNER MERGE JOIN LabInvoice
ON LabCustomer.CustomerID = LabInvoice.CustomerID
WHERE LabCustomer.lname = 'last_name'
```

Highlight and execute this query to force SQL Server to use a merge join strategy for the table join.

13. In the following table, record the statistics SQL Server generated when you forced it to use the merge join strategy.

Statistic	Value
Join Strategy	
Scan Count for the Worktable	
Scan Count for the LabInvoice Table	
Scan Count for the LabCustomer Table	
Logical Reads for the Worktable	
Logical Reads for LabInvoice Table	
Logical Reads for LabCustomer Table	
Total I/O Generated (add the values for all logical reads)	
Number of Indexes Used (if any)	
Names of Indexes Used (if any)	

14. Edit the table join query in the script file so that you can force SQL Server to use the hash join strategy. (Change the join clause to INNER HASH JOIN.) Your query should look like the following:

```
SELECT LabCustomer.CustomerID, LabCustomer.LName,
LabInvoice.Invoice_num
FROM LabCustomer INNER HASH JOIN LabInvoice
ON LabCustomer.CustomerID = LabInvoice.CustomerID
WHERE LabCustomer.lname = 'last_name'
```

Highlight and execute this query to force SQL Server to use a hash join strategy for the table join.

15. In the following table, record the statistics SQL Server generated when you forced it to use the hash join strategy.

Statistic	Value
Join Strategy	
Scan Count for the LabInvoice Table	
Scan Count for the LabCustomer Table	
Logical Reads for LabInvoice Table	
Logical Reads for LabCustomer Table	
Total I/O Generated (add the values for all logical reads)	
Number of Indexes Used (if any)	
Names of Indexes Used (if any)	

16. Based on the values you see for the total logical reads for each join strategy, which join strategy is most efficient? Did the query optimizer select the most efficient strategy?

17. Close all open windows.

Summary

In this lesson, you examined the different execution plans the query optimizer selects given the type of query you're executing and the types of indexes you've defined on your tables. For example, you saw that SQL Server can't use any of a table's indexes if you don't have an index on all of the columns you specify in search conditions with the OR keyword. You also examined the three types of join strategies that SQL Server can implement: nested loop, merge, and hash, and why the query optimizer chooses one strategy over the other.

LESSON 16 REVIEW

16A You've created a table for storing your company's parts inventory. You've created only one index on this table: a clustered index on the parts_num column. Given this information, how do you think SQL Server will retrieve the rows to satisfy the following query?

```
SELECT parts_num, description
FROM parts
WHERE description LIKE 'e%' OR parts_num > 1500
```

The Movies Database Structure

Table Design

The movies database consists of the following tables: movie, category, customer, rental, and rental_detail. The following figures display the column names, data types, and any default values or identity columns for each of these tables.

movie

	Column Name	Data Type	Length	Nullable	Default Value	Identity Seed	Identity Increment
🔑	movie_num	movie_num (int)	4	NOT NULL		100	1
	title	varchar	40	NOT NULL			
	category_num	category_num (int)	4	NOT NULL			
	rating	varchar	5	NOT NULL			
	date_purch	smalldatetime	4	NOT NULL	(getdate())		
	rental_price	smallmoney	4	NOT NULL			
	rented	char	1	NULL	('N')		

Figure A-1: *Movie table.*

category

	Column Name	Data Type	Length	Nullable	Default Value	Identity Seed	Identity Increment
🔑	category_num	category_num (int)	4	NOT NULL		1	1
	description	varchar	20	NOT NULL			

Figure A-2: *Category table.*

customer

	Column Name	Data Type	Length	Nullable	Default Value	Identity Seed	Identity Increment
🔑	cust_num	cust_num (int)	4	NOT NULL		300	1
	lname	varchar	20	NOT NULL			
	fname	varchar	20	NOT NULL			
	address1	varchar	30	NULL			
	address2	varchar	20	NULL			
	city	varchar	20	NULL			
	state	char	2	NULL			
	zip	char	10	NULL			
	phone	varchar	10	NOT NULL			
	join_date	smalldatetime	4	NULL	(getdate())		

Figure A-3: *Customer table.*

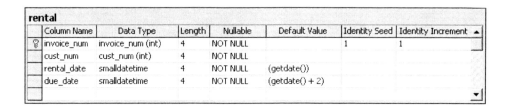

rental							
	Column Name	Data Type	Length	Nullable	Default Value	Identity Seed	Identity Increment
🔑	invoice_num	invoice_num (int)	4	NOT NULL		1	1
	cust_num	cust_num (int)	4	NOT NULL			
	rental_date	smalldatetime	4	NOT NULL	(getdate())		
	due_date	smalldatetime	4	NOT NULL	(getdate() + 2)		

Figure A-4: *Rental table.*

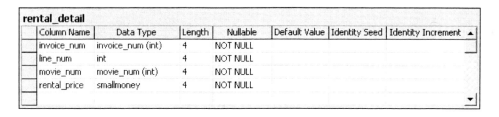

rental_detail							
	Column Name	Data Type	Length	Nullable	Default Value	Identity Seed	Identity Increment
	invoice_num	invoice_num (int)	4	NOT NULL			
	line_num	int	4	NOT NULL			
	movie_num	movie_num (int)	4	NOT NULL			
	rental_price	smallmoney	4	NOT NULL			

Figure A-5: *Rental_detail table.*

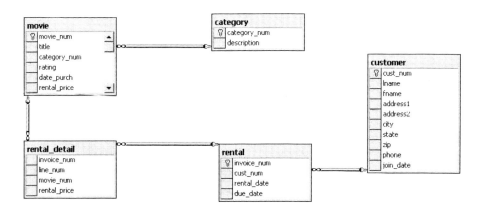

Figure A-6: *Primary key to foreign key relationships.*

Course Script Files

Using the Course SQL Script Files

In the following table, we list the hands-on activities in this course along with the script files you can use to complete these activities. You'll find that most of these script files consist of multiple queries. We've added inline comments to each query file to identify where each query corresponds to a step in the hands-on activity. In order to run the scripts properly, you should highlight the appropriate query for a given step, and then execute that query by pressing [Ctrl]E or clicking the Run Query button on the toolbar in SQL Query Analyzer. Don't simply open the script file and execute the entire file. In many cases, executing the entire script file will generate an error.

Hands-on Activity	Script File
Task 2B-1	create_table.sql
Task 2B-2	insert.sql
Task 2B-3	select.sql
Task 2B-4	permissions.sql
Task 2C-1	variables.sql
Apply Your Knowledge 2-1	select_lab.sql
Apply Your Knowledge 2-2	update_delete_lab.sql
Apply Your Knowledge 2-3	deny_revoke_lab.sql
Apply Your Knowledgw 2-5	execute_lab.sql
Apply Your Knowledge 2-6	statement.sql
Task 3B-1	set_options.sql
Apply Your Knowledge 3-1	create_database.sql
Apply Your Knowledge 3-2	filegroup.sql
Apply Your Knowledge 3-3	increase_size.sql
Apply Your Knowledge 4-2	data_types.sql
Apply Your Knowledge 4-3	movie_tables.sql
Apply Your Knowledge 4-4	modify_table.sql
Task 5B-1	pk_movie.sql
Task 5B-2	fk_movie.sql
Task 5B-3	df_movie.sql
Task 5B-4	ck_movie.sql
Apply Your Knowledge 5-2	pk_constraints.sql
Apply Your Knowledge 5-3	fk_constraints.sql
Apply Your Knowledge 5-4	df_constraints.sql
Apply Your Knowledge 5-5	disable_constraint.sql
Task 6B-1	cl_movie.sql
Task 6B-2	sysindexes.sql
Task 6C-1	rebuild.sql

Hands-on Activity	Script File
Task 6C-2	drop_existing.sql
Apply Your Knowledge 6-2	indexes.sql
Apply Your Knowledge 6-3	dropindex.sql
Task 7A-1	cross_joins.sql
Task 7B-1	multiple.sql
Task 7B-2	self_joins.sql
Task 7B-3	union.sql
Task 7B-4	select_into.sql
Apply Your Knowledge 7-1	inner_joins.sql
Apply Your Knowledge 7-2	outer_joins.sql
Apply Your Knowledge 7-3	multi_table.sql
Apply Your Knowledge 7-4	temp_tables.sql
Task 8A-1	single_value.sql
Task 8B-1	insert_data.sql
Task 8B-2	delete_rows.sql
Apply Your Knowledge 8-1	subqueries.sql
Apply Your Knowledge 8-2	correlated.sql
Apply Your Knowledge 8-3	update_queries.sql
Task 9A-1	create_view.sql
Task 9A-3	drop_view.sql
Task 9A-4	indexed_view.sql
Task 9A-4	partitioned_view.sql
Apply Your Knowledge 9-1	join_views.sql
Apply Your Knowledge 9-2	modify_view.sql
Apply Your Knowledge 9-3	view_change.sql
Task 10A-2	extended_proc.sql
Task 10B-1	create_proc.sql
Task 10C-1	input.sql
Task 10C-2	output.sql
Apply Your Knowledge 10-1	createproc_lab.sql
Apply Your Knowledge 10-4	return_codes.sql
Apply Your Knowledge 10-5	custom_errors.sql
Apply Your Knowledge 10-6	showmovie.sql
Task 11A-1	functions.sql
Task 11A-2	groupby.sql
Apply Your Knowledge 11-1	agg_functions_lab.sql
Apply Your Knowledge 11-2	groupbylab.sql
Apply Your Knowledge 11-3	topvalues.sql
Apply Your Knowledge 11-4	scalar.sql
Apply Your Knowledge 11-5	multi-statement.sql
Apply Your Knowledge 11-6	in-line.sql
Task 12A-2	insert-trigger.sql
Task 12A-3	delete-trigger.sql
Task 12A-4	instead-trigger.sql
Apply Your Knowledge 12-1	insert-trigger-lab.sql

Hands-on Activity	Script File
Apply Your Knowledge 12-2	update-trigger.sql
Apply Your Knowledge 12-3	manage-triggers.sql
Task 13A-1	transactions.sql
Task 13B-2	locking.sql
Task 13B-2	customer.sql
Task 13B-3	lock1.sql
Task 13B-3	lock2.sql
Task 13B-4	tablock.sql
Task 13B-4	tablock2.sql
Apply Your Knowledge 13-1	transactions.sql
Task 14A-1	linked.sql
Apply Your Knowledge 14-1	distqueries.sql
Apply Your Knowledge 14-2	linkedprocs.sql
Apply Your Knowledge 14-3	modify.sql
Task 15A-1	querygovernor.sql
Task 15A-2	showplan.sql
Task 15A-3	graphplan.sql
Apply Your Knowledge 15-1	newcustomer.sql
Apply Your Knowledge 15-1	statslab.sql
Apply Your Knowledge 15-2	cleanindex.sql
Apply Your Knowledge 15-2	indexcovers.sql
Apply Your Knowledge 15-3	hints.sql
Apply Your Knowledge 16-1	gen_labcustomer.sql
Apply Your Knowledge 16-1	cleanindexmovie.sql
Apply Your Knowledge 16-1	and_queries.sql
Apply Your Knowledge 16-2	or_queries.sql
Apply Your Knowledge 16-3	invoices.sql
Apply Your Knowledge 16-3	gen_labinvoice.sql
Apply Your Knowledge 16-3	joinlab.sql

Lesson 1 Answers

Task 1A-1 Page 6

1. **You're planning to install Microsoft Access on your client workstations; your clients will use Microsoft Access to work with a database that's currently stored on your Windows 2000 server. Why should you consider implementing Microsoft SQL Server in this environment?**

    I should consider implementing Microsoft SQL Server because it processes my clients' queries on the server itself. If I use only Microsoft Access, my clients' computers must process queries. Implementing SQL Server enables me to reduce network traffic.

2. **You have a client that is considering downsizing a corporate database from a minicomputer to a Microsoft SQL Server on a microcomputer. Your client is concerned about performance. What features of SQL Server should you describe to your client?**

    Microsoft SQL Server is multi-threaded. It also supports a parallel database architecture so that it can take advantage of multiple processors in a microcomputer. The Standard edition of SQL Server can also address up to 2 GB of RAM and 32 TB of hard-disk space.

Task 1A-3 Page 9

1. **Match each SQL Server utility with the types of tasks you can use it to perform.**

_c_	SQL Server Enterprise Manager	a.	Enables you to configure the server's Network-Library.
_h_	Client Network Utility	b.	Use to track activity on your SQL server.
_f_	bcp	c.	Enables you to configure and manage all SQL servers on your network.
_b_	SQL Server Profiler	d.	Use to query SQL Server at the command line.
_d_	osql	e.	Enables you to automate administrative tasks such as backups.
_g_	Index Tuning Wizard	f.	Import text files into a SQL database.
_e_	Database Maintenance Plan Wizard	g.	Use to automate the creation of indexes for a database.
_a_	SQL Server Network Utility	h.	Use to configure the client's Network Library.

Task 1B-1 Page 20

1. **What is a database? What types of objects can a database contain?**

   A database is a collection of related information. A database consists of tables, indexes, views, stored procedures, and triggers.

2. **Compare and contrast clustered and nonclustered indexes.**

   Both clustered and nonclustered indexes enable you to perform faster searches on a table. A clustered index changes the order of the data within a table; the data is stored in the order of the clustered index's key. In contrast, a nonclustered index doesn't change the order of the data within a table. Instead, a nonclustered index contains the sorted key information for each row and a pointer to the original row within the table.

3. **You would like to create a table named bookstores in the pubs database. Assuming that dbo is the owner of the database and that the database is on your current server, what name should you use to identify this table?**

   I should use the partial name pubs.dbo.bookstores.

4. **Why might you create a clustered index on a view?**

   By default, SQL Server doesn't store the results set of a view unless I define a clustered index. If the view is complex and will use a lot of overhead on my SQL server to retrieve its results set, I'll get better performance by creating a clustered index on the view.

9. **Assuming that you want to access the Customers table in your server's Northwind database, what is the table's fully qualified name?**

   sqlserver#.northwind.dbo.customers.

10. **If you're currently working on your server and you're the owner of the Customers table, what partial names could you use to refer to this table?**

    Answers include: customers, northwind..customers.

12. **What is your current database?**

    My current database is pubs. (We queried this database earlier in the lesson.)

13. **In the following space, write a query to view all rows in the Customers table in the Northwind database (given that your current database is pubs).**

    Because I'm not currently using the Northwind database, I must use at least a partial name to view the rows in the Customers table. For example, I could use the following query:

```
SELECT *
FROM northwind..customers
```

Task 1B-2 Page 24

1. In your own words, define the term metadata.

Metadata is data about data. In other words, metadata consists of information about a database such as what tables it contains, the types of columns, and users of the database.

2. What is the difference between the system catalog and a database catalog?

The system catalog consists of information about all databases on the server and is stored in the master database. Each database contains a database catalog. The database catalog consists of system tables containing information about only that database.

4. What is the role of the sysdatabases table in the master database?

SQL Server uses the sysdatabases table to track information about all of the databases on my server.

Task 1B-3 Page 26

12. Based on the relationships between the tables you see in the diagram, which tables will you need to query if you want to see a list of orders, the dates the orders were placed with the Northwind company, and the names of the customers?

I have to query the Customers and Orders tables.

27. You want to display the results of your query in alphabetical order by company name. Within each company's orders, you would like to see the orders sorted by order date. Of the columns in both tables, which columns should you use to perform this sort?

I should sort on the Company Name column first to sort by company name, and then sort on the Order Date column to sort the orders by order date.

Apply Your Knowledge 1-1 Page 31

2. Based on this diagram, which should you use in a query if you want to see a list of the authors' names and the titles of their books?

I should include the authors, titleauthor, and titles tables in my query to see the authors' names and the titles of their books.

3. How are these tables linked together?

The authors table is linked to the titleauthor table by the au_id column. The titleauthor table is then linked to the titles table by the title_id column.

Task 1C-1 Page 34

1. What is the role of the Net-Library?

The Net-Library enables SQL Server to communicate with clients over a variety of network protocols (including TCP/IP, NetBEUI, and NWLink).

2. **What database APIs does SQL Server support?**

SQL Server supports the OLE DB, ODBC, and DB-Library APIs.

Task 1C-2 Page 36

1. **Why are applications sometimes referred to as 2-tier?**

This term indicates that a portion of the application's layers resides on the server, and the remaining layer(s) reside(s) on the client.

2. **Where do the three layers of an application reside in an Intelligent Server (2-Tier) application?**

The Presentation layer resides on the client, and the Business and Data layers reside on the server.

Task 1D-1 Page 37

1. **You're planning to implement SQL Server on your network. As the database developer, what are some of the tasks you will be responsible for?**

Answers might include: Designing, creating, and managing all databases and their objects, including tables, indexes, views, and stored procedures.

2. **If you're the database developer and not the administrator, what are some of the tasks you aren't responsible for?**

Answers might include: Installing and configuring the server; optimizing the server's performance; monitoring the server by using System Monitor; implementing security; backing up and restoring data; managing replication; transferring data between servers; and monitoring the disk space used by databases.

LESSON 1 REVIEW

Topic 1-A

List two features that make SQL Server a powerful database management system.

Answers include: SQL Server supports multiple operating systems including Windows 98, Windows Me, Windows NT Workstation, Windows NT Server, and the Windows 2000 Server family; SQL Server's security, services, and performance monitoring are integrated with Windows 2000; and SQL Server integrates with all of the Microsoft .NET Enterprise Server applications.

Topic 1-B

In the SQL Server environment, what do the terms database and table mean?

The term database refers to a collection of database objects. The term table refers to a database object that contains the actual data. A table consists of rows and columns.

Topic 1-C

What three layers make up the client/server application architecture?

The client/server application architecture consists of the following layers:

- *Presentation—the user interface;*
- *Business—the application's logic and rules for working with the data; and*
- *Data—the actual database itself, its rules for database integrity, and stored procedures.*

Topic 1-D

List and explain the two login security modes you can implement in SQL Server.

SQL Server supports both Windows and Mixed Authentication modes. With the Windows Authentication mode, my users can log in to SQL Server by using only their Windows 2000 user accounts. In contrast, with Mixed Authentication, users can log in to SQL Server by using either a Windows or a SQL Server login account.

LESSON 2 ANSWERS

Task 2A-2 Page 54

1. **Write an osql statement for logging in to your partner's SQL server by using a trusted connection.**

    osql -S sqlserver# -E.

Task 2B-2 Page 60

1. **Write an INSERT statement for inserting your name into the practice table.**

    I could use the following statement to insert my name into the practice table. I don't have to specify the column names because I'm providing a value for all columns in the row.

    ```
    INSERT INTO practice
    VALUES ('last_name', 'first_name')
    ```

Task 2B-3 Page 61

1. **Write a query for viewing all rows in the practice table.**

    ```
    SELECT *
    FROM practice
    ```

3. **Write a query for listing all rows in the practice table with the first and last names concatenated together. Use Name as the column heading in the results set.**

    ```
    SELECT fname+' '+lname AS 'Name'
    FROM practice
    ```

5. Write a query for sorting all rows in the practice table in descending order by last name.

```
SELECT *
FROM practice
ORDER BY lname DESC
```

Apply Your Knowledge 2-1 Page 66

1. **In SQL Query Analyzer, verify that you have the pubs database selected. Use a stored procedure to view the structure of the authors table in the pubs database. What stored procedure did you use?**

   sp_help authors

2. **In the space below, write a SELECT statement that will enable you to view a list of all authors' first names, last names, and telephone numbers. Concatenate the authors' first and last names and use the column heading Name. Execute this query in SQL Query Analyzer.**

   ```
   SELECT au_fname+' '+au_lname AS Name, phone
   FROM authors
   ```

3. **In the space below, write a SELECT statement for viewing all authors who live in California but not in Oakland. Include the authors' first names, last names, city, and state in your results. Concatenate the authors' first and last names, and use Name for the column heading. Concatenate the city and state columns and use City and State for the column heading. Separate the city and state with a comma.**

   ```
   SELECT au_fname+' '+au_lname AS Name,
          city+', '+state AS 'City and State'
   FROM authors
   WHERE state = 'CA' AND city <> 'Oakland'
   ```

   Execute this query in SQL Query Analyzer. How many rows are in your results?

   10.

5. **In the space below, write a query to select all books with a price greater than 20 dollars. Include the title of the book and its price in your results.**

   ```
   SELECT title, price
   FROM titles
   WHERE price > 20
   ```

   Execute the query in SQL Query Analyzer. How many rows are in your results?

   Three.

6. **In the space below, write a query to select all books with a price of at least 15 and no more than 20 dollars, and year-to-date sales greater than 2000 dollars. Include the title of the book, its price, and year-to-date sales in your results.**

   ```
   SELECT title, price, ytd_sales
   FROM titles
   WHERE (price>=15 AND price<=20) AND ytd_sales>2000
   ```

Execute the query in SQL Query Analyzer. How many rows are in your results?

Five.

7. **In the space below, write a query to determine the average price of all of the books in the titles table.**

```
SELECT AVG(price)
FROM titles
```

Execute this query in SQL Query Analyzer. What is the average price?

14.7662

Apply Your Knowledge 2-2 Page 68

1. **In SQL Query Analyzer, use INSERT to add a new row to the practice table. Use Practice for the first name and User for the last name. What query did you use?**

```
INSERT INTO practice
VALUES ('User', 'Practice')
```

2. **Verify that you inserted the row correctly by using the SELECT statement. Write the query you used in the space below.**

```
SELECT *
FROM practice
```

3. **In the space below, write a query to change the Practice User's first name to Joe. Execute this query in SQL Query Analyzer, and then verify your change with the SELECT statement.**

```
UPDATE practice
SET fname = 'Joe'
WHERE lname = 'User'
```

4. **In the space below, write a query to delete the new row. Execute this query in SQL Query Analyzer.**

```
DELETE FROM practice
WHERE lname = 'User'
```

Task 2B-4 Page 71

2. **In the space below, write the SQL statement for giving the public database role the SELECT, INSERT, UPDATE, and DELETE permissions to the practice table in the pubs database.**

```
GRANT SELECT, INSERT, UPDATE, DELETE
ON practice
TO public
```

Apply Your Knowledge 2-3 Page 73

1. **In the space below, write the SQL statement for denying the DELETE permission from the public database role for the practice table. Execute this query in SQL Query Analyzer.**

```
DENY DELETE
ON practice
TO public
```

3. **Write the SQL statement for revoking the UPDATE and INSERT permissions from the public database role for the practice table. Execute the query in SQL Query Analyzer.**

```
REVOKE UPDATE, INSERT
ON practice
FROM public
```

5. **What's the difference between denying and revoking permissions?**

Revoking a user or role's permissions removes the assignment altogether. So, if a user has permissions through another role, the user can inherit those permissions for the object. In contrast, denying permissions prevents the user or role from exercising those permissions whatsoever.

Apply Your Knowledge 2-4 Page 74

2. **Which function can you use to find the highest price of a book in the titles table in the pubs database?**

```
MAX(column_name)
```

3. **How can you use this function to find the highest price of a book in the titles table of the pubs database?**

```
SELECT MAX(price)
FROM titles
```

4. **In SQL Query Analyzer, use this function to find the highest price of a book. How much is the book?**

22.95

5. **In Books Online, by using the Index tab, find the syntax for the osql utility. What command should you use to run osql, find the highest price of a book in the titles table, and close osql?**

```
osql -E -Q "SELECT MAX(price) FROM pubs..titles"
```

7. **Use the Search tab to search for Transact-SQL tips. What are some of the techniques Microsoft recommends you use to improve the performance of queries?**

Answers include: Send multiple statements as a single batch rather than individually; consolidate statements into a single stored procedure rather than separate procedures; and restrict the use of cursors.

Task 2C-1 Page 77

1. **What query should you use to define a variable named @vlname for storing an author's last name and setting its initial value to Hunter?**

```
DECLARE @vlname varchar(20)
SET @vlname = 'Hunter'
```

2. **How can you use this variable to find an author with this last name in the authors table? (Hint: the name of the last name column in the authors table is au_lname.)**

```
SELECT *
FROM authors
WHERE au_lname = @vlname
```

4. **What query could you use to determine how many logins have occurred on your server since its last startup?**

```
SELECT @@CONNECTIONS
```

Apply Your Knowledge 2-5 Page 80

1. **Write a query to execute a dynamic SQL statement for querying the titles table in the pubs database for all books. Have SQL Server display only the title and price columns, and sort the results in descending order by price. Declare variables for storing the database, table, and columns you want to include in the SELECT statement. Verify that your query works by executing it in SQL Query Analyzer.**

```
DECLARE @vdbase varchar(20), @vtable varchar(20), @vcol1 varchar(20), @vcol2 varchar(20)
SET @vdbase = 'pubs'
SET @vtable = 'titles'
SET @vcol1 = 'title'
SET @vcol2 = 'price'
EXECUTE ('USE '+@vdbase+' SELECT '+@vcol1+', '+@vcol2+' FROM ' +@vtable+' ORDER BY PRICE
DESC')
```

2. **Write a query to insert two new rows into the practice table in the pubs database. Add the necessary commands to have SQL Server treat the query as a batch. Execute the query in SQL Query Analyzer.**

```
INSERT INTO practice
VALUES ('LastName1', 'FirstName1')
INSERT INTO practice
VALUES ('LastName2', 'FirstName2')
GO
```

3. **In SQL Query Analyzer, verify that the new rows were inserted into the practice table. Write the query you used in the space below.**

```
SELECT *
FROM practice
```

Apply Your Knowledge 2-6 Page 83

1. **Write a query to list the books in the titles table. Include the title and year-to-date sales columns in the results set; sort the results set in descending order by the year-to-date sales column. Make sure you include a line to use the pubs database. Use the CASE control-of-flow statement to display messages of your choice based on each book's year-to-date sales. Sort the rows in descending order by year-to-date sales. Record your messages in the following table.**

Condition	Message
year-to-date sales <= 200	
year-to-date sales > 200 and <= 1000	
year-to-date sales > 1000 and <= 5000	
year-to-date sales > 5000	

```
USE pubs
SELECT title, 'Year-to-date sales' =
        CASE
      WHEN (ytd_sales<=200)
        THEN 'message'
      WHEN (ytd_sales>200 AND ytd_sales<=1000)
        THEN 'message'
      WHEN (ytd_sales>1000 AND  ytd_sales<=5000)
        THEN 'message'
      WHEN (ytd_sales>5000)
        THEN 'message'
        END
FROM titles
ORDER BY ytd_sales DESC
```

3. **Use SQL Server Books Online to determine how you can add a case for handling null values in the ytd_sales column for the titles table.**

   I should use the following syntax to handle null values:

   WHEN (ytd_sales IS NULL) then 'message'.

Apply Your Knowledge 2-7 Page 85

1. **In the space below, write the command you should use to execute the sales SQL script. As part of the command, log on to your server using Windows Authentication.**

   osql -S sqlserver# -E -i c:\Data\sales.sql

Task 2C-3 Page 89

1. **Which XML format do you think was used in the query to generate the results set you see in the graphic below? How can you tell?**

```
<row CustomerID="ALFKI" ContactName="Maria Anders" />
<row CustomerID="ANATR" ContactName="Ana Trujillo" />
<row CustomerID="ANTON" ContactName="Antonio Moreno" />
<row CustomerID="AROUT" ContactName="Thomas Hardy" />
<row CustomerID="BERGS" ContactName="Christina Berglund" />
<row CustomerID="BLAUS" ContactName="Hanna Moos" />
```

This query used the FOR XML RAW clause to generate this output. I can tell because each element uses only the generic tag of "row."

2. **You've been asked by the Web development team for your company to provide them with data from your company's customers table in XML format. They don't want the data in hierarchical order, but they would like you to include information about the customers table's schema. What FOR XML clause should you use?**

I should use the clause FOR XML RAW, XMLDATA. This clause enables me to provide the Web development team with the customer information in a non-hierarchical format. Using the XMLDATA keyword enables me to also provide the Web development team with the customers table's schema.

LESSON 2 REVIEW

Topic 2-A

In what scenario would you use osql instead of SQL Query Analyzer?

Because osql enables me to both log on to a SQL server and run a script or query with a single command, I would use osql whenever I want to create a batch file to perform tasks on my server.

Topic 2-B

What are the three categories of SQL statements? Give an example of each.

- *Data Definition Language (DDL) statements:* CREATE DATABASE.
- *Data Manipulation Language (DML) statements:* SELECT.
- *Data Control Language (DCL) statements:* GRANT.

Topic 2-C

How can you document SQL scripts?

I can document SQL scripts by using comments. The comments I use can be inline (on the same line as a SQL statement) or within a block. I must precede inline SQL statements by two hyphens (--). I identify a block of comments by preceding them with /* and ending them with */.

LESSON 3 ANSWERS

Task 3A-1 Page 93

1. **You're planning to implement a customer service application within SQL Server. What components do you need to create to support this application? What file extensions will SQL Server use?**

    I must create a database for storing the necessary database objects, such as tables, indexes, views, and stored procedures. This database must contain at least a primary data file with a file extension of .mdf. I also need to create a transaction log for this database. SQL Server stores the transaction log in a file with the extension .ldf. After I've created the database, the database developer must create the database objects needed for the customer service application.

2. **Explain the function of a transaction log.**

    To protect my databases, SQL Server writes all changes to my database to the transaction log on the server's hard disk before it writes these changes to the database itself. After SQL Server writes the transactions to the transaction log, SQL Server can then write the changes to the database on the hard disk. Because SQL Server always writes to the transaction log first, it can roll back or roll forward any incomplete transactions in the event of a server failure.

Task 3A-2 Page 96

1. **How does SQL Server address the storage space on your hard drive?**

    SQL Server uses disk space in 8 KB pages. It allocates disk space in extents. An extent is a contiguous block of eight pages, for a total of 64 KB.

2. **What factors should you consider when estimating the size of a database?**

    Answers might include: The amount of data stored in the database's tables, the size of the transaction log, and anticipated growth.

3. **At what point does SQL Server use a uniform extent to store a table's data?**

    SQL Server uses a mixed extent to store a table until the table's size exceeds more than eight pages. When a table's size exceeds 64 KB (eight pages), SQL Server allocates the table's next extent as a uniform extent.

Task 3A-3 Page 99

1. **You're responsible for designing the server on which your company will use SQL Server and a customer service database. You want to minimize your administrative workload while still providing the best possible performance for your server. What should you do?**

    Because implementing multiple data files and filegroups increases the administrative workload, I should implement either a RAID 5 or RAID 10 disk array. This strategy enables my server to take advantage of reading and writing to multiple disks simultaneously without requiring me to plan and implement multiple files/ filegroups.

Apply Your Knowledge 3-1 Page 102

1. **Given the information in the following table, write the syntax you should use to create this database by using Transact-SQL. Notice that this database contains only one data file and it's stored in the primary filegroup.**

Parameter	Value
Database name	movies
Primary data file's logical name	movies_data
Primary data file's path and file name	C:Program Files\Microsoft SQL Server\mssql\Data\movies_data.mdf
Database initial size	25 MB
Database maximum size	40 MB
Database file growth increment	1 MB
Transaction log logical name	movies_log
Transaction log path and file name	C:Program Files\Microsoft SQL Server\mssql\Data\movies_log.ldf
Transaction log initial size	6 MB
Transaction log maximum size	8 MB
Transaction log file growth increment	1 MB

```
USE master
CREATE DATABASE movies
ON
 PRIMARY (NAME = movies_data,
 FILENAME =
   'C:\Program Files\Microsoft SQL Server\mssql\Data\movies_data.mdf',
 SIZE = 25MB,
 MAXSIZE = 40MB,
 FILEGROWTH = 1MB)
LOG ON
 (NAME = movies_log,
 FILENAME =
   'C:\Program Files\Microsoft SQL Server\mssql\Data\movies_log.ldf',
 SIZE = 6MB,
 MAXSIZE = 8MB,
 FILEGROWTH = 1MB)
```

Apply Your Knowledge 3-2 Page 105

1. **In SQL Query Analyzer, design and execute a query to add a filegroup named Data to the movies database. Write the query you used in the following space.**

```
USE master
ALTER DATABASE movies
ADD FILEGROUP Data
```

2. **Design and execute a query to add a data file with a logical name of movies_data2 and a physical file name of movies_data2.ndf. Create this file with an initial size of 10 MB, and don't specify a maximum size (so that the file growth is unlimited). Add this file to the Data filegroup. Write the query you used in the following space.**

```
ALTER DATABASE movies
ADD FILE
 (NAME = movies_data2,
 FILENAME =
    'C:\Program Files\Microsoft SQL Server\mssql\Data\movies_data2.ndf',
 SIZE = 10 MB)
TO FILEGROUP Data
```

Task 3B-1 Page 108

10. **Write and execute a new query to reconfigure the movies database for multi-user access. Record the query you used in the space below.**

```
ALTER DATABASE movies
SET MULTI_USER
```

11. **Write and execute a query to configure the movies database to use the Simple Recovery Model. Record the query you used in the space below.**

```
ALTER DATABASE movies
SET RECOVERY SIMPLE
```

Task 3B-2 Page 109

5. **In the following space, write a query for displaying information about only the movies database.**

```
sp_helpdb movies
```

Apply Your Knowledge 3-3 Page 112

2. **You want to increase the size of the movies database by increasing the size of the movies_data2 secondary data file from 10 MB to 15 MB. What SQL statement should you use?**

```
USE master
ALTER DATABASE movies
MODIFY FILE
        (NAME = 'movies_data2',
         SIZE = 15MB)
```

5. **You want to increase the maximum size of the movies database's transaction log from 8 MB to 10 MB. What SQL statement should you use?**

```
USE master
ALTER DATABASE movies
MODIFY FILE
        (NAME = 'movies_log',
         MAXSIZE = 10MB)
```

Apply Your Knowledge 3-4 Page 114

2. **What percentage of the movies database's log file is currently in use?**

Approximately 5 percent of the movies database's log file is in use.

Apply Your Knowledge 3-5 Page 117

2. **Record the changes you made to the script in the following space.**

```
USE master
CREATE DATABASE movies
ON
 PRIMARY (NAME = movies_data,
 FILENAME =
   'C:\Program Files\Microsoft SQL Server\mssql\Data\movies_data.mdf',
 SIZE = 25MB,
 MAXSIZE = 40MB,
 FILEGROWTH = 1MB),
 FILEGROUP Data (NAME = movies_data2,
 FILENAME =
   'C:\Program Files\Microsoft SQL Server\mssql\Data\movies_data2.ndf',
 SIZE = 15MB)
LOG ON
 (NAME = movies_log,
 FILENAME =
   'C:\Program Files\Microsoft SQL Server\mssql\Data\movies_log.ldf',
 SIZE = 6MB,
 MAXSIZE = 10MB,
 FILEGROWTH = 1MB)
```

LESSON 3 REVIEW

Topic 3-A

What formula can you use to estimate how big you should make a database's transaction log?

Microsoft recommends that I initially configure the size of a transaction log as 10 to 25 percent of the database size.

Topic 3-B

You would like to make sure that your database's transaction log doesn't use all of the available disk space on your server. How can you prevent this from happening?

I can prevent a transaction log from using all of the available disk space by configuring it with a size limit. I limit the size by specifying the maxsize parameter as part of the CREATE DATABASE statement.

Topic 3-C

What are some of the management tasks you might perform on databases?

Answers might include: Expanding the size of a database or its transaction log; shrinking a database; and deleting a database.

LESSON 4 ANSWERS

Task 4A-1 Page 122

1. **Given the structure of the following tables, what changes should you make to normalize their design?**

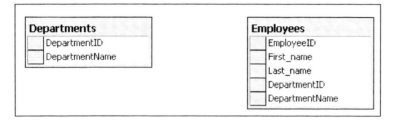

I should remove the DepartmentName column from the Employees table.

2. **As a consultant, you've been asked to analyze the design of a database for a local junior college. One of the complaints the college administration has is that they have students that take more than five classes, but the design of the Students table enables them to enroll students in only five classes. You can see the structure of two of the database's tables in the following graphic. How should you normalize the design of these two tables? Do you need any additional tables to improve the design of this database?**

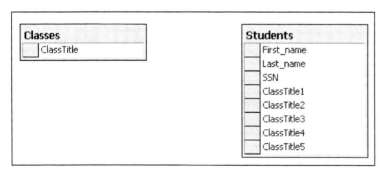

In order to normalize these tables, I should first remove the ClassTitle1, ClassTitle2, ClassTitle3, ClassTitle4, and ClassTitle5 columns from the Students table. Next, I should add an identification number for each class in the Classes table. Finally, I should create an enrollment table. I'll use this table to store a row for each class in which a student is enrolled. This table should have two columns: one for storing the class identification number, and the other for storing the student's social security number.

Apply Your Knowledge 4-1 Page 130

1. What columns and data types will you use in the movie table?

Column Name	Data Type
movie_num	int
title	varchar(40)
category_num	int
rating	varchar(5)
date_purch	smalldatetime
rental_price	smallmoney

2. What columns and data types will you use in the customer table?

Column Name	Data Type
cust_num	int
lname	varchar(20)
fname	varchar(20)
address1	varchar(20)
address2	varchar(20)
city	varchar(20)
state	char(2)
zip	char(10)
phone	varchar(10)
join_date	smalldatetime

3. What columns and data types will you use in the category table?

Column Name	Data Type
category_num	int
description	varchar(20)

4. What columns and data types will you use in the rental table?

Column Name	Data Type
invoice_num	int
cust_num	int
rental_date	smalldatetime
due_date	smalldatetime

5. What columns and data types will you use in the rental_detail table?

Column Name	Data Type
invoice_num	int
line_num	int
movie_num	int
rental_price	smallmoney

6. **What, if any, user-defined data types do you think you should create? Why?**

    Because I reference the movie_num, category_num, cust_num, and invoice_num columns in multiple tables, I might want to create user-defined data types for these columns in order to ensure that they're consistent across all tables. I should use the integer data type for all of these user-defined data types.

Apply Your Knowledge 4-2 Page 132

2. **Write a query for creating a user-defined data type named movie_num based on the integer data type; don't permit nulls in this data type.**

```
sp_addtype movie_num, 'int', 'NOT NULL'
```

4. **In SQL Query Analyzer, create user-defined data types named category_num, cust_num, and invoice_num based on the integer data type; configure these data types to not permit nulls.**

```
EXEC sp_addtype category_num, 'int', 'NOT NULL'

EXEC sp_addtype cust_num, 'int', 'NOT NULL'

EXEC sp_addtype invoice_num, 'int', 'NOT NULL'
```

5. **What query can you use to view a list of the user-defined data types in the movies database?**

    I can use either of the following queries:

```
SELECT *
FROM systypes
```

```
sp_help
```

Apply Your Knowledge 4-3 Page 135

1. **In the following space, write the CREATE TABLE statement for creating the movie table. Don't permit null values in any columns. Use the following table to define the columns and their data types.**

Column Name	Data Type
movie_num	movie_num IDENTITY(100,1)
title	varchar(40)
category_num	category_num
rating	varchar(5)
date_purch	smalldatetime
rental_price	smallmoney

```
CREATE TABLE movie
(movie_num movie_num IDENTITY(100,1),
title varchar(40) NOT NULL,
category_num category_num NOT NULL,
rating varchar(5) NOT NULL,
date_purch smalldatetime NOT NULL,
rental_price smallmoney NOT NULL)
```

3. Customer:

Column Name	Data Type	Permit Nulls?
cust_num	cust_num IDENTITY(300,1)	No
lname	varchar(20)	No
fname	varchar(20)	No
address1	varchar(30)	Yes
address2	varchar(20)	Yes
city	varchar(20)	Yes
state	char(2)	Yes
zip	char(10)	Yes
phone	varchar(10)	No
join_date	smalldatetime	No

```
CREATE TABLE customer
(cust_num cust_num IDENTITY(300,1),
lname varchar(20) NOT NULL,
fname varchar(20) NOT NULL,
address1 varchar(30),
address2 varchar(20),
city varchar(20),
state char(2),
phone varchar(10) NOT NULL,
join_date smalldatetime)
```

Category:

Column Name	Data Type	Permit Nulls?
category_num	category_num IDENTITY(1,1)	No
description	varchar(20)	No

```
CREATE TABLE category
category_num category_num IDENTITY(1,1),
description varchar(20) NOT NULL)
```

Rental:

Column Name	Data Type	Permit Nulls?
Invoice_num	invoice_num IDENTITY(1,1)	No
cust_num	cust_num	No
rental_date	smalldatetime	No
due_date	smalldatetime	No

```
CREATE TABLE rental
(invoice_num invoice_num IDENTITY(1,1),
cust_num cust_num NOT NULL,
rental_date smalldatetime NOT NULL,
due_date smalldatetime NOT NULL)
```

Rental_detail:

Column Name	Data Type	Permit Nulls?
invoice_num	invoice_num	No
line_num	int	No
movie_num	movie_num	No
rental_price	smallmoney	No

```
CREATE TABLE rental_detail
(invoice_num invoice_num NOT NULL,
line_num int NOT NULL,
movie_num movie_num NOT NULL,
rental_price smallmoney NOT NULL)
```

4. **Verify the structure of all tables by using the `sp_help` stored procedure.**

```
EXEC sp_help 'movie'
EXEC sp_help 'customer'
EXEC sp_help 'category'
EXEC sp_help 'rental'
EXEC sp_help 'rental_detail'
```

Apply Your Knowledge 4-4 Page 138

1. **In the space below, write a SQL statement for adding a column named phone with a data type of varchar(15) to the practice table.**

```
ALTER TABLE practice
ADD phone varchar(15)
```

3. **Execute a query to verify the structure of the table.**

```
sp_help 'practice'
```

4. **Write a query to add a column named description with a data type of varchar(20) to the practice table. Don't permit null values in this column.**

```
ALTER TABLE practice
ADD description varchar(20) NOT NULL
```

5. **Execute this query in SQL Query Analyzer. What must you do to fix this query so that it will run properly?**

I must add a default value for the description column. SQL Server requires that I include a default value whenever I configure a column to not permit nulls by using the ALTER TABLE statement.

6. **Revise the query you wrote in step 4 so that it will run properly. If necessary, refer to Books Online to find the correct syntax. Write the revised query in the space below.**

```
ALTER TABLE practice
ADD description varchar(20) NOT NULL DEFAULT 'test'
```

8. **Write a SQL statement for dropping the column named phone from the practice table.**

```
ALTER TABLE practice
DROP COLUMN phone
```

Apply Your Knowledge 4-5 Page 139

1. **Write a query for deleting the practice table.**

   `DROP TABLE practice`

LESSON 4 REVIEW

Topic 4-A

List the parameters you must configure when you add a column to a table.

For each column in the table, I must define a column name, data type, size, and whether the column can accept null values. Depending on the data type I choose, I might not be required to specify a size for the column.

Topic 4-B

You want to add a column named comments with a data type of text to the customer table in the movies database. What query should you use?

```
ALTER TABLE customer
ADD comments text
```

LESSON 5 ANSWERS

Apply Your Knowledge 5-1 Page 145

1. **Given the structure of the movie table, what types of constraints do you think you should use on the movie table?**

Column Name	Data Type	Permit Nulls?
movie_num	movie_num IDENTITY(100,1)	No
title	varchar(40)	No
category_num	category_num	No
rating	varchar(5)	No
date_purch	smalldatetime	Yes
rental_price	smallmoney	No

I should configure the movie_num column as the table's primary key. I should also configure a foreign key constraint between the category_num column in the movie table and the same column in the category table. Finally, I should consider creating a check constraint on the rating column and specify the permitted values as G, PG, R, NC17, and NR. I could also create a default constraint on the date_purch column of GETDATE( ).

2. **What types of constraints do you think you should use on the customer table?**

Column Name	Data Type	Permit Nulls?
cust_num	cust_num IDENTITY(300,1)	No
lname	varchar(20)	No
fname	varchar(20)	No
address1	varchar(20)	Yes
address2	varchar(20)	Yes
city	varchar(20)	Yes
state	char(2)	Yes
zip	char(10)	Yes
phone	varchar(10)	No
join_date	smalldatetime	No

I should configure the cust_num column as the table's primary key. In addition, I could define a default constraint of GETDATE( ) on the join_date column.

3. **What types of constraints do you think you should configure on the category table?**

Column Name	Data Type	Permit Nulls?
category_num	category_num IDENTITY(1,1)	No
description	varchar(20)	No

I should configure the category table with a primary key constraint on the category_num column.

4. **What types of constraints do you think you should configure on the rental table?**

Column Name	Data Type	Permit Nulls?
invoice_num	invoice_num IDENTITY(1,1)	No
cust_num	cust_num	No
rental_date	smalldatetime	No
due_date	smalldatetime	No

I should configure a primary key constraint on the invoice_num column and a foreign key constraint between the cust_num columns in the rental table and the customer table. In addition, I might want to set a default constraint on rental_date of the current date by using the GETDATE( ) function. I could also create a default constraint on the due_date column based on my company's rental terms. For example, if my company rents movies for two days, I could configure the due_date column with a default constraint of GETDATE()+2. Another constraint I could implement is a check constraint to make sure that the value in the due_date column is after the rental_date.

5. What types of constraints do you think you should configure on the rental detail table?

Column Name	Data Type	Permit Nulls?
invoice_num	invoice_num	No
line_num	int	No
movie_num	movie_num	No
rental_price	smallmoney	No

I should configure a foreign key constraint between the invoice_num columns in the rental_detail and rental tables. I should also configure a foreign key constraint between the movie_num columns in the rental_detail and movie tables. Finally, I could set a default constraint on the rental_price column (I would typically use programming such as through a trigger to look up the rental price in the movie table and insert it into the rental_detail table).

The rental_detail table doesn't need a primary key column because each row doesn't have a unique number assigned to it. Instead, each row is linked to the rental table by the invoice_num column. In addition, I can have multiple rows for each invoice number.

Apply Your Knowledge 5-2 Page 151

1. Record the query you used in the space below.

```
ALTER TABLE customer
ADD CONSTRAINT PK_customer
PRIMARY KEY NONCLUSTERED (cust_num)
```

2. Record your query below.

```
ALTER TABLE category
ADD CONSTRAINT PK_category
PRIMARY KEY NONCLUSTERED (category_num)
```

3. Record your query below.

```
ALTER TABLE rental
ADD CONSTRAINT PK_rental
PRIMARY KEY NONCLUSTERED (invoice_num)
```

4. Use `sp_helpconstraint` along with each table name to verify your tables' primary keys.

```
EXEC sp_helpconstraint 'customer'
EXEC sp_helpconstraint 'category'
EXEC sp_helpconstraint 'rental'
```

Task 5B-2 Page 154

2. How will SQL Server handle cascading updates and deletes for the FK_movie constraint?

SQL Server won't permit me to update or delete a row from the category table if it has corresponding rows in the movie table. By default, SQL Server configures a foreign key constraint to not support cascading referential integrity unless I specify otherwise.

Apply Your Knowledge 5-3 Page 155

1. **Write the query you use in the space below.**

```
ALTER TABLE rental
ADD CONSTRAINT FK_rental
FOREIGN KEY (cust_num)
REFERENCES customer(cust_num)
```

2. **Write your query in the space below.**

```
ALTER TABLE rental_detail
ADD CONSTRAINT FK_detail_invoice
FOREIGN KEY (invoice_num)
REFERENCES rental(invoice_num)
ON DELETE CASCADE
```

3. **Write your query below.**

```
ALTER TABLE rental_detail
ADD CONSTRAINT FK_detail_movie
FOREIGN KEY (movie_num)
REFERENCES movie(movie_num)
```

Apply Your Knowledge 5-4 Page 157

1. **Write your query below.**

```
ALTER TABLE customer
ADD CONSTRAINT DF_customer_join_date
DEFAULT GETDATE() FOR join_date
```

2. **Write your queries in the following space.**

```
ALTER TABLE rental
ADD CONSTRAINT DF_rental_rental_date
DEFAULT GETDATE() FOR rental_date
```

```
ALTER TABLE rental
ADD CONSTRAINT DF_rental_due_date
DEFAULT GETDATE()+2 FOR due_date
```

Task 5B-4 Page 159

3. **In the space below, write a query for adding a check constraint to the rental table to make sure that the value in the due_date column is equal to or later than that of the rental_date column.**

```
ALTER TABLE rental
ADD CONSTRAINT CK_rental
CHECK (due_date >= rental_date)
```

Task 5B-5 Page 161

7. **In the space below, write a SQL query for disabling checking of the primary key to foreign key relationship between the authors and titleauthor tables.**

```
ALTER TABLE titleauthor
NOCHECK CONSTRAINT FK__titleauth__au_id__05419C6AF
```

12. **In the following space, write a query to enable constraint checking on the titleauthor table:**

```
ALTER TABLE titleauthor
CHECK CONSTRAINT FK__titleauth__au_id__0519C6AF
```

Apply Your Knowledge 5-5 Page 164

1. **Given the constraints on the tables in the movies database, in what order do you think you should import data into those tables?**

    Category, movie, customer, rental, rental_detail.

5. **Based on the data in the movie and category tables, write a query that will conflict with the foreign key constraint FK_movie. (If necessary, use** `sp_helpconstraint 'movie'` **to view the properties of this constraint.) Execute this query to verify that you receive an error. Write your query in the following space.**

    Answers will vary. Here's one query I can use:

```
UPDATE movie
SET category_num = 25
WHERE movie_num = 150
```

LESSON 5 REVIEW

Topic 5-A

Explain the difference between declarative data integrity and procedural data integrity.

With declarative data integrity, I use constraints to make sure that my users input valid data into your tables. Constraints are implemented as part of the tables themselves. With procedural data integrity, I validate data by using programs such as stored procedures and triggers to make sure that my users enter valid data.

Topic 5-B

List two differences between the primary key and unique constraints.

Answers might include: I can define only one primary key per table, but I can define multiple unique constraints per table. I can't configure primary key columns to permit nulls, whereas I can configure unique constraint columns to permit nulls.

LESSON 6 ANSWERS

Task 6A-1 Page 172

1. **Name two advantages to implementing a clustered index.**

   Answers might include: A clustered index enables SQL Server to store the rows of the table in order by the index key, so data retrieval is much faster because the rows are already stored in order; the query processor is optimized when it uses a clustered index; SQL Server requires fewer I/O operations to retrieve data from a table on which I've defined a clustered index than from a heap.

2. **On what type of columns should you base a clustered index?**

   I should base a clustered index on columns containing values for which I would like SQL Server to return a group of rows rather than only one row. For example, it's better to base a clustered index on customer names rather than customer account numbers.

3. **Explain the B-tree architecture for indexing.**

   The B-tree architecture consists of a root level page, one or more levels of non-leaf level pages, and leaf-level pages. SQL Server uses each level of the index to narrow down its search until it can retrieve the data.

Apply Your Knowledge 6-1 Page 174

1. **The movies database and its associated programs will be used for online transaction processing. What types of reports do you think you will generate from its tables? For example, you might want to print a report that lists all of the rented movies that are due back in today. When you list a report, indicate which table (or tables) you will use to generate that report.**

   Answers might include:
   - *A list of movies by category (comedy, drama, etc.)—tables: movie and category.*
   - *A list of movies by title—table: movie.*
   - *A list of customers sorted by name—table: customer.*
   - *A list of customers sorted by zip code—table: customer.*
   - *Rentals per customer—tables: customer, rental, rental_detail, and movie.*
   - *Rentals by area of the city (ZIP code)—tables: customer, rental, rental_detail, and movie.*
   - *Rentals by movie category—tables: rental, rental_detail, movie, and category.*

2. **Do you think you need any additional indexes? If so, list the table, the columns you will include in the index, indicate whether the index will be clustered or nonclustered, and explain why you need it. For example, you might want to create a clustered index on the title column of the movie table. This is because you might want to be able to retrieve a list of all movie numbers for a particular title—and clustered indexes are optimized for retrieving a group of rows.**

   I should create clustered indexes whenever I think I will perform frequent queries that retrieve a group of rows. So, at a minimum, I should create the following clustered indexes:
   - *Customer—I should create a clustered index on either the ZIP code or lname plus fname columns. I should choose between these two keys based on which query I think I will perform more often: a search of the customer table by name or by ZIP code. Given that I should try to keep my clustered index key as*

small as possible, I should probably create a clustered index on the ZIP code column (and create a nonclustered index on the lname and fname columns). The ZIP code column is a better choice because I will use it to return a range of rows. In contrast, an index on the lname and fname columns will typically be used to return only a single row.

- *Movie—I should consider creating a clustered index on the title column. Because the movie table contains multiple copies of the popular movies, I can use this index to retrieve a list of all of the copies of a particular title.*

- *Rental—Clustered index on the cust_num column. Use this index to find all invoices on file for a particular customer. (Each customer could have more than one invoice on file.)*

- *Rental_detail—Clustered index on the invoice_num column. Use this index to find the line item details for each invoice. (Each rental invoice might have multiple line items.)*

I could also create nonclustered indexes on the foreign key columns in order to speed up table joins between the foreign key and primary key tables. At a minimum, I should create the following indexes:

- *Customer—Nonclustered index on lname and fname. I will use this index to retrieve customer lists in alphabetical order.*

- *Movie—Nonclustered index on category_num. I should create this index because the category_num column is a foreign key linked to the primary key column in the category table. This index will help me speed up table joins.*

- *Rental_detail—Nonclustered index on movie_num. I should create this index because the movie_num column is a foreign key linked to the primary key column in the movie table.*

Apply Your Knowledge 6-2 Page 179

1. **In SQL Query Analyzer, create a clustered index on the customer table based on the ZIP code column. Name the index CL_zip. Write your query in the following space.**

```
CREATE CLUSTERED INDEX CL_zip
ON customer (zip)
```

2. **On the customer table, create a nonclustered composite index based on the lname and fname columns. Name the index NC_lname_fname. Write your query here.**

```
CREATE NONCLUSTERED INDEX NC_lname_fname
ON customer (lname, fname)
```

3. **On the rental table, create a clustered index based on the cust_num column. Name the index CL_cust_num. Write your query in the following space.**

```
CREATE CLUSTERED INDEX CL_cust_num
ON rental (cust_num)
```

4. **On the rental_detail table, create a clustered index on the invoice_num column. Name the index CL_invoice_num. Record your query here.**

```
CREATE CLUSTERED INDEX CL_invoice_num
ON rental_detail (invoice_num)
```

5. **On the rental_detail table, create a nonclustered index on the movie_num column. Name the index NC_movie_num. Write your query here.**

```
CREATE NONCLUSTERED INDEX NC_movie_num
ON rental_detail (movie_num)
```

6. **On the movie table, create a nonclustered index on the category_num column. Name the index NC_category_num.**

```
CREATE NONCLUSTERED INDEX NC_category_num
ON movie (category_num)
```

Apply Your Knowledge 6-3 Page 181

1. **In SQL Query Analyzer, attempt to drop the index named PK_movie from the movie table. Record the query you used and its results in the following space.**

   I used the query DROP INDEX movie.pk_movie. *Although I can execute this query, SQL Server doesn't permit me to drop an index based on a primary key by using the* DROP INDEX *statement. Instead, I must drop the primary key constraint, and SQL Server will then drop the index as well.*

2. **Drop the clustered index named CL_title from the movie table. Record your query here.**

```
DROP INDEX movie.CL_title
```

3. **Re-create the index named CL_title. (This index is based on the title column of the movie table.)**

```
CREATE CLUSTERED INDEX CL_title
ON movie(title)
```

Task 6B-2 Page 182

3. **Look at the indid column for the category table. What types of indexes have you defined on the category table? How can you tell?**

   I've defined only nonclustered indexes for this table. I can tell because the first row for the category table has an indid value of 0, which means that the table is a heap. In addition, the two other indexes for the category table have indid values of 2 and 3, which means that they are nonclustered indexes.

4. **What types of indexes have you defined on the movie table? What are the names of the indexes?**

   I've defined both a clustered index (CL_title) and two nonclustered indexes (PK_movie, NC_category_num).

Task 6C-1 Page 186

4. **How full are the CL_title index's pages? What statistic do you use to find this information?**

   The CL_title index's pages are 97.62% full. I find this information by looking at the Avg. Page Density (Full) statistic.

9. **The Scan Density [Best Count: Actual Count] for the CL_title index (and thus the movie table) is now 50 percent. Is this a problem?**

   It depends on the role of the table. If it's part of an OLTP system, having a lower scan density (such as 50 percent) means that SQL Server won't have to split pages as often as I add data to the table. In this scenario, a lower scan density helps improve performance. On the other hand, if the table's part of a DSS system, having a lower scan density means that SQL Server must do more work to retrieve the table's pages. In a DSS system, a lower scan density hurts performance.

Apply Your Knowledge 6-4 Page 193

2. **When the Index Tuning Wizard is done, observe the recommended indexes for the movies database. Did the wizard recommend any new indexes? If so, what performance increase can you expect as a result?**

    Given the queries I used in the previous task and the current indexes on my tables, the Index Tuning Wizard doesn't recommend any new indexes. I see that each of the recommended indexes the Index Tuning Wizard suggested already exists in my database.

Task 6C-4 Page 196

5. **Use the results set you see for the CL_title index to complete the following table.**

Statistic	Value
Total Number of Rows in Table	156
Total Number of Rows Sampled	156
Density	0.0
All Density	.008

Given the information you recorded in the table, how selective is this index? Is it more or less selective then the PK_movie index?

This index is selective because it has a value that's pretty close to zero. It isn't as selective as the PK_movie index, which had an All Density value of .006.

10. **Use the results set you see for the NC_state index to complete the following table.**

Statistic	Value
Total Number of Rows in Table	23
Total Number of Rows Sampled	23
Density	0.0
All Density for State column	0.125

Given the information you recorded in the table, how selective is this index? Should you keep this index? Why or why not?

This index isn't highly selective because it has a value that's greater than 0.10. I probably shouldn't keep this index because it isn't highly selective, which means it might be faster if SQL Server retrieved results for queries based on the state column by performing a table scan.

Lesson 6 Review

Topic 6-A

In what scenario should you choose to implement a nonclustered index? How about a clustered index?

I should implement nonclustered indexes whenever I want to optimize queries that retrieve only a few number of rows or even a single row from a table. I should implement a clustered index whenever I want to optimize queries that retrieve multiple rows from a table.

Topic 6-B

What is the role of the fill factor in an index? How should you configure the fill factor for OLTP and DSS environments?

SQL Server uses the fill factor to determine how full to fill the index pages when it creates an index. If my database will be used in an OLTP environment, I should use a lower fill factor to allow room for growth. If my database will be used in a DSS environment, I should use a higher fill factor because my system will have few changes to the data.

Topic 6-C

What is the easiest way for you to create and maintain the index statistics for all of a database's indexes?

The easiest way to create and maintain index statistics for a database's indexes is to enable both the Auto Create Statistics and Auto Update Statistics options for a database.

Lesson 7 Answers

Apply Your Knowledge 7-1 Page 202

2. **In SQL Query Analyzer, select the movies database. Design and execute a query to display the invoice number, rental date, and the customer's first and last names for all of the movie rentals. Sort the results by the rental date column. Hint: You can use `CONVERT(CHAR(10), rental_date, 101)` to display the rental date in the format month/day/year. You can also concatenate the customer's first and last name columns. Record your query in the following space.**

```
USE movies
GO
SELECT r.invoice_num, CONVERT(CHAR(10), r.rental_date, 101) AS 'rental date', c.fname+'
'+c.lname as 'name'
FROM rental AS r INNER JOIN customer AS c
ON r.cust_num = c.cust_num
ORDER BY r.rental_date
```

3. **What query did you use?**

```
SELECT r.invoice_num, r.rental_date, rd.line_num, rd.movie_num
FROM rental AS r INNER JOIN rental_detail AS rd
ON r.invoice_num = rd.invoice_num
ORDER BY r.invoice_num
```

4. **Design and execute a query to list the titles and the category descriptions for all movies with a rating of PG. List each movie only once, and sort the list of titles in alphabetical order. Record your query below.**

```
SELECT DISTINCT m.title, c.description
FROM movie AS m INNER JOIN category AS c
ON m.category_num = c.category_num
WHERE m.rating = 'PG'
ORDER BY m.title
```

How many PG titles does your store have?

Twenty-five.

5. **Refer to the database diagram for the pubs database. Design and execute a query to display the store name and their discount percentage. Sort the results by the store name column. (Note: This query returns only one row in the results set.) What query did you use?**

```
USE pubs
GO
SELECT s.stor_name, d.discount
FROM stores AS s INNER JOIN discounts AS d
ON s.stor_id = d.stor_id
ORDER BY s.stor_name
```

6. Record your query below.

```
USE pubs
GO
SELECT t.title, r.royalty
FROM titles AS t INNER JOIN roysched  AS r
ON t.title_id = r.title_id
WHERE r.royalty > 20
ORDER BY r.royalty DESC
```

How many titles have royalty percentages greater than 20 percent?

Eleven.

Apply Your Knowledge 7-2 Page 204

1. **In SQL Query Analyzer, select the movies database. Design and execute a query to display category, description, and movie title. Include all categories whether the store has movies in a category or not. Sort the results by category description. What query did you use?**

```
USE movies
SELECT c.category_num, c.description, m.title
FROM category AS c LEFT OUTER JOIN movie AS m
ON c.category_num = m.category_num
ORDER BY c.description
```

For which movie categories do you not find any movies in stock?

Biography, documentary, fantasy, and musical.

2. **Design and execute a query to display a list of all movies and the invoices (if any) on which they have been rented. Include the movie's title and the invoice number in the results set. Sort the results by movie title. Write your query below.**

```
USE movies
SELECT m.title, r.invoice_num
FROM movie AS m LEFT OUTER JOIN rental_detail AS r
ON m.movie_num = r.movie_num
ORDER BY m.title
```

3. **Based on the pubs database, design and execute a query to list publishers' names and titles of books. Display all publishers in the results set whether they have published a book or not. Sort the results by publisher name. (Use a right outer join.) What query did you use?**

```
USE pubs
SELECT p.pub_name, t.title
FROM titles AS  t RIGHT OUTER JOIN publishers AS p
ON t.pub_id = p.pub_id
ORDER BY p.pub_name
```

How many publishers do not have any published titles yet?

Five.

4. Using the pubs database, design and execute a query to display a list of all stores and any discounts on file. Include the store name and their discount (if any) in the results. Sort the results by store name. What query did you use?

```
USE pubs
SELECT s.stor_name, d.discount
FROM stores AS s LEFT OUTER JOIN discounts AS d
ON s.stor_id = d.stor_id
ORDER BY s.stor_name
```

Task 7A-1 Page 205

3. How many rows are in the results set?

    2,184.

4. When would you use a cross join?

    I might use a cross join to generate a large amount of data for a table.

Apply Your Knowledge 7-3 Page 207

1. In SQL Query Analyzer, design and execute a query to display movie rentals by category. Include the title and category description in the results. Sort the results by the category description. (You should see 525 rows in the results set.) What query did you use?

```
USE movies
GO
SELECT m.title, c.description
FROM rental_detail AS rd INNER JOIN movie AS m
ON rd.movie_num = m.movie_num
INNER JOIN category AS c
ON m.category_num = c.category_num
ORDER BY c.description
```

2. Design and execute a query to display a list of movies rented by each customer. Include the customer's first and last names and the movie titles in the results. Sort the results by customer name. (Hint: This query requires that you join four tables together. You should see 525 rows in the results set.) What query did you use?

```
USE movies
SELECT c.fname+' '+c.lname AS 'Customer Name', m.title
FROM customer AS c INNER JOIN rental AS r
ON c.cust_num = r.cust_num
INNER JOIN rental_detail AS rd
ON r.invoice_num = rd.invoice_num
INNER JOIN movie AS m
ON rd.movie_num = m.movie_num
ORDER BY c.lname, c.fname
```

3. **Based on the pubs database, design and execute a query to display a list of titles and their authors. Include each author's first and last names and the book titles in the results. Sort the results by name. (You should see 25 rows in the results set.) What query did you use?**

```
USE pubs
GO
SELECT a.au_fname+'  '+a.au_lname AS 'Author Name', t.title
FROM authors AS a INNER JOIN titleauthor AS ta
ON a.au_id = ta.au_id
INNER JOIN titles AS t
ON ta.title_id = t.title_id
ORDER BY a.au_lname, a.au_fname
```

Task 7B-4 Page 211

5. **How many rows do you have in the G_movie table?**

Twenty-one.

Apply Your Knowledge 7-4 Page 212

1. **Design and execute a query for creating a local temporary table for storing all movies with a rating of PG. Use an appropriate name for a local temporary table. Include the Title and Movie Number columns in the table. What query did you use?**

```
SELECT title AS title, movie_num AS movie_num
INTO #PG_movie
FROM movie
WHERE rating = 'PG'
```

2. **Write a query to view all rows of your new table. Execute this query in SQL Query Analyzer.**

```
SELECT *
FROM #PG_movie
```

4. **Can you query your new table in this second connection? (Execute SELECT * FROM #PG_movie.) Why or why not?**

I can't query the new table in this second connection because local temporary tables are available only in the current session. When I open a second Query window, I establish a new session with the server.

6. **Design and execute a query for creating a global temporary table for storing all movies with a rating of "R." Use an appropriate name for a global temporary table. Include the title and movie number columns in the table. Execute this query. What query did you use?**

```
SELECT title AS title, movie_num AS movie_num
INTO ##R_movie
FROM movie
WHERE rating = 'R'
```

7. **Write a query to view all rows of your new table. Execute this query in SQL Query Analyzer. Record your query below.**

```
SELECT *
FROM ##R_movie
```

8. **Open a second connection to your server. Can you query your new table? Why or why not?**

I can query the new table because global temporary tables are available to all current user sessions.

LESSON 7 REVIEW

Topic 7-A

What types of joins can you use to query multiple tables? When would you use each type?

I can use three types of joins: inner, outer, and cross. I should use an inner join when I want to link two tables together such that the results set will contain only those rows with matching values in both tables. I use an outer when I want to link two tables together, but I want the results set to contain not only the rows that match the join condition, but also any unmatched rows from one or the other of the tables. I should use a cross join when I want to create a results set that consists of a combination of every row in the first table with every row in the second table. I can use cross joins to generate data for testing purposes.

Topic 7-B

Why might you use the UNION keyword in a query? What are some of the restrictions to using the UNION keyword?

I should use the UNION keyword whenever I want to combine the results sets from multiple SELECT statements into a single results set. In order to use the UNION keyword, the tables referenced in each of the SELECT statements must have similar data types, the same number of columns, and the same column order in each line of the query.

LESSON 8 ANSWERS

Task 8A-1 Page 217

4. **How many movies have prices that are less than the average price?**

Seventy-eight.

Apply Your Knowledge 8-1 Page 219

1. **By using the pubs database, design and execute a query to list the title and royalty percentage of the book(s) with the highest royalty percentage. What query did you use?**

```
USE pubs
SELECT title, royalty
FROM titles
WHERE royalty = (SELECT MAX(royalty)
                     FROM titles)
```

    How many books are in your results set?

    I have two titles with a royalty percentage of 24 percent: You Can Combat Computer Stress and The Gourmet Microwave.

2. **Based on the pubs database, design and execute a query to list all books with sales in the sales table. Record your query in the following space.**

```
SELECT title
FROM titles
WHERE title_id IN (SELECT title_id
                       FROM sales)
```

    How many books have sales on file?

    A total of 16 books have sales on file.

3. **What query could you use to achieve the same results as step 2 by using a JOIN statement instead of a nested subquery? Execute this query in SQL Query Analyzer to verify that you get the same results. Write your query in the following space.**

```
SELECT DISTINCT title
FROM titles RIGHT OUTER JOIN sales
ON titles.title_id = sales.title_id
```

4. **Why should you consider using a table join instead of a subquery when they both generate the same results set?**

    I should use a table join whenever possible because SQL Server can retrieve a join's results set more efficiently than that of a subquery.

Apply Your Knowledge 8-2 Page 221

1. **In SQL Query Analyzer, design and execute a correlated subquery with the EXISTS keyword. By using the movies database, write a query that displays a list of customer names and numbers if they have rented any movies. Sort the results by customer name. What query did you use?**

```
USE movies
GO
SELECT fname+'  '+lname, cust_num
FROM customer AS c
WHERE EXISTS (SELECT *
                 FROM rental AS r
                 WHERE c.cust_num = r.cust_num)
ORDER BY c.lname, c.fname
```

How many customers have rented movies?

204 customers have rented movies.

2. **Design and execute a correlated subquery to display a list of all customers who rented movies between 8/1/99 and 8/31/99. What query did you use?**

```
SELECT fname+'  '+lname, cust_num
FROM customer AS c
WHERE EXISTS (SELECT *
              FROM rental AS r
              WHERE c.cust_num = r.cust_num
              AND (rental_date >= '8/1/99'
                   AND rental_date <= '8/31/99'))
ORDER BY c.lname, c.fname
```

How many customers are on the list?

48 customers rented movies in the month of 8/99.

Task 8B-2 Page 224

2. **How many rows does this query delete?**

Twenty-three.

Apply Your Knowledge 8-3 Page 225

1. **In SQL Query Analyzer, design and execute a query to list the titles and rental prices of any movies that haven't rented. Note: The movie table contains more than one copy of many of the movies. Write your query so that it will return a list of only those movies for which none of the copies have rented. (Hint: You'll need to use a subquery that contains an outer join between the movie and rental_detail tables.) You'll find that only one movie hasn't rented. What query did you use?**

```
USE movies
GO
SELECT title, rental_price
FROM movie
WHERE title NOT IN (SELECT m.title
                    FROM movie AS m
                    RIGHT JOIN rental_detail AS rd
                    ON  m.movie_num = rd.movie_num)
```

2. **Design and execute a query to reduce the price of any movie by 20 percent if it hasn't rented. (Remember, you want to reduce the price only if all copies of a movie have not rented. Don't reduce the price of a movie if some of its copies have rented.) Note: Because the smallmoney data type supports four decimal places, SQL Server will calculate the decrease in the rental price column to four digits of precision. You can round the rental price to two digits of precision by using ROUND(rental_price * .8, 2) in your formula. What query did you use?**

```
UPDATE movie
SET rental_price = ROUND(rental_price * .8, 2)
WHERE title NOT IN (SELECT m.title
                    FROM movie AS m
                    RIGHT JOIN rental_detail AS rd
                    ON  m.movie_num = rd.movie_num)
```

3. **Repeat the query you wrote in step 1 to verify that you've lowered the prices.**

```
SELECT title, rental_price
FROM movie
WHERE title NOT IN (SELECT m.title
                    FROM movie AS m
                    RIGHT JOIN rental_detail AS rd
                    ON  m.movie_num = rd.movie_num)
```

4. **Design and execute a query to list the titles of all movies that have rented and their rental price even if one of the copies of a specific title hasn't rented. What query did you use?**

```
SELECT title, rental_price
FROM movie
WHERE title IN (SELECT m.title
                FROM movie AS m
                RIGHT JOIN rental_detail AS rd
                ON  m.movie_num = rd.movie_num)
```

5. **Design and execute a query to increase the price of all copies of movies that have rented by 10 percent. Record your query below.**

```
UPDATE movie
SET rental_price = ROUND(rental_price * 1.1, 2)
WHERE movie.movie_num IN (SELECT movie_num
                          FROM rental_detail)
```

6. **Repeat the query you wrote in step 4 to verify that you've increased the prices of the movies that have rented.**

```
SELECT title, rental_price
FROM movie
WHERE title IN (SELECT m.title
                FROM movie AS m
                RIGHT JOIN rental_detail AS rd
                ON  m.movie_num = rd.movie_num)
```

LESSON 8 REVIEW

Topic 8-A

What are some of the reasons why you might choose to use subqueries instead of table joins?

I can use subqueries as a technique to break up complex queries into their separate components. I can then make sure each of the components works before trying to execute the complex query as a whole. In addition, subqueries enable me to query tables based on the results of a query. For example, if I want to list all of the movies in the movie table with rental prices that are greater than the average rental price—and I don't know the average rental price—I can use the following subquery to find the answer:

```
SELECT title, rental_price
FROM movie
WHERE rental_price > (SELECT AVG(rental_price)
                      FROM movie)
```

Topic 8-B

In what scenario might you use the `INSERT...SELECT` statement instead of only the `INSERT` statement?

I should use the `INSERT...SELECT` statement whenever I want to insert a number of rows into a table based on specific values. If I use the `INSERT` statement by itself, I must write an `INSERT` statement for each row I want to insert into a table.

LESSON 9 ANSWERS

Apply Your Knowledge 9-1 Page 234

1. **In the movies database, create a view that contains the title and category number of each movie with an 'R' rating. Name the view R_MovieView. What query did you use?**

```
USE movies
GO
CREATE VIEW dbo.R_MovieView
AS
SELECT title, category_num
FROM movie
WHERE rating = 'R'
```

2. **Use the SELECT statement to display the rows in the view. Record your query here.**

```
SELECT *
FROM R_MovieView
```

3. In the movies database, create a view that contains the movie_num, title, and category description columns. Name the view MovieCategoryView. What query did you use?

```
CREATE VIEW dbo.MovieCategoryView
AS
SELECT m.movie_num, m.title, c.description
FROM movie AS m JOIN category AS c
ON m.category_num = c.category_ num
```

4. Use the **SELECT** statement to verify the view. Display the results in order by title. Display each title only once. Record your query here.

```
SELECT DISTINCT *
FROM MovieCategoryView
ORDER BY title
```

5. Create a view consisting of each customer's first name, last name, invoice number, and rental date. Name the view RentalsView. (Note: This view will create a row for every invoice. If you have a customer who has rented movies more than once, you'll see their name listed once for each rental invoice when you use this view.) What query did you use?

```
CREATE VIEW dbo.RentalsView
AS
SELECT c.fname, c.lname, r.invoice_num, r.rental_date
FROM customer AS c JOIN rental AS r
ON c.cust_num = r.cust_num
```

6. Use the **SELECT** statement to verify the RentalsView view. Display the customer's first and last names in a single column. Sort the results by customer name. (You should see multiple rows for customers who have rented movies more than once.) What query did you use?

```
SELECT fname+' '+lname AS Name, invoice_num, rental_date
FROM RentalsView
ORDER BY lname, fname
```

Apply Your Knowledge 9-2 Page 237

1. Write and execute a query for modifying the MovieCategoryView to add the rating column from the movie table. What query did you use?

```
ALTER VIEW dbo.MovieCategoryView
AS
SELECT m.movie_num, m.title, c.description, m.rating
FROM movie AS m JOIN category AS c
ON m.category_num = c.category_num
```

2. Write and execute a query to verify that MovieCategoryView now contains the rating column. What query did you use?

```
SELECT *
FROM MovieCategoryView
```

3. What is an advantage to using **ALTER VIEW** instead of dropping and re-creating a view?

Using the ALTER VIEW statement enables me to change a view yet maintain any permissions I've assigned to users for that view. If I drop and re-create a view, I must re-create the permissions.

Task 9A-3 Page 238

1. Write and execute a query for dropping the view named MyTitleView from the pubs database. Record your query in the following space.

```
USE pubs
DROP VIEW MyTitleView
```

Apply Your Knowledge 9-3 Page 240

1. In SQL Query Analyzer, design and execute a query to create a view named MovieView. Configure dbo as the owner of the view. Include the title, category_num, rating, and rental_price columns in the view. What query did you use?

```
USE movies
GO
CREATE VIEW dbo.MovieView
AS
SELECT title, category_num, rating, rental_price
FROM movie
```

2. Can you use this view to insert data into the movie table? (Hint: You can review the structure of the movie table by looking at it in the movies database diagram or by executing the query `sp_help movie`.)

    Yes, because SQL Server automatically generates the values in the movie_num and date_purch columns of the movie table.

3. Design and execute a query to insert a new movie into the table by using the view. Use values of your choice. (To choose a movie category number before you add the row, you can use the query `SELECT * FROM category` to view a list of categories.)

```
INSERT INTO MovieViewVALUES('title', category_num, ' rating', price)
```

4. Verify that your new movie was added to the table by using a `SELECT` statement against the MovieView. (Your new movie will appear in alphabetical order because you've defined a clustered index on the title column.) Write your query here.

```
SELECT *
FROM MovieView
```

    *(I could also use SELECT * FROM MovieView WHERE title = 'title'.)*

5. What query did you use?

```
SELECT *
FROM movie
WHERE title = 'title of your choice'
```

Task 9A-4 Page 242

3. Can you create a clustered index based on this view? Why or why not?

    No, I can't create a clustered index on this view because the view's definition doesn't include the WITH SCHEMABINDING option. Also, I haven't used a valid two-part name for the movie table.

Task 9A-5 Page 244

7. Into which table do you think SQL Server inserted the row?

Because the storeID in the INSERT statement is '001', SQL Server inserted the row into the store1 table.

LESSON 9 REVIEW

Topic 9-A

You would like to prevent anyone from reading the statement you used to build a view. What should you do?

I can prevent users from displaying a view definition by encrypting it. I encrypt a view definition by adding the WITH ENCRYPTION clause after the CREATE VIEW statement as follows:

```
CREATE VIEW view_name
WITH ENCRYPTION
AS
SELECT statement
```

LESSON 10 ANSWERS

Task 10A-1 Page 249

5. In what scenario would you use the sp_helptext stored procedure?

I should use sp_helptext to view the text (SQL statements) contained in unencrypted views, defaults, stored procedures, rules, or triggers.

Task 10A-3 Page 253

1. How does a stored procedure differ from a SQL script file?

A stored procedure differs from a script file in that after SQL Server parses and compiles a stored procedure, it caches the execution plan in its procedure cache. From this point on, each time I run the stored procedure, SQL Server can retrieve it from cache. As a result, SQL Server doesn't have to parse and compile the stored procedure again—where it must do so each time you run the statements in the script file.

2. What scenarios will cause SQL Server to automatically parse and recompile a stored procedure?

Answers might include: When I restart my server; make changes to the structure of a table or view referenced in the stored procedure; generate new index statistics; drop an index that was used by the execution plan; or I force SQL Server to recompile the stored procedure.

Apply Your Knowledge 10-1 Page 258

1. By using the movies database, design a query for listing the customer name, invoice number, and rental date. (You can use CONVERT(CHAR(10), rental_date, 101) to format the date.) Sort the results by customer name and rental date. After you've tested the query, create a stored procedure based on this query and name it RentalsByCustomer. What query did you use?

```
USE movies
GO
CREATE PROC dbo.RentalsByCustomer
AS
        SELECT c.fname+' '+c.lname AS name, r.invoice_num,
        CONVERT(CHAR(10), r.rental_date, 101) AS 'rental date'
        FROM rental AS r JOIN customer AS c
        ON r.cust_num = c.cust_num
        ORDER BY c.lname, c.fname, r.rental_date
GO
```

4. Check the statements in your stored procedure by using `sp_helptext`. What query did you use?

```
sp_helptext RentalsByCustomer
```

5. Verify that the stored procedure you created in step 1 works by running it. What command did you use to run the stored procedure?

    I can use either EXEC dbo.RentalsByCustomer *or* RentalsByCustomer.

7. By using the movies database, design a query for listing the category description, title, and rating for all movies that have rented. Sort the results by category description and title. After you've tested the query, create an encrypted stored procedure based on this query and name it RentalsByCategory. (Hint: You must use a three-table join in your SELECT statement.) What query did you use?

```
USE movies
GO
CREATE PROC dbo.RentalsByCategory
WITH ENCRYPTION
AS
        SELECT c.description, m.title, m.rating
        FROM rental_detail AS rd JOIN movie AS  m
        ON rd.movie_num = m.movie_num
        JOIN category AS  c
        ON m.category_num = c.category_num
        ORDER BY c.description, m.title
GO
```

10. Verify that you can't read the stored procedure's definition by using `sp_helptext`. (You should see a message stating that the object's comments are encrypted.) What query did you use?

```
sp_helptext RentalsByCategory
```

11. Verify that your stored procedure works by running it.

```
EXEC dbo.RentalsByCategory
```

Apply Your Knowledge 10-2 Page 260

2. **Add the necessary commands to your script file to modify the RentalsByCategory stored procedure to add the date you purchased the movie to the results set. Save your changes to a new script file named newcategory.sql. Record your new query in the following space.**

```
USE movies
GO
ALTER PROC dbo.RentalsByCategory
WITH ENCRYPTION
AS
  SELECT c.description, m.title, m.rating,
   CONVERT(CHAR(10), m.date_purch,101) AS 'purchase date'
  FROM rental_detail AS rd JOIN movie AS m
  ON rd.movie_num = m.movie_num
  JOIN category AS c
  ON m.category_num = c.category_num
  ORDER BY c.description, m.title
GO
```

4. **Verify that your stored procedure works by running it.**

```
EXEC RentalsByCategory
```

Task 10C-1 Page 262

4. **Write and execute a query to run the stored procedure; specify a value of your choice for the @rating parameter by reference. What query did you use?**

```
EXEC MovieByRating @rating = 'G'
```

5. **Write and execute a query to execute the stored procedure; specify a value for the @rating parameter by position. What query did you use?**

```
EXEC MovieByRating 'PG'
```

Apply Your Knowledge 10-3 Page 263

1. **In SQL Query Analyzer, open the input.sql script file. Modify the script so that it alters the stored procedure. Add an IF statement to check to see if the @rating parameter is null or if it isn't G, PG, R, NC17, or NR. (Hint: Use the NOT IN keywords.) Have the stored procedure display a message if the @rating parameter isn't set correctly, and then exit the stored procedure. Save the changes to a file named newmovierating.sql (choose File→Save As). Record your changes here.**

```
ALTER PROCEDURE dbo.MovieByRating
@rating varchar(5) = null
AS
 IF @rating IS NULL
 OR @rating NOT IN ('G', 'PG', 'R', 'NC17', 'NR')
   BEGIN
     PRINT 'Please provide a movie rating. For example: '
     PRINT 'Use "G", "PG", "R", "NC17", or "NR".'
   RETURN -- ENDS running the stored procedure
 END
 SELECT rating, title
 FROM movie
 WHERE rating = @rating
 ORDER BY title
GO
```

Task 10C-2 Page 265

3. **In the above query, what type of parameters are @x and @y? How do they get values?**

Because @x and @y are input parameters, I must specify values for them when I run the stored procedure. I can specify values for @x and @y either by reference or position.

Apply Your Knowledge 10-4 Page 268

1. **In SQL Query Analyzer, by using the movies database, design a stored procedure for listing the invoice number, title, and the date rented for a specific movie number. Sort the results by the rental date. Name your stored procedure MoviesRented. Include an input parameter in the stored procedure so that you can input the movie number when you run it. Have your stored procedure return the number of rows in the results set as a return status code. (Hint: You'll need to join the movie, rental, and rental_detail tables.) What query did you use?**

```
CREATE PROCEDURE dbo.MoviesRented
@movie_num movie_num = null
AS
   SELECT r.invoice_num, m.title,
     CONVERT(CHAR(10),r.rental_date,101) AS 'rental date'
   FROM rental AS r JOIN rental_detail AS rd
   ON r.invoice_num = rd.invoice_num
   JOIN movie AS m
   ON rd.movie_num = m.movie_num
   WHERE rd.movie_num = @movie_num
   ORDER BY r.rental_date
   RETURN (@@rowcount)
```

2. **Design and execute a new query to call the MoviesRented stored procedure, display all of the movie rentals for a specific movie number (such as 155), and display the number of rows returned by the RETURN statement. What query did you use?**

```
DECLARE @answer smallint
EXEC @answer = MoviesRented 155
SELECT ' Total number of rentals for this movie is: ', @answer
```

Apply Your Knowledge 10-5 Page 272

1. **In SQL Query Analyzer, use the sp_addmessage stored procedure to create a custom error message. You will use this error message to notify users if they attempt to delete a movie for which there are rentals on file. Assign the error message a message number of 50001, a severity level of 10, and configure it to write a message to the Application log. Use a message text of your choice. What query did you use?**

```
sp_addmessage
@msgnum = 50001,
@severity = 10,
@msgtext = 'You cannot delete this movie. This movie has rentals on file.',
@with_log = 'true'
```

2. **Use the sp_addmessage stored procedure to create another custom error message. You will use this error message to record the name of the user who deletes a movie from the movie table. Assign the error message a message number of 50002, a severity level of 10, and configure it to write a message to the Application log. Use a message text of your choice, but include a variable to display the user name. What query did you use?**

```
sp_addmessage
@msgnum = 50002,
@severity = 10,
@msgtext = 'Movie record deleted by %s.',
@with_log = 'true'
```

3. **Execute a query to view only your new custom messages in the sysmessages table. Record your query below.**

```
SELECT *
FROM master..sysmessages
WHERE error > 50000
```

4. **Create a stored procedure named DeleteMovie to delete a movie from the movie database. Configure the stored procedure to accept an input parameter for the movie number. Have your stored procedure generate an error if you try to delete a movie for which there are rentals on file; generate the second error message if you successfully delete a movie from the file. What query did you use?**

```
CREATE PROC dbo.DeleteMovie
@movie_num movie_num = null
AS
IF EXISTS (SELECT movie_num FROM rental_detail WHERE movie_num=@movie_num)
        BEGIN
           RAISERROR(50001, 10, 1)
           RETURN
        END
DELETE FROM movie
WHERE movie_num = @movie_num
DECLARE @username char(30)
SELECT @username = suser_sname()
RAISERROR(50002, 10, 1, @username)
GO
```

5. **Execute the DeleteMovie stored procedure. Usc 105 as the value for the input parameter. Record the results below.**

```
EXEC DeleteMovie 105
```

I can't delete this movie because it has rentals on file in the rental_detail table.

7. **Execute the DeleteMovie stored procedure for a movie that has not rented. Record the results below.**

```
EXEC DeleteMovie movie_number
```

I see a message stating that the movie was deleted by my user account.

LESSON 10 REVIEW

Topic 10-A

List and describe the three types of stored procedures supported in SQL Server.

SQL Server supports system, extended, and user-defined stored procedures. System stored procedures enable me to perform many of the administrative tasks on my server. System stored procedures typically have names that begin with sp_. Extended stored procedures are actually DLLs that extend the functionality of SQL Server. Extended stored procedures have names that begin with xp_. User-defined stored procedures are ones that I define to perform virtually any task on the server.

Topic 10-B

How can you view the definition of a stored procedure? How can you determine on which objects a stored procedure depends?

I can view a stored procedure's definition by executing sp_helptext procedure_name. *I can list the objects on which a stored procedure runs by executing* sp_depends procedure_name.

Topic 10-C

What's the difference between an input parameter and an output parameter? Give an example of when you might use each.

An input parameter enables me to specify a value for use within the stored procedure. For example, I can use an input parameter to accept a value for a movie rating. I can then use this value in a WHERE clause to display only those movies with a specific rating. An output parameter enables me to return a value from a stored procedure to either the calling stored procedure or a SQL batch. For example, I can use an output parameter to return the number of rows in a table to the calling stored procedure.

Topic 10-D

You would like SQL Server to recompile a stored procedure the next time you run it. What should you do?

I should run the following query: EXEC sp_recompile procedure_name.

Lesson 11 Answers

Apply Your Knowledge 11-1 Page 282

1. **What is the average price of movies with a G rating? What query did you use?**

The average rental price is 2.3471.

```
USE movies
GO
SELECT AVG(rental_price) AS 'Average Rental Fee'
FROM movie
WHERE rating = 'G'
```

2. **What's the title and price of the highest-priced movie? (Hint: You must use a subquery to find this information.) What query did you use?**

The Godfather is the highest-priced rental at 5.49.

```
USE movies
GO
SELECT title, rental_price
FROM movie
WHERE rental_price = (SELECT MAX(rental_price)
                      FROM movie)
```

3. **How many authors live in Utah? (Use the pubs database.) What query did you use?**

   Two authors live in Utah.

   ```
   USE pubs
   GO
   SELECT COUNT(*)
   FROM authors
   WHERE state = 'UT'
   ```

4. **What is the highest royalty percentage paid to an author? (Hint: Query the roysched table.) What query did you use?**

   24 percent.

   ```
   USE pubs
   GO
   SELECT MAX(royalty) AS 'Highest Royalty Percentage'
   FROM roysched
   ```

5. **What's the total year-to-date sales for all titles in the Pubs database? What query did you use?**

   97,446.

   ```
   USE pubs
   GO
   SELECT SUM(ytd_sales) AS 'Total YTD Sales'
   FROM titles
   ```

Task 11A-2 Page 284

3. **How can you fix this query?**

   Add a GROUP BY rating clause.

Apply Your Knowledge 11-2 Page 286

1. **Design and execute a query based on the movies database that shows the total rental price collected for each invoice in the rental_detail table. What query did you use?**

   ```
   USE movies
   GO
   SELECT invoice_num, SUM(rental_price) AS 'Total Rental Price'
   FROM rental_detail
   GROUP BY invoice_num
   ```

2. **Design and execute a query on the movies database that shows all invoices and their total rental price where the total price was more than $4.00. (You should get 22 rows in the results set.) What query did you use?**

   ```
   USE movies
   GO
   SELECT invoice_num, SUM(rental_price)  AS 'Total Rental Price'
   FROM rental_detail
   GROUP BY invoice_num
   HAVING SUM(rental_price) > 4
   ```

3. **Design and execute a query that lists the category and average rental price of movies in the Comedy category. (The category_num for Comedy is 1.) What query did you use?**

```
SELECT category_num,
    AVG(rental_price) AS 'Average Rental Price'
FROM movie
GROUP BY category_num
HAVING category_num = 1
```

4. **Design and execute a query that lists the average rental price of movies by category. Include the category description in the results set and sort the results by the description. (Hint: You must join two tables in this query.) What query did you use?**

```
SELECT c.description,
    AVG(m.rental_price) AS 'Average Rental Price'
FROM movie AS m JOIN category AS c
ON m.category_num = c.category_num
GROUP BY c.description
ORDER BY c.description
```

5. **Design and execute a query that shows all customer names who have rented movies, and the total price of each customer's rentals. Sort the results in order by last name and then first name. (Hint: You must join three tables in this query.) What query did you use?**

```
SELECT c.fname, c.lname,
    SUM(rd.rental_price) AS 'Total Rental Price'
FROM rental_detail AS rd JOIN rental AS r
ON rd.invoice_num = r.invoice_num
JOIN customer AS c
ON r.cust_num = c.cust_num
GROUP BY c.lname, c.fname
ORDER BY c.lname, c.fname
```

Apply Your Knowledge 11-3 Page 288

1. **By using the movies database, write and execute a query to list the titles of the top three movies based on rental price. What are they? (Hint: Make sure you use the DISTINCT keyword so that you get three unique titles.) What query did you use?**

The Godfather, Alien, and Aliens.

```
USE movies
GO
SELECT DISTINCT TOP 3 title, rental_price
FROM movie
ORDER BY rental_price DESC
```

2. **Use the movies database to write and execute a query listing the top three invoice numbers based on total money spent renting movies. Which invoices are they? What query did you use?**

Invoice numbers 243, 244, and 254.

```
USE movies
GO
SELECT TOP 3 invoice_num, SUM(rental_price)
FROM rental_detail
GROUP BY invoice_num
ORDER BY SUM(rental_price) DESC
```

3. Use the pubs database to write and execute a query listing the titles and prices of the top five most expensive books. What is the title and price of the most expensive book? What query did you use?

The book's title is "But Is It User Friendly?" and its price is 22.95.

```
USE pubs
GO
SELECT TOP 5 title, price
FROM titles
ORDER BY price DESC
```

Apply Your Knowledge 11-4 Page 292

1. In the pubs database, create a function named fn_AvgPrice to calculate the average price of books for a specific book type. Define the function so that you can use the book type as an input parameter. Base the function on the titles table. If necessary, use the Object Browser window or SQL Server Enterprise Manager to review the structure of the titles table. What query did you use?

```
USE pubs
GO
CREATE FUNCTION fn_AvgPrice
(@type varchar(12))
RETURNS money
AS
BEGIN
        DECLARE @avg money
        SELECT @avg = avg(price)
        FROM titles
        WHERE type = @type
        RETURN @avg
END
```

2. Execute a query to find out what types of books are in the titles table. What query did you use?

```
SELECT title, type
FROM titles
ORDER BY type
```

3. Execute a **SELECT** query to view the average price for a book type. What query did you use?

```
SELECT dbo.fn_AvgPrice('psychology')
```

4. Execute a query that uses the fn_AvgPrice in a **WHERE** clause. Design the query to display the title, type, and price columns for titles with a price greater than the average price for a book type. What query did you use?

```
SELECT title, type, price
FROM titles
WHERE price > dbo.fn_AvgPrice('psychology')
```

5. **Design and execute a query that enables you to display the title, type, and price columns for titles with a price greater than the average price for a book type. Include only those titles that have the same book type as that of the function. Record your query in the space below.**

```
SELECT title, type, price
FROM titles
WHERE price > dbo.fn_AvgPrice('psychology')
AND type = 'psychology'
```

Apply Your Knowledge 11-5 Page 294

3. **Design and execute a query to test this function. What query did you use?**

```
SELECT *
FROM dbo.fn_AuthorState('ca')
```

4. **Design and execute a query that uses a value for the state abbreviation that doesn't exist in the authors table. What happens when you execute this query?**

I don't see any rows in the results set.

Apply Your Knowledge 11-6 Page 295

1. **Design and execute a query to create an inline table-valued function named fn_Rentals. Design this query so that you can use it to find all rental invoices with a total value greater than a dollar value you specify. Include the invoice_num and the total value of the rentals. (Hint: You'll need to use SUM(rental_price) to find the total value of the rentals.) What query did you use?**

```
USE movies
GO
CREATE FUNCTION fn_Rentals
    (@rentals money)
RETURNS TABLE
AS
RETURN (SELECT invoice_num,
            SUM(rental_price) AS 'Total Price'
        FROM rental_detail
        GROUP BY invoice_num
        HAVING SUM(rental_price) > @rentals)
```

2. **Design and execute a query to test the fn_Rentals function. What query did you use?**

```
SELECT *
FROM dbo.fn_Rentals(7.50)
```

LESSON 11 REVIEW

Topic 11-A

In what scenario must you include a GROUP BY clause when you use an aggregate function? Give an example of a query that includes a GROUP BY clause.

I must include the GROUP BY clause whenever I want to use an aggregate function on groups of rows from a table instead of all rows. As a rule of thumb, I must use the GROUP BY clause if I specify a column name in the SELECT statement along with an aggregate function. The following example enables me to display the highest-price movie within each movie rating:

```
SELECT rating, MAX(rental_price)
FROM movie
GROUP BY rating
```

Topic 11-B

In what scenario should you create a multi-statement table-valued function instead of an inline table-valued function?

I should create a multi-statement table-valued function if I want to be able to use multiple statements within a BEGIN and END code block to define the function. For example, I should create a multi-statement table-valued function if I want to use the CASE statement as part of the function's definition.

LESSON 12 ANSWERS

Task 12A-1 Page 301

1. **What's the difference between a constraint and a trigger?**

   While I can use both a constraint and a trigger to enforce data integrity, a constraint prevents me from inserting, changing, or deleting data that violates the constraint. In contrast, a trigger checks the data only after I've inserted, changed, or deleted the data. Triggers provide me with much greater flexibility for validating the data because they support programming logic. In contrast, I specify a constraint at the column or table level, and I can't add programming logic to the constraint.

2. **What are two triggers you might use in the movies database?**

   Answers include: A DELETE trigger to perform cascading deletes of invoices in the rental and rental_detail tables; a DELETE trigger to perform cascading deletes of a customer and the customer's invoices; and an UPDATE trigger to change a movie's number in the movie and rental_detail tables.

Task 12A-2 Page 304

7.   Add a query to the insert-trigger.sql script file to view the definition of the audit_inserts trigger. What query did you use?

```
sp_helptext audit_inserts
```

Apply Your Knowledge 12-1 Page 305

3.   Create an INSERT trigger on the rental_detail table that will set the rented column to Y for a movie whenever a customer rents it. Name the INSERT trigger movie_rental. (Hint: Your INSERT trigger should use an UPDATE statement to update the movie table. You will need to join the movie table to the inserted table on the movie_num column as part of the UPDATE statement.) What query did you use?

```
CREATE TRIGGER dbo.movie_rental
ON rental_detail
FOR INSERT
AS
UPDATE movie SET rented = 'Y'
FROM movie AS m JOIN inserted AS I
ON i.movie_num = m.movie_num
```

7.   Design and execute a query to check to see if your INSERT into the rental_detail table caused your trigger to fire. What query did you use?

I can check by verifying that SQL Server updated the movie's rented column and set it to Y to indicate that the movie is rented. I can use the following query:

```
SELECT movie_num, title, rented
FROM movie
WHERE movie_num = 105
```

Task 12A-3 Page 307

9.   You want to delete an invoice. Given that to delete an invoice you must delete it from both the rental and the rental_detail tables, from which table must you delete the invoice first?

I must delete the invoice's row (or rows) from the rental_detail table first and the rental table second. I can't delete the invoice from the rental table first because SQL Server won't let me delete rows in a primary key table that are referenced by rows in a foreign key table.

10.   You've decided to define a DELETE trigger to delete an invoice from both the rental and rental_ detail tables. On which table must you define the DELETE trigger?

I must define the DELETE trigger on the rental_detail table.

Apply Your Knowledge 12-2 Page 310

2.   You're planning to create an UPDATE trigger on the roysched table to record changes to the audit_trail table. Which logical table should you use to copy the data into the audit_trail table?

I should use the inserted table. I would use the deleted table only if I wanted to record a copy of the data prior to the change that fired the UPDATE trigger.

3. **Design and execute a query to create an UPDATE trigger on the roysched table. Configure the trigger so that SQL Server will fire it only if a user changes the royalty column. Have the trigger add a row to the audit_trail table to record the changes. Name your trigger dbo.audit_updates. What query did you use?**

```
CREATE TRIGGER dbo.audit_updates
ON roysched
FOR UPDATE
AS
IF UPDATE (royalty)
BEGIN
        INSERT audit_trail (title_id, royalty)
        SELECT title_id, royalty
        FROM inserted
END
```

4. **Write and execute a query that will cause SQL Server to fire your UPDATE trigger. (Hint: Use the title_id you inserted in Task 12A-2, step 5.) What query did you use?**

```
UPDATE roysched
SET royalty = 50
WHERE title_id = 'PC9999'
```

5. **Verify that your UPDATE trigger recorded a row in the audit_trail table. What query did you use?**

```
SELECT *
FROM audit_trail
```

Apply Your Knowledge 12-3 Page 314

1. **In SQL Query Analyzer, use the pubs database. Design and execute a query to temporarily disable the audit_updates trigger. What query did you use?**

```
ALTER TABLE roysched
DISABLE TRIGGER audit_updates
```

2. **Design and execute a query to verify that SQL Server doesn't fire your UPDATE trigger. Record your query below.**

```
UPDATE roysched
SET royalty = 35
WHERE title_id = 'PC9999'
```

3. **Verify that SQL Server didn't add a row in the audit_trail table. What query did you use?**

```
SELECT *
FROM audit_trail
```

4. **Design and execute a query to re-enable the audit_updates trigger. What query did you use?**

```
ALTER TABLE roysched
ENABLE TRIGGER audit_updates
```

LESSON 12 REVIEW

Topic 12-A

In what scenario would you choose to implement a check constraint instead of a trigger? In what scenario would you choose to implement a trigger instead of a check constraint?

I should use a check constraint whenever the rules for enforcing data integrity are relatively simple. For example, it's more efficient to use a check constraint to make sure that users enter a movie rating of G, PG, R, NC17, or NR than it is to define a trigger. I should implement a trigger whenever the rules for enforcing data integrity are complex. For example, I can use a trigger to set the value for the rented column to Y in the movie table whenever I add an invoice for a customer movie rental to the rental table.

LESSON 13 ANSWERS

Task 13A-1 Page 320

4. **What do you think the value of the @@trancount system function will be at the end of this script?**

The @@trancount variable will have a value of 1 because I don't have a COMMIT TRAN statement in the script. As a result, SQL Server will consider the transaction as still open when I execute this script.

8. **Why is SQL Server unable to process your query?**

SQL Server can't process this query because the transaction to update the movie's title hasn't completed. SQL Server has locked this row in the movie table.

9. **What do you think the current title of movie number 105 is?**

The current title of movie number 105 hasn't changed because my transaction hasn't been committed. Its title is still "Godfather The".

Apply Your Knowledge 13-1 Page 322

2. What query did you use?

```
BEGIN TRAN
 SELECT 'The current number of open transactions is: ',
   @@trancount
 SELECT 'The current last name of customer number 2 is: ',
   lname
 FROM customer
 WHERE cust_num = 2

 UPDATE customer SET lname = 'Johnson'
 WHERE cust_num = 2

 SELECT 'After the UPDATE statement, the last name of customer 2 is:',
   lname
 FROM customer
 WHERE cust_num = 2

ROLLBACK TRAN

 SELECT 'After the roll back statement, the last name of customer 2 is: ',
   lname
 FROM customer
 WHERE cust_num = 2

 SELECT 'The current number of open transactions is: ',
   @@trancount
```

Task 13B-2 Page 330

5. What is your current transaction isolation level?

By default, SQL Server configures my transaction isolation level as READ COMMITTED. *This means that if I execute a query against a row that a user is currently updating, until the user's transaction is committed and the exclusive lock released, I won't be able to read that row. The* READ COMMITTED *transaction isolation level honors exclusive locks on rows.*

LESSON 13 REVIEW

Topic 13-A

What is the difference between explicit and implicit transactions?

I must begin an explicit transaction with the BEGIN TRAN *statement and end it with either the* COMMIT TRAN *or* ROLLBACK TRAN *statement. In contrast, I don't mark the beginning of a transaction in implicit transactions. The beginning of the transaction is implied based on the SQL statement I execute. SQL Server doesn't commit implicit transactions until I use the* COMMIT TRAN, COMMIT WORK, *or* ROLLBACK TRAN *statement.*

Topic 13-B

What techniques can you use to control resource locking?

I can control resource locking by setting session-level locking or table-level locking. Session-level locking enables me to control how SQL Server handles locks for my entire session. Table-level locking enables me to control how SQL Server handles locks for a single transaction.

LESSON 14 ANSWERS

Task 14A-2 Page 343

13. Why does your login fail?

My login attempt fails because I'm logged in to my local SQL server as sqluser#, but this login account doesn't exist on my partner's server. So, my local server can't log in to the linked server by using my login account.

14. How should you fix this problem?

I should fix this problem by either creating a duplicate login account for sqluser# on my partner's server or by defining a linked server login name with the sp_addlinkedsrvlogin stored procedure.

Apply Your Knowledge 14-1 Page 347

1. **In SQL Query Analyzer, design and execute a query to list all movies on your partner's server with a category number of 4 (comedy). Don't use a pass-through query. What query did you use?**

```
SELECT *
FROM sqlserver#.movies.dbo.movie
WHERE category_num = 4
```

2. **Design and execute a query to list all customers in alphabetical order on your partner's server. Use a pass-through query. What query did you use?**

```
SELECT *
FROM OPENQUERY(sqlserver#, 'SELECT *
                    FROM movies.dbo.customer
                    ORDER BY lname, fname')
```

3. **Design and execute a query to join the movie table on your partner's server with the category table on your server. Include the movie title and the category description in the results set. Sort the results by category description and then movie title. Don't use a pass-through query. What query did you use?**

```
USE movies
GO
SELECT c.description, m.title
FROM sqlserver#.movies.dbo.category AS c JOIN movie AS m
ON c.category_num = m.category_num
ORDER BY c.description, m.title
```

4. **Design and execute a query to create a new local table named partner_movie in your movies database. Use the `SELECT INTO` statement to populate this table with movies that have a rating of G from your partner's movie table. Verify the contents of the partner_movie table when you are done. What queries did you use?**

```
SELECT *
INTO partner_movie
FROM sqlserver#.movies.dbo.movie
WHERE rating = 'G'
GO

SELECT *
FROM partner_movie
```

Apply Your Knowledge 14-2 Page 348

1. **In SQL Query Analyzer, design and execute a query to list all stored procedures on your partner's server. What query did you use?**

```
EXEC sqlserver#.movies.dbo.sp_stored_procedures
```

2. **Design and execute a query to list the definition of one of the stored procedures. What query did you use?**

```
EXEC sqlserver#.movies.dbo.sp_helptext stored_procedure_name
```

3. **Run one of your partner's stored procedures. If necessary, provide the appropriate values for any input parameters. (Use the appropriate stored procedure to view the definition of the stored procedure to determine if you need any input parameters.) What query did you use?**

```
EXEC sqlserver#.movies.dbo.MovieByCategory
```

Apply Your Knowledge 14-3 Page 350

1. **In SQL Query Analyzer, design and execute a query to insert yourself as a customer in your partner's customer table. (Hint: You don't need to provide values for the cust_num and join_date columns.) What query did you use?**

```
SET XACT_ABORT ON
BEGIN DISTRIBUTED TRAN
 INSERT INTO sqlserver#.movies.dbo.customer
 (lname, fname, address1, address2, city, state, zip, phone)
 VALUES ('Ferrer', 'Henri', '123 Someplace', ' Suite 101',
 'New Orleans', 'LA', '70130', '5041234566')
COMMIT TRAN
```

2. When your partner has completed step 1, verify that you can see your partner's name in your own customer table. What query did you use?

```
SELECT *
FROM customer
WHERE lname = 'partner's_last_name'
```

Lesson 14 Review

Topic 14-A

How do you define an SQL server as a linked server?

I define an SQL server as a linked server by using the `sp_addlinkedserver` *stored procedure. Here's the syntax:*

```
sp_addlinkedserver
@server = 'linked_server_name',
@srvproduct = 'SQL Server'
```

Topic 14-B

How can you configure a distributed query to be processed by the linked server instead of your local server?

I specify that I want the linked server to process my query by using the OPENQUERY *function in place of the table name in my query. Use the following syntax:*

```
SELECT * FROM OPENQUERY(linked_ server_name, 'query')
```

Lesson 15 Answers

Apply Your Knowledge 15-1 Page 360

6. How many times did SQL Server access this table? How can you tell?

SQL Server accessed this table one time. I can tell by looking at the Scan Count statistic.

7. What is the Cache Hit Ratio for this query? How do you calculate this value?

The Cache Hit Ratio is 100 percent. I can calculate this value by using the formula (Logical Reads - Physical Reads)/Logical Reads. In this statement, SQL Server retrieved all of the table's pages by using logical reads, so the Cache Hit Ratio is 100 percent.

Task 15A-1 Page 361

4. **What value do you see for the CPU time? (Look at the SQL Server Execution Times at the end of the results set.)**

   Answers will vary depending on the classroom hardware.

5. **Given the value you see for the CPU time, what value should you use if you want the query governor to prevent this query from executing? (Notice that SET STATISTICS TIME ON displays the value for CPU time in milliseconds, but you specify the value for the query governor in seconds.)**

   Answers will vary.

Task 15A-2 Page 363

4. **How will SQL Server retrieve the results of this query?**

   SQL Server will retrieve the results by performing an index seek against the nonclustered index named NC_category_num.

6. **How will SQL Server retrieve the results of this query?**

   SQL Server will retrieve the results by performing a clustered index seek of the clustered index named CL_title.

8. **How will SQL Server retrieve the results of this query?**

   SQL Server will retrieve the results by performing a clustered index scan of the clustered index named CL_title. SQL Server is essentially performing a table scan because the movie table doesn't have an index on the rating column.

10. **How will SQL Server retrieve the results of this query?**

    SQL Server will retrieve the results by performing a table scan of the category table. SQL Server is using a table scan because the table doesn't have a clustered index nor does it have a nonclustered index on the description column.

Task 15A-3 Page 366

7. **How did SQL Server retrieve this query? (Hint: Point to the movie.CL_title node to determine the action SQL Server performed with this object.)**

   It used a seek of the table's clustered index. The clustered index on the movie table is already in order by movie_num, so using this index to retrieve the query's results set is the fastest method for retrieving the data.

9. **What steps does SQL Server perform to retrieve this query's results set?**

   SQL Server first performs a scan of the movie table's clustered index to find rows. It then used a filter operation to restrict the rows so that the results set contains only those movies with a PG rating.

11. **How does SQL Server retrieve this query's results set?**

    SQL Server first performs a scan of the category table. It uses a table scan because no indexes are available to help optimize this query. Next, it sorts the results set to display the categories in order by description.

Apply Your Knowledge 15-2 Page 369

9. **In the table below, use the information you see on the Messages and Execution Plan tabs in the Results pane to record the query's statistics. This information tells you how SQL Server executed the query by using the clustered index.**

Statistic	Value
Scan Count	*1*
Logical Reads	*3*
Index or Table Scan	*Index*
Type of Index Operation	*Clustered Index Seek*

13. **In the table below, use the information you see on the Messages and Execution Plan tabs in the Results pane to record the query's statistics. This information tells you how SQL Server executed the query using the nonclustered index.**

Statistic	Value
Scan Count	*1*
Logical Reads	*7*
Index or Table Scan	*Index*
Type of Index Operation	*Nonclustered Index Seek*

14. **Given the statistics you see in steps 9 and 13, which index is more efficient for this query? Why?**

The clustered index is more efficient because SQL Server uses less I/O (fewer logical reads) to retrieve the query's results set.

18. **In the table below, use the information you see on the Messages and Execution Plan tabs in the Results pane to record the query's statistics. This information tells you how SQL Server executed this new query using the clustered index.**

Statistic	Value
Scan Count	*1*
Logical Reads	*3*
Index or Table Scan	*Index*
Type of Index Operation	*Clustered Index Seek*

21. **In the table below, use the information you see on the Messages and Execution Plan tabs in the Results pane to record the query's statistics. This information tells you how SQL Server executed this new query using the nonclustered index.**

Statistic	Value
Scan Count	*1*
Logical Reads	*2*
Index or Table Scan	*Index*
Type of Index Operation	*Nonclustered Index Seek*

22. Given the statistics you see in steps 18 and 21, which index is more efficient for this query? Why?

For this new query, the nonclustered index is more efficient. The nonclustered index requires fewer I/Os to retrieve the results set because SQL Server can satisfy the requirements of the query by using the nonclustered index keys instead of accessing the table's data pages directly.

25. In the table below, use the information you see on the Messages and Execution Plan tabs in the Results pane to record the query's statistics. This information tells you how SQL Server executed this third query using the clustered index.

Statistic	Value
Scan Count	*1*
Logical Reads	*50*
Index or Table Scan	*Index*
Type of Index Operation	*Clustered Index Seek*

28. In the table below, use the information you see on the Messages and Execution Plan tabs in the Results pane to record the query's statistics. This information tells you how SQL Server executed this third query using the nonclustered index.

Statistic	Value
Scan Count	*1*
Logical Reads	*10*
Index or Table Scan	*Index*
Type of Index Operation	*Nonclustered Index Seek*

29. Given the statistics you see in steps 25 and 28, which index is more efficient for this query? Why?

For this third query, the nonclustered index is significantly more efficient. The nonclustered index requires fewer I/Os to retrieve the results set because SQL Server can satisfy the requirements of the query by using the nonclustered index keys instead of accessing the table's data pages directly.

Because this query retrieves a greater number of rows, the advantage to having a nonclustered index that covers the query becomes clearer: the nonclustered index contains all of the information SQL Server needs to satisfy the query (the CustomerID column, in this scenario). Because the nonclustered index contains only the index key values on its pages, SQL Server can fit more rows per page. In contrast, the clustered index can't fit as many rows per page (because each row contains all of the table's columns). As a result, SQL Server must retrieve and process more pages in order to retrieve the query's results set.

Task 15B-1 Page 373

1. After analyzing your users' queries, you've determined that the majority of the queries retrieve the Contact Name and Phone columns from the Customers table. You've defined a clustered index on the customers table's SalesRepID column. Should you create an index to improve the performance of these queries? If yes, what factors should you consider when selecting the index's key?

I should create a composite index to improve the performance of these queries. The order of the columns in the composite index's key should reflect the order the columns are queried.

2. **You have created an index to help improve the performance of a query. You'd like to determine whether SQL Server is using the index and its impact on performance. What should you do?**

I should use the SET SHOWPLAN_ALL ON *statement to verify that SQL Server is using the index to retrieve the query's results set. I could also use the* SET STATISTICS IO ON *statement to see the I/O operations SQL Server must perform when processing the query.*

Apply Your Knowledge 15-3 Page 375

1. **Design and execute a query to use the movies database and list each movie's title, rating, and category from the movie table in order by category. Include the** SET SHOWPLAN_ALL ON **statement so that you can see how SQL Server will process this query. What query did you use? How will SQL Server retrieve this query's results set?**

```
USE movies
GO
SET SHOWPLAN_ALL ON
GO
SELECT title, rating, category_num
FROM movie
ORDER BY category_num
```

SQL Server will retrieve this query's results set by using a clustered index scan of the CL_title index.

2. **Write a query to list each movie's title, rating, and category from the movie table in order by category; include a hint in your query. (You can use** sp_helpindex movie **to identify the name of the index you want to use.) What query did you use?**

```
SELECT title, rating, category_num
FROM movie WITH (INDEX(NC_category_num))
ORDER BY category_num
```

SQL Server will now retrieve this query's results set by performing a nonclustered index scan of the NC_category_num index.

3. **Turn off the display of the query execution plan.**

SET SHOWPLAN_ALL OFF

LESSON 15 REVIEW

Topic 15-A

You would like to determine how many I/O operations SQL Server must perform to retrieve the results set for a complex query. What should you do?

I should execute the SET STATISTICS IO ON *statement and then execute my query. SQL Query Analyzer will then display the number of logical reads and physical reads my server performs to retrieve the query's results set.*

Topic 15-B

What steps should you take before you resort to adding table hints to a query?

I should first make sure that my index statistics are current. In addition, I should recompile my stored procedures. I should also consider the design of my queries and evaluate the effectiveness of my indexes.

LESSON 16 ANSWERS

Apply Your Knowledge 16-1 Page 379

8. **Record the information you see in the Results pane's Execution Plan and Messages tabs in the following table.**

Statistic	Value
Number of Rows Retrieved	9
Scan Count	2
Logical Reads	15
Number of Indexes Used (if any)	2
Names of Indexes Used (if any)	NC_LName; and NC_SalesRepID

10. **Record the information you see in the results pane's Execution Plan and Messages tabs for this new query in the following table.**

Statistic	Value
Number of Rows Retrieved	374
Scan Count	1
Logical Reads	3
Number of Indexes Used (if any)	1
Names of Indexes Used (if any)	NC_LName
Does this Index Cover the Query?	Yes

12. **Record the information you see in the results pane's Execution Plan and Messages tabs for this new query in the following table.**

Statistic	Value
Number of Rows Retrieved	149
Scan Count	1
Logical Reads	3
Number of Indexes Used (if any)	1
Names of Indexes Used (if any)	NC_SalesRepID
Does this Index Cover the Query?	Yes

14. **Record the information you see in the results pane's Execution Plan and Messages tabs for this new query in the following table.**

Statistic	Value
Number of Rows Retrieved	3500
Scan Count	1
Logical Reads	8
Number of Indexes Used (if any)	1
Names of Indexes Used (if any)	NC_CustomerID
Does this Index Cover the Query?	Yes

15. **In the following table, summarize the results of each of the queries so that you can compare your results.**

Statistic	Complete Query	LName Only	SalesRepID Only	CustomerID Only
Number of Rows Retrieved	9	374	149	3500
Scan Count	2	1	1	1
Logical Reads	15	3	3	8
Names of Indexes Used	NC_LName; and NC_SalesRepID	NC_LName	NC_SalesRepID	NC_CustomerID
Number of Indexes Used	2	1	1	1

Given these statistics, why do you think the query optimizer didn't use the NC_CustomerID index when it selected the execution plan for the complete query (the query consisting of three search conditions)?

SQL Server doesn't use the NC_CustomerID index for this query because the search condition isn't selective enough. The search condition returns 3,500 rows.

Compare the number of logical reads SQL Server performs for the queries with only one search condition to the query with all three search conditions. Why is the I/O higher for the query with all three search conditions?

The I/O is higher for the query with all three search conditions because SQL Server had to access the table directly by using a bookmark lookup. In other words, SQL Server couldn't retrieve the rows by accessing the nonclustered indexes' pages. Instead, SQL Server accessed the table directly. In contrast, with each of the queries that used only one search condition, SQL Server could retrieve the data by using only the relevant nonclustered index's pages.

17. **In the following table, record the information you see in the results pane's Execution Plan and Messages tabs for this new query. In addition, record the information for the original three search condition query so that you can compare the results.**

Statistic	Value for New Query	Value for Query with All Three Search Conditions
Number of Rows Retrieved	9	9
Scan Count	2	2
Logical Reads	6	15
Number of Indexes Used (if any)	2	2
Names of Indexes Used (if any)	NC_LName; and NC_SalesRepID	NC_LName; NC_SalesRepID

Why does this new query use less I/O than the original query?

SQL Server doesn't use as much I/O for the new query because it can retrieve this query's results set by using only the two indexes; it doesn't have to access the LabCustomer table directly. In contrast, for the query with the three search conditions, SQL Server must first use the indexes and then query the LabCustomer table directly to retrieve the query's results set.

20. **In the following table, record the information you see in the results pane's Execution Plan and Messages tabs for this new query.**

Statistic	Value
Number of Rows Retrieved	1
Scan Count	3
Logical Reads	10
Number of Indexes Used (if any)	3
Names of Indexes Used (if any)	NC_SalesRepID; NC_LName; and NC_CustomerID
Do the Indexes Cover the Query?	Yes

Why does SQL Server use all three indexes to retrieve this query's results set?

SQL Server uses all three indexes because the CustomerID search condition is much more selective in this query. The CustomerID > 9500 eliminates 9500 of the rows in the LabCustomer table.

23. **In the following table, record the information you see in the results pane's Execution Plan and Messages tabs for this new query. In addition, record the information for the three search condition query from step 20 so that you can compare the results.**

Statistic	Value for New Query	Value for Query with All Three Search Conditions
Number of Rows Retrieved	1	1
Scan Count	1	3
Logical Reads	4	10
Number of Indexes Used (if any)	1	3
Names of Indexes Used (if any)	CL_CustomerID	NC_SalesRepID; NC_LName; and NC_CustomerID

Did creating a clustered index improve the performance of this query? How can you tell?

The clustered index improved the performance of this query. I can tell because SQL Server used fewer I/O operations to retrieve the results set for this query.

Apply Your Knowledge 16-2 Page 386

6. Look at the graphical execution plan. How did SQL Server retrieve this query's results set? Why does the query optimizer select this method?

SQL Server retrieved the query's results set by performing a table scan because I haven't defined an index for one of the search conditions (TerritoryID). With an OR *query, SQL Server always performs a table scan if no index is available for one of the search conditions.*

7. Record the information you see in the results pane's Execution Plan and Messages tabs for this OR **query in the following table.**

Statistic	Value
Number of Rows Retrieved	*1000*
Scan Count	*1*
Logical Reads	*44*
Number of Indexes Used (if any)	*0*
Names of Indexes Used (if any)	*None*
Does the Index Cover the Query?	*No*

9. Look at the graphical execution plan. How did SQL Server retrieve this query's results set? Why does the query optimizer select this method?

Even though this query is more selective, SQL Server still retrieved the query's results set by performing a table scan because I haven't defined an index for one of the search conditions (SalesRepID).

10. Record the information you see in the results pane's Execution Plan and Messages tabs for this OR **query in the following table.**

Statistic	Value
Number of Rows Retrieved	*2*
Scan Count	*1*
Logical Reads	*44*
Number of Indexes Used (if any)	*0*
Names of Indexes Used (if any)	*None*
Does the Index Cover the Query?	*No*

11. Compare the values you see in the tables in step 7 and step 10. Do you see any difference in these queries' execution plans? Why or why not?

No. Both queries used the same number of logical reads to retrieve the results set even though one query returns 1,000 rows and the other returns only a few rows. This is because I haven't created an index that covers one of the search conditions in both queries.

14. Look at the graphical execution plan. How did SQL Server retrieve this query's results set? Why does the query optimizer select this method?

SQL Server retrieved the query's results set by using both the NC_CustomerID and CL_SalesRepID indexes.

15. **In the following table, record the information you see in the results pane's Execution Plan and Messages tabs for this OR query.**

Statistic	Value
Number of Rows Retrieved	2
Scan Count	2
Logical Reads	8
Number of Indexes Used (if any)	2
Names of Indexes Used (if any)	NC_CustomerID; and CL_SalesRepID
Does the Index Cover the Query?	Yes

16. **Compare the values you see in the tables in step 10 and step 15. (These are the results for the same query but with different indexes.) Do you see any difference in these queries' execution plans? Why or why not?**

Yes. The second query (where I have indexes on the CustomerID and SalesRepID columns) uses much less I/O than the query for which I have only one index. That's because the query optimizer can't use an index that covers only one of the search conditions in an OR clause.

19. **Record the information you see in the results pane's Execution Plan and Messages tabs for this query in the following table.**

Statistic	Value
Number of Rows Retrieved	35
Scan Count	35
Logical Reads	105
Number of Indexes Used (if any)	1
Names of Indexes Used (if any)	NC_CustomerID
Do the Indexes Cover the Query?	Yes

20. **The values generated by STATISTICS IO indicate that SQL Server used a total of 105 logical reads to retrieve the data. What steps do you think generated this I/O on your server?**

SQL Server first scanned the table once for each of the values in the IN clause of my query (for a total of 35 I/O). Next, it read the leaf-level pages of the nonclustered index to find the row identifier (RID) for each row (which generated another 35 I/O operations). Finally, SQL Server used a bookmark lookup operation to retrieve the rows (which generated the final 35 I/O operations).

21. **How would the execution plan change if you created an index that covered this query?**

SQL Server would eliminate the bookmark lookup step in the query's execution plan if I created an index that covers this query.

Apply Your Knowledge 16-3 Page 393

10. **Look at the execution plan for the table join query. What join strategy did the query optimizer select for this query? Why do you think it selected this strategy?**

The query optimizer used a nested loop join strategy to retrieve the results set. It chose the nested loop join strategy because the LabCustomer table is much smaller than the LabInvoice table. SQL Server finds only one row in the LabCustomer table and then looks for matching rows in the LabInvoice table.

11. In the following table, record the statistics generated for this query.

Statistic	Value
Join Strategy	Nested Loop
Scan Count for the LabInvoice Table	1
Scan Count for the LabCustomer Table	1
Logical Reads for LabInvoice Table	2
Logical Reads for LabCustomer Table	2
Total I/O Generated (add the values for all logical reads)	4
Number of Indexes Used (if any)	2
Names of Indexes Used (if any)	CL_Name; and CL_CustomerID

13. In the following table, record the statistics SQL Server generated when you forced it to use the merge join strategy.

Statistic	Value
Join Strategy	Merge
Scan Count for the Worktable	1
Scan Count for the LabInvoice Table	1
Scan Count for the LabCustomer Table	1
Logical Reads for the Worktable	1
Logical Reads for LabInvoice Table	18
Logical Reads for LabCustomer Table	2
Total I/O Generated (add the values for all logical reads)	21
Number of Indexes Used (if any)	2
Names of Indexes Used (if any)	CL_Name, and CL_CustomerID

15. In the following table, record the statistics SQL Server generated when you forced it to use the hash join strategy.

Statistic	Value
Join Strategy	Hash
Scan Count for the LabInvoice Table	1
Scan Count for the LabCustomer Table	1
Logical Reads for LabInvoice Table	63
Logical Reads for LabCustomer Table	2
Total I/O Generated (add the values for all logical reads)	65
Number of Indexes Used (if any)	2
Names of Indexes Used (if any)	CL_Name; and CL_CustomerID

16. Based on the values you see for the total logical reads for each join strategy, which join strategy is most efficient? Did the query optimizer select the most efficient strategy?

The most efficient join strategy is the nested loop join. Yes, the query optimizer selected the most efficient join strategy.

Lesson 16 Review

Topic 16-A

You've created a table for storing your company's parts inventory. You've created only one index on this table: a clustered index on the parts_num column. Given this information, how do you think SQL Server will retrieve the rows to satisfy the following query?

```
SELECT parts_num, description
FROM parts
WHERE description LIKE 'e%' OR parts_num > 1500
```

Because I haven't created an index on the description column, SQL Server will use a table scan to retrieve the results set for this query.

aggregate functions

Functions that enable you to summarize data. The result of these functions is a single value.

atomicity

A state in which SQL Server either performs all of a transaction's modifications or none of them.

batch

A series of SQL statements you send to the server so that the server can process them together.

built input

The smaller of two tables in a hash join.

check constraint

A range of values that you define for a column to force users to enter only those values into the column.

clustered index

An index that changes the way SQL Server stores the rows in a table. This index isn't a separate database object. Instead, SQL Server uses this index to determine the order in which it stores the rows that make up a table. You can define only one clustered index per table.

covering index

A nonclustered index where the index key consists of all of the values you select in a query. For example, if you execute the query SELECT movie_num, title, rating FROM movie, a covering index for this query must use the movie_num, title, and rating columns as its index key.

data integrity

The state in which all of the information stored in a database is accurate. If a table contains inaccurate data, your database has lost its data integrity.

database

A collection of related database objects such as tables, views, and indexes. Each database in SQL Server consists of at least one data file and a transaction log file.

declarative data integrity

The process of enforcing data integrity through an object's definition. For example, you can use constraints, defaults, and rules to enforce declarative data integrity.

default constraint

A value that you assign to a column. SQL Server automatically fills in the column with this value during data entry. You can always override the default value by entering another value into the column.

dirty read

Occurs when one transaction reads another transaction's uncommitted changes. As you'll see in this lesson, you can configure SQL Server's locking such that it's possible for this scenario to occur.

extent

An allocation of disk space made up of eight contiguous 8 KB pages for a total of 64 KB.

File Header page

The first page in the first extent of a file. SQL Server uses this page to store information about the file, including the name of the database to which it belongs, the filegroup, and sizing information.

filegroup

A collection of one or more database data files. You use filegroups to group data files together so that you can administer them as a single unit.

foreign key

The column or group of columns in one table that match the primary key column or columns of another table.

GLOSSARY

fully qualified name
An object name that contains the server, database, owner, and object names. Because this name consists of four components, you'll sometimes hear the fully qualified name for an object referred to as the four-part object name.

Global Allocation Map (GAM) page
SQL Server uses this page to keep track of all extents within a file and identifies whether or not each extent is allocated.

heap
A table without a clustered index.

inconsistent analysis (nonrepeatable read)
Occurs when a transaction reads a row multiple times and retrieves different values.

input parameter
A value that you pass into a stored procedure.

keys
The column (or columns) on which you've indexed a table.

lost updates
An update that gets lost when one user's update overwrites another user's update.

materializing
The process of retrieving the rows and columns from one or more tables to display the results set for a view.

Net-Library
A Dynamic Link Library (DLL) that enables a client and a SQL server to communicate over a specific network protocol.

nonclustered index
A separate database object that contains the key columns on which you want to index a table, along with a value to identify each row in the table. A nonclustered index doesn't change the order of the actual rows in the table.

normalization
The process of organizing the information in tables within a relational database in order to minimize the duplication of data across those tables.

output parameter
A value SQL Server passes out of a stored procedure. This value is typically generated by a statement within the stored procedure.

page
The minimum block of disk space that SQL Server copies from your server's hard disk to RAM, and vice versa. In SQL Server 2000, SQL Server uses 8 KB pages.

Page Free Space (PFS) page
SQL Server keeps track of the available space in the file's pages within the PFS page. Each PFS page can keep track of a maximum of 8,000 contiguous pages in the file. If necessary, SQL Server adds multiple PFS pages to keep track of free space.

parameter
A programming entity that enables you to send information to or retrieve information from a stored procedure.

partitioning column
The column in each table you reference in a partitioned view that you use to ensure that each table's data is mutually exclusive.

phantom
Occurs when one transaction adds a new row while another transaction is in the midst of updating several rows.

GLOSSARY

primary key
One or more columns that you use to uniquely identify each row in a table.

probe input
The larger of two tables in a hash join.

procedural data integrity
The process of enforcing data integrity through programming techniques. Triggers and stored procedures are examples of procedural integrity techniques.

procedure cache
The memory in which SQL Server stores compiled query execution plans.

row density
A measure of the number of rows stored on a data page. A high row density means that you have a greater number of rows per page. In contrast, a low row density means that you have only a few rows per page.

Secondary Global Allocation Map (SGAM) page
SQL Server uses the SGAM page to keep track of all mixed extents, along with whether or not each mixed extent has at least one free page.

SQL
Structured Query Language is a language you use to add, modify, retrieve, and delete data from a relational database management system.

system stored procedures
Stored procedures written by Microsoft that are installed when you install SQL Server 2000. You can use these stored procedures to perform most of the administrative tasks on your server.

table
An object within a database that contains rows and columns of information.

Transact-SQL
Microsoft's enhanced version of ANSI SQL-92.

variable
A programming entity to which you assign a value.

virtual directory
A virtual directory is an alias to a folder that can be accessed through your IIS server.

YOUR NOTES:

INDEX

with Windows 2000, 4

K

keys, 168-172

L

locks
  basic, 324
  coexistence of locks, 325
  configuring a lock timeout, 333-334
  deadlocks, 335-336
  managing, 324-328, 329-333
  session-level, 329-330
  special use, 325
  table-level locking, 334-335
  viewing current, 326
login accounts
  creating, 40-42
lost updates, 324-328

M

management tasks, 36-37
Microsoft Distributed Transaction
    Coordinator
    See: MSDTC
monetary data types, 128
MSDTC, 349

N

naming conventions
  designing, 57
Net-Library, 32-33
nonclustered index, 17-18
nonclustered indexes, 171
normalization, 120-121

O

object permissions, 70
objects
  identifying, 19-20
  naming, 56-57
optimizing queries

designing indexing to optimize,
    373
  using indexes, 368-372
Osql, 53-55
output parameter, 261-262

P

page, 94
Page Free Space page
    See: PFS page
parameter, 261-262
partitioning column, 243-245
permissions
  configuring, 42-46
  validating, 44
PFS page, 95-96
phantom, 324-328
primary key constraints
  defining, 148-149
probe input, 391-392
procedural data integrity, 144-147
procedure cache, 248-250
programming
  local variables, 76
  Transact-SQL, 75-76
  variables, 75-76

Q

queries
  analyzing OR queries, 385-389
  analyzing performance, 378-385
  analyzing table join queries, 389-395
  forcing a join strategy with hints,
      392
  hash joins, 391-392
  merge joins, 390-391
  nested loop joins, 390
query optimizer
  displaying query statistics, 357-359
  exploring, 356-360
  limiting long-running queries,
      361-362
  overriding, 374-375
  SHOWPLAN_ALL, 362-364

SHOWPLAN_TEXT, 362-364
understanding, 356-357
using the graphical execution plan,
    364-368

R

registering servers, 9-11
reliability, 5
replication, 4-5
results
  sorting, 61
retrieving metadata, 23-24
row density, 183-188
rules
  creating, 159

S

scalability, 4
scripts, 80
Secondary Global Allocation Map
    page
    See: SGAM page
security, 37-40
server achitecture, 33
SGAM page, 95-96
sotred procedures
  modifying, 259-260
  running the first time, 251-253
special data types, 128-129
SQL, 2-3
SQL Profiler, 190-192
SQL Query Analyzer, 12-16, 50
SQL scripts
  comments, 84
  creating, 84-85
SQL statements
  batches, 78-79
  BEGIN...END, 81
  CASE, 82
  combing results of multiple
      SELECT, 208-209
  control-of-flow, 81-83
  dynamic, 77-78
  executing, 77-80

INDEX